Ceramics Monthly's Guide to

MATERIALS & GLAZES

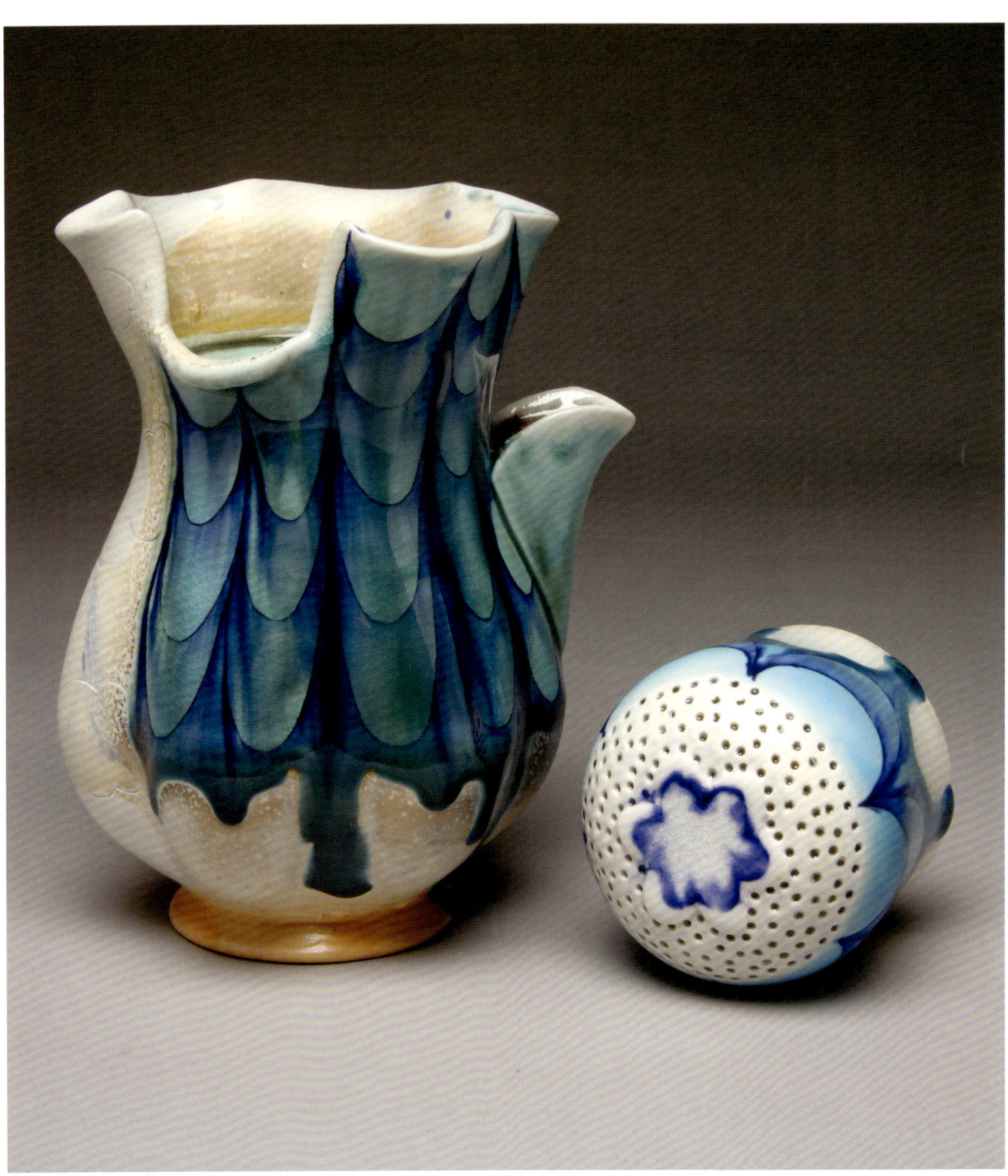

Julia Galloway's ewer with cup, multiple slips and glazes, soda fired to cone 6.

Ceramics Monthly's Guide to

MATERIALS & GLAZES

Edited by Jessica Knapp

The American Ceramic Society
600 N. Cleveland Ave., Suite 210
Westerville, Ohio 43082

www.CeramicArtsDaily.org

The American Ceramic Society
600 N. Cleveland Ave., Suite 210
Westerville, OH 43082

ISBN: 978-1-57498-377-7 (Paperback)

ISBN: 978-1-57498-587-0 (PDF)

Publisher: Charles Spahr, Executive Director, The American Ceramic Society

Managing Director: Sherman Hall

Editor: Jessica Knapp

Design and Graphic Production: Melissa Bury

Frontispiece: Julia Galloway's ewer with cup, mid-range soda-fired porcelain and glazes.

Cover Image: Detail of the glaze surface on Julia Galloway's ewer.

Contents

SECTION 1: Understanding Material 1

CHAPTER 1: Feldspar Overview *by Dave Finkelnburg* 2

CHAPTER 2: Fluxes *by Dave Finkelnburg* 5

CHAPTER 3: Kaolin and Ball Clay *by Dave Finkelnburg* 8

Calcined Kaolin *by Dave Finkelnburg* 9

CHAPTER 4: Glass Formers 11

Silica *by Dave Finkelnburg* 11

Boron in Glazes *by Matt Katz* .13

CHAPTER 5: Additions 16

Chrome Oxide *by John Britt* 16

Cobalt *by Dave Finkelnburg* 17

Copper Oxide *by John Britt* 18

All About Iron *by John Britt* 19

Ceramic Stains *by John Britt* 21

Opacifiers *by Dave Finkelnburg* 23

Silicon Carbide: The Stuff of Stars *by Mark Chatterley* 25

Suspenders and Binders for Glaze *by David Pier* 26

SECTION 2: Studio Application 31

CHAPTER 1: In the Studio: Practical Physics 32

Mesh Size *by John Britt* 32

Solubility *by Dave Finkelnburg* .35

Viscosity *by Tina Gebhart* 38

In the Bucket: The Key to Consistent Glazes
by Richard A. Eppler with Mimi Obstler 41

Raw Glazing, Single Firing *by Steven Hill* 46

CHAPTER 2: In the Kiln 49
Heatwork *by Dave Finkelnburg* 49
Pyrometric Cones *by Tina Gebhart* 50
Glaze on Clays *by David Pier* 53
Glaze Fit *by Dave Finkelnburg* 54
Glaze Melt and Seal Point *by Dave Finkelnburg* 56
Carbon Trapping *by Dave Finkelnburg* 57
Matte Glaze *by David Pier* 60
Cooling *by Dave Finkelnburg* 62
Faster Firing *by Dave Finkelnburg* 64
Glaze Unity Formula *by Dave Finkelnburg* 67
Testing Standards *by Dave Finkelnburg* 70

SECTION 3: Recipes, Research, and Techniques **75**

CHAPTER 1: Low Fire 76
Lusters *by Johanna DeMaine* 76
Colorful World of Majolica *by Linda Arbuckle* 80
Polychrome Glazes *by Joan Bruneau* 84
Low-fire Slip and Glaze *by Martina Lantin* 85
Low-fire Red Glaze *by Dave Finkelnburg* 86

CHAPTER 2: Mid Range 87
Chrome Red/Green Glazes *by John Britt* 87
Glazes with Iron *by John Britt* 90
Celadons at Six *by John Britt* 91
Mid-Range Reduction: It's Not Just Cooler, It's Cool *by John Britt* 95
Atmospheric-like Effects for Electric Firing *by Steven Hill* 101
Opaque Glazes *by John Britt* 107
Versatile Cone 6 Glazes *by Julia Galloway* 108
Expanding Your Palette in Mid-range Firing *by Yoko Sekino-Bové* 111

Ceramic Stains in Glaze *by John Britt* 115
Crater Glazes *by Mark Chatterley*. 117
Snowflake Crackle *by John Britt* 119

CHAPTER 3: High Fire 124
Copper Glazes *by John Britt* 124
Experiments in Peach Bloom *by John Britt* 126
Cobalt Glaze Recipes for Purple and Green *by Dave Finkelnburg* 133
High-fire Red Glazes *by Dave Finkelnburg* 134
The New World of Crystalline Glazes *by Diane Creber*. 135
Oil Spot and Hare's Fur Glazes *by John Britt*. 141
Strontium/Barium Matte Glazes *by Dave Finkelnburg* 145
Soda Surfaces *by Nolan Baumgartner* 147
Woodfire Glazes *by Matt Schiemann*. 149
Ash Glazes and Overglazes for Cone 10 Firing *by Robert Briscoe* 150

SECTION 4: Troubleshooting **153**
Blistering *by Johanna DeMaine* 154
Bloating *by Dave Finkelnburg*. 156
Glaze Crawling *by Phil Berneburg* 158
Pinholing *by Dave Finkelnburg* 161
Underfired Glazes *by Alisa Liskin Clausen* 163

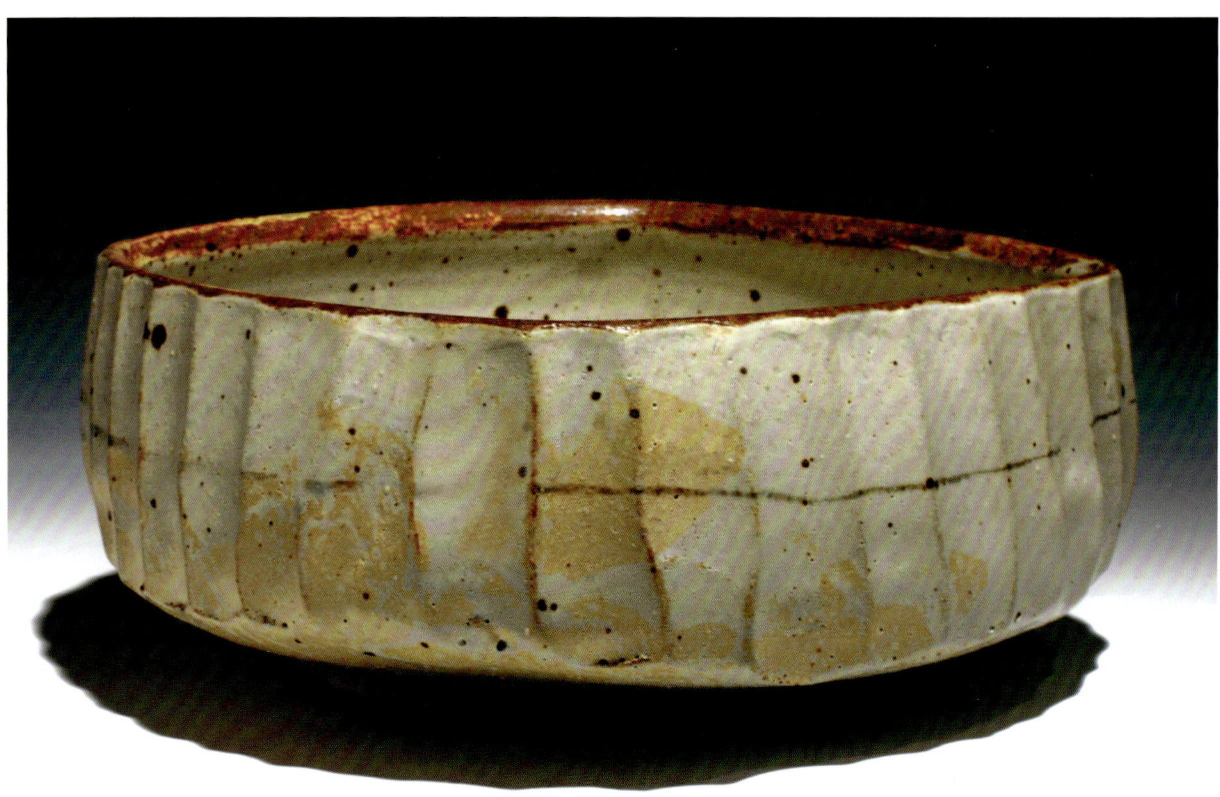

Robert Briscoe's salad bowl, white ash glaze wash over heavy white bisque slip, overglaze stains, fired to cone 10 in reduction.

Preface

When most of us start working with clay, we're introduced to the material and processes in an experiential rather than analytic way. We learn the forming skills needed, then learn to properly apply slips, stains, and glazes. If we're lucky, we also get to see how clay is made, glazes are mixed, and kilns are fired, but it can be hard to squeeze in that kind of learning in an introductory class. Often beginning students pull ready-to-use clay from a bag or storage area, use commercial underglazes and glazes or premixed shop glazes to finish the surface, and place the glazed bisque onto shelves in a kiln room. Several days later, everyone checks those same shelves to find the unloaded fired work ready to be admired and taken home. The interactions between and transformation of the materials remains pretty mysterious.

My introduction to clay followed this path, and I started to learn abut the technical side of the medium slowly as I tested how the standard shop glazes interacted with one another, and how they changed when I added colorants and other materials to them, and mixed up test batches of new recipes I found in books.

The numerous questions that came out of testing materials, mixing new glazes, and making lots of mistakes were often overwhelming, as was the amount of time it all required. There are so many factors that affect a specific outcome that learning why it happened, and how to repeat or avoid it can be a challenge no matter how much experience you have in the studio. Invariably, when faced with a failure, the following questions came up: How did people ever figure out what each material in this glaze recipe does? What characteristic of the finished clay or glaze are each of these powders responsible for? Where/what do the materials came from/start out as? What makes all of them work (or not work) together? I found that I needed to learn a lot more about the materials, their characteristics, and the ways they interacted in order to answer these questions.

This book is designed as a reference guide to help you understand the results you're getting in the studio, investigate new surfaces at all temperature ranges, and to expand your knowledge of ceramic materials and processes. The goal is to provide the basic background on many of the more common materials we use and the ways we work with them in the studio so you can feel more comfortable experimenting with making your own glazes, trying a new technique or firing temperature, or altering tried and true glazes to find new possibilities or make them work better for you.

The collection of articles were selected from both the Techno File section of *Ceramics Monthly* as well as technical and glaze-focused features that have been published in the magazine over the last five years. While not intended to be exhaustive, it provides an overview of ceramic materials from the raw state to the fired glassy surface. Feel free to read from front to back, or if you're a more experiential learner, skip to the section that interests you most, and use the navigation guides throughout the book to find related scientific information or practical studio applications. Dive in and see what's possible.

—Jessica Knapp

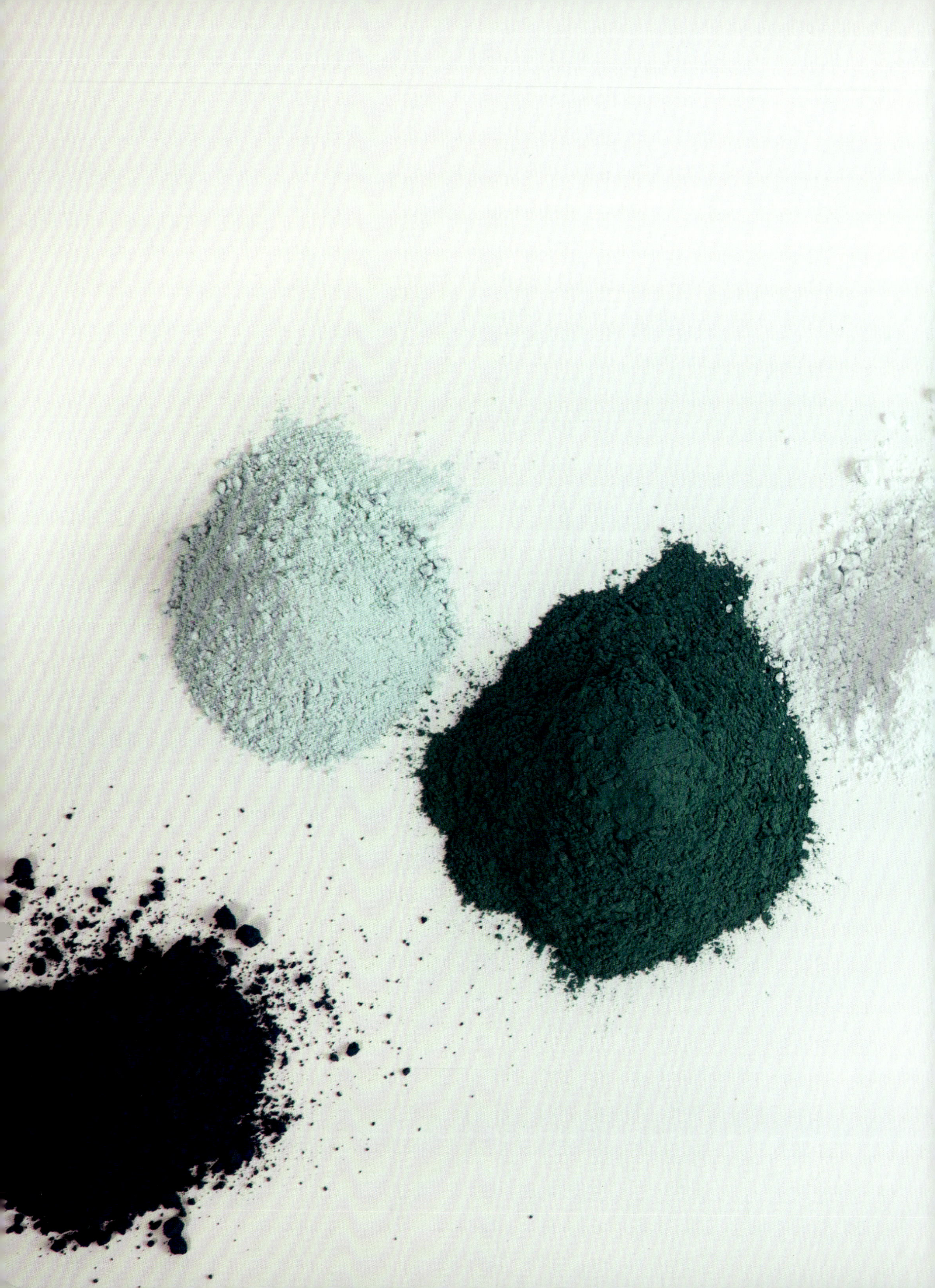

SECTION 1

Understanding Materials

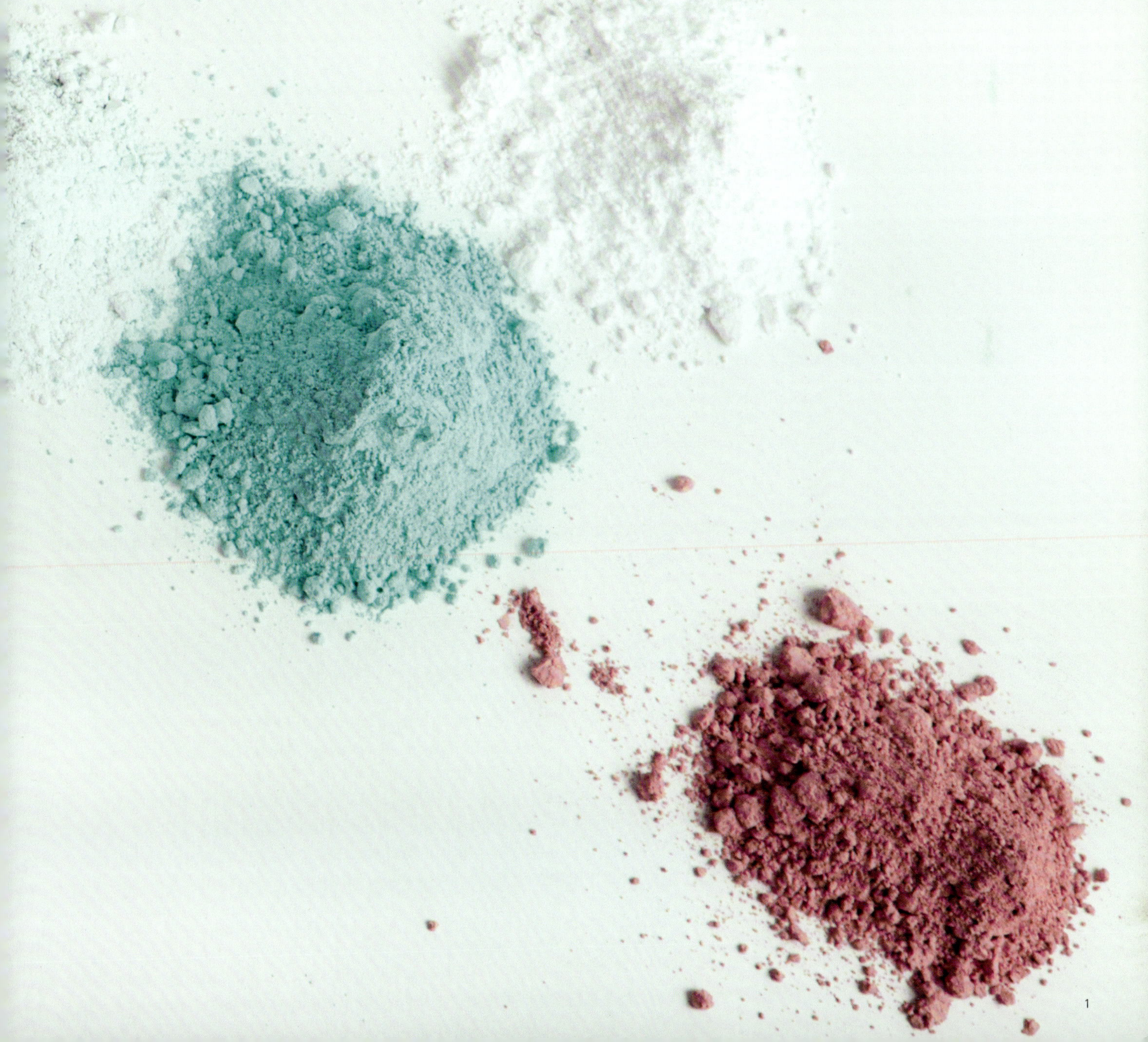

CHAPTER 1

Feldspar Overview

by Dave Finkelnburg

Defining the Terms

Albite: Pure sodium feldspar with the chemical formula $Na_2O{\cdot}Al_2O_3{\cdot}6SiO_2$. Very rare in nature.

Custer Feldspar: Potassium-rich feldspar that can be described as a natural frit because it provides relatively insoluble sodium and potassium oxide. Sodium and potassium oxides start their fluxing actions at 1472°F (800°C)—well before other fluxes commonly used, if present in the right amounts, control the production of cristobalite. Source: Ron Roy.

Feldspar: Any of a group of natural crystalline aluminum silicate minerals containing sodium, potassium, calcium, lithium or barium. Alkali feldspars (those containing sodium and potassium) are used most in ceramics.

Frit—A synthetic source of glaze flux and frequently of alumina and silica, manufactured by melting the ingredients together, cooling the resulting glass, and grinding it to a fine powder.

Lepidolite: A naturally occurring mica mineral containing about 4% lithium oxide plus about 9% potassium oxide.

Orthoclase and Microcline: The two crystalline forms of pure potassium feldspar, both with the chemical formula $K_2O{\cdot}Al_2O_3{\cdot}6SiO_2$. Very rare in nature.

Petalite: A lithium aluminum silicate mineral with a high silica content, more than 4% lithium oxide, and relatively insignificant amounts of other fluxes.

Potash Feldspar: Potassium-rich feldspar. Potash feldspars may contain, in total, more than 14% sodium and potassium oxides by weight.

Spodumene: A lithium-aluminum silicate mineral currently available with well over 7% lithium oxide.

A Natural Frit

As a crystalline mineral precipitated from molten rock over geologic time, feldspar is definitely not a designer material. Feldspar is sometimes called a natural frit and is composed entirely of crystals, but a commercial frit is made up of a finely ground glass manufactured with a specific composition. More energy is needed to melt crystals than glass, so to give it time to melt, feldspar requires a somewhat slower firing, most often to higher temperatures. While a frit can be manufactured with any desired ratio of flux, alumina, and silica, with feldspar what you mine is what you get. Thus feldspar is a sort of good-news bad-news story.

The good news is that the natural laws controlling how silicon, aluminum, and oxygen link to form the feldspar crystal ensure that the ratio of silica and alumina in *pure* feldspar is fixed.* More good news is that the flux elements exist in a fixed ratio to the alumina and silica.

Part of the bad news, however, is that nature permits sodium and potassium to occupy that flux amount in infinitely variable proportions to one another. The amount of either in a given feldspar depends entirely on what was handy when the feldspar precipitated from the molten rock in the earth's crust. Virtually every alkali feldspar deposit on earth has at least some difference in analysis.

In scientific terms, albite and microcline/orthoclase can form a solid solution. That is, an alkali feldspar can theoretically vary from 100% sodium to 100% potassium as its flux constituent. Soda feldspars actually tend to have at least 30% of their flux as potassium, while potash feldspars usually have at least 15% of their flux as sodium.

The rest of the bad news is that feldspar most commonly occurs as a rock, usually along with mica, quartz, and other minerals. In a feldspar mine, the rock is ground to a powder and sophisticated techniques are used to separate the minerals. How well and how consistently mining companies clean and concentrate the feldspar that artists use has virtually nothing to do with artists and focuses on the folks who buy 100-ton rail-car loads of feldspar to make literally millions of tons of glass per year. Quality control good enough to make beer bottles may not be as good as we would like in the studio, but who is ultimately the bigger end user of feldspar—studio artists or folks molding beer bottles? Feldspar is ultimately an industrial mineral and we have to accept that its quality is controlled by what's good enough for industry.

* (Note the difference in the ratio of silica and alumina between feldspars, spodumene, and nepheline syenite. There is less silica in the latter two. The crystal structure explains this. This also explains the differences between potash feldspars to nepheline syenite and spodumene.)

Making Adjustments in the Glaze Lab

Commercial frits have generally consistent analyses. Naturally occurring feldspars are less consistent and subject to change over time. While all raw materials should be tested before use, this needs to be a requirement before using each new batch of feldspar in the studio.

When feldspar is added to a clay body, it helps to melt very fine quartz into a glass phase that provides strength in the fired body. The amount of feldspar needed in a stoneware body depends entirely upon the flux level of the clays composing the body. For a fixed recipe of clays, various amounts of feldspar are tested to achieve a body with the desired level of vitrification from a given firing cycle.

The difference in silica content between Custer and G-200HP feldspars (see graph on previous page) is enough to change glaze fit. While these two potash feldspars can generally be substituted one-for-one, if one wants precise control of glaze chemistry, then a more accurate substitute for Custer is G-200HP plus 3% silica. When an existing feldspar disappears or a new one enters the market, some substitution such as this is likely to be necessary to achieve consistent results.

Time is also a factor. The landscape varies and as industry excavates from one mine to another the composition of feldspar changes along with it. The feldspar you were using five or ten years ago is most likely not exactly the same as what you are using today, even if it is the same brand name. Fusion button tests of the new and old material will guide you in whether and how to substitute other materials to accommodate the new feldspar's chemistry. To start:

1 Get a full chemical analysis of the new and old feldspars, if they are available.

2 Fire fusion buttons (a few grams of feldspar pressed into a small mold such as a crucible) of both materials side by side to get a visual indication of the differences in the two materials. Note color changes, melting temperatures, opacity, and surface effects.

3 Adjust recipes as these differences indicate and fire recipe tests to confirm that the adjustments are correct.

Some ceramic artists use chemistry to adjust clay and glaze recipes before testing. Others rely entirely on testing. The method chosen may say something about an artist's working style, but not the results, both methods work equally well.

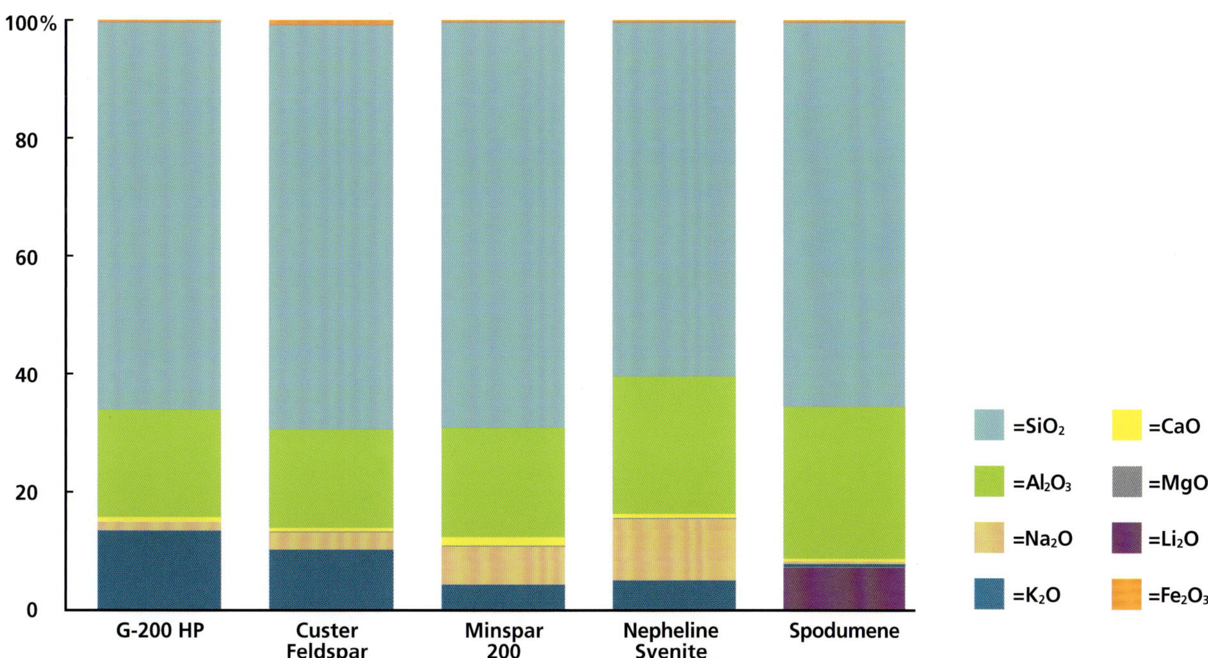

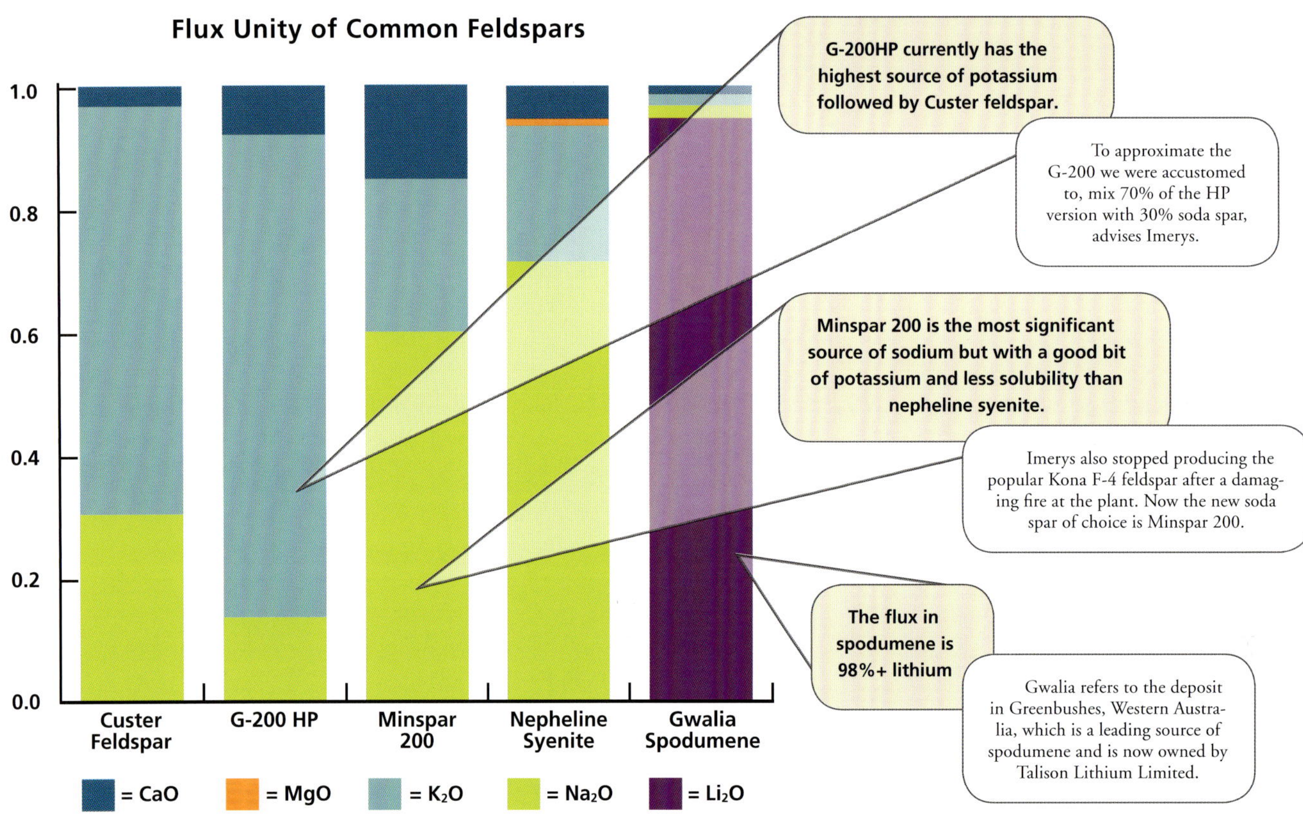

Lifespan of Feldspars

Bernard Leach used Varcoe feldspar in a clay body recipe he published in *A Potter's Book* in 1940. Have you ever heard of that feldspar? Not likely. Varcoe and Sons was sold to English China Clays, Ltd., and Leach's feldspar disappeared from the market.

Have you ever heard of Oxford feldspar? Daniel Rhodes' book *Clay and Glazes for the Potter*, published in 1957, used a feldspar from Oxford County, Maine, in almost every clay and glaze recipe. Oxford feldspar, too, is long gone. In the fifth edition of *Ceramics: A Potter's Handbook*, Glenn C. Nelson listed analyses of nine feldspars. None are available today. Feldspars such as Keystone, Kingman, K200, Kona F-4, A-3, Bell, Eureka, Chesterfield, Buckingham, and most recently G-200, have all vanished.

Currently there are five common feldspars available in the US: G-200 HP ("HP" for high potassium), Custer, Minspar 200, Nepheline Syenite, and Talison Spodumene (formerly Gwalia). The relatively subtle differences in their chemical compositions are shown on page 3.

CHAPTER 2

Fluxes

by Dave Finkelnburg

Defining the Terms

Alkalis: The group of chemical elements that includes lithium, sodium, and potassium. These are the most powerful ceramic fluxes and work at the lowest temperatures. They also tend to lend brighter colors to glazes.

Alkaline Earths: The group of flux elements that includes magnesium, calcium, strontium, and barium. While suitable for all temperatures, these fluxes are used in larger amounts at higher temperatures. They also tend to produce more muted glaze colors.

Ceramic Flux: A chemical compound containing elements that help ceramic materials melt. In other words, a material which, when mixed with other ceramic materials, lowers the temperature at which the mixture melts. Atoms of a powerful flux, say sodium, flow into a particle of silica to dissolve it. Heat provides the energy for this flow to occur. The extent of silica dissolution by fluxes is a function of peak firing temperature.

Coefficient of Thermal Expansion (CTE): The distance any material expands per unit of length upon heating (or shrinks upon cooling) one degree of temperature. A typical CTE of fired stoneware is about 0.000007 inches (in scientific notation, 7×10-6) per inch per °F. A typical CTE of porcelain is ~6×10-6/. While the numbers indicating CTE stay the same whether one measures length in inches or millimeters, it is important to note the temperature scale (°F or °C) and keep that consistent for both clay and glaze. A higher CTE means a material shrinks more, a lower one means it shrinks less.

A firm appreciation of fluxes is key to understanding how clay and glazes fire into ceramic art. Fluxes help things melt. Ceramic fluxes lower the melting points of other ceramic materials to temperatures that allow us to use affordable amounts of energy and common equipment and materials. To understand fluxes, though, we need to know what fluxes are and how they work.

Clay, for pottery and ceramic art, is mostly the mineral kaolinite. If pure, kaolinite will not melt unless heated to 3200°F (1760°C). However, if kaolinite is mixed with a flux, it will begin to melt at a much lower temperature. Fluxes let us fire work at temperatures as low as 1200°F (650°C)— about what you'd find in an open bonfire. Developing clay bodies and glazes that will fire to specific temperatures requires understanding and controlling the use of fluxes.

The subject of fluxes can seem intimidating at first. By breaking fluxes down into logical groups, though, they soon become manageable.

Science

As soon as any ceramic material starts to melt, atoms making up the material are freed to move about within the liquid formed. Atoms of any given element within the liquid will move from areas of high concentration of the element to areas of lower concentration. It's like they try to get away from all the neighbors who are just like them and go where the nearest neighbors are not like them. This is the driving force that causes flux elements to diffuse and help dissolve quartz particles in a clay body. There's a lot more going on, of course. Melting of ceramic materials is a complex process. It's important to understand, though, that the chemical composition of the materials in a clay body or glaze ultimately control the temperature and speed of melting.

We often use chemical nomenclature—RO and RO_2—to define our materials (where the letter *R* is user defined). Since *R* is not used by any element on the periodic table, it can be used to denote an unknown element in a chemical formula. In ceramics, *R* refers to one or more of the flux, glass forming, or glass modifying elements we most commonly work with.

We classify flux elements generally as alkali and alkaline earths, and while some fluxing characteristics are specific to each group, many are not. The alkaline earth fluxes fire at a higher temperature while the alkali fluxes melt at a lower temperature and promote brighter colors.

FLUXING OXIDES	MELTING TEMP.	CHARACTERISTICS	COLOR AND SURFACE	SOURCE MATERIAL
Li_2O (Lithium Oxide)	1333°F (723°C)	can reduce the viscosity and increase fluidity, most reactive flux, strong color response, low expansion/contraction, small particle size	blue with copper, pinks and warm blues with cobalt, textural, variegated effects	lithium carbonate, petalite, spodumene
Na_2O (Sodium Oxide)	1688°F (920°C)	strong flux, high expansion/contraction rate causing crazing, begins to volatilize at high temperatures	copper reds in reduction and copper blues in oxidation	soda feldspar, nepheline syenite, frits
K_2O (Potassium Oxide)	1305°F (707°C)	stable, predictable, and active flux, a heavy oxide, high expansion/contraction, crazing in high amounts	promotes bright colors in a broad range	potash feldspar, frits
CaO (Calcium Oxide)	5270°F (2910°C)	very active flux in medium/high temp glazes, can harden glaze, intermediate expansion, not an effective flux below cone 4	glossy brown/black to yellow, generally matt surfaces	whiting, wollastonite, feldspars, colemanite, dolomite
MgO (Magnesium Oxide)	5072°F (2800°C)	refractory at lower temps, low expansion and crazing resistance, poor response in bright colored glazes	matt, 'fatty matt' and 'hare's fur' tactile surface	magnesium carbonate, dolomite, talc
SrO (Strontium Oxide)	4406°F (2430°C)	useful at lower temps for high gloss and craze resistant glazes, similar expansion and behavior to calcium	satin matt surfaces through a fine crystalline mesh	strontium carbonate
BaO (Barium Oxide)	3493°F (1923°C)	very active in small amounts, larger amounts can be refractory and leachable	blues with copper, milky streaks and cloudy effects	barium carbonate, frit
ZnO (Zinc Oxide)	3272°F (1800°C)	auxiliary flux in oxidation atmospheres, dramatic color response, low expansion/ contraction rate	can produce opacity due to the development of a crystal mesh surface	zinc oxide

Alkali fluxes are grouped under the label R_2O because it takes two alkali atoms to balance the electrical charge of one oxygen atom. Thus lithium, sodium, and potassium (abbreviated Li, Na, and K) form the oxides Li_2O, Na_2O, and K_2O.

Lithium, sodium, and potassium all brighten glaze colors. However, lithium also promotes clearer transparent glazes and lowers both the melting point and the viscosity of glazes even more than sodium or potassium. Lithium also contributes to a harder fired glaze surface than either of those fluxes.

Lithium dramatically lowers the linear coefficient of thermal expansion (CTE) of glazes and clay bodies. This is part of why lithium is so useful in reducing susceptibility of flameware to thermal shock. However, the amount of lithium used must be carefully controlled. Too much lithium in a glaze is certain to cause that glaze to shiver from most ordinary clay bodies. Too much lithium also causes the formation of crystals, effectively turning a clear glaze opaque.

Magnesium is the only flux that has a lower CTE than lithium. Potassium and sodium have CTEs on the order of five times larger than that of lithium and the remaining alkaline earth fluxes (calcium, barium, and strontium) have CTEs twice as large as lithium.

Alkaline earth fluxes are labeled RO because it takes only one alkaline earth atom to balance the electrical charge of one oxygen atom. Thus magnesium, calcium, strontium, and barium (abbreviated Mg, Ca, Sr, and Ba) form the oxides MgO, CaO, SrO, and BaO.

For use in glazes, alkaline earth fluxes are all available as carbonates. Calcium carbonate, often called whiting, is made by grinding ordinary limestone to a very fine powder. Magnesium is also found in limestone, notably as the variable mineral dolomite, theoretically 54% calcium carbonate and 46% magnesium carbonate. Both limestone and dolomite are abundant and inexpensive. Strontium and barium, on the other hand, occur most commonly as sulfate minerals and are converted to carbonates by expensive chemical processes. That's why they are much more costly.

Both chemically, and in their effects on glazes, strontium and barium are closely related to calcium and magnesium, the most common alkaline earth elements in glazes. However, each of these fluxes have different effects on glaze melting, crystal formation, glaze fit, and the response of colorant oxides. Strontium and barium both brighten glossy glazes, barium even more than strontium. In both cases the brightness is a result of the effect of strontium and barium on the refractive index of a glaze, the angle at which light is reflected by the surface of the fired glaze. Strontium, compared to calcium, somewhat lowers the temperature at which a glaze melts. Barium, on the other hand, somewhat raises the glaze melting temperature in comparison to calcium

All carbonate glaze ingredients decompose on heating and give off carbon dioxide. Thermal decomposition of barium and strontium carbonates in glazes is reported to occur at relatively high temperatures (around cone 02). This is in stark contrast to magnesium carbonate, which decomposes well below red heat, and calcium carbonate, which decomposes completely by cone 010. The higher thermal decomposition temperatures of strontium and barium carbonates occur because of the high bond strengths between the flux elements, carbon, and oxygen.

A common starting point for fluxes in glossy glazes is, in flux unity, to use 0.7 moles of alkalis (70% of the flux atoms) and 0.3 moles of the alkaline earth element calcium (30% of the flux atoms). If the proportion of calcium is increased, or if more than half the calcium is replaced by magnesium, barium, or strontium, satin to matte glaze finishes can be produced. **Note:** A glaze containing several alkaline earth fluxes can be less likely to produce the tiny crystals that form satin and matte surfaces than a glaze with only one.

Because characteristics beyond general melting temperatures and color response are not particular to one group or another, use these chemical associations carefully. The chart on page 6 provides an overview of the effects of the different fluxes. In particular, be aware that the influence of a flux element on glaze color defies classification. For example, magnesium-containing flux materials turn cobalt powerfully purple. In a typical NaKCa-silicate glaze cobalt produces blue. If you begin to remove Ca and replace it with Mg, though, the color will shift to purple. Eventually one can produce a very gorgeous bubble gum grape color without changing the amount of cobalt a bit! Copper is sensitive to different combinations of a number of different fluxes, producing at times blue, yellow, or green. These and other color effects of fluxes must be learned, studied and tested one flux at a time.

Safety with Barium and Strontium

The most important thing to know about these fluxes is that strontium carbonate is not radioactive (that's strontium 90) and barium carbonate is an effective rat poison. Yes, this glaze ingredient—a fine white powder—is dangerously toxic to people! Using barium carbonate safely requires taking proper precautions to avoid inhaling its dust. It also goes without saying that it must be kept out of the reach of children and pets, either as the powder or in the mixed glaze, as well as away from any area where it might be accidentally added to food or drink.

Confusion about barium's toxicity can occur because barium sulfate, an acid-insoluble compound, is used internally in humans in medical applications. At least some barium has been reported to be leachable from most if not all glazes.

CHAPTER 3

Kaolin and Ball Clay

by Dave Finkelnburg

Defining the Terms

Kaolinite: The clay mineral in kaolin, kaolinite is also the principal clay mineral in ball clays. Kaolinite occurs in nature as a hydroxylated aluminum silicate crystal with the chemical formula $Al_2Si_2O_5(OH_4)$. That means kaolinite contains alumina (Al_2O_3), silica (SiO_2), and some hydroxyl (OH) groups. The hydroxyl groups are bound up in the aluminum silicate crystal lattice and are driven off, as water, by heating to at least 1166°F (630°C).

Quartz: A silica mineral with a hexagonal crystal structure and a chemical composition of SiO_2.

Mica: A hydrous aluminum disilicate. Typically the parent mineral of earthenware clays (rather than kaolinite).

Facts and Formation

While clay mineralogy is complex, and kaolinite can also form in other ways, it is useful to think of kaolinite simply as altered feldspar. Most of the clay on earth began life as molten rock that solidified slowly into feldspar and mica. In cases where those minerals are exposed to water for long periods of time, the flux atoms are slowly leached out and the relatively pure aluminum-silicate crystal structure is left behind. In this way, feldspar is altered into kaolinite clay. The leaching or alteration leaves flat, plate-like kaolinite crystals that, under very high magnification, are seen to be in stacks.

When this kaolinite (weathered feldspar) is found right where it was formed, the clay deposit is kaolin. Besides kaolinite, the kaolin also contains quartz, feldspar, mica and other minerals found in the parent rock.

Sometimes kaolin is very near or at the surface of the earth or becomes exposed over time. Surface deposits of kaolin are quite soft and may be eroded by wind or, more often, by water. Erosion moves the stacks of ka-

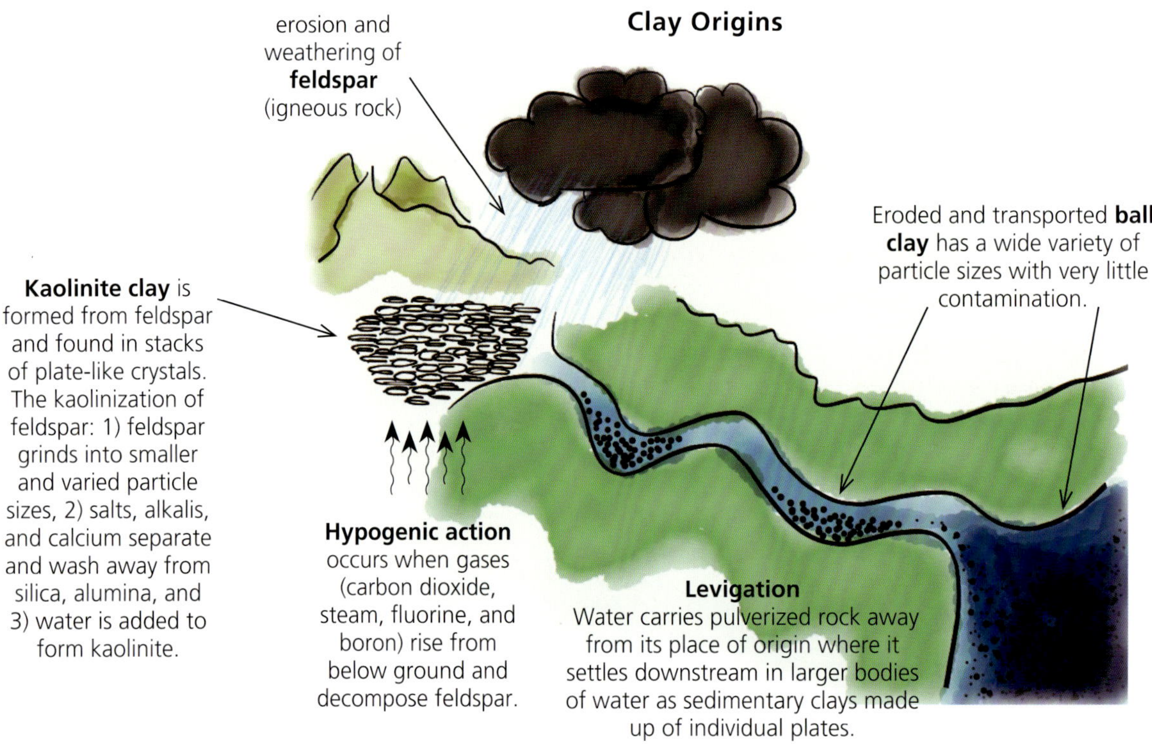

olinite crystals downhill or downwind. In this process of transportation, the stacks literally break down. The stacks split apart into shorter stacks or individual plates and the plates break into smaller pieces.

Significant accumulations of kaolinite transported by erosion are what we call ball clay. Because of its unique properties, it is logical to assume that ball clay is a particular clay mineral. That isn't true. Technically speaking, all ball clays are mostly kaolinite, the same clay mineral that makes up kaolins. The majority of ceramic clays used around the world are kaolins. If ball clay is mainly kaolinite, what makes ball clay different than ordinary kaolin? The answer is particle size.

Very importantly, ball clays have a very wide mix of particle sizes, including very fine clay particles. Ball clays settle in deposits that are relatively uncontaminated except for plant matter. A common misconception is that more contaminated deposits are often earthenware. Typically, the parent mineral of earthenware is mica rather than feldspar. Thus earthenware is high in iron and the clay minerals tend to be mostly illite and chlorite rather than kaolinite.

When ball clay deposits form, there may be significant fine quartz sand transported in the same way and to the same location as the ball clay. As a result, ball clays are highly variable in their quartz content, which can range from a few percent to 15% or more. In cases where glaze fit is important, it is essential to adjust the quartz added to a clay-body recipe if the ball clay is replaced with a substitute. This is because increasing quartz content reduces fired-body expansion.

Calcined Kaolin

Defining the Terms

Calcining: Heating a material to drive off that part of the material which turns to a gas and is lost as a vapor at or below the calcining temperature.

Dehydroxylation: Loss of structural hydroxyl ions as water molecules on heating.

Hydroxyl Group: An atom of hydrogen (with the chemical symbol H) and an atom of oxygen (with the chemical symbol O) bonded together (thus having the chemical symbol OH) and bound to another atom or compound.

Loss on Ignition (LOI): Loss of weight, as a percent of the weight of a bone-dry sample, upon heating to a temperature at which volatile materials escape. Heating is typically continued until the weight of the sample ceases to change.

Take Control of Shrinkage

Why would one want to use calcined clay? The answer is because any wet clay shrinks as it drys. However, the same clay, when calcined, shrinks less during the process of drying.

In the case of glazes, drying shrinkage can become problematic as the clay content of the glaze rises above 10% of the recipe. If a glaze contains so much clay that it shrinks too much as it air dries, it will crack and may even fall off the ware. Calcined clay does not behave in the same way, yet delivers the same amount of silica and alumina as the raw clay originally called for, so the recipe has the benefit of high alumina and silica but the application and drying properties of a recipe containing a lesser amount of clay.

Single firers commonly use what are called slip glazes for application to leather-hard ware. Slip glazes have intentionally high shrinkage so they shrink with the greenware to which they are applied. When converting a greenware slip glaze to a glaze to be applied to bisqueware, calcined kaolin is frequently substituted for some of the clay fraction to prevent shrinkage cracks.

Slip glazes are essentially a slurry of clay and water containing a small amount of quartz plus feldspar or other fluxes. Such a slip-glaze recipe will typically contain from 25% to as much as 70% clay. Slip-glaze recipes that have a clay content on the low end of the range usually also contain bentonite because a small amount of it gives the glaze a relatively high shrinkage.

To achieve the high silica and alumina content of a slip glaze with a high clay content, yet avoid the shrinkage involved, some of the raw clay in the recipe can be replaced with calcined clay. Slightly less calcined clay than raw clay is used because the calcining process drives off water and makes the calcined clay lighter for the same amount of alumina and silica it contains. In other words, calcined clay contains more alumina and silica per gram than uncalcined clay does.

The benefits of reduced shrinkage when using calcined clay comes with a trade off. Wet clay is a relatively plastic material. Calcined clay is not.

Science of Calcining

Clay minerals are composed almost entirely of alumina and silica with some water bound up in the crystal lattice of the clay. Other minerals may contaminate any given clay deposit, and those minerals can modify the properties of the clay. However, in all cases calcining the clay to drive off bound water will reduce that clay's future firing shrinkage.

The practical definition of calcining clay is heating it until all free water evaporates, all organic contamination is burned off, and all lattice-bound water is driven off.

Most pottery clays, wherever they are found in the world, are kaolins. Kaolinite gives up its lattice-bound water at about 1166°F (630°C). That dehydroxylation temperature is approximately cone 020, far below the ordinary temperature range for a first firing of 1652–1940°F (900–1040°C).

Most studio artists either buy calcined kaolin or make their own by placing raw kaolin in a shallow bowl and firing it in a bisque firing. Care must be used to avoid over-calcining the clay. If kaolin is calcined at too high a temperature, say cone 04, the resulting calcine can contain hard lumps of clay. Such lumps don't distribute their alumina and silica content as thoroughly within the glaze matrix. These lumps can only be broken up by grinding.

Industry has found that calcining kaolin to 1292°F (700°C) is sufficient. That's slightly less than cone 018.

Heating kaolinite above its dehydroxylation temperature causes the clay to lose weight as water in the clay crystal lattice evaporates. The theoretical weight loss of water from calcining kaolinite is approximately 13.2% of the original weight. Because of the loss of weight, when replacing 100 grams of raw kaolin, 86.8 grams of calcined kaolin will produce the same fired result.

If one were to calcine a ball clay or any other clay, the alumina and silica would be more concentrated in the calcined version. However, most ball clays, while their clay fraction is entirely or almost entirely kaolinite, also contain a fair amount of quartz and other contaminants. For example, OM4 ball clay is about 13–14% quartz.

The percentage of weight loss on calcining OM4 ball clay is less than for calcining pure kaolinite. If calcining other clays, it might be prudent to weigh a sample carefully, calcine it in a vitrified vessel, and weigh the sample carefully again soon after cooling to determine the actual percent weight loss for that clay. The reason for weighing the sample soon after firing is to prevent humidity from the air being absorbed by the calcined clay and affecting the accuracy of the measurement.

CHAPTER 4

Glass Formers

Silica

by Dave Finkelnburg

Silica is the single most important ingredient in traditional ceramics. Silicates are so common (they comprise about 50% of the earth's crust) that their value may be overlooked—but that would be a mistake. In clay bodies, silica contributes to translucency, whiteness, hardness, and fired strength. In glazes it provides durability, gloss, and resistance to crazing. Silica is found in multiple forms and the different names can be confusing. Here's the foundation for understanding what silica is and what it does in ceramics.

Silica Limits in Glazes

The bar charts below show concentration of primary glaze components by weight percentage. Notice that, as the temperature increases, more silica is required to keep the glaze from running off the ware during firing.

Defining the Terms

Silica: Silicon dioxide, SiO_2, is the primary glass former in clay and glazes. Vitrification, fluidity, transparency, opacity, melting point, and other properties of silica glass are controlled by adding flux and/or refractory elements and materials. Silica's melting point is 3110°F (1710°C).

Quartz: A relatively pure form of silica (typically 99.7% SiO_2) derived originally from igneous rocks. Washed quartz sand, either as is or ground to a fine powder, is used around the globe as a silica source in clay bodies and glazes. Quartz is also the specific term for the primary phase of silica.

Flint: A silica mineral formed in sedimentary sea bed deposits. True flint is somewhat impure silica compared to quartz, typically containing up to 10% impurities. The impurities include magnesium, calcium, and organic carbon. It is prepared by washing, calcining, and grinding. While flint, once widely used in Britain for clay and glazes has been almost completely replaced by ground quartz, its name persists and ceramic artists worldwide frequently use the word flint as a synonym for ground quartz.

Glass former: An oxide which is able to retain the amorphous property of its molten state when setting to a solid. Other minerals return to a crystalline state as they cool. Boron and phosphorus are also in this category. The terms silica and glass former are not synonymous.

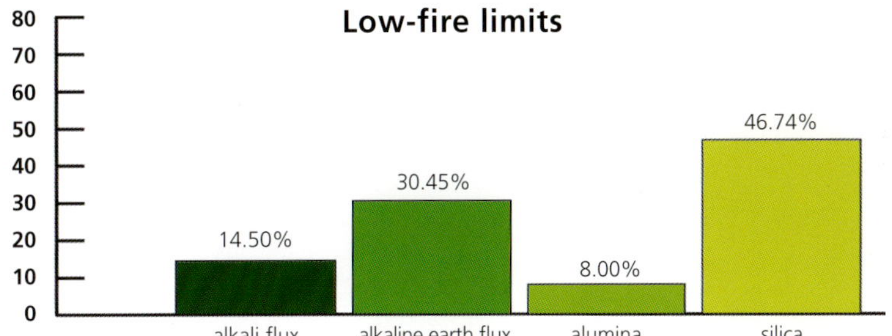

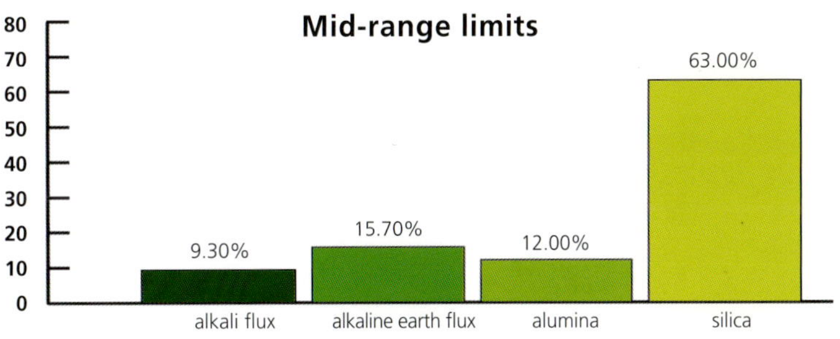

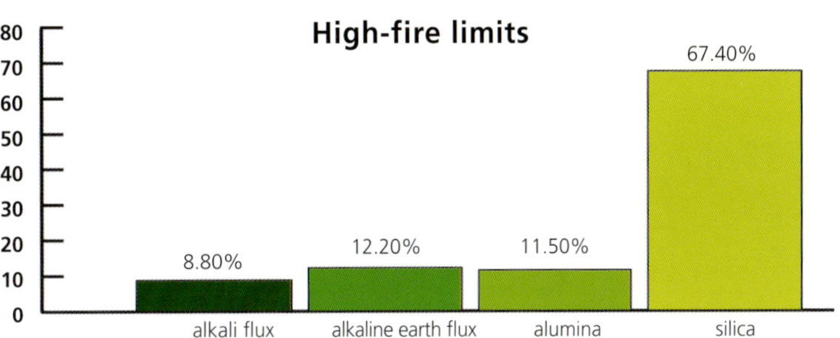

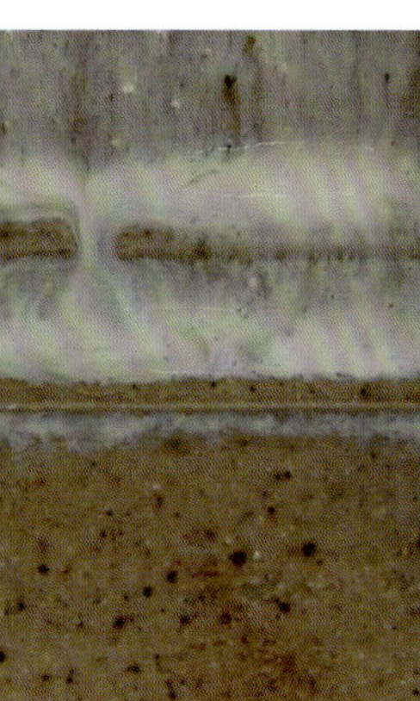

NUKA GLAZE

(cone 10 reduction/oxidation)

Cornwall Stone	34.5 %
Wood Ash (unwashed)	41.5
Silica	24.0
	100.0 %

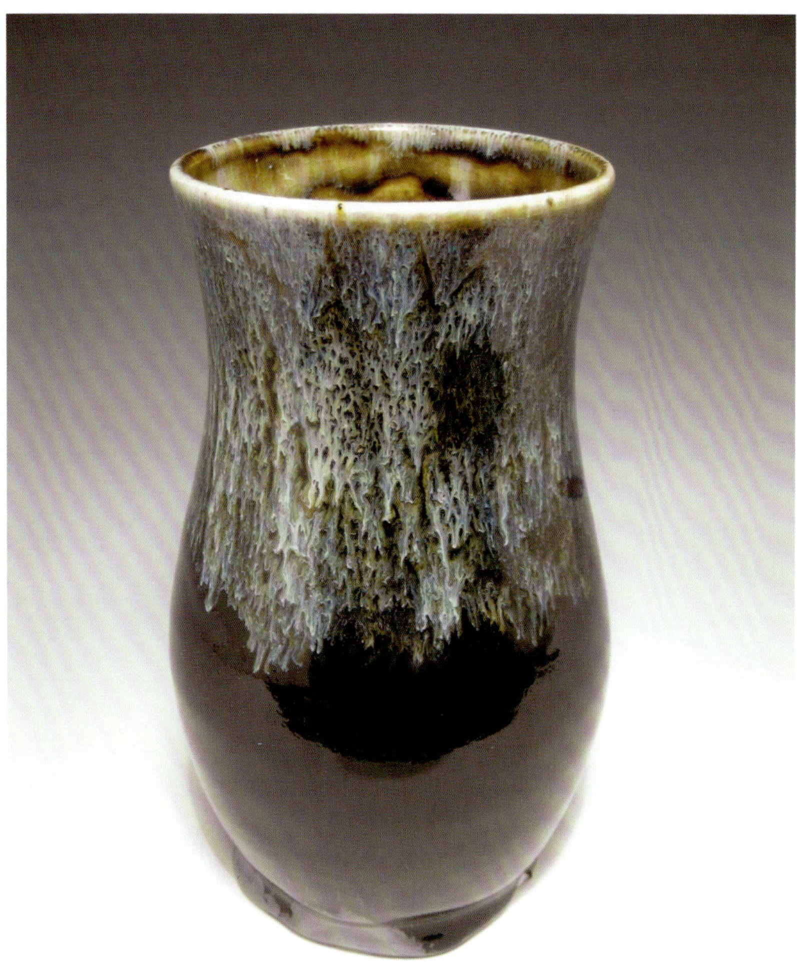

A nuka glaze is often an iridescent, milky, white or light chun blue glaze. The color comes from slight impurities in the feldspar, ash, and from unmelted silica. True Japanese nuka glazes are made with rice hull ash, which contains over 75% silica. With low alumina, high silica, and high KNaO, nukas fall outside the matrix limits of a stable glaze. Despite this, they are not toxic as they contain no metallic colorants. A traditional nuka recipe would be 4 parts rice straw ash, 3 parts wood ash, and 3 parts feldspar.

Recipe and glaze images supplied by John Britt.

Boron in Glazes

by Matt Katz

Define the Terms

Boron: A low-temperature glass former.

Intermediate: Materials that perform similarly to the major group of glass formers and modifiers but also contain properties of other groups. For example, iron functions predominately as a colorant, but in heavy concentrations can play the role of a flux.

Boron is one of the most, if not the most, misunderstood material in ceramics but it doesn't need to be. What exactly does it do? Where does it come from? How should we use it? These questions permeate the mysteries of boron but are easily answered.

Glass Former or Flux?

Boron is very basic in function and it performs in a predictable manner. However, boron usage in the US for the last 50 plus years has been dominated by Gerstley borate, a raw material that is prized for its unpredictability. This has left at least a couple generations of ceramists with varying levels of confusion about the true nature of boron and a collection of recipes that don't work without this particular material.

Boron is found primarily in Turkey, as an element in the mineral borax ($Na_2O{\cdot}3B_2O_3{\cdot}10H_2O$), and California (Boron, California, to be specific), where the largest mine in the state produces half of the world's boron.

All glazes are based on only eleven oxides. These are the oxides of silicon, aluminum, lithium, sodium, potassium, magnesium, calcium, strontium, barium, zinc, and boron. There are others, but they are all relegated to the role of colorants, additives, or the relatively unused, such as the dreaded lead. These basic eleven elements make up 99% of glazes. The first ten can be simplified further into two groups—glass formers and fluxes. This leaves us with boron. Which is it, a glass former or a flux?

If you look at the version of the periodic table of the elements below, as used by glass scientists, boron is grouped with silicon and four other glass formers. It is above aluminum, which can substitute, within limits, for silica in a glass network.

All of the fluxes (except for zinc) are found in the first two columns of the table. They are the alkalis in the first column and the alkaline earths in the second. The elements in each column act similarly to each other and slightly different than the elements in the other column, yet all are

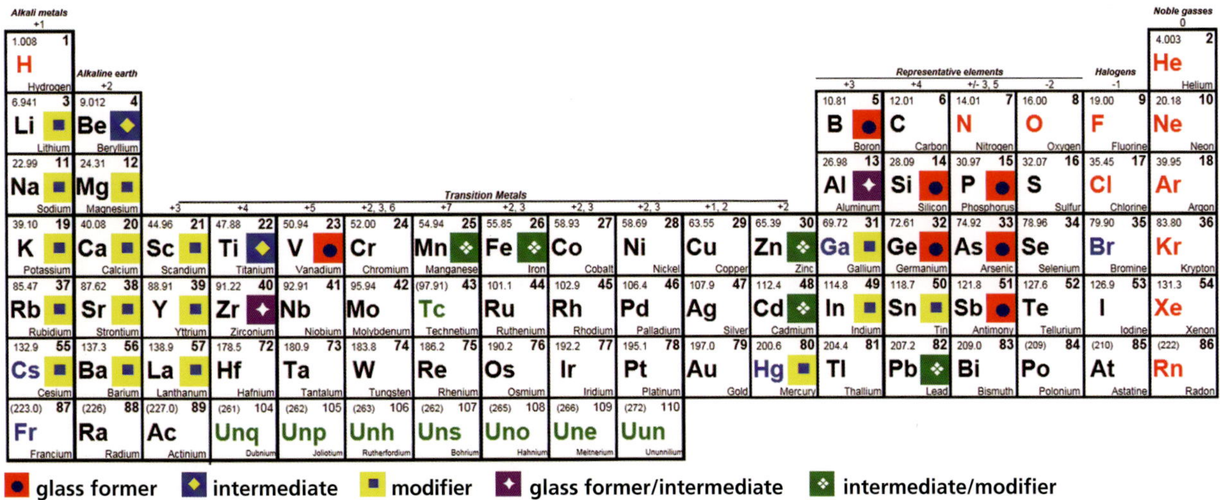

Periodic Table of Elements—oxide glass forming classification.

fluxes. The function of true fluxes is to lower the melting temperature of glass formers. In the process, fluxes also influence color, strength, and the chemical and mechanical durability of glazes.

Historically, many have declared that boron is a flux because we use it to make glazes melt at low (cone 04) and mid-range (cone 6) temperatures. Here's where the confusion comes from. The fact is that boron is a glass former. We know this because pure boron oxide will make a glass on its own, just like pure silica will. Where boron differs from silicon is that boron oxide forms a glass at a dramatically lower temperature than silica.

All glazes require silica, and it is by leaps and bounds the most prevalent material in all glazes, regardless of temperature or type. Silica is the second most abundant material on earth after iron, making it cheap and plentiful. Boron, on the other hand, is a minor player. Boron is not pragmatic as a primary glass former for many reasons; material sources are all limited for reasons such as solubility, common availability, and cost. There are no glazes that are composed exclusively of boron; it is, at best, an accessory. Yet understanding boron for mid- and low-temperature glazes (even high-temperature), is very useful.

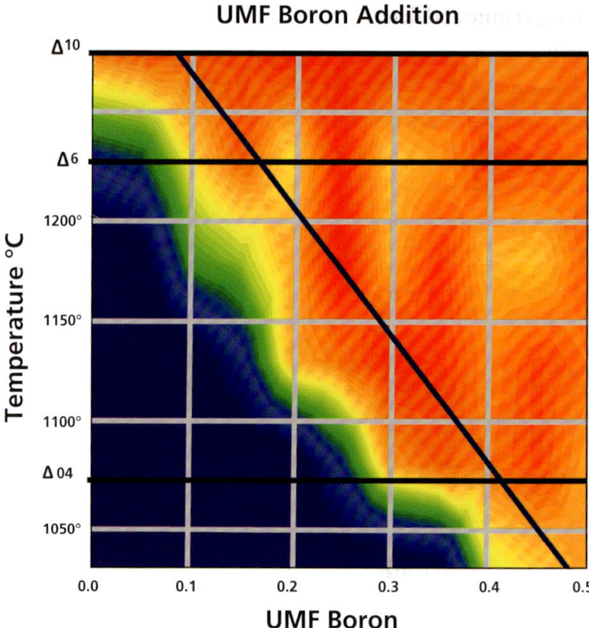

Boron Glaze Limits. The above chart indicates amounts of boron needed to make a glaze melt based on the desired firing temperature. Orange/red suggests a glossy melt, purple/blue areas indicate underfired surfaces.

Sources

For many years, the major source of boron has been Gerstley borate. This is a naturally occurring deposit of the minerals colemanite ($2CaO{\cdot}3B_2O_3{\cdot}5H_2O$), ulexite ($NaCaB_5O_9{\cdot}8H_2O$) and bentonite ($3Al_2O_3{\cdot}SiO_2{\cdot}H_2O$). Gerstley borate is an exciting material for ceramists as the two borate materials (colemanite and ulexite) melt at different times in the firing, leading to the "breaking" effect of the glaze.

When it was feared that Gerstley's availability would be limited (the mine was closed for safety reasons) a variety of materials sold as Gerstley substitutes came onto the market. There are also two other types of borate materials: frits, and soluble sources. The soluble materials, boric acid ($B_2O_3{\cdot}3H_2O$) and borax, are very effective boron sources. The problem with these materials is they are very soluble in water, meaning that the boron dissolves in the water of the glaze. As glazes dry, the water is absorbed into the bisqued clay body rather than remaining in the glaze. This can change the melting performance of the body (over melting) and the glaze (under melting).

For this reason, frits are the favored sources for boron. Frits are wonderful materials as they provide all the boron required in a stable, minimally soluble form. Frits are essentially glazes that have been batched, melted, and then ground to a powder by the frit manufacturer. There are a huge number of frits out there, but in the US our palette is often limited to Ferro's 31XX series, including 3110, 3124, 3134, and 3195. Each of these frits does something different but they are all very simple and bring in various amounts of boron.

Boron and UMF

The function of silica, alumina, and fluxes are well understood in the unity molecular formula (UMF) or Seger formula, thanks to the work of R.T. Stull. However, boron, as a bit player, did not receive any attention in his work. All high-temperature glazes require silica, alumina, an alkaline earth, and an alkali. Boron is not required for a cone 10 glaze. At Alfred University, Dr. Bill Carty and I have put a lot of effort into defining how to best utilize boron from a UMF perspective. We believe that one can predict the amount of boron needed to make a glaze melt based on the desired firing temperature.

The graph on this page shows the amount of boron required at any temperature. The purple-blue areas are underfired, while the red/orange areas are very glossy. The vertical axis is temperature in celsius and the horizontal axis is UMF boron additions to a standard glaze. By finding the desired temperature and determining the position on the oblique line, you can figure out the corresponding required UMF boron level at that temperature. This chart applies from cone 06 to cone 10. As a general rule, we define the required amount of boron as an additional 0.1 mole (via UMF) of boron for every 50°C below cone 10 (1305°C). Boron is an exceptionally good material for adding to glazes as it makes glasses at lower temperatures that are just as strong and resistant to wear and chemical leaching as the best cone 10 glazes.

THE PERFECT CONE 04 GLOSS

Ferro Frit 3124	90 %
EPK Kaolin	10
	100 %

Add 10% Zircopax for a white glaze.

MATT AND DAVE'S CRAZE-FREE GLOSS

Cone 10

Whiting	5.42 %
Ferro Frit 3124	40.46
G200 HP	14.37
EPK Kaolin	27.20
Silica	12.55
	100.00 %

Cone 10 to Cone 6—The First Step

A glaze temperature conversion is no easy feat. It takes knowledge and experience to successfully convert a glaze recipe that works at one temperature so it works as well at another. There are a lot of subtle factors in the chemistry of a glaze that dictate its color, texture, and performance. That said, here is a quick start with fast results, helped in part by boron.

1. Take a cone 10 glaze that you are fond of and mix three 100 gram batches of it.

2. Add Ferro frit 3124 to the cups: 5% to one, 10% to the second, and 15% to the third.

3. Apply each test recipe to its own flat test tile. Place each in a disposable, unglazed clay-run catcher.

4. Fire the tiles, propped at a 45° angle, to cone 6.

5. Select the glaze that ran the least in the kiln.

This is just a first step to adjusting your glaze to a lower temperature, but it should be a good starting place for creating a glaze that looks similar. By using a frit, you are introducing boron as a material that will not alter the basic nature of the glaze but will still contribute the boron needed to lower the firing temperature.

CHAPTER 5

Additions

Chrome Oxide

by John Britt

Defining the Terms

Chrome Oxide (Cr_2O_3): An amphoteric/refractory that melts at 4109°F, and volatilizes at 2192°F. It is a green powder used by potters that doesn't dissolve well in a glaze melt, resulting in opaque, mainly green colors. Red, pink, gray, brown, and orange colors are also possible.

Iron Chromate (Fe_2O_3 Cr_2O_3 or $FeCrO_3$): An iron–chromium ore commonly used to produce grays. It gives opacity and can be used with cobalt, iron, and manganese oxides to produce blacks. With tin in oxidation, it can develop a pinkish gray.

Potassium Dichromate ($K_2Cr_2O_7$): A bright orange crystalline material that is generally used at low-temperatures to create bright reds with lead frits in oxidation. It is toxic and soluble.

Amphoteric: A material capable of acting as an acid (glass-former) or a base (alkaline flux) in a glaze. Acts as a bridge between the two depending on the situation.

Safety

While there is no legal limit set for safe leaching of chrome in glazes, potters should be aware that the legal level of allowable chrome oxide deemed safe for drinking water is 0.1 mg/L (ppm). Because chromium can have different valences, its toxicity and carcinogenic effects vary greatly. It is volatile at higher temperatures and is a toxic fume (fugitive chrome). Care should be taken when handling and firing chrome compounds.

Chrome oxide is a very powerful colorant that can at times be fickle.

Properties and Characteristics

Chrome oxide comes to potters as a bright green powder derived from iron chromate. It is a very powerful colorant—even 0.1% can give a green color (see right). Chrome is unaffected by oxidation and reduction but sometimes glazes that use chrome oxide appear to be affected by reduction because they also contain other oxides to influence their color and those are affected by reduction (like tin oxide, copper oxide, etc.)

Chrome oxide is an amphoteric oxide, which means it plays an intermediate role between fluxes and silica. It is generally very refractory and not very soluble in a glaze melt but sometimes it acts as a flux, e.g. as with the acidic tin oxide. The exact color it produces depends on the role chrome is fulfilling in the glaze. For example, in high alkaline or high boron glaze bases, when less than 1% chrome is added, it can dissolve well and give bright glossy transparent greens, (see Odyssey series 0.15/0.5% on page 89). In a zinc (zinc chromate) base it produces browns (see Chun glazes). In a high calcium or high strontium base without zinc, it can produce pinks, or crimson to burgundy colors (see Raspberry and Cranberry glaze on page 87). In a glaze that contains tin oxide, adding chrome pushes it toward shades of pink. The colors of chrome-tin pinks can be quite variable but consistent chrome-tin colors can be achieved by using commercial stains where the chrome and tin combination have been pre-melted together.

Less than 1% chrome oxide usually disperses in a glaze melt but occasionally it may cause speckling. To disperse the color evenly, depending on the stiffness of the base, it may require ball milling.

Find mid-range recipes that use chrome to make both red and green glazes.

Cobalt

by Dave Finkelnburg

Cobalt is an extremely powerful colorant that almost always produces an intense blue, but it doesn't have to be that way all the time. This oxide is actually quite versatile and can make glazes that run the gamut from green to purple, pink to blue violet, blues mottled with red, pink, and even an intense black. There are four major factors that can affect a glaze's color: the clay and slip beneath it, kiln atmosphere, fired temperature, and the glaze composition, including the colorants.

Defining the Terms

Oxide: A chemical compound containing at least one oxygen atom as well as at least one other element. Oxides result when an element combines with oxygen. Some raw materials are used in oxide form (like black cobalt oxide) while others form oxides during the firing process. In a glaze firing the oxygen usually comes from air, though in a fuel-fired kiln it may also come from carbon monoxide and carbon dioxide.

Carbonate: The compound of carbon and oxygen in a 1:3 ratio that gives a negatively charged ion. It is generally insoluble. When fired, the carbonate breaks down and CO_2 goes up the chimney, leaving behind an oxide.

Valence Electrons: The unbound, shared electrons that move among atoms rather than moving within a single atom.

Mole: The base unit of measure for the amount of substance, either atoms or molecules. This unit is used in unity molecular formulas for glazes.

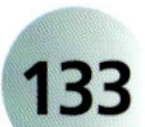

See high-fire green and purple glazes made with cobalt.

Just Like Taking a Little Slice out of a Rainbow

When a fired glaze is exposed to light, the color of the glaze will depend entirely on which wavelengths of the light are absorbed by the valence electrons in the glaze colorants. The energy level of the valence electrons determines which photons it will absorb (absorb them all and you have black) or emit (emit them all and you have white). Emit only one wavelength and you have that color, just like taking a little slice out of a rainbow. Cobalt in a fired glaze usually absorbs all wavelengths of visible light except blue and thus a glaze containing cobalt is blue (see below).

However, two or more colorants in a glaze interact so that the wavelengths of light absorbed are different for the combination than for either colorant by itself. The interaction between atoms of one colorant, say cobalt, and another, say chrome, alters the energy level of the valence electrons of both elements. That is why we may add both cobalt (blue) and chrome (green) to get a glaze that is turquoise.

Flux elements such as sodium, stabilizers such as alumina, and even some glass formers also influence valence electrons. Because the glass formed in the glaze firing controls the interaction of the glaze elements, what you see in the mixed glaze is almost never the color you get in the fired glaze.

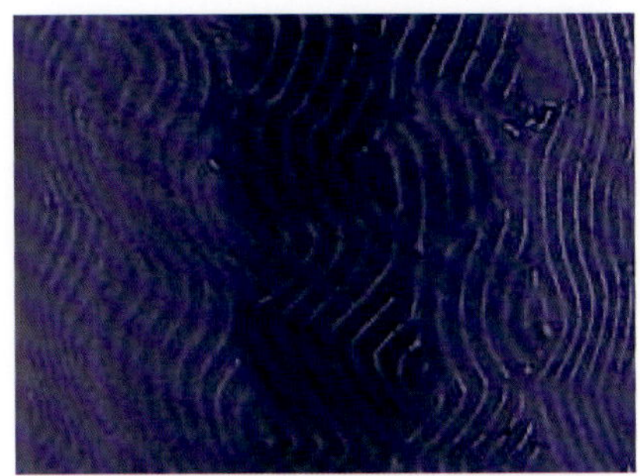

More Cobalt Facts

- Cobalt Oxide: CoO is 1.4 times stronger than cobalt carbonate
- Cobalt Carbonate: Co_3O_4 (mix of CoO and Co_2O_3)
- CoO and Co_3O_4, although mainly thought of as colorants, are also strong fluxes
- Melting point (oxide): 328°F (1805°C), not yet volatile even at 2552°F (1400°C)
- Strongest coloring oxide: 0.25% noticeably blue in a transparent base glaze, used in a wide array of decal inks, underglaze colors, body stains, and colored glazes
- Soluble in glaze melt, thus it has little or no opacifying effect
- Very fine particle size, gives more uniform color in glazes
- Atmosphere and firing temperature do not change the color
- Very dependable color results in both oxidation and reduction conditions, and in fast and slow firing
- Toxic (inhalation and ingestion)

Copper Oxide

by John Britt

Defining the Terms

Copper Oxide—Black Copper Oxide (Cupric) CuO; melts at 2419°F (1326°C). Red Copper Oxide (Cuprous) Cu_2O; melts at 2255°F (1235°C). Cupric oxide decomposes at 1847°F (1008°C) to cuprous oxide and oxygen. It is an active flux, so adding it to a glaze may cause the glaze to run. It has high coefficient of expansion/contraction, which may increase crazing in larger amounts. It is toxic, volatile (fume hazard), and can leach into food. It can migrate through a clay body, and almost any copper glaze with a matte black surface will leach copper in the presence of acidic liquids. It can also cause pinholing.

Copper Carbonate—The idealized formula for this green powder is $CuCO_3$, but the material may come as a variety of compounds and may contain impurities. $Cu_2(OH)2CO_3$ (Malachite) may be a more accurate formula representation. Since it is reactive chemically, it disperses better in a glaze thus giving more even results than copper oxide. It off gasses and can cause pinholes or blisters in a glaze. At approximately 572°–608°F (300°–320°C) copper carbonate releases carbon dioxide and water, and then at 1922°F (1050°C) it loses more oxygen as it restructures. Copper carbonate makes greens in amounts of 5% or less, blacks above 5%, and at 0.3–0.8% it makes blues in oxidation and copper reds in reduction. Approximate conversion: 5% copper carbonate = 3.6% black copper oxide = 3.24% red copper oxide.

Copper Sulfate—This blue crystal is an agricultural fungicide. It is soluble in water, starts decomposing at 302°F (150°C), loses four water molecules by 392°F (200°C), then changes to copper oxide and sulfur trioxide by 1202°F (650°C). Often used in pit and low-temperature saggar firings. Produces grays in soluble salt firings as well as pinks and reds in heavy reduction.

Copper Chloride—Often used in water soluble metal salt firing (aka *water coloring* on porcelain). Produces burgundy colors in pit and saggar firings.

Copper Filings—Chips of copper metal. Copper filings are sometimes sprinkled in or on a wet glaze to give black spots with flashes of red on the perimeter.

Copper oxide is an active metal that combines easily with oxygen, which means that it is very sensitive to oxidation and reduction atmospheres. It produces a very wide range of colors in glazes, from greens (delicate light greens to turquoise (1) to deep emerald green(3)), to red (2), pink, blue, black, yellow, and copper luster.

Sourcing Copper

Copper was one of the first metals worked by humans (6000–4000 BCE). It shows up in glass as early as 2000 BCE and in glazes of the Han Dynasty (200–25 BCE).

Some of the most famous copper green glazes are known as Oribe, which comes from Furuta Oribe, a general and tea master during the Japanese Keicho period (1596–1615 CE). Another popular copper glaze is a copper red. It most likely came about from the accidental reduction of copper green glazes fired in a wood-burning kiln. Some of the early sources of copper in glazes are believed to be from spraying water onto hot bronze. This produces a black flaky substance composed of copper oxide and tin oxide (the metals in bronze), which was then finely ground and used to produce copper reds. Copper red colors include strawberry, oxblood, flambé, black-red, peach bloom, apple red, rose carmin, etc.

There are four major sources of copper in glazes: Black copper oxide (CuO); red copper oxide (Cu_2O); copper carbonate ($CuCO_3$); and copper sulfate ($CuSO_4$), which dissolves in water. Each has different properties that can make a significant difference in the outcome of the glaze. Copper carbonate is the most commonly used form. It disperses well in a glaze slop and melts well in glazes to give uniform color. Black copper oxide has a larger particle size that doesn't melt well and can cause specking in glazes. Red copper oxide is the strongest form and has a hydrophobic coating (oleic acid surfactant) that keeps it from reoxidizing in the air. Because of this coating, it won't mix with water and simply floats on the surface. This can be corrected by adding several drops of liquid soap, which breaks the surface tension and allows it to disperse.

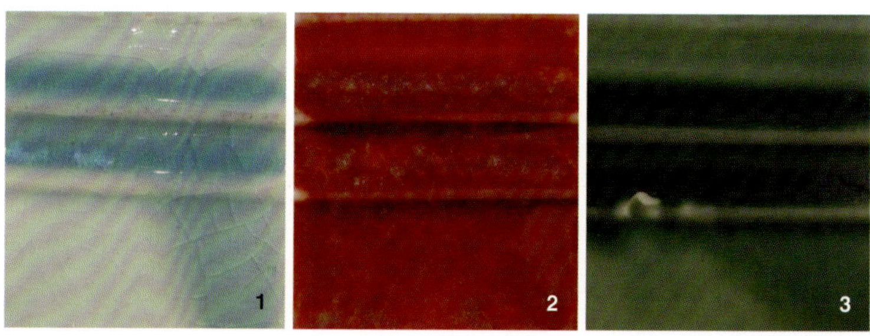

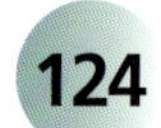

See high-fire recipes for red, green, blue purple and mottled black glazes that use copper as the main colorant.

All About Iron

by John Britt

Defining the Terms

Iron—The fourth most common element in the earth's crust and the most common element (in terms of mass) on the planet, comprising 35% of the earth's core.

Melting Point: 2795°F (1535°C)

Toxicity: Non-toxic

Iron is everywhere in many different forms, but that doesn't mean it has to be boring—or even brown.

Forms of Iron

Iron oxide is the most common colorant in ceramics. It is so ubiquitous that it is very difficult to find a material without some iron—it's found in almost everything from feldspars to kaolin to ball clays, earthenware clays, and many colorants. In fact, many materials require expensive processing to reduce the amount of iron to acceptable levels.

Iron is a very active metal that combines easily with oxygen. That means it is very sensitive to oxidation and reduction atmospheres, producing a wide range of glaze colors and effects from off white, light blue, blue, blue-green, green, olive, amber, yellow, brown, russet, tea-dust, black, iron saturate, iron spangles, iron crystalline (goldstone/tiger's eye), oil spot, hare's fur, kaki (orange), leopard spotted kaki, tan, black seto, pigskin tenmoku, shino, gray (Hidashi), iridescent, silver, gold, etc. Iron also plays a major role in clay bodies, slips, terra sigillata, and flashing slips.

There are three major forms of iron used in ceramics: red iron oxide (Fe_2O_3), black iron oxide (FeO or Fe_3O_4), and yellow iron oxide ($FeO(OH)$). There are different mesh sizes and grades, and each contains varying degrees of impurities that can make a significant difference in the results you get.

The most interesting thing about iron is that it can act both as a refractory and a flux. As red iron oxide, Fe_2O_3, it is an intermediate or amphoteric similar in structure to alumina (Al_2O_3) and acts as a (refractory/stabilizer). But if it is reduced to black iron oxide (FeO) it acts as a flux similar in structure to calcium oxide (CaO). What this means is that a tenmoku glaze with 10% red iron oxide will be a stiff black glaze if fired in oxidation because the iron oxide acts as a refractory. But, if the same glaze is fired in reduction that 10% Fe_2O_3 will be reduced to FeO, changing it to a flux, which will make it a glossy brown/black glaze that may run.

Another interesting property of iron oxide is that if it is fired in oxidation it will remain Fe_2O_3 until it reaches approximately 2250°F (approximately cone 8) where it will then reduce thermally to Fe_3O_4 on its way to becoming FeO. The complex iron oxide molecule simply cannot maintain its state at those temperatures. This results in the release of an oxygen atom that will bubble to the surface of the hot glaze and pull a bit of iron with it. When it reaches the surface the oxygen releases the iron as it leaves the glaze, creating spots with greater concentrations of iron oxide. This is what creates an oil spot glaze. This reaction can easily be seen through the spy hole of a kiln or with draw tiles. There is an obvious and unmistakable bubbling. If heated further, these spots begin to melt and run down the pot, creating a distinctive "hare's fur" effect.

***Synthetic and Spanish Varieties of Red Iron Oxide** (see page 22)
Synthetic Red Iron Oxide is produced by calcining black iron oxide particles in an oxidation atmosphere. They are then jet milled, which produces "micronized" red iron oxide particles that are approximately 325 mesh. This type of red iron is very heat stable (up to 1832°F (1000°C). This differs from black iron oxide, which changes color at 365°F (180°C) from black to brown to red as it oxidizes. The color of red iron oxide changes from light pinkish to red to dark purplish red as the particle size increases.

Spanish red iron oxide is bacterially ingested iron oxide that is micronized. The Tierga mines in Spain found that their iron sulfide was inadequate for steel making (which accounts for 95% of the iron market). After some time a worker noticed that the iron in a pool of rain water turned a brighter shade of red after it was heated. This turned out to be caused by a bacterium that uses iron sulfide as an energy source. The bacterium changes the state of the iron, which is then put into evaporative ponds where it forms green crystals. These are then roasted to produce Spanish red iron oxide.

Sources of Iron

Form & Chemical Name	Characteristics	Most Common Use
Red Iron Oxide Fe_2O_3 ferric iron, Hematite	Most common form of iron and is a finely ground material that disperses well in glaze slurries, contains 69.9% Fe in the chemical formula, sold as: • Natural Red Iron Oxide or Brown 521 (85% purity) • Spanish Red Iron Oxide* (83–88% purity) • Synthetic Red Iron Oxide* (High Purity Red Iron or Red 4284) (96–99% purity). Very fine 325 mesh. Sometimes sold as the brand name Crocus Martis or Iron Precipitate.	Used in glazes, washes, slips, engobes, terra sigillatas, and clay bodies, used to make celadons, tenmoku, kaki, iron saturates, etc. Normally used from 1–30% in glazes.
Black Iron Oxide FeO ferrous oxide, wustite	Strongest form of iron, containing 72.3% Fe in the chemical FeO, sold as: • Natural Black Iron Oxide (85–95% purity) 100 mesh; is black in color and has a larger particle size. In glazes it's prone to speckling but this is easily eliminated by ball milling. • Synthetic Black Iron Oxide (99% purity) 325 mesh	Used in glazes, washes, slips, engobes, and terra sigillatas; used to make celadons, tenmoku, kaki, iron saturates, etc.
Yellow Iron Oxide FeO (OH) ferric oxide hydrate, Geothite	Weakest form of iron, containing 62.9% Fe in the chemical formula, has a high LOI of 12%, sold as: • Synthetic Iron Oxide (96% purity) 325 mesh • Yellow Ochre or Natural Yellow Iron Oxide (35% purity) contains impurities of calcium carbonate, silica, and sometimes manganese dioxide	Used in glazes, washes, slips, engobes, terra sigillatas, and clay bodies; used to make celadons, temmoku, kaki, iron saturates, etc.; sometimes yellow ochre is added to porcelain to make "dirty" porcelain (5–9%)
Umber, Burnt Umber	Calcined umber, which is a high-iron ochre material containing manganese	Used in glazes, washes, slips, engobes, terra sigillatas or claybodies to make a range of reddish-brown colors; darker than sienna and ochre (yellow iron)
Sienna, Burnt Sienna	Calcined Sienna, which is a high-iron ochre material with less manganese than umber	Used to make browns in glazes, washes, slips, engobes, terra sigillatas or clay bodies
Iron Chromate Cr_2FeO_4	Contains chrome and iron oxide (ferric chromate); toxic— absorption, inhalation, and ingestion	Used to make dark colors in glazes, slips, engobes or clay bodies; can give gray, brown, and black; can give pink halos over tin white glazes
Ferric Chloride/ Iron Chloride $FeCl_3$	Water soluble metal salt; toxic—corrosive/caustic, affects liver, inhalation and ingestion	Used in low-fire techniques, like pit firing, aluminum foil saggars, horse hair and raku techniques; also used in water coloring on porcelain techniques
Iron Sulfate (Copperas) $FeSO_4$	Water soluble metal salt, soluble form of iron, (aka Crocus Martis)	Salt used in water coloring on porcelain, raku, and low-fire soda
Iron Phosphate $FePO_4$		Rarely used but can be used to develop iron red colors; sometimes used instead of bone ash as a source of phosphate without the calcium in synthetic bone ash (TCP or tri-calcium phosphate)
Rutile (light, dark, and granular) TiO_2	Most common natural ore of titanium, containing various impurities including iron (up to 15%)	Used in glazes, washes, slips, engobes, and terra sigillatas to give yellows, tans, greens, blues, and milky, streaky, mottled textures; also used to produce crystalline glaze effects
Illmenite (powdered and granular)	Naturally occurring ore containing iron and titanium, higher in iron than rutile (when 25% or more iron is present)	Commonly used to produce speckles in glazes or clay bodies
Iron Clays $FeTiO_3$	e.g., Redart, Albany slip, Alberta Slip, Barnard Slip (aka Blackbird Slip), Michigan slip, Lizella, laterite, and other assorted earthenware clays	Used in glazes, slip glazes, slips, engobes, terra sigillatas, and claybodies to make a range of reddish-brown colors
Magnetic Iron Oxide Fe_3O_4 Magnetite	Iron scale or iron spangles—coarse, hard particles that resist melting and chemical breakdown	Gives speckles in clay bodies and glazes

90 See mid-range and high-fire recipes for glazes that use iron as the main colorant.

Ceramic Stains

by John Britt

Defining the Terms

Frits: Ceramic materials that have been mixed, fused/melted/sintered together in a kiln, quenched, and ground to a specific size. They can be used as part of a glaze recipe (e.g. Ferro frit 3134) or added to coloring oxides, or stains to assist in melting.

Spinel: Mineral with alkaline oxide and amphoteric oxide. RO/R_2O_3. Gemstones are an example of natural spinels while in ceramics, these spinels are used to produce commercial colorants because they are chemically stable in molten glass. A purple can be created by combining cobalt and alumina oxide, $CoAl_2O_3$, into a cobalt aluminate stain.

Stains: **1)** Coloring oxides suspended in water (a.k.a. an oxide wash). May also contain frit and/or kaolin (usually EPK). **2)** Commercial ceramic colored powders that are used in glazes, clay bodies, and slips/engobes. Prepared coloring oxides that are fritted, reground, and colored with organic dyes to simulate fired color.

Ceramists today are spoiled. It wasn't that long ago that getting the colors and surfaces you wanted took a lifetime of work to achieve. But today because of the developments in modern stain technology, we have practically every color in the rainbow at our finger tips.

Properties and Characteristics

Historically, potters made glaze from feldspar, ash, and whatever iron-rich clays were available locally. This usually meant brown pots, or occasionally another earth-tone color. Then they began using metal oxides—like copper, chrome, manganese, iron oxides—and blending them with opacifiers to create colors. There is historic evidence that colored frits were used at least as early as 2600 BCE. Egyptian blue was a combination of silica, limestone, sodium, and copper oxides. This required a great deal of knowledge about glaze chemistry and firing to achieve the desired colors. And this knowledge was something that was in short supply, so potters basically accepted the glazes they stumbled upon and liked enough to build a body of work around.

Stains are a mixture of ceramic oxides and coloring metal oxides that are melted in kilns, quenched, ground to specific mesh size (some are acid washed), and colored with organic dyes to simulate the fired color. Essentially they are fritted colorants. They are made and manufactured for several reasons: to provide a consistent and stable form of colorant that doesn't dissolve in the glaze melt as easily as coloring metal oxides; to make colorants safer to use than raw metal oxides (commercial stains are less soluble in water); to allow repeatable and consistent results with minimal effort; and to allow you to fine tune your color selection to get the color you want at a reasonable cost. They can appear expensive, but time is money. Consider the countless hours of glaze testing that would be necessary without the consistency of a dependable commercial stain, then the prices are more reasonable.

Commercial stain companies provide a detailed list of what oxides are present in each stain. The exact recipe is

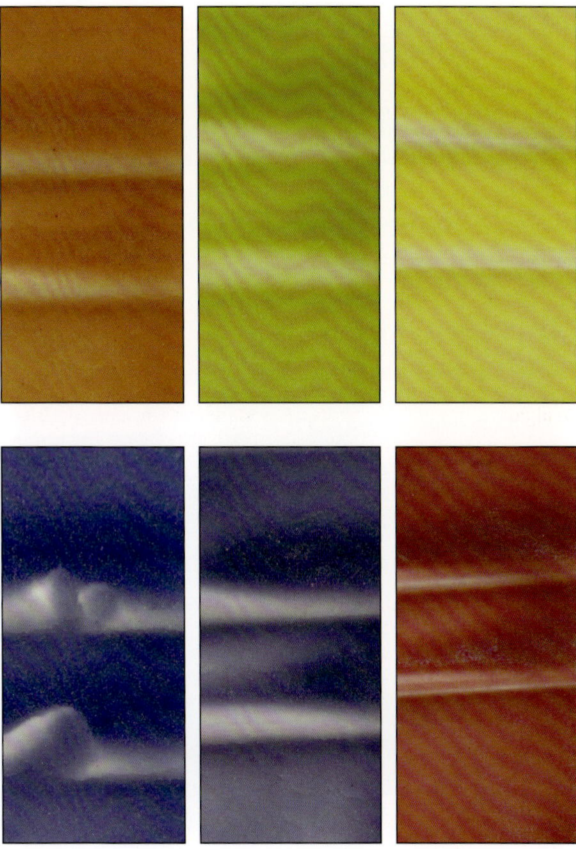

proprietary, but knowing what oxides are used in a given stain can give you great clues as to how a color is achieved or how to encourage or prevent particular effects. For example, there are several different black stains. One is Best Black while another choice is Cobalt-Free Black. If you are using a white glaze with a black-stained glaze next to it, you may notice that a blue line develops at the overlap. If you don't want that line, you can look in the stain chart and choose the black stain without cobalt—the cause of the blue line. This chart also tells the base glaze structure that is necessary for each stain to work. Before deciding on a color, it is advisable to look at the reference notes associated with that stain. Sometimes called the *Base Glaze Guide*, this information indicates the specific requirements to achieve each color. For example, the name is listed, followed by the oxides it contains, and finally a list of numbers such as 3, 5, and 9; each indicating information important to the mixing, firing, etc., to that stain: #3: Maximum firing limit 2300° F (1260°C), #5: Do not use zinc in glaze, and #9: Glaze must contain 6.7–8.4% CaO (12–15% $CaCO_3$). Each manufacturer will have a full list of reference notes for their stains.

Each color is not guaranteed in all bases, and being aware of these reference notes will help you achieve greater success. Stains are not meant for all firing conditions and are generally designed for neutral or oxidation firing atmospheres (although some may work in reduction atmospheres). Because stains contain coloring metal oxides along with other ceramics materials like opacifiers, silica, and alumina, adding them to certain glaze bases can cause a glossy glaze surface to turn matte.

Stains are generally added at 5–8% in a glaze and 15–25% in slips and clay bodies. At 8% most of the glazes are opaque and flat but if you add smaller amounts of stain (1–3%) it is possible to get transparent colors, including some very nice transparent celadon-colored glazes, when fired in an electric kiln or similar neutral atmosphere.

Encapsulated (Inclusion) Stains

Specialty stains, called encapsulated stains, allow potters to get colors that were once not possible with traditional stains. These stain types, also known as inclusion stains or inclusion pigments, are zirconium silicate with cadmium sulfoselenide crystals (Ca/Se). Dave Finkelnburg explains in "Low-fire Red Glaze" on page 86, "The discovery of the encapsulation process (the melting of the colorants into a zirconium silicate glass at high temperatures) has now made the many hues of yellow through red reliable at temperatures through cone 10 in both oxidation and reduction atmospheres." The addition of 3% zirconium silicate will produce an even brighter color. These stains are refractory at higher temperatures, they do not melt much, if at all.

As Tony Hansen writes on Digital Fire (www.digitalfire.com), "Encapsulated stains are not, as the name suggests and some misunderstand, a zircon capsule around an otherwise unstable compound. Rather they are manufactured by sintering to form a crystalline matrix (in a process called encapsulation)." Inclusion stains have specific firing temperatures and duration of firing protocols as well as warnings about not ball milling the stains (which will allow release of cadmium and/or selenium). If the fired glaze surface is damaged it can release the crystals.

Finkelnburg also states that cadmium stains can produce food-safe colors; however, under certain circumstances, it can be leached from the fired glaze. He adds that a sample of any cadmium-stain-tinted glaze used on potential food surfaces should be tested for leaching by a qualified laboratory.

115 See mid range glaze recipes that work well with a variety of commercial ceramic stains

Opacifiers

by Dave Finkelnburg

Defining the Terms

Metal Marking: Abrasion of eating utensils by the surface of ceramic dinnerware that leaves dark lines visible on the glaze surface.

Opaque: Not capable of allowing light to pass through.

Opacifier: In ceramics an ingredient, or combination of ingredients, that makes a glaze opaque to varying degrees.

Translucent: Capable of allowing light to pass through, but with significant distortion; semi-transparent.

Zircon: A naturally-occurring crystal form of zirconium silicate.

For millennia ceramic artists have covered their work with glazes that concealed the fired clay beneath. Seems easy, right? Because a glaze begins as molten glass, it is more likely to be transparent, so formulating an opaque glaze requires a surprising amount of attention to detail.

Considering the Nature of Light

To be adequately opaque for ceramic use, a glaze must reflect and scatter, rather than transmit, the light that falls upon it. To understand how light scatters, consider the nature of light.

Light cannot pass through a totally opaque material. A sheet of steel and a wall of concrete are examples of opaque materials. An opacifier, however, is not necessarily opaque. If it is not opaque, then how does an opacifier render a ceramic glaze opaque?

In a vacuum all light, say sunlight, for example, travels in a straight line from its source. When it encounters some material, the light is scattered; that is, it is either reflected back at an angle of less than 180 degrees or deflected forward at an angle greater than 180 degrees.

Few materials are totally opaque (reflect all light). If we slice them thinly enough, some light will pass through virtually all glazes. However, that light may be heavily scattered. That means the formerly straight beam of light changes direction when it hits some surface in the glaze.

The surfaces on and within glazes that scatter light are most often those of small crystals. These crystals, which opacify glazes, may be zirconium silicate (zircon) ground to a fine powder and added to the recipe. An alternative is to design the recipe and firing conditions so crystals will form in the glaze, either when it melts or as it cools. Wood-fired and wood-ash glazes are almost always opacified in this way.

In some cases, glazes are opacified by the formation of separate glass phases or by the addition of specific chemicals that do not fully dissolve in the glaze. Tin is the most common example of the latter method of opacification. The first attempts by European artists to duplicate the fine white porcelains imported from China relied on

Testing Opacifiers

JOHN'S 10x SERIES #12

Cone 6

Ingredient	%
Talc	10 %
Whiting	10
Ferro Frit 3134	10
Ferro Frit 3195	10
Custer Feldspar	10
Spodumene	10
Ball Clay	10
Kaolin	10
Silica (200 mesh)	10
Silica (325 mesh)	10
	100 %

2% Zircopax · 4% Zircopax · 6% Zircopax · 8% Zircopax · 10% Zircopax

2% Tin Oxide · 4% Tin Oxide · 6% Tin Oxide · 8% Tin Oxide · 10% Tin Oxide

2% Titanium Dioxide · 4% Titanium Dioxide · 6% Titanium Dioxide · 8% Titanium Dioxide · 10% Titanium Dioxide

low-fire clay bodies and low-fire, lead-fluxed, tin-opacified white glazes.

If the cooling portion of a firing cycle is slow enough, crystals will always precipitate from highly flux-rich glazes. At high-fire temperatures, calcium, magnesium, and barium, if present in a sufficient proportion, all produce such crystals. At mid-range, sodium, potassium, and lithium do likewise. While there is considerable overlap in the temperatures at which these fluxes dissolve and later precipitate, zircon opacifiers work at all firing temperatures.

A separate glass phase must have chemistry sufficiently different than that of the surrounding glass in order to have a different physical structure. Opalescence in phosphorous-rich glazes is an example of phase separation causing light scattering.

Titanium, either pure or in the form of rutile, while it's usually added as a colorant, can also be a glaze opacifier. Depending on its concentration and particle size in the glaze, its effect will vary. Finally, an abundance of fine bubbles in a cooled glaze will render it translucent to opaque.

Metal Marking and Zircon

Zircon is currently the most common glaze opacifier. It has been sold under many names over the years—Ultrox, Zircopax, and Superpax are such names. Zircon is mined from naturally occurring mineral sands, which are then cleaned and ground to different levels of fineness. Particle size and chemical purity vary depending on source and processing.

The recipe amount of zircon used for glaze opacification and whitening is usually less than 15% of the batch weight, sometimes much less. Where other light-scattering crystals also form in the glaze, 3–5% zircon may be sufficient.

While zircon is exceptionally effective as an opacifier, it can be problematic when added to glazes used on dinnerware. That's because zircon contributes to metal marking.

Metal marking on glazes opacified with zircon occurs because the opacifier is much harder than eating utensils. Unsightly gray lines on the glaze surface are evidence that knives, forks, and spoons have been drawn across the pottery. When the metal marks cannot be removed by washing it's because the metal has been left in tiny pits in the glaze. The pits are created when the hard zircon is dragged out by the use of the eating utensils.[1]

Glossy and matte glazes opacified by means other than zircon typically do not suffer from permanent metal marking. That's because eating utensils, while softer than zircon, are harder than most glazes.

Testing for Resistance to Knife Marking[2]

The best test for knife marking is simply to use your pottery yourself. It is always easier to see on white or light colored glazes and you will know after a few months whether or not this is a problem for a particular glaze. This test takes time and an accelerated version would be useful. Perhaps the easiest test is to take any coin, knife, or metal tool and firmly drag that metal across the glazed surface to be tested. After a few tries with both a glossy and a matte glaze you will learn how much pressure to use to leave metal marks. Repeat several times and examine the surface carefully. The marks you see (if any) are tiny particles of the metal which have been abraded by the ceramic surface. They will lodge in microscopic crevices of the glaze and can be easy or difficult to remove (1). If you can remove them by rubbing with your thumb, they are probably at a satisfactory level. The best situation is, of course, not to have made any visible marks. Sometimes the marks will not come off even after vigorous scrubbing with a scouring powder. If they are this difficult to remove, the glaze should not be used on surfaces subject to metal contact such as plates, the insides of bowls and cups, etc. It is also important to point out that a glaze that is attacked by acids or bases will metal mark worse over time. The etching from the acids/bases will leave a rougher surface that will abrade metal more easily and be more difficult to clean.

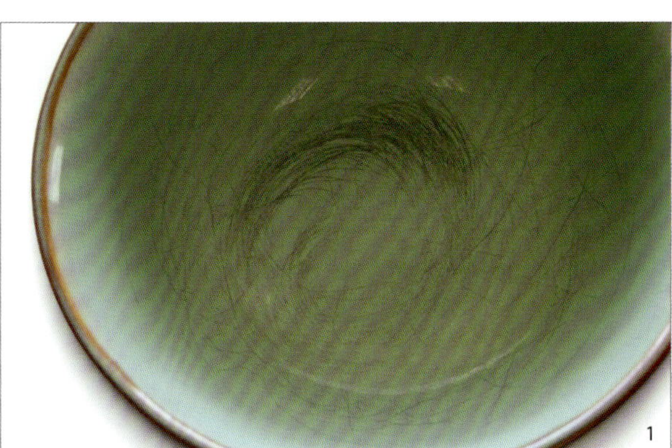

1

[1]Metal Marking of Dinnerware Glaze: Correlation with Friction and Surface Roughness, Hyojin Lee, Dr. William M. Carty, Robert J. Castilone, in: "Whitewares and Materials: Ceramic Engineering and Science Proceedings," Volume 25, Issue 2, 2004.

[2]Exerpted from *Mastering Cone 6 Glazes* by John Hesselberth and Ron Roy. The book is available on Apple's iBooks app or, a black-and-white version, at www.thebookpatch.com. To learn more check out www.masteringglazes.com.

107 Find more glaze recipes that work well with various opacifiers.

Silicon Carbide: The Stuff of Stars

by Mark Chatterley

Defining the Terms

Silicon Carbide (SiC): A hard compound composed of silicon and carbon, also called carborundum that is used as an abrasive in grinding applications. It is also a refractory and is used for making kiln furniture.

Localized Reduction: Producing reduction effects in a glaze while firing in an oxidizing atmosphere. The reduction is achieved through the inclusion of small amounts of silicon carbide (approximately 0.3% should work, depending on the colorant used) in the glaze or slip. The silicon carbide remains unaffected in a glaze until above 1832°F (1000°C), but after that point the molten glaze around it causes the bonds between the silicon and carbon to break. These separate molecules seek to bond with oxygen to create silica and carbon monoxide or dioxide. The silica becomes part of the glaze melt, and the carbon gases bubbls to the surface of the glaze and escape. —Definition excerpted from *The Potter's Dictionary of Materials and Techniques* by Frank Hamer

carborundum brick Grinding blocks made from silicon carbide and designed for abrading glaze drips from kiln shelves and smoothing the bottom of fired ware.

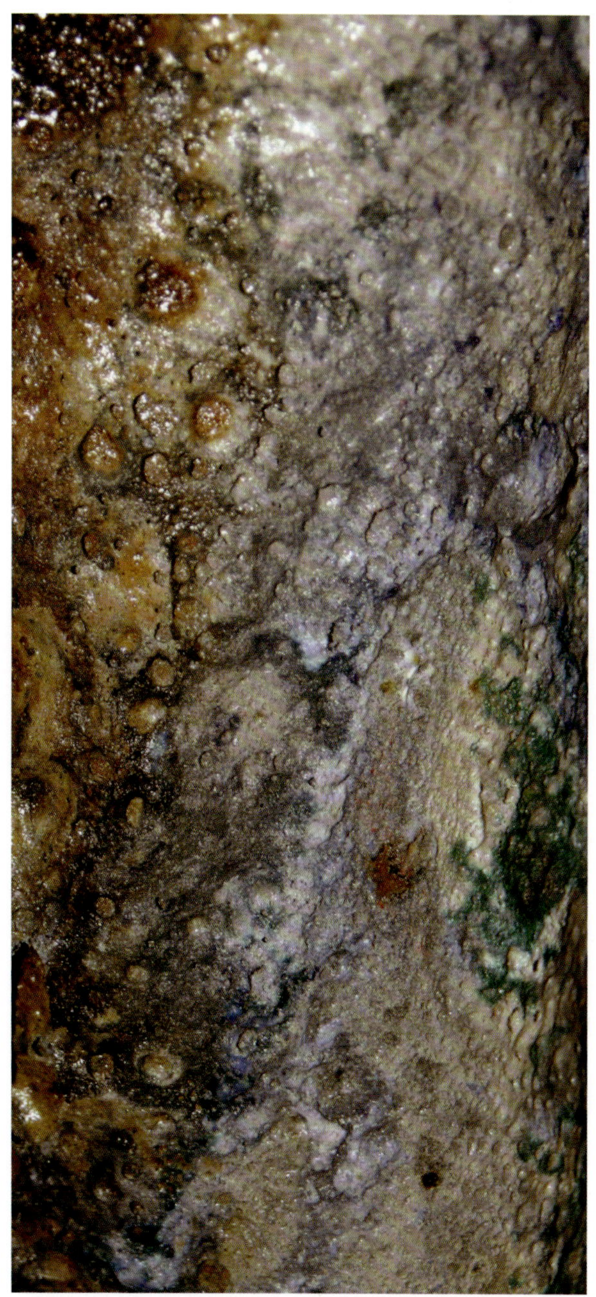

Silicon carbide, or carborundum, is an interesting material. It was first discovered in 1893 in an attempt to make artificial diamonds. It is found naturally in a rare material called moissanite that comes from meteors (astronomers and astrophysicists speculate that carbon stars have silicon carbide dust floating around them). However, the silicon carbide we use is man made. This chemical has a wide range of industrial uses, from grinding wheels and bullet-proof vests to electronic circuits and kiln shelves. I find it interesting that a material that has such a high temperature range for a kiln shelf will react in a glaze.

Some potters have used small amounts (0.5%, 500 mesh) in copper red glazes to enhance reduction. This happens because when the SiC bond is broken, the carbon molecule wants to stabilize by using an oxygen molecule from the copper oxide. But in larger amounts, it creates bubbles in the form of carbon gas coming through the glaze. What happens when it is fired is that carbon gas is released (looking for oxygen to bond with), leaving the silica behind. This is why I suggest starting with a shiny glaze when experimenting.

Glazes made with silicon carbide are not food safe.

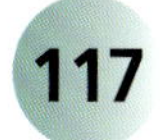

117 See mid-range crater glaze recipes made by adding silicon carbide to base glazes.

Suspenders and Binders for Glaze

by David Pier

Defining the Terms

Gum: In the context of glaze chemistry, organic compounds derived from plants, bacteria, or fungi, that act as suspenders and/or binders. In many ceramics studios, the word is also often applied to the mineral suspenders.

Suspender: Any additive whose primary purpose is to slow or eliminate settling, and sometimes to prevent the glaze from settling as hard. Most suspenders are also binders.

Binder: Any additive whose primary purpose is to harden the dry, unfired glaze coat.

Organic: Chemicals mostly made of carbon. Unlike most glaze chemicals (which are inorganic minerals), organic compounds can be food for bacteria and therefore must either be used up quickly once mixed or mixed with an antibacterial preservative.

Brushability: Desirable properties for brushing glazes are a) slower drying time to make for smooth brush marks; b) reduced surface tension to allow glaze to flow into fine detail (a few drops of common dish soap will reduce the surface tension of any glaze. The small mineral content of this soap is unlikely to affect the fired appearance); and c) harder drying to prevent lifting and flaking from additional brush passes.

Viscosity: The resistance of a fluid to deformation such as from stirring or pouring. Water is an example of a low viscosity liquid and honey of a high viscosity liquid.

Fluidity: The opposite (reciprocal) of viscosity. Water has higher fluidity than honey.

Thixotropy: The property of some clays and glazes that are solid or semi-solid (gelled) under static conditions to become dramatically more fluid when stirred or otherwise agitated. Thixotropy is closely related to the terms *shear thinning* and *pseudoplasticity*, but only the term thixotropy is commonly used in ceramics studios, even when actually referring to shear thinning.

Shear Thinning: Very similar to thixotropy, but whereas thixotropic materials become increasingly more fluid with continued but constant shear rate, shear thinning fluids only become more fluid with increasing shear rate. For any thixotropic or shear thinning material there is a yield value, a minimum shear stress that must be applied for viscosity to decrease (think of how hard you have to whack the bottle of thixotropic ketchup).

Pseudoplasticity: A more general fluid mechanics term that encompasses both thixotropy and shear thinning.

Potent additives can make your life much easier and increase your glazing success. The drudgery of extensive stirring and the flaws from fragile unfired glaze coatings can be put behind you.

Gaining Control of the Mix

A suspender is simply any additive whose primary purpose is to slow or eliminate settling. They typically work by absorbing a huge amount of water, thereby thickening (increasing the viscosity of) the glaze. A binder is any additive whose primary purpose is to harden the dry, unfired glaze coat. Binders usually make it easier to apply multiple and thick glaze coats. Most of these materials function as both suspenders and binders; there is only one common material that is exclusively a binder, and that's gum arabic.

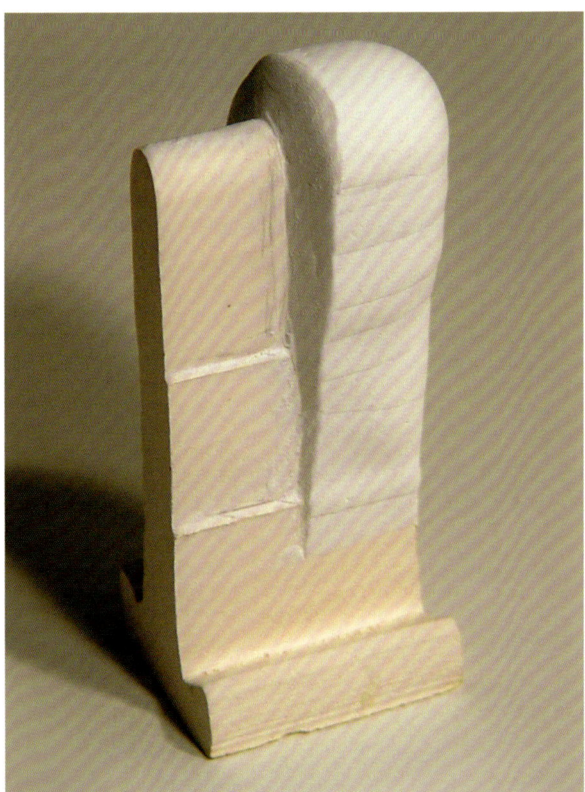

Repeatedly dipped in a simple glaze (100% frit with 3% added MAGMA), the above tile shows how a good binder allows unlimited glaze layering as well as carving. The glaze on the left half of the tile was carved away without chipping the remaining glaze.

Add to an Existing Wet Glaze

a) Calculate/estimate the maximum amount of suspender you might end up using in the batch. If you end up mixing more than you need, consider mixing in a preservative.
b) Add suspender powder to hot water; for every 20 grams suspender add to about 80 ml of hot water, then add a little more water bringing the concentrate to a total of 100 ml.
c) Mix with a hand blender, or wait a few hours for the mixture to thoroughly combine into a gel/syrup; depending on the suspender it might take some time, even overnight.
d) Add gel/syrup in small increments to your glaze.
e) Mix together with an electric mixer until the suspender is thoroughly dispersed.

Add Suspender to a Dry Glaze Batch

a) Calculate and weigh out an appropriate quantity of suspender, add preservative if necessary. (Typically .5–2%; for the example below we are using .75%)
b) Mix suspender (and preservative powders) with the glaze dry ingredients. The combination and mixing of dry ingredients will prevent the suspender from clumping.
c) Use hot water unless contraindicated by another ingredient. The hotter the water, the faster the dispersion will be.
d) Add the dry mixture to a normal amount of water for the glaze batch (the glaze will be thicker than normal). Wait a few hours to ensure full dispersion and absorption then sieve the glaze as usual.

CMC Gel/Syrup to Wet Glaze

Mixed Wet Glaze (approximate amounts)	CMC Gum Gel/Syrup (approximate amounts)
4 oz.	add ¾ tsp.
20 oz.	add 3¾ tsp.
40 oz.	add 2½ Tbsp.
1 Gallon	add ½ cup
3 Gallons	add 1½cups

Dry CMC Gum to Dry Glaze

Mixed Glaze Dry Ingred. (approximate amounts)	Dry CMC Gum (approximate amounts)
100 grams	add .75 grams
500 grams	add 3.75 grams
1000 grams	add 7.5 grams
3500 grams	add 26 grams
10,000 grams	add 75 grams

Only flocculents can sometimes improve suspension while actually worsening binding. Therefore, for the rest of this discussion, the word suspender will mean suspender/binder.

Because suspenders absorb so much water, glazes containing them shrink more when drying. This can sometimes lead to cracking and crawling, especially when suspenders are used in quantities exceeding the recommended ranges, but more often suspenders actually decrease cracking because their binding power increases cohesiveness and because they dry slowly, which gives the glaze more time to adjust to the stress of shrinking.

These additives can be broadly divided into organic and mineral categories. Mineral suspenders are clay-like minerals and are, by far, the most frequently used (when added to clay bodies they increase plasticity, but mixed up by themselves they are not plastic and so are not clay). They can be used as the only suspending material in a glaze. Their effects on suspension are more dramatic than on binding, but they do improve binding. They become part of the fired glaze, but because their chemical composition is similar to clay (and they are typically used at only about 2% of dry ingredients) they usually do not noticeably alter the final appearance. The most common mineral suspenders are bentonite and Veegum-T. There are many different sources of bentonite, varying somewhat in strength and quite a bit in iron and other impurity content. In most circumstances the different mineral suspenders can be used interchangeably, perhaps with a small adjustment in quantity to account for different potencies. Mineral suspenders usually exhibit thixotropy, which means that they gel when not being stirred. This improves suspension more than simply increasing the viscosity, sometimes completely preventing any settling.

Organic suspenders, usually called gums, are usually even more potent in most ways than the mineral suspenders. They also have the advantage of almost completely burning out and therefore leaving the fired glaze unaltered. Many of them also are more effective binders than the mineral suspenders. One drawback is that they will rot after several days to months if there is no preservative. Not only do they lose effectiveness, but it makes a nasty stink. This rotting is easily prevented by the addition of a preservative. There are some preservatives sold specifically for this, but they are quite toxic to people as well as to the bacteria. I have found the best preservative is one you already have in your studio: copper carbonate. It only requires 0.04% of total dry batch (0.4g $CuCO_3$ per 1000g

Glaze Additives

MATERIAL	TYPICAL USAGE RATE*	REQUIRES PRESERVATIVE?	TOXICITY	IMPORTANT PROPERTIES
Bentonite, White Bentonite	.5%–3%	No	Inhalation Hazard	More properly sodium bentonite. Most common suspender. Mineral suspender and binder. Some bentonites contain enough iron to change the color of glazes. Calcium bentonite is sometimes used in clay bodies, but it does not aid in glaze suspension.
Veegum-T	.4%–2%	No	Inhalation Hazard	High purity and high potency bentonite produced by the R.T. Vanderbilt company. It has almost no iron impurity.
Veegum Cer	.2%–2%	Yes	Inhalation Hazard	Mixture of Veegum-T (for suspension) and CMC gum (for binding and brushability). More potent than either Veegum-T or CMC alone.
Bentone MA Bentone EW (aka Macaloid)	.4%–2%	No	Inhalation Hazard	Purified hectorite mineral suspenders produced by Elementis Specialties. Potent mineral suspenders with properties essentially the same as Veegum-T. Some grades have low iron similar to Veegum-T.
CMC gum	.05%–2% (powder)	Yes	None	A chemically modified cellulose gum (specifically, sodium carboxymethylcellulose gum—adding a tiny amount of soluble sodium to your recipe.) Most useful as a binder and brushing aid, aiding in smooth brushstrokes due to longer drying times. As a suspender, it slows settling instead of preventing it, since it does't exhibit thixotropy. The small sodium content can actually deflocculate any clay in the recipe, thereby reducing thixotropy, actually worsening settling over time. The same slow drying that can aid in brushing is often a nuisance in a dipping glaze, as the glaze can remain wet beyond a minute. Since CMC is manufactured in various grades, it doesn't always work as expected. Sometimes sold already mixed as a concentrated syrup, although there is no standard concentration.
MAGMA gum	.05%–3% (Typical glaze usage is .4%–1%)	Yes	None	Thixotropic organic gum blend. Can indefinitely suspend even a zero clay glaze when used at 3%. Strong binder
Starch, e.g. Sta-Flo liquid laundry starch	1%–100%	Yes	None	Poor suspender at low concentrations, mostly used for binding and improved brushability. Expensive compared to gums because so much starch is required to match the strength of gums.
Gum Arabic/ Acacia Gum	3%–30% (dry powder)	Yes	None	Binder/hardener only. Increases drying time. Does not significantly increase viscosity of glaze. In addition to binding, it reduces surface tension of liquid, allowing easier flow into fine detail. Also commonly sold already mixed as a liquid, mostly for use in watercolor painting, although there is no standard concentration.
Other food gums (guar, locust, bean, konjac, tragacanth, xanthan, etc.)	.1%–2%	Yes	None	Most food gums will behave very much like CMC gum, although usually without the deflocculation. Potency varies between different gums and even between different batches of the same gum. Most do not exhibit thixotropy. Some are available in the vitamin area of grocery stores.
Glycerin and propylene glycol	1%–100%	Yes	None	Very weak suspenders, used primarily to improve brushability. Does not increase drying shrinkage. Not very cost effective compared to gums.
Ethylene glycol (auto antifreeze)	1%–100%	Yes	Toxic through skin absorption or ingestion	Very weak suspender, used primarily to improve brushability. Very toxic and not very cost effective.
Flocculents (e.g. Epsom Salts, calcium chloride)		Some do	Varies	Chemicals that are sometimes used to aid in glaze suspension. They increase the water holding power of clays, bentonites, and similar materials, but not of organic gums. Flocculents typically make the dry glaze coat more fragile.

dry glaze) to indefinitely prevent rotting. This amount of copper, if properly dispersed, is almost never visible in the fired glaze.**

Suspenders, most dramatically the organic gums, also slow the drying of glazes. Sometimes this is an advantage, as it allows easier brushing, or touching up of drips after dipping. Too slow, though, and glazing takes longer, since it is hard to put the piece down until the glaze has dried. If you start your experimentation with usage levels at the lower end suggested in the chart, and then work your way up, you will find the quantity that balances suspending, binding, and drying time to best suit your work habits. CMC gum is particularly potent in slowing drying.

CMC gum is the most common gum and is typically used in brushing glazes, as it is better at binding and slowing drying than it is at suspending. CMC doesn't exhibit thixotropy, and can actually reduce any thixotropy already present, so it only slows rather than prevents settling. Much of CMC's prevalence is due to CMC having been available for many decades before most of the other gums. A recently introduced organic gum, MAGMA, exhibits strong thixotropy and can prevent settling of any glaze, indefinitely, without as much slowing of drying time as CMC. Because of the thixotropy, MAGMA is more or less suitable for different brushing techniques. (MAGMA is suitable for all applications, but CMC is often preferable for brushing since it provides smoother brushstrokes due to slower drying. However, that should be weighed against the potential for dripping of CMC glazes on dipped pots.)***

There are many other organic gums available, although not usually from ceramic suppliers. Most of them behave similarly to CMC gum, although potency varies widely.

Tips for Smooth Mixing

If you leave these additives out of your slips and glazes, they'll look pretty much the same after the firing as if you had put them in. So why bother? Imagine big buckets of glazes that only need a few seconds of stirring, even if they have been sitting unused for over a year. Imagine unfired glazes that never chip because they are as hard as the bisque they are applied to! It isn't magic that makes commercial, ready-to-use glazes so easy to use; it's the additives. Most of these materials are sold as dry powders. If you sprinkle them into your already-mixed glazes, you'll get little globs that will hinder rather than help glazing. If you try to sieve them, you'll be trying all day and night. Below are two basic methods of adding suspenders to your slip or glaze while avoiding clumping and excess water.

*Lower for higher clay glazes, higher for lower clay glazes.

**Of course, copper is quite toxic to people, too, but it is not normally absorbed through the skin in large quantities. All normal precautions should be taken with this copper. This demonstrates how potent a toxin copper can be.

***MAGMA was developed by the author. He no longer has any financial interest in it.

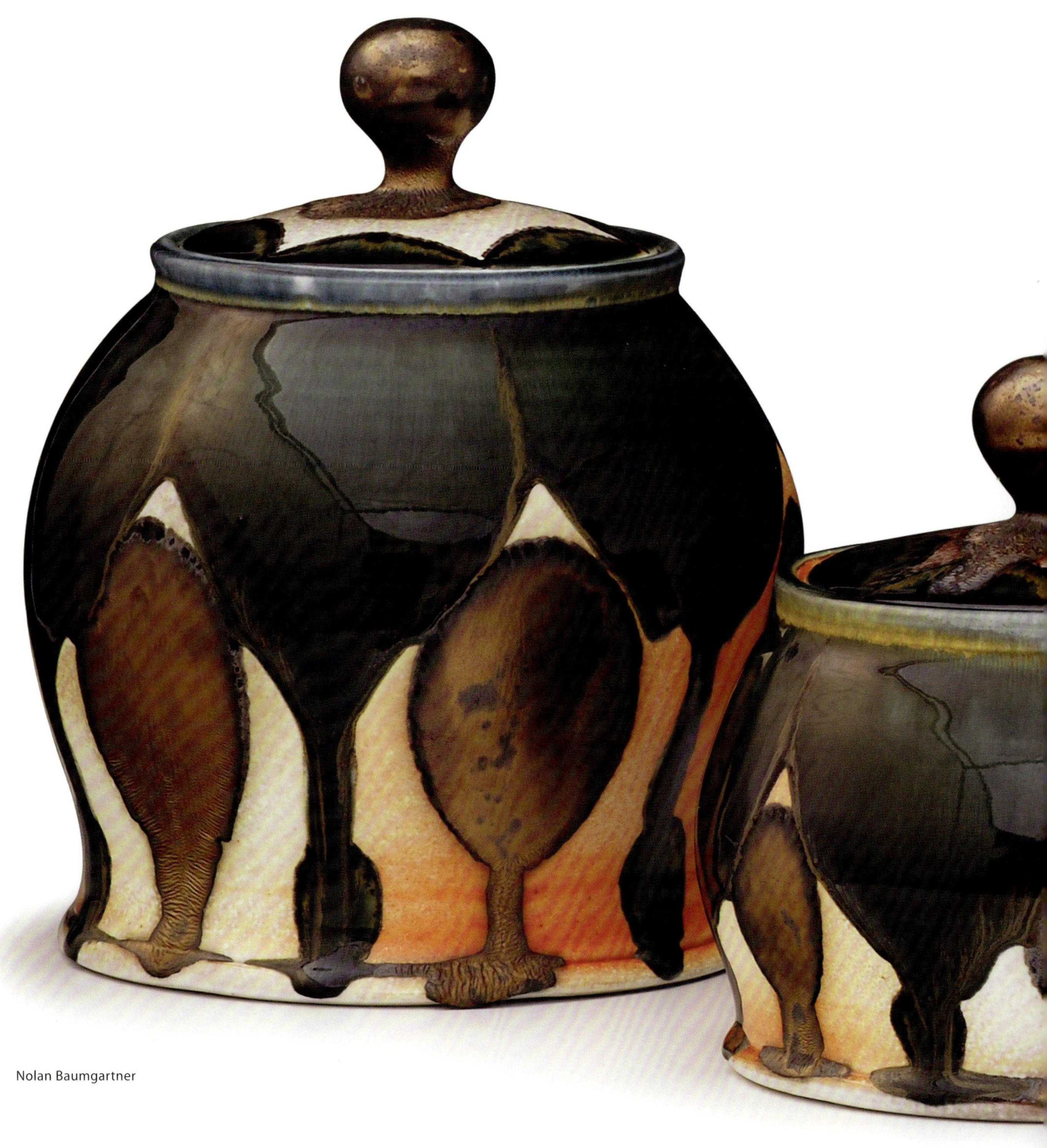

Nolan Baumgartner

SECTION 2

Stuido Application

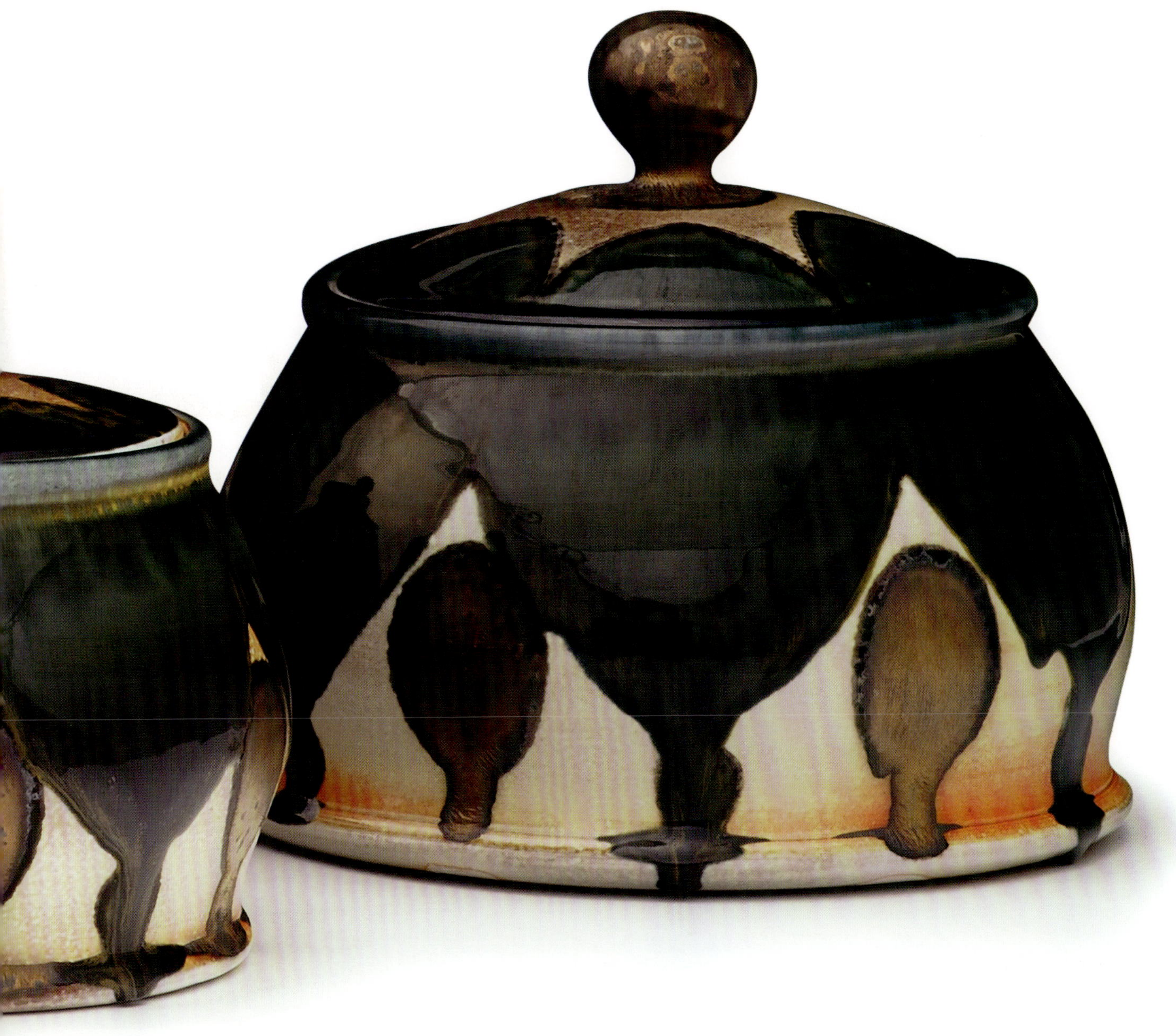

CHAPTER 1

In the Studio: Pracitcal Physics

Mesh Size

by John Britt

Defining the Terms

Mesh Size—A count of the number of strands per inch in a screen that is used to grade the particle size of the material. Theoretically, in a 100-mesh material sample, approximately 95% of the particles should pass through a 100-mesh sieve (this means that 1–5% of the particles will remain in the pan). A larger mesh-size number indicates smaller particles so 100-mesh particles are larger than 200-mesh particles. In ceramics, mesh sizes generally range from 25 to 325 mesh, smaller particles are referred to in microns.

Micron—A unit of length one-millionth of a meter or one twenty-five thousandth of an inch.

Particle Size—Also called grain size. It is relevant in terms of how long the particle will take to dissolve in a glaze melt and also in terms of plasticity, shrinkage, and strength of a clay body.

Sieve—A device with a screen or mesh bottom used to separate out coarse or unwanted particles. Most glazes are sieved twice through an 80-mesh sieve. Can be done dry or wet.

Potters often buy whatever selection of materials suppliers provide without thinking about the consequences or even the potential artistic possibilities. Using the correct particle size and distribution for the job you are doing requires some basic knowledge of material properties followed by some creative experimenting.

Size Matters

Size, on many levels, makes a big difference in both clay bodies and glazes. For example, if you have a glaze recipe that calls for 30% silica and you used 325-mesh silica, it would create a smooth and glossy glaze, but if you used silica sand (40 mesh), you would have a rough and crusty glaze.

Mesh sizing originally referred to the number of threads per linear inch of mesh, which presumed the same number of holes. Of course, thread size caused variance so uniform international standards measured in micrometers have been adopted. So a 100-mesh sieve has 100 square holes per inch which measure 0.152 mm (or 152 microns). Theoretically, in a 100-mesh sample, 95% of the particles should pass through a 100-mesh sieve. A higher mesh size number indicates smaller particles so 100-mesh particles are larger than 200-mesh particles. If you continue to add more and more threads to a screen, eventually you will clog all the holes. So anything beyond 325–500 mesh is usually described in microns.

Because the sieve hole is a square, the size of the diagonal is larger than the width and length. Larger particles can make it through the diagonal and that is why you often sieve several times.

Describing a material as 100 mesh is not very precise as you don't know the size of the 95% of particles that passed through the sieve. A more precise notation has been established which uses -/+ signs. So a particle that is "-80 /+100"means that 95% of the particles passed through(-) the 80 mesh sieve but were retained(+) by the 100-mesh sieve. In ceramics, grogs are often listed more precisely as 12–48, (or -12/+48) which shows the range of particle size.

Today, because our grinding technology is vastly improved, the particle size (expressed as mesh size) is much different than it was just 50 years ago. For example, 50 years ago the standard silica for glazes was 200 mesh, which meant that 95% of the particles passed through a 200-mesh sieve. We do not know exactly how fine 95% of the particles were, we just know that they passed through the 200-mesh sieve. But now that same 200-mesh silica is much finer because our grinding ability is so much better. So the 95% of the particles that passed through the sieve are much finer and that affects the melting of those particles. Using 200-mesh silica now may be closer to using 325 mesh back in the day. Knowing the particle distribution may help and is generally available from many suppliers. For example, Minspar 200 lists that 87% of particles are finer than 30 microns; 72% are finer than 20 microns; 40% are finer than 10 microns; and 19% smaller

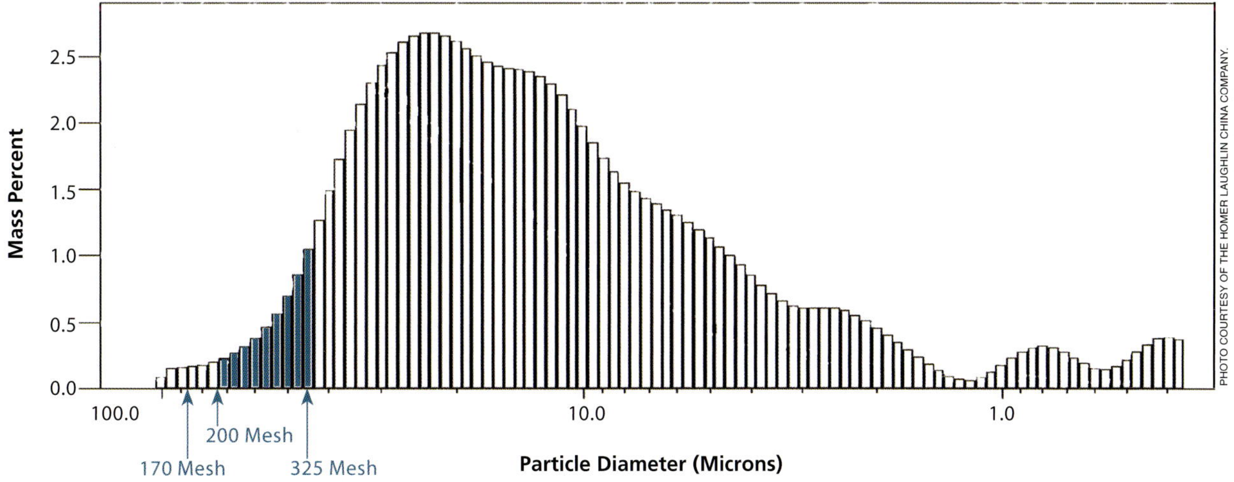

Minspar 200

PARTICLE SIZE	% RETAINED
20 mesh	0.0
30 mesh	0.0
40 mesh	0.0
100 mesh	trace
140 mesh	trace
170 mesh	0.1
200 mesh	0.3
325 mesh	3.6
30 micron	9.0
20 micron	15.0
10 micron	32.0
5 micron	21.0
< 5 micron	19.0

Typical sieve analysis of a 50 pound bag of 200-mesh Minspar 200 (a soda feldspar mined by Imerys Minerals in North Carolina). Note that 3.6% of the material passes through the 200-mesh screen but is retained by the 325-mesh screen, so very little of the material is actually graded at precisely 200 mesh.

than 5 microns. The graph below shows the variation in particle size of a sample of Minspar 200, ranging from 100 microns to less than 1.0 micron, with the vast majority between 3 and 50 microns.

Clay Bodies

Although clays are described as 200 mesh, many are actually much finer than 325 mesh (40 microns). For example, in a 200-mesh sample of EPK, approximately 55-65% of kaolin particles are less than 2 microns, while approximately 81% of ball clay particles are less than 2 microns and many can be as low as 0.1 microns or 400 times smaller than 325 mesh.

Porcelain bodies are often difficult to throw because the particles (kaolin, feldspar, and silica) in the body are all approximately 200 mesh or less, making it a homogenous clay body. Stoneware bodies, however, are a mix of various clays and particle sizes. They contain fire clays, which are 25–50 mesh; ball clays, which are 200 mesh; and then grogs, which can be 12–80 mesh.

Grog is often added to sculptural bodies to give them strength and reduce shrinkage. Val Cushing lists a proportion of: 12% fine grog, 3% medium grog, and 15% coarse grog, for a total of 30%. This is how you can produce non-shrinking sculptural clay bodies. In a plastic clay body this proportion of mixed mesh-size grog helps fill all the voids and avoids micro-cracking around larger particles.

Grog is often listed by the largest particle size, for example 30 mesh. This tells you the size of the largest particle but not the smallest. Some grogs are listed as 30–80 mesh, meaning that the largest particles are 30 mesh and the smallest are 80 mesh.

Glazes

Melting particles in glazes can be compared to dissolving sugar in tea. The particle size of the sugar makes a big difference in the amount of sugar that will dissolve into the tea and thus how sweet it is. For example, two sugar cubes will not dissolve as easily as the same weight of crystallized sugar and certainly won't dissolve as easily as

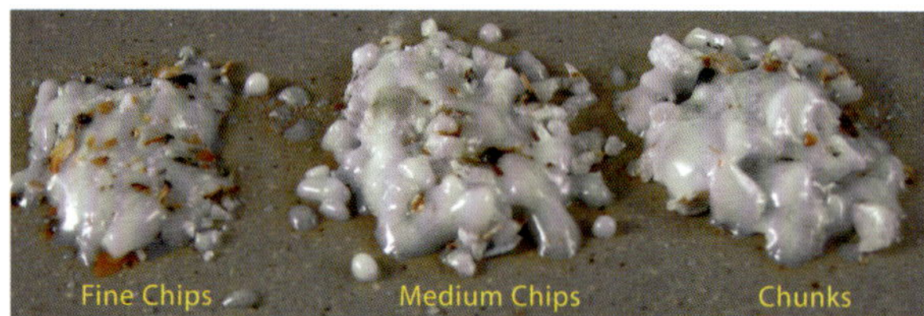

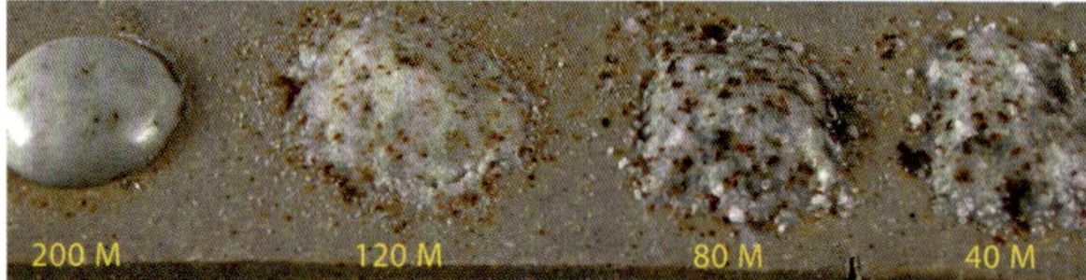

Melt tests showing various grades of unprocessed feldspars, fired to cone 10 in reduction.

the same weight of powdered sugar. This is because there is more surface area per weight in the fine particles and they enter the melt easier. In glazes, the same principle applies; 325-mesh silica will go into the melt easier than the same amount of 200-mesh silica.

Mesh size can be related to other properties, like solubility. For example, nepheline syenite has two grinds available to potters, 270 mesh and 400 mesh. Theoretically the 400 mesh would go into the glaze melt better than the 270 mesh. But because it is slightly soluble, using the finer 400 mesh (more surface area) will also cause the glaze slurry to deflocculate quicker and the glaze will settle out and hard pan more easily. So there's a trade off.

The mesh sizes in some materials are kept large to create specific effects, like granular illmenite or granular rutile. These create intentional speckles used in glazes like Jackie's Speckled Lavender. Other materials, like silicon carbide, are specific sizes to encourage cratering in glazes. Some sculptural low-fire glazes may specify sand in the glaze to add texture. In the case of Bleeding Cake, the sand is used to get a surface that looks like Red Velvet Cake.

Colorants

Mesh size can make a big difference with colorants. For example, when making a blue celadon, if you use 100-mesh black iron oxide (an old-school way of mixing blue celadon with a coarse grind) you might get speckling. This can be corrected by ball milling the colorant in a small amount of the glaze for several hours then adding it to the whole batch. But by simply changing the colorant to synthetic red iron oxide (a very fine type of iron at 325 mesh) which goes into the melt more easily without ball milling, you get no speckling.

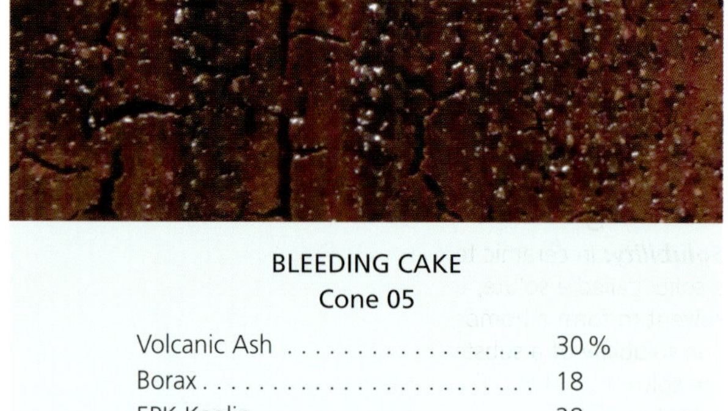

BLEEDING CAKE
Cone 05

Volcanic Ash	30 %
Borax	18
EPK Kaolin	28
Sand	15
	100 %
Add: Yellow Iron Oxide	5 %
Red Iron Oxide	5 %

Apply thick. To make it look wetter, sprinkle on borax after dipping.

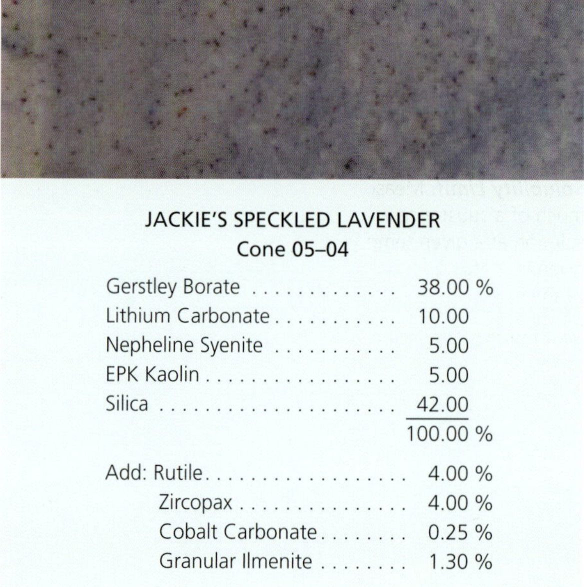

JACKIE'S SPECKLED LAVENDER
Cone 05–04

Gerstley Borate	38.00 %
Lithium Carbonate	10.00
Nepheline Syenite	5.00
EPK Kaolin	5.00
Silica	42.00
	100.00 %
Add: Rutile	4.00 %
Zircopax	4.00 %
Cobalt Carbonate	0.25 %
Granular Ilmenite	1.30 %

Routinely putting glazes through a ball mill (approximately 2 hours) is also a good way to smooth out a glaze batch by slightly grinding the particles, but grinding glazes for too long (beyond 4 hours) will reduce the particle/mesh size too much and cause the glazes to crawl. The most efficient grinding is when there is just enough material in the ball mill to fill all the voids and just cover the grinding media. If ball milled too long, the small particles in the glaze will shrink excessively when they melt and cause crawling. Ball milling is usually done wet with glazes but can be done dry.

Solubility

by Dave Finkelnburg

Defining the Terms

Solubility: In ceramic terms, the property of a solid, called a solute, to dissolve in a liquid solvent to form a homogeneous solution. The solubility of a substance depends on the solvent used and the temperature. The extent of the solubility of a substance in a specific solvent is measured as its saturation, where adding more solute does not increase the concentration of the solution.

Solute: A substance which is dissolved by a solvent to form a solution.

Solution: A homogeneous mixture composed of two or more substances.

Soluble: A measure of how much of something (a solute) will be dissolved by a liquid (the solvent) to form a solution.

Saturation: When a solution contains 100% of its capacity to hold a particular element or compound in solution.

Solubility Limit: Measurement of how much of a substance will dissolve into a solution at a given temperature, usually given in mass of the substance per volume of the solvent such as grams/liter.

Scumming: A deposit of soluble salts on the surface of unglazed and bisque ware (most often red earthenware). The salts, dissolved in the water in the clay body, crystallize when they are left behind on the surface of the ware as the water from the body evaporates. This can happen during initial drying after forming or it can happen later after the clay is fired and subjected to repeated wet-dry cycles in use. This problem can usually be dealt with by the addition of barium carbonate to the clay body during mixing.

Solubles and Scum

A solid dissolves in a liquid because the attraction forces between atoms and molecules of the solid and liquid are greater than the attraction forces within the solid itself. Concentration of a solute, viscosity, and temperature of the solution affect the rate at which the solute dissolves, but not its solubility, which is determined by the strength of the attraction forces mentioned above. Weak bonds between the atoms or molecules of a solute allow it to be dissolved. In general, if the bonds are ionic (electrostatic attraction, typical of all salts) the material will be soluble. Covalent bonds, where electrons are actually shared between atoms, are unlikely to be broken without adding significant energy. This is not absolute because the strength of the covalent bonds vary. As an example, whiting is not soluble in water but if it's calcined, the resulting CaO converts to Ca(OH)2 in water and is slightly water soluble (0.19 g/100 mL).

While magnesium sulfate (Epsom salts) is easy to dissolve, whiting is extremely difficult and quartz cannot be dissolved at all in water under ordinary conditions.

Add a teaspoon (about 50 grams) of Epsom salts to a quart of water and it will soon dissolve. However, one can only add about five teaspoons of Epsom salts to a quart of water before the solution becomes saturated and no more Epsom salts will dissolve. If a solution contains more of a soluble element than the solution's solubility limit, the element will precipitate (or crystallize) out of the solution. That's why crystals can form over time in a bucket of glaze, and this changes the chemistry of what is still in solution.

Sugar will dissolve faster in water if the water is heated. Will that work with Epsom salts? Oddly enough, no. At room temperature Epsom salts are slightly less soluble than at near freezing! Lithium carbonate is also less soluble at higher temperatures. Soda ash, on the other hand, is about three times as soluble in water at room temperature as at 32°F. These examples help show that temperature does affect solubility but not necessarily as one might expect. Why don't all materials react the same to temperature? We don't know and one should not assume that raising the temperature of the solution raises solubility. Materials that are soluble in a glaze in summer may precipitate in winter, or vice versa, forming crystals entirely unrepresentative of the glaze batch that are big enough to affect the fired glaze.

The Good, the Bad, and the Ugly

Knowing which glaze ingredients are at least partly soluble in water can help avoid having a glaze that settles to a hard, dense layer in the bottom of a container. This "hard panning" is caused by soluble materials that deflocculate the glaze. Sources of the solubles can include feldspars and frits (over time frits dissolve slowly) but the worst offenders are highly

Troubleshooting Solubility

SOLUBILITY ISSUES	DESCRIPTIONS/CAUSES	SOLUTIONS
Hard Panning	The gradual settling of glaze while in storage due to the soluble materials deflocculating the glaze.	Add 1/4–1% (of dry batch weight) Epsom salts or 2% bentonite. Either will usually slow the settling.
Temperature	Solubility increases with temperature (most of the time.) Potters generally see this in their studios during the change of seasons as glaze buckets are continually affected.	For materials which are more soluble at higher temperatures, use hot water when mixing to speed up the dissolving.
Crystal Development	If concentration of something in the glaze is right on the edge of forming crystals, then falling temperatures (like from winter weather) may cause crystals to precipitate. Crystals also form due to saturation.	Know the solubility limit for suspect materials, and formulate glazes to stay below that limit.
Scumming/ Efflorescence	White residue that appears on the surface of various wares and is caused by soluble salts in the clay which crystallize at the surface as water evaporates. Deposits are visible when the soluble salt concentration is higher than .5%. Deposits intensify with an ambient temperature increase or with a decrease in relative humidity. During firing, the salts become oxides and on cool bisque appear as a removable dust. On a hot bisque, these salts can flux the body and can't be removed. Glazes can absorb the scummed oxides or may not absorb into the ware at all due to over-fluxing.	Some salts in the clay can be rendered harmless by the addition of ¼% to 2% of barium carbonate. The barium carbonate is only slightly soluble and must be added into the clay during the mixing stage as adding to pre-mixed clay and wedging is insufficient.

soluble wood ash and soda ash. Glazes stored for very long periods of time are best made without the latter two ingredients unless they also contain plenty of clay, bentonite, or Veegum. Besides these ingredients, glazes with feldspars and frits will hard pan less if dosed with a small quantity of a flocculant such as calcium chloride or Epsom salts. Use between 0.1 and 1% of a flocculant by weight of the dry glaze ingredients.

Being able to identify soluble ingredients can also help determine the cause and remedy for scumming. Irregular blotches of gray to white to pale yellow are left on the surface of the dried ware. So, what's wrong with scumming? The scum is usually calcium sulfate, sometimes contaminated with iron sulfate that has migrated to the surface by evaporation. The calcium fluxes the clay surface during firing, producing a glazed effect. This is most objectionable on terra cotta where no glaze had been intended.

Removal of scum from bone dry clay can only be done with difficulty. Wiping the surface carefully with a dilute acid solution such as vinegar in water may be sufficient. Scumming may be avoided by adding up to 2% barium carbonate to the dry clay body before mixing. This can convert the calcium sulfate in the clay to much less soluble calcium carbonate. Alternately, preparing the clay as a dilute slurry and removing the excess water with a filter press will usually remove enough of the solubles to prevent scumming.

It is possible for scumming to be used for positive effects. The most common example is found in the firing of carbon-trap glazes. In fact, carbon trapping relies on scumming to work. In shino glazes with a high soda-ash content, sodium is dissolved into the glaze slurry. When the water in the glaze evaporates from the ware, sodium is left behind, forming a crust on the glaze surface. Potters can control where the evaporation of the sodium deposits occur. This involves putting wax, cloth, paper, or plastic over some or all of the glaze surface to slow and direct evaporation, or allowing fans, sun, or wind to speed and direct the evaporation. Anything that slows evaporation on part of the clay surface will reduce

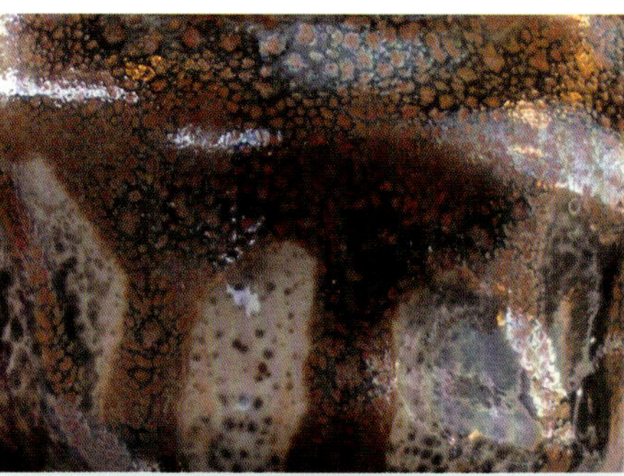

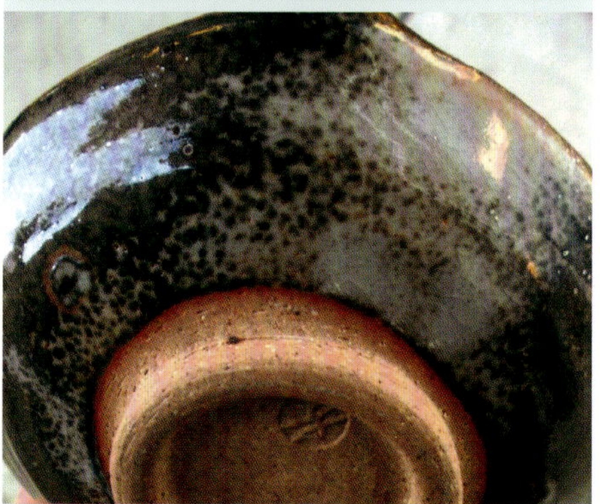

SHINO GLAZE

Cone 6 reduction

Soda Ash	10 %
Spodumene	40
Nepheline Syenite	40
EPK Kaolin	10
	100 %

Apply very thinly for an almost salt-glazed look. Tends to be bland in oxidation, an addition of 4% rutile warms it up a bit.

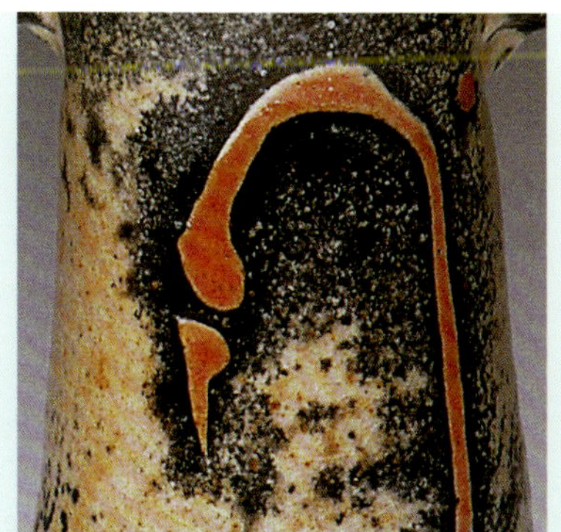

Detail of vase by Malcolm Davis, porcelain with Malcom Davis Shino Glaze.

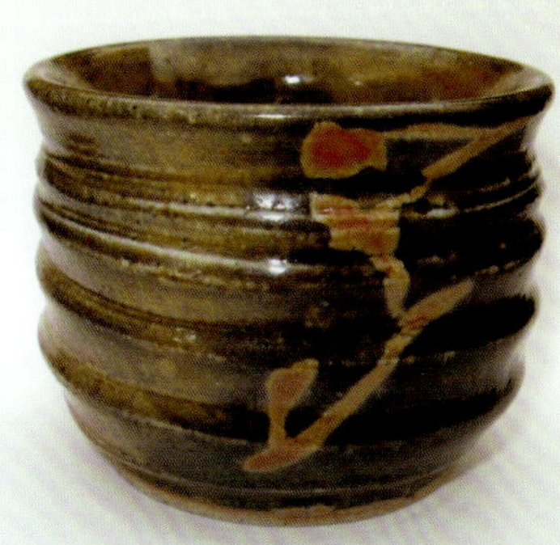

Cup by Dave Finkelnburg, stoneware with Malcolm Davis Shino Glaze.

MALCOLM DAVIS SHINO GLAZE

Cone10 reduction

Ingredient	%
Soda Ash	17.27 %
Kona F-4 Feldspar	9.82
Nepheline Syenite	40.91
EPK Kaolin	18.18
OM 4 Ball Clay	13.82
	100.00 %

carbon trapping there during the firing. Careful placement of the ware while drying can produce irregular patterns of sodium deposits. Additionally, care must be used to avoid disturbing the accumulated sodium scum as the pots are loaded in the kiln.

Just before the sodium scum melts, the kiln is thrown into heavy, sooty reduction. The scum melts before the rest of the glaze melts and this traps in the carbon. The kiln atmosphere is then changed just close to a neutral atmosphere to permit any untrapped carbon to burn off. When this is done before the remainder of the glaze melts, the result is a pattern of dark to light areas on the work depending on the degree of carbon trapping that occurs. The fired ware will be blackest where the scum was the heaviest.

On the cup I made that is pictured above, wax resist brushed onto the damp glaze produced an orange coloration. In drying there is very little soda ash scumming where the wax has been applied, so that portion of the glaze melts at a higher temperature than the glaze with a scum on it. There is an intermediate amount of scum on the left side of the piece compared to the right side, the result of stacking the piece close to another on the left. The heaviest scum melts first, and if the timing is right, traps the most carbon. The firing is timed to, hopefully, oxidize away the carbon that has not yet been trapped, leaving the wax resist portion with no black. It is possible to do this oxidation too early and get no trapping anywhere, or too late and the whole piece will remain black.

Viscosity

by Tina Gebhart

Define the Terms

Double Layer: The two charged layers surrounding a particle in suspension. The first layer, resulting from direct electrostatic charge attraction, is on the surface of that particle. The second layer is outside that and is composed of ions attracted from the surrounding solution.

Double Layer Compression: If more ions or stronger charge ions are available to neutralize the attraction between the two charged layers surrounding a particle in suspension, the second layer ends closer to the particle. This allows for surface-charge repulsion in particles, but allows them to be closer together, in a network. Clay particles normally have both electrostatic attractions and repulsions, as well as gentler attractions of Van der Waals forces, which attract based on proximity of particles, like a kind of gravity. This is similar to the idea that opposites attract; the compression state harnesses both properties to make a strong network, much like a strong community.

Peaking: Showing meringue-like points when a slip is stretched.

Poise: The cling of the glaze to the bisque ware during application. Officially a unit of measure for viscosity, but is often used in our field to describe the hang time and application activity of glaze/slip (i.e. physical drips, curtaining, and flowing away from edges on application).

Solids Loading: The actual amount of solid material/particulate in the suspension, regardless of the viscosity. Density of the suspension; mass per volume. The mass of ceramic material in the suspension, regardless of the viscosity.

Suspension: Liquid with particles floating within it. Slips and glazes are suspensions.

Solution: Liquid with a homogenous mixture of materials dissolved in it.

Super-Saturated Solution: A solution with enough of a material dissolved that the liquid cannot contain any more of that material. It is beyond its saturation point. Additional material will not dissolve, but falls to the bottom of the solution as solids/precipitates.

Viscosity: Resistance to flow, or anti-flow. Low viscosity flows a lot. High viscosity flows only a little or not at all.

How thickly or thinly we batch our glazes and slips can determine how much ceramic material is applied to our work. Changes to viscosity can determine whether shrinking, cracking, or application drips occur, and changing the viscosity does not have to mean adjusting the water content.

Finding the Flow

Glazes and slips are suspensions and behave with some amount of fluidity. This fluidity is a continuum, ranging from flowing-like-water to nearly-wedge-able. The formal term used to describe this property is viscosity.

Viscosity is the resistance to flow in a fluid or a fluid-like material. A high-viscosity fluid is thick and relatively non-flowing; a low-viscosity fluid is thin and flows with ease. We commonly use the terms thick and thin to describe these fluid states because a high-viscosity glaze typically applies a thick coating of material, and a low-viscosity glaze typically applies a thin coating. The terms high viscosity and low viscosity are more specific and clear than thick and thin, because they cannot be misunderstood as a measurement of an application layer thickness. *Applied thick* can mean *applied while in a high viscosity state*, or *applied so that there is more ceramic material present*, i.e. *a thicker coating*, and these meanings are not always interchangeable.

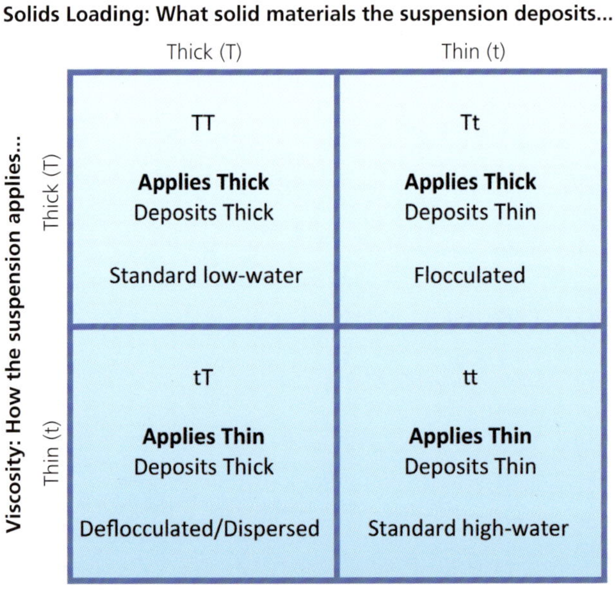

Solids Loading: What solid materials the suspension deposits...

Viscosity: How the suspension applies...	Thick (T)	Thin (t)
Thick (T)	TT **Applies Thick** Deposits Thick Standard low-water	Tt **Applies Thick** Deposits Thin Flocculated
Thin (t)	tT **Applies Thin** Deposits Thick Deflocculated/Dispersed	tt **Applies Thin** Deposits Thin Standard high-water

Visco-Loading Punnett Square:
Interaction of Viscosity and Solids Loading

1 Visco-Loading Punnett Square. The solids loading of a suspension batch illustrating the potential combinations of viscosity state and solids loading levels. A standard low-water mix looks thick, applies thickly, and deposits thickly—whereas a low-viscosity mix with higher solids loading (deflocculated/dispersed) looks thin, applies thinly, but deposits thickly.

When applying a suspension, the application process is the *how,* and the actual physical layer that results is the *what.* Viscosity determines *how* the suspension moves during application—*how* it applies. We can also call this property *poise.* Solids loading, the amount of solid material in the suspension, determines the physical thickness of a resultant suspension application—what material is deposited (1).

Measuring viscosity in ceramic suspensions can be a deceptive thing, because of the issue introduced above, that physical viscosity may not match the solids loading. The methods below are standard ways of measuring viscosity, each of which has some advantages and disadvantages. For ideal control in your suspension, any of these should be combined with specific gravity measurements to keep the solids loading consistent.

The Finger Test

This is a simple, non-numerical test performed by dipping one's finger into the well-mixed suspension. The finger is removed and the ceramist judges the remaining coating of suspension by eye. Judgment is based discerning the forms of the cuticle, fingernail, and skin folds through the ceramic material layer while it is still wet. Seeing the skin surface/color through the layer (visual sheerness) generally indicates very low viscosity; seeing no discernible form details, where the finger looks like a corn dog, is very high viscosity. Nuances of seeing some form details, with no sheerness, are the typical indicators of "just right" viscosity.

Pros: This test is quick, and tools are readily available. Cons: The measurements of low and high viscosity are relative to the particular suspension. Familiarity and practice with that particular suspension are needed to establish accurate judgment. This is not quantitative, and not easily transferable from person to person.

Drip Cup (Ford Cup or Zahn Cup)

These are cups of a standard volume that have a hole of standard size (there are multiple standard sizes) in the base, allowing a suspension to flow out. Drip cups have a ladle handle making them easy to dip and withdraw from the suspension bucket. A given volume of the suspension flows out of the hole, that flow time is recorded, and that time indicates the viscosity of that material.

Pros: This testing method is accurate for viscosity proper, and is consistent across different materials, slips, and glazes. Viscosity results can be well quantified, and data/accuracy is transferable between people and studios. Cons: Can be more physically awkward due to multiple tools (cup, timer) and simultaneous handling. Standard drip cups cannot be used with very high-viscosity suspensions.

Hydrometer

This is a glass bobber that floats at a certain depth depending on the viscosity of the suspension. Normally a hydrometer is used to measure the density (specific gravity) of a solution. When used to measure a suspension, a hydrometer is more effectively measuring viscosity (as will be apparent if used in a suspension before and after Darvan is added). This tool must still be paired with the long-hand specific gravity measurements below for full control. Hydrometers are made with different measurement ranges for different applications.

Pros: This testing method is fast, simple to use, and is quantifiable. Relative accuracy can be transferred between people/studios. Cons: Finding a hydrometer of the desired range in the desired length (so that it fits into your bucket) can be a slight challenge.

Specific Gravity

Specific gravity is a measurement to pair with the above viscosity measurements. Given that potential viscosity shifts may or may not indicate more or less water, we must check the amount of solids loading by measuring the specific gravity. A given volume of the suspension is weighed against the same volume of water, and the relationship between these two weights indicates how much particulate is present in the suspension. Traditionally, the volume used for testing specific gravity is 100mL, and this allows for comparison in a universal measurement system. (Ideal terra sigillatas have a specific gravity of 1.1–1.2 whereas standard glazes and traditional slips may be in the range of 1.4–2.0.) Water is 1.0 in this system, and is the standard of measure.

If a suspension has a different specific gravity than usual, even if it has the same viscosity measurements in a Zahn cup or with a hydrometer, it will not deposit the same, even if it seems to apply the same, because it has a different solids loading. The simple addition of water is the most direct method of adjusting viscosity and is the primary difference between plastic clay and slip. Sometimes a water addition brings with it undesirable changes, such as increased shrinkage on drying, problems with cracking, a shift in the poise of the material, or creating a gradient in the suspension application layer where the application is actually thinner on edges and ridges than it is elsewhere.

We may want that suspension to apply with a low-viscosity nature, such as flowing off of high points, or a high-viscosity nature, where it clings well over edges. We may, at the same time, want the resultant suspension layer to be thin or thick because the look of that fired material is different in those

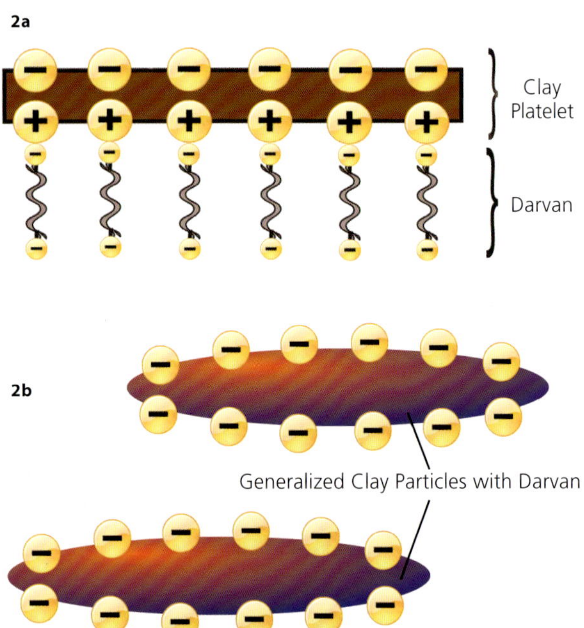

2a, 2b: Diagrams of clay particle charges and Darvan. (a) Mechanics of Darvan's attachment to clay platelets. (b) Negative surfaces repel/flow. **3** Relationship of deflocculant additions to viscosity[2]..

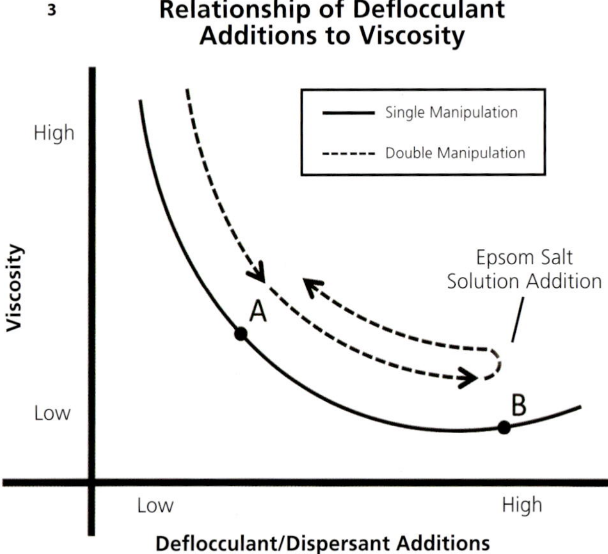

different states. What if we need a glaze to cling while applying, yet we need the look of the physically thin glaze? Or vice versa? Knowing how to increase or reduce viscosity will give you the best of both worlds during the glazing process.

Additions of deflocculant will reduce the viscosity of a suspension, and can allow it to act like it has more water without having more water. That suspension will then apply with a thin application nature, yet cling to the artwork in a thicker deposit (1). This can be a helpful characteristic to have in a slip used for attachments or for slip trailing, where shrinkage from high water levels can cause cracking or loss of the three-dimensional effect.

Small additions of a flocculant (like Epsom salts) can increase the viscosity of a suspension, allowing for more cling during application without much affecting the overall thickness of the layer applied. This allows artwork to be evenly coated with a generally thin layer—less material applied, but less flowing during the application process. This can be a helpful change when using persnickety glazes that normally show even the slightest difference in application layer thickness, such as drips and thickness gradients.

Darvan

Adding Darvan (typically Darvan 811 for slips, Darvan 7 for glazes) affects the surface charge on clay particles[1], causing them to repel each other. This repulsion, much like magnets aimed toward one another, increases fluidity of the particles because of reduced friction, therefore reducing the viscosity of the suspension. As John Gill says, "Darvan makes water wetter." Casting slips rely on this effect of increased flow and decreased water, which allows more casting cycles before the plaster molds become water saturated (2a and 2b).

Viscosity Curve: Casting and Stick-Up Slip

Casting slips typically reside around point A on the viscosity curve (3). At point B, larger material particles (silica, feldspar, frit) will often settle out. An addition of a saturated Epsom Salt solution will move the material back to point A, and the slip becomes an excellent attachment/trailing/meringue slip. In this slip, we have higher solids loading (more particles per volume) as well as high flow (as compared to the solids loading in a standard slip) with high cling (compressed double layer, with dispersion and flocculation).

Footnotes 1: Carty, William. *The Colloidal Nature of Kaolinite.* The American Ceramic Society Bulletin, 78.8 1999, p. 74–75. 2: Generalized and modified from chart of: Carty, William. *A Critical Review Of Dispersants For Whitewares Applications. Science of Whitewares II. Ed.* Carty & Sinton, The American Ceramics Society, 2000, p. 162.

In the Bucket: The Key to Consistent Glazes

Excerpted from Understanding Glazes,
by Richard A. Eppler with Mimi Obstler

After chemical formulation of a glaze, the three most important factors for success are application, application, and application. The flow characteristics (how it sprays, brushes, dips, etc.) are what govern application, but the flow of material cannot be understood through a simple measurement of viscosity, because there are far too many variables at work. This excerpt is meant to be an overview of those variables that are most important in studio ceramics including rheology, binders, deflocculants, flocculants, surface area, and suspension agents.

Rheology

Rheology is the science of how a liquid responds to force. For our purposes this typically means whether a glaze sticks on a surface, drips off or runs off in sheets, and whether it smooths out or shows brush strokes. Flocculants and deflocculants modify glaze rheology.

It is rare for any slip or glaze—that is any mixture of ground frit and raw materials suspended in water—to be usable as is, particularly with any degree of reproducibility. The rheological properties (viscosity, thixotropy, etc.) of the mixture are influenced by the particle sizes and shapes of the various components, and these flow properties can change with time.

Control is needed over the thickness of coating and evenness of application of a glaze. Hence, additions of rheology modifiers are required to control sedimentation (settling out over time), improve wetting properties on and bonding to the ware body, control drying time, prevent drying cracks, and improve green strength. Command of these properties provides the means to control the application process and, therefore, final results.

Most additives often influence more than one of the rheological properties. These properties are also somewhat dependent on details of the water and other raw materials, the person, the processing equipment (mixers, mills, spray guns, etc.), and the methods used in preparation and application. Thus, several trials are usually required to find a suitable combination of additives for a given glaze and application procedure at a particular location. However, once you have a suitable combination of additives that works for you, that combination of additives will be usable in almost all the glazes you prepare, apply, and fire by the same procedure.

The rheological property of most immediate concern is the viscosity (resistance to flow) of the slip (see page 38 for more information). The viscosity of simple liquids, such as water, used in making ceramic slips is said to be Newtonian. If we push a fluid down a pipe or a channel, a stress develops between the moving fluid and the stationary container through which it is flowing. When we say that a liquid is Newtonian, we mean that the stress is proportional to how fast the fluid is moving. The constant of proportionality is the viscosity. Thus, viscosity indicates the resistance to flow due to friction between the molecules of the fluid and its stationary container.

Viscosity measurement of ceramic slips can be performed several ways. The most widely used instrument in industry for ceramic suspensions is the variable-speed rotating cylinder viscometer. However, an indication of viscosity can be obtained from a simple flow test. Apply a level teaspoon of glaze slip to a nonabsorbing substrate (e.g., a glass panel). For comparative purposes the applications should be arranged in a row along one side of the panel. The glass panel is then raised to an incline of 45 degrees. Once the glaze flows have stopped moving, the lengths of flow are measured. The greater the length, the lower the viscosity.

Initially, at low concentration of solid particles, the effect of adding solid particles to a liquid is merely to gradually increase the viscosity, as the liquid media has to flow around the solid particles. At a concentration of solids above 5–10 percent by volume, the solid particles begin to interfere with each other. They become entangled in each other as the flow rate (stirring) is increased. Thus, the viscosity increases as the flow rate increases. This is called dilatant flow, and it basically means that the faster you stir, the more viscous a fluid becomes. Dilatant flow is characteristic of large particles. Either polymer additives or agglomerates of ceramic particles, especially clays, can produce dilatant flow. This is an additional reason (beyond avoiding crawling defects) for limiting clay additions to the amount needed for suspension of the solid particles, as dilatant flow is often undesirable in a glaze.

Binders

Though some glaze compositions high in clay content can be easily handled in the green state, most can easily be damaged in preparing the ware for firing. The binder acts as a temporary cement that holds the glaze particles on the surface until firing. The binder must be strong enough to permit handling of the ware in the dried-but-not-fired state, but soft and pliable enough to accommodate the drying shrinkage without cracking off the ware. Thus, lower-viscosity grades are preferred for glaze hardening. It is almost never possible to use the same grade of binder for glazes as is used for binding a ceramic body, where the high-viscosity grades are more effective.

The amount of binder added can range up to 3 percent, but 0.5 percent is typical. Excessive amounts make the coating brittle and introduce shrinkage upon firing. Therefore, one should add the least amount of binder that will permit handling without difficulty. The ideal binder burns away freely below 400°C (752°F) without ash, and doesn't cause shrinkage or disruption of the coating.

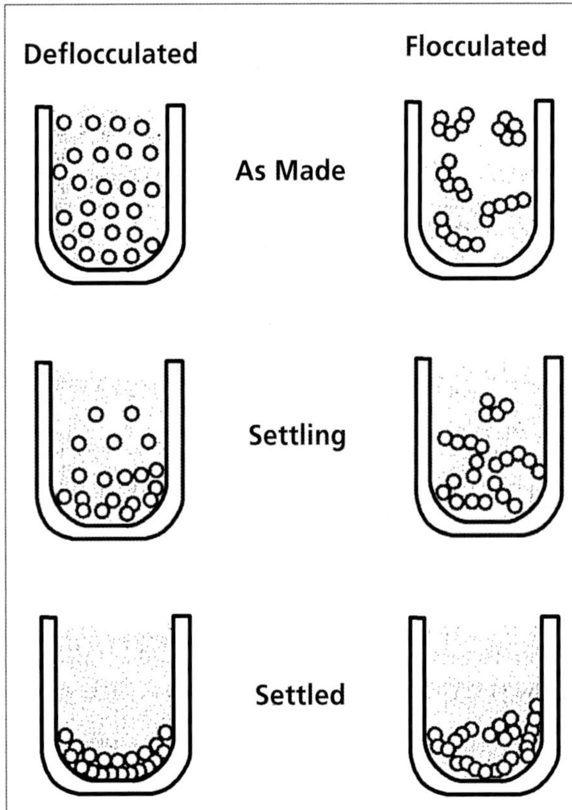

A flocculated glaze will settle out in a layer of particles that is less dense than a flocculated glaze, making it easier to remix. It will also result in a glaze layer on ware that is less dense, possibly requiring multiple applications in order to achieve the desired results.

Both natural gums and synthetic polymers (plastics) are used as binders, sometimes mixed, but the most commonly used binders are cellulose ethers (water-soluble derivatives of cellulose; carboxymethyl cellulose—trade name CMC). They are chosen as coating hardeners because their properties are more consistent than natural gums and starches. In a glaze of stable flocculation (i.e., a stable arrangement of the suspended particles in the slip), there is an improvement in the stability of the viscosity. Hence, coatings of consistent and controllable thickness can be applied by various techniques. Drying shrinkage is also predictable.

The physical properties of the binder are affected by temperature, pH, and the presence of electrolytes and preservatives. Vigorous stirring permits solution of the binder in cold water. Usually a 10 percent solution is made up, from which additions up to 1 percent are made to the coating slip, or to the water being used to make the slip. Mechanical stress and heat can degrade the binders, but small quantities (up to 5–10 gallons of slip) can be milled or mixed without damaging the binders.

There are side effects to using binders that cannot be ignored. CMC, although a preferred binder, also acts as a deflocculant in most glazes. Because they are organic cellulose solutions, glazes containing these organic binders require protection against biological and mold attack if kept more than a couple days.

Natural gums are carbohydrate polymers of high molecular weight. Gum tragacanth is a natural hydrophilic (water loving) gum found on a bush in much of Asia. It is only partially soluble in water, where it swells to form first a gel (a viscous jelly-like product), and then a sol (a liquid colloidal dispersion). These sols have low surface tension and are useful as coating stabilizers.

Starch has wide application in industry as a thickener, extender (i.e., a filler), and adhesive. However, the large amount of ash remaining after firing is a major limitation to its use in ceramics.

There is a range of polyvinyl alcohol compounds (PVA) that are efficient binders. Low-molecular-weight versions disperse more readily and are necessary for glaze applications. Additions of up to 1 percent to the glaze produce tough, coherent layers. Wetting agents (soaps) improve the use of polyvinyl alcohol. Other possibilities include alginates (seaweed), water-soluble acrylics, and resin emulsions (a stable mixture of resins).

Deflocculants

In a glaze mixture, the solid particles can either be individually dispersed or agglomerated into flocs (loosely bonded aggregates of particles). Stokes Law shows that heavier particles, or agglomerates, settle out much faster than small particles. Therefore, control of the dispersion of the particles in a mixture is critical.

This control is achieved by adding materials that are called deflocculating electrolytes, or deflocculants. Their action in the suspension may be compared to magnets, having a north and south pole, or a positive and negative charge. For example, when dissolved in water, sodium nitrite has a positive charge on the sodium and a negative charge on the nitrite. Clay in suspension carries a negative charge. As a result, the positively charged sodium will adhere to the clay particle surface. This charged clay, with sodium ion, will in turn attract water, forming a three-part sphere known as a clay micelle. Instead of a small clay particle moving about freely in water, there is now a much more bulky shape of lower density, which cannot move with the same freedom as the original clay particle. Hence, the slurry becomes able to suspend larger quantities of the heavier frit and other solid particles.

Though all deflocculants work the same way, they vary in effectiveness and in the balance between improving suspension of the solids in the liquid and altering viscosity (resistance to flow), or set (the ability of a suspension to adhere to a vertical surface, and not run off). Thus, some of the milder agents may increase set, whereas the overall effect of some strong agents is to produce a free-flowing suspension of lower viscosity.

The amount of deflocculant needed depends upon the viscosity of the slip needed for the application process you have chosen (dipping, spraying, brushing), plus the desire to maximize the amount of solids applied to the ware. The higher the density of application, the less the amount of water to be removed in drying, and the less the glaze will shrink upon firing. See the example on page 44.

Flocculants

Flocculants are less often used in industry, but are widely used in the studio. The figure on page 42 shows that flocs (loosely bonded aggregates of particles) settle to less dense coatings. Hence, flocculants like Epsom salts and calcium chloride can be used to control coating density. Second, and more important, ions (charged particles) can be leached from most glaze materials, given sufficient time. These ions tend to be the alkalis (soda and potash) that thin the slip to a viscosity below that needed for application. This often occurs during storage. Flocculants can counteract this trend and restore a glaze to the viscosity needed for the application process. Flocculants are generally very powerful, so they are used in very small quantities, from 0.005 to 0.1 percent.

Surface Area

The most important factor in glaze suspension is the amount of surface area of the glaze solids. Frit, ground quartz, feldspar, and whiting are relatively coarse glaze ingredients, on the order of 45 microns (45 millionths of a meter) in diameter. These coarse materials have about one square meter of surface area per gram of material. Kaolins and ball clays, in contrast, are much smaller and finer, roughly 1 to 10 microns in diameter, with a surface area of 15 to 30 square meters per gram. They also tend to be plate-shaped, which gives them a lot of surface area for their weight. Bentonite and VEEGUM® are less than one micron in diameter, and may have 30 to 100 square meters of surface area per gram of material. Just like dust in air, fine clay particles tend to settle extremely slowly in water if they ever settle at all. While chemically inert, these powerful glaze suspenders prevent coarser glaze materials from settling out. A good starting point for testing glaze recipes is to use a minimum of 10% kaolin or ball clay or 1% bentonite. Use care in dispersing and hydrating fine clays to prevent them from clumping. Don't use too much clay; it can make a glaze suspend well, but dry too slowly.

Suspension Agents

If a glaze is to be applied from an aqueous slip, its formulation must include an amount of colloidal material (material with a plate-like shape, and particle size less than 1 micron) that provides the means to suspend the other heavier-than-water components in the slip. The most common suspending agent is clay. Clays come in three general classes: kaolins, ball clays, and montmorillonites.

Kaolins are white burning and are comparatively pure kaolinite. They are moderately powerful suspending agents. They find use primarily in white and light-colored coatings, where the impurities in ball clays cannot be tolerated.

Ball clays are less pure, often containing substantial free silica and/or micas in addition to kaolinite. Many contain

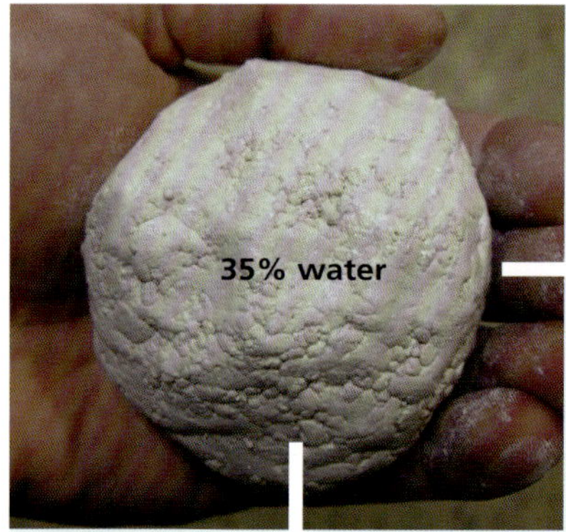

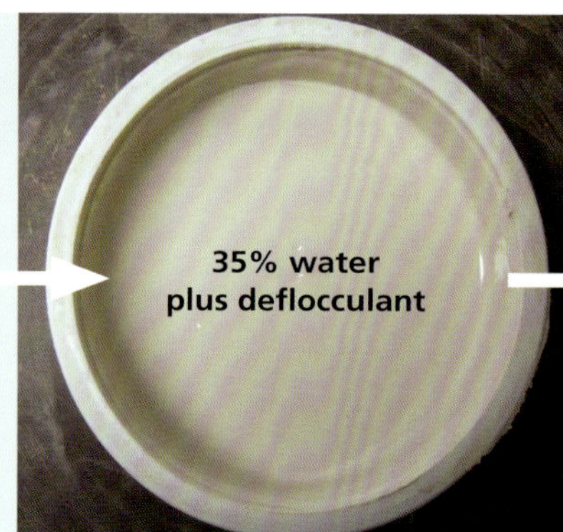

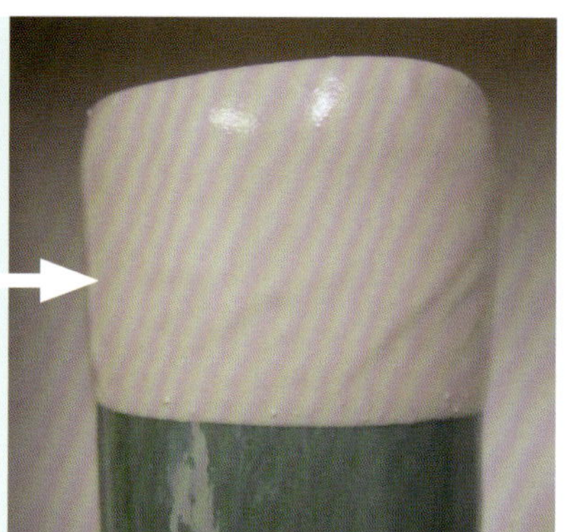

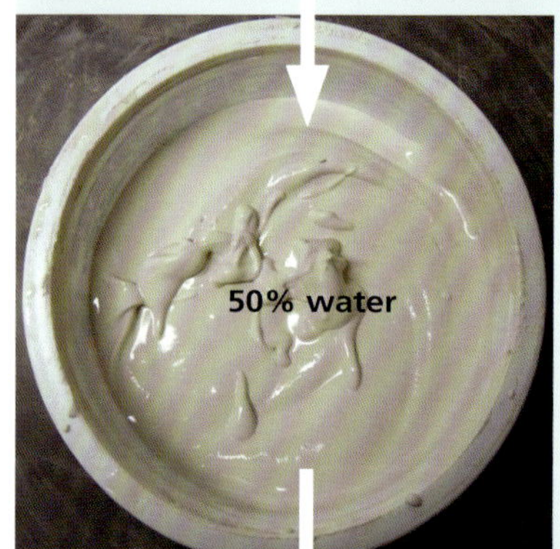

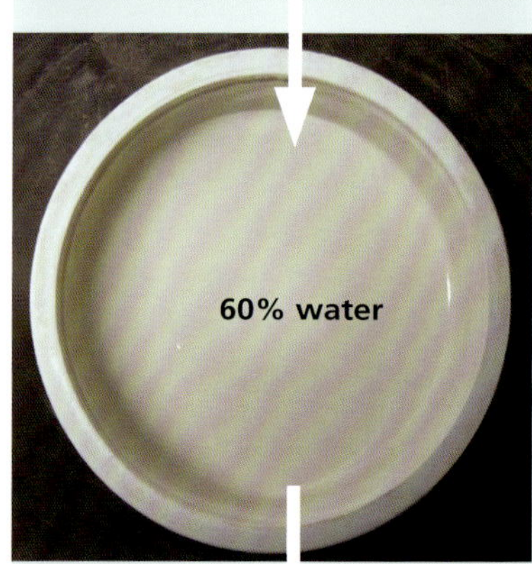

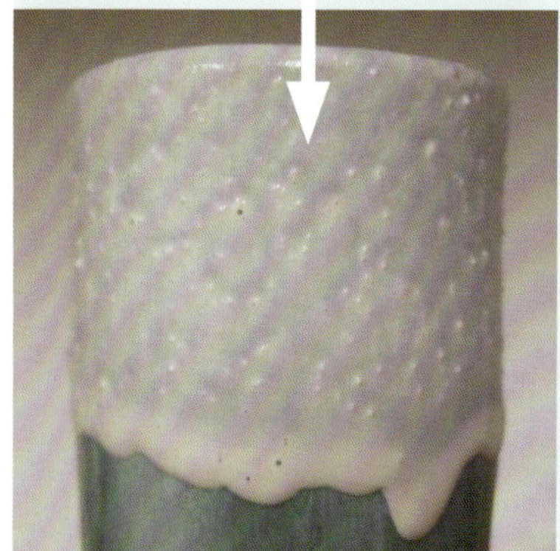

Deflocculants and Glaze Fluidity

The image at the upper left shows a glaze batch with just enough water to bind it together. In this case, it is 35% water by weight. This result is a very soft ball that will gradually slump when placed on a flat surface. The addition of several drops of deflocculant (sodium silicate) made it possible for the mixture to become fluid to the point that the surface of the mixture became flat immediately after stirring. The amount of deflocculant and water necessary will vary by recipe, and will depend largely on the specific materials used in the glaze batch.

Water was then added to a second batch of the same glaze, at 5% increments (by weight). The glaze was thoroughly mixed with each addition, until the same level of fluidity was reached in the bucket. For this recipe, 60% water by weight was necessary to achieve a flat surface in the bucket immediately after mixing.

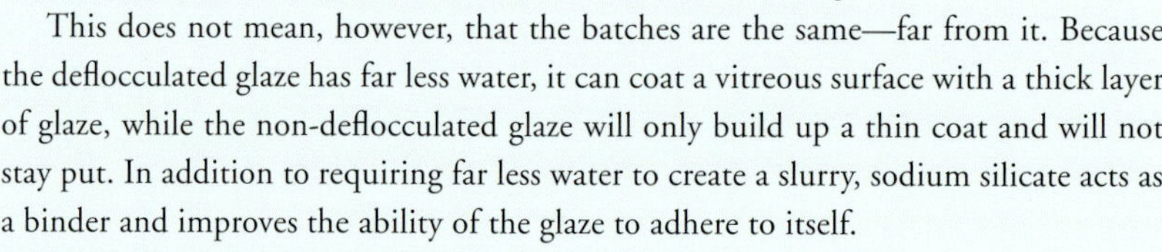

This does not mean, however, that the batches are the same—far from it. Because the deflocculated glaze has far less water, it can coat a vitreous surface with a thick layer of glaze, while the non-deflocculated glaze will only build up a thin coat and will not stay put. In addition to requiring far less water to create a slurry, sodium silicate acts as a binder and improves the ability of the glaze to adhere to itself.

Most of the time, we are not glazing vitreous surfaces in studio practice, so what would be the point of deflocculating a glaze? The answer is application, especially if you are looking for a thicker layer of glaze. Increasing the fluidity of a glaze while decreasing the water content allows a thicker coating of solids to be deposited on the ware surface (whether vitreous or bisque). While a glaze slurry can be mixed thicker using less water than is typical (like the one with 50% water by weight on the left) in order to adhere to a vitreous surface or produce a thicker layer, it will still contain considerably more water than the deflocculated glaze and is therefore more likely to shrink and crack off the surface or cause crawling problems.

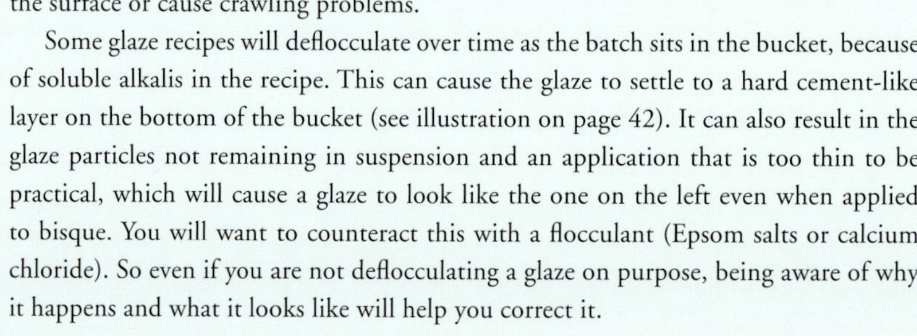

Some glaze recipes will deflocculate over time as the batch sits in the bucket, because of soluble alkalis in the recipe. This can cause the glaze to settle to a hard cement-like layer on the bottom of the bucket (see illustration on page 42). It can also result in the glaze particles not remaining in suspension and an application that is too thin to be practical, which will cause a glaze to look like the one on the left even when applied to bisque. You will want to counteract this with a flocculant (Epsom salts or calcium chloride). So even if you are not deflocculating a glaze on purpose, being aware of why it happens and what it looks like will help you correct it.

substantial concentrations of iron oxide and titania, and are thus darker burning. Therefore, they can alter the color and color purity of the glaze. Since 70–80 percent of their total particles are less than 1 micron, they are more powerful suspending agents than kaolins.

Clay additions (either kaolin or ball clay, or some combination) up to 12 percent by weight are often used. If no other suspending agents are used, at least 3 percent by weight of clay is required. However, excessive clay additions are to be avoided! Too much clay will cause excessive glaze shrinkage on drying, leading to crawling defects.

Bentonite and hectorite are the names given to a class of montmorillonite clays that have higher-than-normal water content and very fine particle size. They are somewhat difficult to disperse in water, but once dispersed they collect a very high water concentration around the particles, forming strong gels that are up to five times more effective in suspension power than normal clay. As a result, they are effective at concentrations of 0.5 to 2.0 percent, well below the 10 percent or more used with more conventional clays. Bentonite is particularly useful with a fully fritted glaze, which can be formulated in many cases with 99 percent frit and 1 percent bentonite. Unlike organic agents, bentonite does not degrade due to bacterial action. Combinations of 0.5 to 1.0 percent bentonite with 3–7 percent kaolinite or ball clay are also possible.

Most of the materials previously discussed as binders also have some suspending power and can be considered as suspending agents as well. Similarly, the various clays have some binding capability, particularly when present in large quantity.

An additional complication to flow behavior is time dependence. Some materials, catsup for example, require force to get moving, but little or no force to keep moving. If the flow rate in such materials is reversed, the material does not immediately require force to continue moving. It continues to flow for a while with little or no external force. This time dependence is called thixotropy. It's a fascinating phenomenon—but it's a different topic.

This article was excerpted from Understanding Glazes, *by Richard A. Eppler with Mimi Obstler, published by the American Ceramic Society. For further information and other resources, go to http://ceramics.org/acers-bookstore/whitewares-glazes/.*

26 See "Suspenders and Binders for Glaze" for more information on specific materials.

Raw Glazing, Single Firing

by Steven Hill

Defining the Terms

Blister: A broken gas bubble, frozen in the glaze, usually with sharp edges and caused by outgassing in the firing.

Crawling: When glaze pulls back as it melts, revealing bare clay. In single firing, it is usually caused by not enough clay in the glaze formula.

Delamination: The tendency of the clay body to separate as the water from glazing penetrates from both sides and meets in the center of the wall. The result looks similar to bloating in a fired piece, but it happens during glaze application on raw ware, rather than during firing. A crack will often accompany the surface bump.

Flaking: Severe crawling where glaze flakes off the pot before it is fired.

Outgassing: The escape of gases from clay bodies during firing. Carbonates, sulfates, nitrates, lattice-bound water, and organic contaminants volatilize during the early stages of glaze firing. In twice-fired ware this will occur during the bisque, with the early part of the glaze firing as the backup, but in single-fired wares everything must volatilize during the glaze firing.

Pinholing: Blisters that have burst and typically have smooth, melted edges.

Clay Forming Considerations

Raw glazing considerations start with good forming techniques and well-balanced ware. It is important to not make the walls overly thin. Delicate, thin walls made to showcase translucency are better suited for bisque firing. Having a generous wall thickness, although not too thick, with a lightly compressed rim is optimum. Excessively thin pots are fragile to handle when raw and more likely to succumb to the rigors of glazing. As water absorbs into the body, cracks are much more likely to form around feet or perhaps perpendicular to the rim.

Additionally, as the water from glazing is absorbed into the body, delamination can occur, leaving as few as one or a whole series of bumps on the fired ware that looks a bit like bloating, except that it will occur as you glaze, instead of during the firing.

Glaze Application

When raw glazing ceramic ware, the application is critical. It is certainly possible to dip and pour, but submersing raw pots in a bucket of glaze will test the limits of the clay-body strength, both in handling and in the amount of water absorption the body goes through. It is far more advantageous to spray glaze onto your raw pots. When spraying, part of the moisture evaporates between the spray gun and the pot, so there is less water absorption and subsequently less expansion and contraction of the clay body. Also, other than flipping a form over to glaze the underside of a belly or the inside of the foot ring, pots

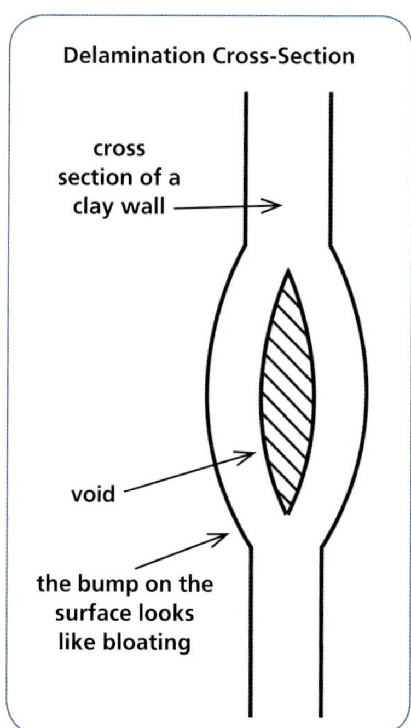

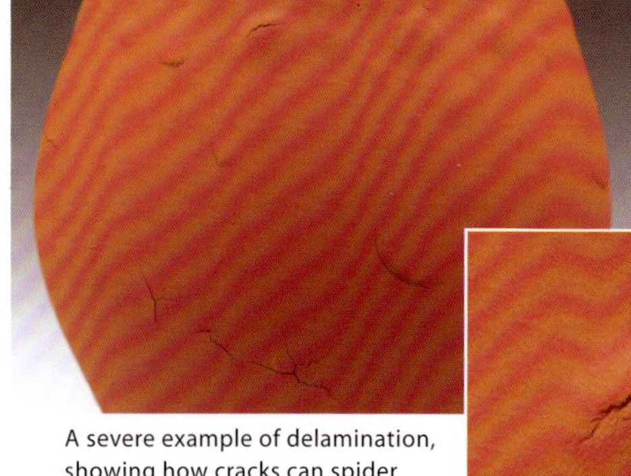

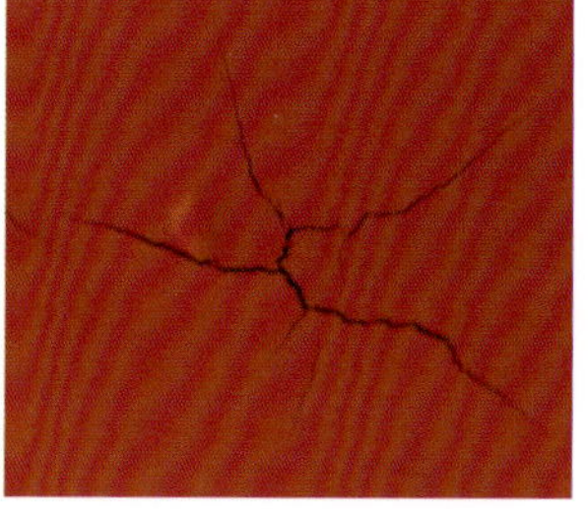

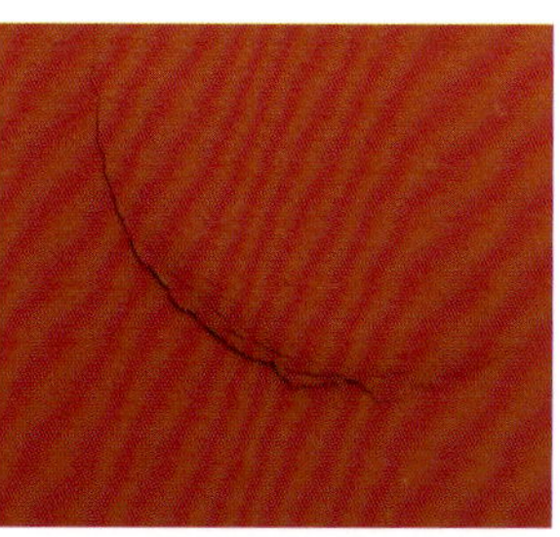

A severe example of delamination, showing how cracks can spider web through or be like a half moon around the edge of the delamination bump.

usually sit on a banding wheel throughout the spraying process, so there is less chance of breaking fragile ware through excessive handling.

I don't recommend glazing pots that are mostly dry although still damp in the bottom, as they are likely to crack around their wet/dry interface, because of a discrepancy in water absorption. My choice is to glaze bone dry, as it allows me to glaze at the end of my work cycle. If you glaze when the pots are leather hard, you must glaze when they are ready to avoid problems. Also, since leather-hard pots are still shrinking, the glazes must have somewhat higher clay content to accommodate the shrinkage.

Clay Body and Glaze Formulation

I have approached the topic of clay body formulation from two opposing directions over the course of my career. My original inclination was to use tight bodies, with a high percentage of ball clay. My theory was that the small particle size, with correspondingly small pores, would prevent the body from absorbing too much water and swelling during glazing. From 1972–1995 I formulated and mixed my own bodies, with anywhere from 25–75% ball clay. If I wanted a coarser texture I would simply add grog to the mixture. Then in 1995 I began working with Laguna B-Mix, an extremely tight body with bentonite added for plasticity. B-Mix is very strong in its raw state and was very effective at blocking the absorption of water. It glazed like a champ, but was much more likely to cause glaze blistering, due to outgassing during the firing. The down side of extremely tight bodies for single firing is that they block the gasses from escaping before glazes melt just as effectively as they block water absorption.

Since 2008, I have been working in porcelain with consistent fired results. I attribute this to the fact that porcelain is made of approximately 50% non-plastics (flint and feldspar). When it does absorb water, it doesn't swell up as much as the high-ball clay bodies I was using. Porcelains are also less prone to outgassing, since kaolin has less organic contamination than ball clays or fire clays. Also, prior to vitrification, porcelain remains quite open, allowing gasses to easily escape before glazes melt. Currently I am using both Standard 257 English Porcelain and Coleman Porcelain.

Fortunately, most mid-range and high-fire glazes can be successfully raw glazed, as long as the formula has a high enough clay content. When you glaze a raw pot, the pot will expand due to the absorption of water. As the water evaporates, the pot contracts back to its original size. If there is not enough clay in the glaze, it will not contract with the pot and potentially lead to crawling and or flaking off the pot before firing.

So, how much clay is necessary? I have used glazes with practically no clay, but have added 2–3% bentonite to compensate. In general I prefer at least 5% clay and 2% bentonite in my glazes, but your results may vary.

Firing Raw Pots

Rule #1: Never blow up a pot.

Everyone knows what happens if a bisque is fired too fast during the early stages. Moisture turns to steam, which cannot escape quickly enough and pots explode. It's bad enough when this happens in the bisque. In a glaze firing one exploding pot can ruin a significant portion of a kiln load, with shards stuck to surfaces all around the offending culprit. So it is important to fire slowly past the boiling point, remembering that just because the air is 212°F doesn't mean that the middle of the body is that hot. Fire slowly to about 450°F to ensure that the core temperature of the ware is above the boiling point.

Rule #2: There has to be enough time for outgassing to occur before glazes begin to sinter and melt.

If you fire too quickly through this zone (approximately 1400° –1900°F), the net result can be blisters frozen in the glazed surface. Not all clays and glazes are equally susceptible to blistering, so each combination must be tested. As a general rule, the dirtier the clay, the slower this part of the firing needs to be. If blistering is a problem for you, start by limiting temperature rise to approximately 100°F an hour (or possibly even less) from 1400°–1900°F.

Bisque firing was an outgrowth of the Industrial Revolution, allowing less skilled workers to glaze in factory settings. Prior to this, pots were single fired, so there is a wealth of experience proving that it does work.

If you think you want to single fire for the potential monetary savings, then you might be frustrated. Even though you will only be firing once, the firing will be somewhat extended, using more fuel. And yes… there will be inevitable losses associated with single firing.

I have never believed that single firing has any appreciable effect on the color or texture of glazes. I can say, however, that my aesthetic development has evolved in tandem with the technical needs of glazing raw pots. So, if I stopped single firing today, my pots wouldn't tell on me. If I had never single fired, however, my aesthetic development would likely have taken a somewhat different path.

Single Firing	Ramp	End Point	Hold
1	200°F/hour	220°F	30 minutes to 3 hours depending on the wetness and/or thickness of the work.
2	100°F/hour	450°F	no hold
3	400°F/hour	2060°F	no hold
4	100°F/hour	2160–2190°F	60 minutes. This temperature is about cone 5, but with an hour soak cone 6 should fall. Due to kilns being calibrated differently, some tweaking may be required.
5	9999°F/hour	1700°F	60 minutes
6	50°F/hour	1600°F	60 minutes
7	50°F/hour	1500°F	no hold, kiln off

This schedule is set up for computerized electric kilns, but because thermocouples are generally not very accurate devices, your kiln could be calibrated differently, so always use guide cones.

This schedule works well for porcelain. Porcelain is a clean clay body with large pores (before firing), which allows gasses to escape easily. If you are firing stoneware, switch to 100°F an hour temperature rise at approximately 1500°F, to allow time for the volatiles to escape before the glazes melt.

The firing cycle presumes that you will be working with an extended programmed cooling cycle. I do this to give more time for microcrystalline development in my glazes. If you choose to not use a cooling cycle, switch segment 4 to 1000°F/hour to cone 6.

105 Find recipes for both single firing and achieving atmospheric-like effects in electric kilns.

CHAPTER 2
In the Kiln

Heatwork

by Dave Finkelnburg

Defining the Terms

Heatwork: The effect of temperature applied over time in a firing. The work done by effective heat transfer to wares is the result of ramp rate and peak temperature. Heatwork can be visualized as the area under a graph that shows the time versus temperature of a firing.

Pyrometric cone: A device used to measure heatwork by bending a predictable amount after exposure to a combination of heat and time. The way we (ceramic artists) measure heat.

Grain boundary slip: The process of solid particles in a material sliding past each other as a result of a force applied to the material. Cones bend and ware slumps because a glass phase forms and permits particles of the cone or ware to move past each other under the force of gravity.

Measuring Heatwork

Why, if a perfectly good thermocouple is installed in a kiln, would an artist also want to put pyrometric cones in a firing? What do those cones accomplish? Why use them? Each cone within a temperature range has a separate chemical and physical composition designed to permit the cone to bend over under the force of gravity at a particular temperature when heated at a specific rate.

For practical purposes, a pyrometric cone is simply a sophisticated blend of finely ground glaze ingredients. As those ingredients begin to melt, liquid first forms on the surfaces of some of the particles. The force of gravity lets individual particles slide past each other on this liquid film, allowing the cone to bend in a reliable, predictable manner.

This deformation of the cone due to grain boundary slip occurs because part of the cone melts to a glass phase. The relatively weak liquid glass is not strong enough to keep the cone erect any longer so the cone, which is manufactured with a slight lean, begins to bend. This bending does not begin at a specific temperature, but rather at a combination of temperature and time.

Because an infinite combination of kiln heating rates and times can occur in any kiln, a cone can only be expected to bend at a specific temperature if it is heated at precisely the rate prescribed by the cone manufacturer. Thus, given the variability of firings, a cone cannot be considered a scientific measure of temperature. Rather, it can be inferred from the appearance of the cone that a particular combination of time and temperature has been reached in the kiln.

To Soak or Not to Soak?

A soak is a period of time in a kiln firing cycle during which temperature is held constant. Some processes in a firing are temperature dependent while others are time dependent.

Achieving a uniform temperature in ceramic ware is a time dependent process. A soak may be used at any point in a firing to reduce the difference between the surface and internal temperature of ware in a kiln.

Temperature dependent processes include organic burn off, driving off chemically bound water, mullite formation, and silica melt. A soak at any of the different temperatures critical to these processes may be useful. Additionally, once a glaze is melted, it will become

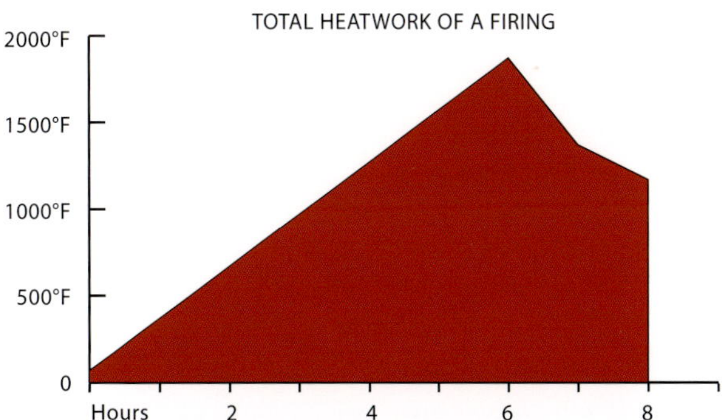

The area below the line on the graph represents this firing's total heatwork, which is a combination of time and temperature. If one of these measures is increased, the other is decreased to maintain the same heatwork. Note that heatwork continues into the cooling part of the firing.

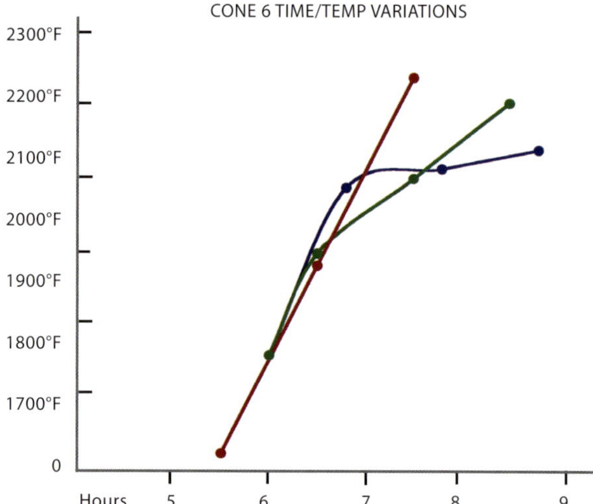

Assuming an initial heating rate of 300°F/hour up to 1725°F, the graph above shows that cone 6 will drop at very different temperatures depending on the heating rate during the final hours of a firing. At a rate of 270°F/hour the cone drops at 2269°F after 2 hours (red line); at 108°F/hour the cone drops at 2232°F after 3 hours (green line); and at 27°F/hour, the cone drops at 2165°F after 3.5 hours (blue line). *Data: Edward Orton Jr. Ceramic Foundation.*

less viscous (flow easily), as temperature increases. The viscosity of a molten glaze is temperature dependent. A soak may be used to hold the viscosity of a melted glaze constant while time passes so that the glaze may flow or smooth out. This type of soak is often used to improve the final surface appearance of a glaze. In kilns for which the atmosphere is controlled, different degrees of oxidation and/or reduction may be used during the soak to further influence the appearance of the glaze surface.

How does one soak without over firing? Once a particular cone is down, and temperature is held constant for 15 minutes, the next numbered cone will go down. So, adding a 15 minute soak at peak temperature will have the effect of increasing the firing by one cone. This means, of course, one should start the soak before the maximum desired cone drops, using the above rule of thumb to estimate when to begin soaking. Adjust the kiln burners or digital controller to slow or arrest the temperature rise. By the end of the soak, the target cone should be fully bent to a 90° angle.

Pyrometric Cones

by Tina Gebhart

Defining the Terms

Bending Face: The flat plane of a cone opposite the spine, also the shortest of all its planes. When stood up on its own base, the cone leans toward the bending face.

Cone abbreviations: c/6, ^6, 6

Glass Phase: The part of a clay body or glaze that has melted; the glass portion.

Melt Viscosity: The viscosity of the glaze phase at any given point of the firing.

Pyrometric Cone: Literally "fire measuring" cone. Used during a firing to parallel heatwork occurring within ceramic wares.

Pyroplastic Deformation: Literally "fire-bending." Bending of a clay body during firing, due to low melt viscosity in the glass phase.

Spine: The longest and thickest edge of the cone, opposite the cone's bending face.

A pyrometer measures temperature, but pyrometric cones measure heatwork. What is a cone, how does it work, and what does any of this have to do with synchronized swimmers?

Cones: A Continuum from Clay to Glaze

There is an old saying that you plant peas when lilac leaves are the size of mouse ears. Planting according to an indicator plant takes advantage of the complex growth triggers in plants and follows them instead of measuring individual factors (day and night temperatures, rainfall, day length, soil temperatures). We allow the lilac bush to be our effective guide. We wait for the visual indicator of lilac leafing, and then we plant the peas.

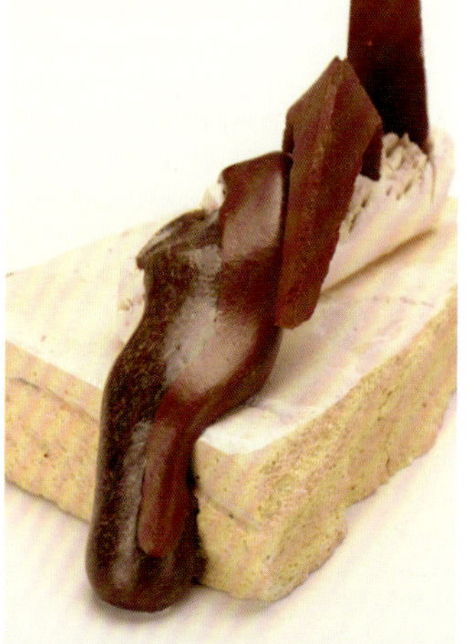

Stages of cone melt (left to right): Fluid glaze, stiff glaze (or engobe), and bending clay.

Pyrometric cones are the equivalent of indicator plants when it comes to firing work. They are made of the same ceramic materials as our wares, so cones respond to firing the same way our clays and glazes do. Cones are designed to respond at consistent intervals that, when the cones are used correctly, will remain consistent throughout the kiln and from one firing to the next.

Cones have been engineered to respond to two things, the first is low melt viscosity. As the heatwork in the kiln increases, the cone begins to melt. It develops a glass phase, and as it does, that glass phase becomes less viscous. It begins to flow.

Cones are engineered to respond to gravity as well. The cone form is designed with a spine that is the longest and strongest edge. It positions the cone in an 8° tilt away from vertical when the cone is stood on its base. In this tilted position, gravity takes hold of the cone and pulls. As heatwork increases and the glass-phase viscosity drops, gravity's effect on the cone becomes apparent, and it bends toward its bending face—much like a bowl on the wheel when the clay is too soft, and the flare becomes too wide. The cone is having a precision flop.

In the example, the bowl is soft not because of melt viscosity, but water content. During firing, a bowl can present mechanics that are truly parallel to the cone, due to glass-phase development and gravity. This is pyroplastic deformation in its classic sense, the bending of clay due to low-viscosity glass phase.

Cones exist theoretically on a continuum between glaze and clay. Fire clay hot enough, and it will be a glaze. Fire that same clay a little less hot, and it will bend if in the proper position. Systematize the compositions with great enough precision, and those clay cones will bend in a continuum like a team of synchronized swimmers cascading into a pool.

The Cone System

The cone numbering system has a virtual zero in the center. Much like negatives numbers in math, cones farthest left of zero are lower heatwork than those closer to zero. These numbers on the left have an 0 ("oh") in front of them. This 0 is not just a place holder. It is spoken, not as zero, but as "oh." Cone 04 is very different than cone 4. Always say the "oh." It indicates left-of-zero.

Cones are made for a range of heatwork measurements. The standard spectrum for studio ceramics spans cone 022 to cone 12, covering four firing ranges: ultra-low-, low-, mid-, and high-fire. Ultra low includes firing for lusters, overglazes, enamels, decals, and glass work (1). The bold-faced cones (018, 04, 6, and 10) are team captains of their zones, the archetypal cone used in that firing range.

Using Cones Well

Pyrometric cones have several practical uses in the ceramics studio. As firing measurement, witness cones (viewed through a kiln spy/peep hole) are the most accurate measure of a kiln's firing progress, and for deciding when to shut down the kiln. Since cones act like clay and glaze, some ceramic artists fire "cones only" (often for wood, salt, and raku)—no pyrometers, kiln sitters, etc.

Cones are good safety nets in both computer- and sitter-fired kilns. In addition, they are important for calibrating your kiln sitters and customized firing schedules. Using cone packs throughout a kiln can give information about the evenness of the heatwork throughout the kiln, and stacking adjustments can be made to minimize cone differences. Even atmosphere and ventilation information can come from your cones (bloating, color change, hardshelling).

Always wear appropriately rated welding goggles when viewing cones in a kiln firing. Prolonged exposure to infrared light and intense heat can be damaging to both the retina and cornea.

Advantages of Good Cone Pack Form

A good cone pack gives you relative information about your current firing. A great cone pack gives you consistent, calibrated, reliable, and comparable information across

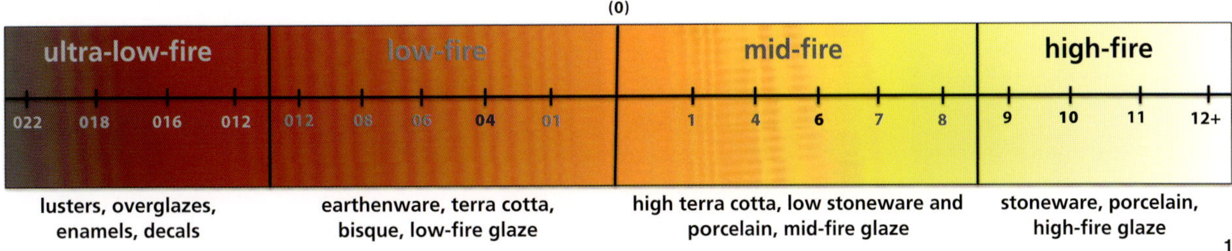

1

Cone Pack Language

Bending: Curve exaggerates, but tip is still higher than halfway. Bending can also refer to the whole range of cone movement; tipping, halfway, and down are the primary degrees of bending.

Down: A fully matured cone. The tip is touching the top of the cone pack, or is level with the base of the cone and the cone has formed an arched shape.

Flat: Negative space below the cone has flattened substantially or become non-existent.

Guard Cone: One pyrometric step beyond the target cone, this cone helps the firer prevent overfiring. This cone should not bend. If the target cone goes down too fast, this cone will indicate if the firing is between cones, or has progressed to the next cone.

Halfway: The cone's tip is at half the height of its original position, or as compared to the next cone in the pack.

Past Half: The cone's tip has traveled below halfway, and points downward.

Sitter Cone: Small cone put into a kiln sitter. When it bends, a sitter cone mechanically triggers kiln shut-off.

Soft: Bending face and spine have become slightly curved, becoming just perceivable by the trained firer's eye.

Standing: Cone is fully erect with all edges/faces still plumb. Shaped like an unfired cone.

Target Cone (or Firing Cone): The firing should bend this cone to a decided degree. For full maturity of this number, this cone's tip should be down.

Tipping: Face and spine are more obviously curved. Cone's tip is distinctly lower than the next cone in the pack.

Warning Cone (or Guide Cone): One pyrometric step before the target cone. It alerts the firer to pay attention.

Witness Cones: Large cones put inside the kiln to be seen through the peep hole, often used in series of multiple cones called packs.

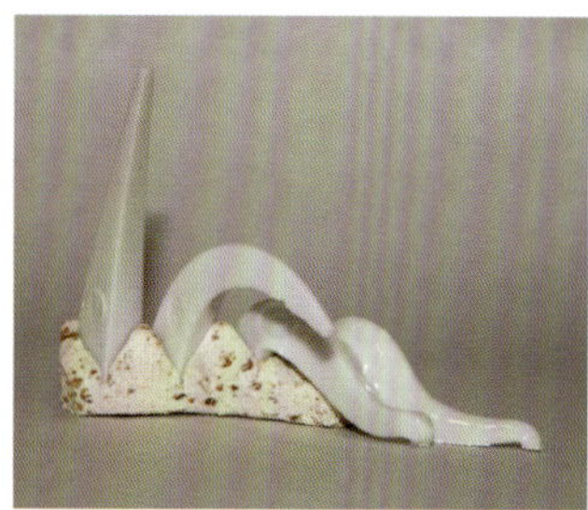
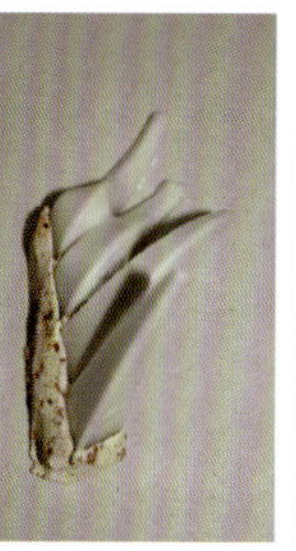
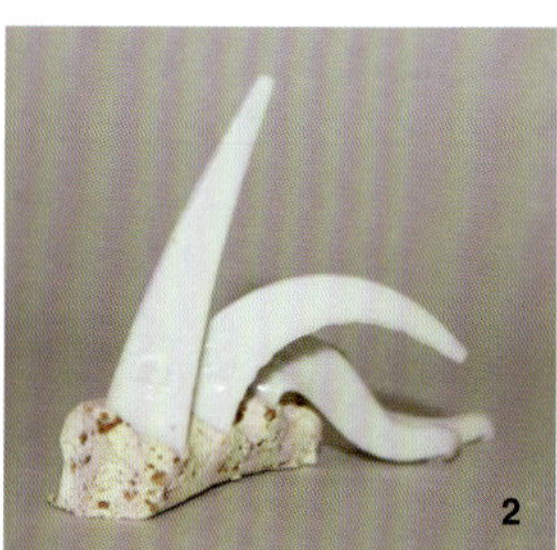

2 Cones can bend freely when aligned properly with spines and side faces in a continuous line, allowing easier and more accurate reading of the bend.

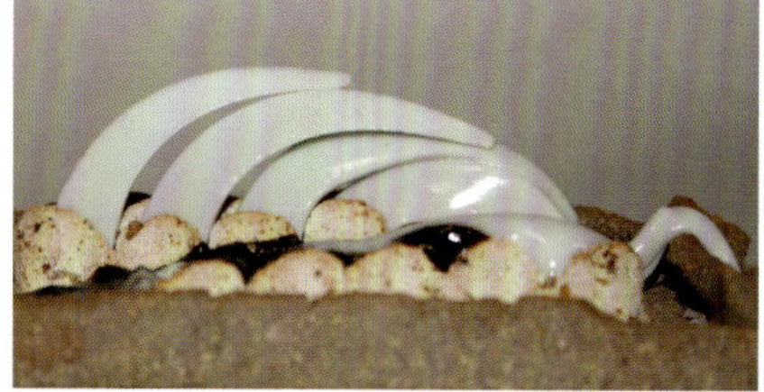
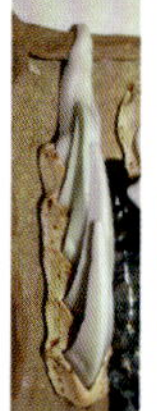
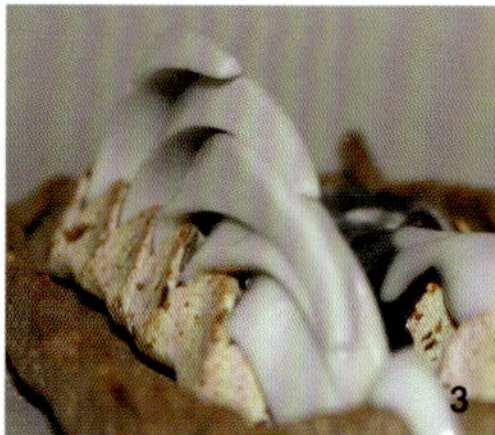

3 Cones will hit each other when aligned bending-face-to-spine, making it impossible to discern how far cone 11 has bent. The far left cone here is cone 11. Is it bent halfway? Or would cone 11 be down if cone 10 were not holding it up?

all of your firings. To get the most out of your witness cone packs, you should always:

1) *Build your cone pack with at least a warning cone, a target cone, and a guard cone.* Know where you are aiming to fire. Know when that point is approaching, and know how much higher the firing has gone if the target cone has fallen faster than expected.

2) *Build cone packs with all the cones' spines aligned with either their left or right faces.* This allows them to fall slightly forward instead of directly to the side and to fall fully and uninterruptedly to the down position, instead of landing on each other. Too often I see quickly made cone packs where all of the bending faces point right into the prior cone. The firer inevitably questions the cone pack: Is that cone 10 halfway, or is cone 9 just holding it up?

3) *Set each cone with two inches exposed so that gravity works on it properly.* Less exposed, and the cone will fall later than its standard. Too much exposed cone may allow the cone to fall too soon, and/or run the risk of the cone simply falling out of the pack.

4) *Angle the cone to 8° from vertical.* The base is designed to put the cone in this position. Simply hold a cone upright, flush with the tabletop, and set your cones in the cone pack to match the angle. If your cones are set at greater than 8°, they will fall sooner and slightly faster. If set less than 8°, the cones may backbend, or fall in the wrong direction entirely.

5) Record the behavior of the cone pack throughout the firing, particularly in combustion kilns (gas, wood, oil). Doing this for all firings allows you to compare results of your firing adjustments, fuel/combustion settings, and stacking arrangements. Recording in consistent log language for your cone readings can help when sharing firing information.

Glaze on Clays

by David Pier

Defining the Terms

Interface Layer: The layer under the glaze where the body and glaze have fused into each other. It is a gradation from pure body to pure glaze (unless the glaze was applied thinly). Also called the clay-glaze interface, body-glaze layer, glaze-body interlayer, intermediate layer, buffer layer, or boundary layer.

Iron Sulfide: Mineral that is present in most geologically old, iron-bearing clays, such as those used in most stoneware bodies. In raw clay it is visible as very small black specks. It is the primary cause of iron spots.

At some point, you've probably been surprised by the appearance of a glaze coming out of the kiln. Your application wasn't too thick or too thin, and the kiln was fired correctly, so what happened? It may have been your clay!

The Interface Rendezvous

The interface layer is the layer between the clay and glaze where the two have penetrated into each other during the glaze firing, resulting in a gradation from pure clay to pure glaze. In stoneware and porcelain, this layer is often thicker than the pure glaze layer on the top. If the glaze is applied thinly, then there might be no pure glaze layer at all. In low-fire ware this interface layer is usually thinner, in large part explaining why there are fewer surprises with low-fire glazing.

The interface layer has properties dictated by the exact combination of clay and glaze. It might be similar to what you would get if you mixed the clay and glaze together before firing, but there will also be more complicated interactions due to the gradated composition and due to crystals growing up through the layer starting at the clay side. The interface layer, affected by the composition of the clay, can push the glaze to matte or gloss, especially where it is thin.

The interface can be a different color than the unglazed clay, altering the apparent color of translucent and transparent glazes. A good example is titanium in the body turning iron blue (blue celadon) glazes into the more common green celadon. Since iron will only go blue when in low concentration along with the near total absence of titanium, only special low titanium clays, such as Grolleg kaolin, prevent a green interface.

Even without effects from the interface layer, the color of the clay with can be different with and without glaze, particularly in reduction firing. This is because the color of the bare clay is actually a thin oxidized layer that forms during the cooling phase after the fuel is turned off. Oxygen won't penetrate the glaze very far once it is fully melted, so the clay covered by the glaze will maintain a fully reduced color. In the most common case, iron containing bodies are some shade of red/brown where unglazed and some shade of gray where glazed.

Many bodies contain small particles of iron sulfide and other impurities. The melting of these particles into the interface layer is responsible for most iron spots, something that is most common in stoneware. Different glaze ingredients will mask or exaggerate iron spots, and the iron spots will often show through an otherwise opaque glaze, so even opacity won't always hide body effects.

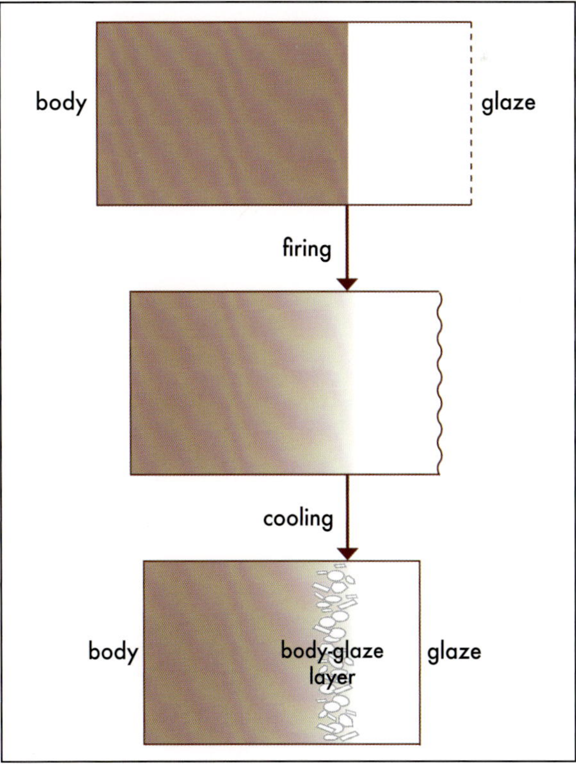

The body can affect the gloss of a glaze, even if it doesn't turn it matte. This is a subtle but important effect that often gets ignored, since people tend to consider gloss a yes or no condition, when actually gloss varies quite a bit. Much of this variance is due to the composition of the glaze, but bodies with large particles with different expansion/contraction rates (coefficients of expansion) than the rest of the body can cause tiny dimples or bumps in the glaze surface as the body and glaze cool. Silica sand has a particularly strong effect. As the body cools, silica contracts more than the rest of the body, so any particle near, or in, the interface pulls the glaze above it below the surrounding surface. This is why when you look into a hot kiln the glazes usually look perfectly glossy and smooth, but they aren't so glossy when you unload the kiln.

Know Your Inner Layer

Now that you know what to look for, you might end up trying different clays rather than glaze to get the results you want. If you need or want to continue using a clay that doesn't give you the glaze results you want, then you can make an underglaze slip that can change the texture and color background for your glaze. Usually this is done to make a smoother and whiter background, but you can go in other directions for decorative effects. Imagine a smooth body with a slip pattern painted with textured slip. An opaque glaze over such a clay/slip combo would show the slip-painted pattern in subtle texture.

When selecting and testing underglaze and slip recipes, keep in mind that you are adding a third variable to the glaze fit problem. Watch for unintended crazing and shivering effects. Sometimes you can simply thin a clay body with water, such as a porcelain, for use as an underglaze on another body, such as a stoneware. The textured underglaze recipe above can get you started.

TEXTURED UNDERGLAZE

For use at all cones onleather-hard clay or greenware

Dried clay-body trimmings	92 %
35-mesh grog	8
	100 %

For brushing, add water until you have a thick creamy consistency.

Glaze Fit

by Dave Finkelnburg

Defining the Terms

Glaze Fit: The difference in the amount of shrinkage per unit temperature (experienced upon cooling) by a fired clay body and the shrinkage per unit temperature of the glaze fired onto the same body. The scientific measure of this shrinkage is called the coefficient of thermal expansion (CTE). Thus, glaze fit is the difference between the CTE of the glaze and body.

Crazing: Cracks in a glaze, seen as lines that appear to be across the glaze surface. It occurs as a result of glaze tension.

Shivering: The spontaneous breaking away of bits of a glaze from the fired clay body underneath. Shivering will occur first on rims and other outside edges, as a result of excess glaze compression.

Though many are unaware of it, poor glaze fit can reduce the strength of a fired ceramic piece to as little as one-fifth the strength of a similar piece with ideal glaze fit. While good glaze fit seldom occurs by accident, it can be planned for and controlled. Some ceramic artists use glaze fit to induce crazing as a decorative technique (crackling) while others artists may want to avoid a "crackle" glaze.

Tight Pants and Fast Cars

If a fired clay body shrinks less than the glaze (the Coefficient of Thermal Expansion (CTE) of the clay is less than the CTE of the glaze), the glaze is in tension. The best way to visualize this is to think of a tight-fitting pair of pants, where the human body is the clay body and the pants are the glaze. If a glaze shrinks more than the clay body, the glaze is in tension (the pants are too tight). A glaze has enough strength to handle a little tension. However, it doesn't stretch very well at all. If the glaze is in too much tension, it cracks—literally pulls apart from itself. This is most likely to occur on surfaces where the tension accumulates across a distance until the tension exceeds the strength of the glaze and it cracks (crazes).

Both glass and fired clay are brittle. Brittle materials are very strong in compression. Visualize the Lamborghini dealer who supported an entire 3100-pound car on only four teacups! However, it takes a lot less force (per unit area) to pull a brittle material apart than to crush that same material. Thus, we say brittle materials are "weak" in tension. All crazing occurs when a glaze is in tension.

Since a glaze is a thin layer of glass melted and "frozen," on the surface of a fired ceramic body, the glaze is a brittle material bonded to another brittle material. If the glaze and the body shrink and expand at exactly the same rate, we say they fit. Both seldom do, except by conscious effort of the artist.

If a fired clay body shrinks more than its glaze (the CTE of the glaze is less than the CTE of the body), the glaze is in compression. Excessive glaze compression will force pieces of the glaze to literally pop off the body. We call this shivering and it doesn't occur nearly as often as crazing, partly because it takes greater CTE mismatch to cause shivering. Visualize this by thinking about the pants again. If the pants are way too loose they may fall down, so there is a weak resemblance to shivering in both meanings of the word! A little glaze compression may be good, say 15%, because it actually makes the fired ware stronger. However, if there is too much compression the glaze shivers.

Troubleshooting for Glaze Fit

Detecting crazing is not necessarily easy, especially with dark, opaque, or matt glazes. Use bright light and a simple, inexpensive, 10-power magnifying glass (often called a hand lens) to spot craze lines.

Understanding the real causes of crazing and shivering are a requirement to achieving a desired glaze fit or, in the case of crazing, misfit. There is a lot of misleading folklore regarding crazing. For example, many believe crazing is caused by cooling ware too fast. While rapid cooling through the quartz inversion temperature between 1100° and 1000°F (593-538°C) may damage ware, rapid cooling below 1000°F (as long as it doesn't cause damage due to thermal shock) cannot cause crazing. Rather, it simply reveals the CTE mismatch that will eventually cause a glaze to craze. All slow cooling accomplishes is possibly slowing down the occurrence of crazing so it isn't so dramatic when one opens the kiln.

In functional ware, shivering is dangerous. Potters don't want to have small bits of sharp glass popping off their pots into people's food or drink. The most likely place to observe shivering is on rims and edges. The sharper the edge or rim, the more likely shivering is to occur there if a glaze is in compression.

In order to change glaze fit, it is first necessary to understand whether to increase or decrease the CTE of the glaze, body, or both. There are only two ways to change glaze fit. One is chemical; change either the glaze recipe or the body recipe so the CTE of the glass in the glaze or body changes. In almost every case, it's easier and more effective to adjust the glaze recipe than the clay body recipe. The second way to change glaze fit is to increase or decrease the vitrification (amount of glass formed) in the clay body. Firing to a higher temperature dissolves more silica from any clay body containing quartz. The glass formed will have a lower CTE than the quartz did. Firing hotter will lower the CTE of the body, typically pushing it farther from the CTE of the glaze increasing the likelihood of crazing. To correct shivering you either have to increase the CTE of the glaze so it expands/contracts more, or reduce the CTE of the body, so it expands/contracts less. To avoid changing your clay body recipe, you will need to fire hotter. Note that if the first (or bisque) firing is hotter than the glaze firing, often the case for low fire, then the first firing is the one you would need to adjust. Underfiring, of course, will tend to promote crazing but reduce shivering, assuming the glaze still melts fully. Adjusting glaze recipes to fix glaze fit is a topic much larger than this page. Summarizing briefly, though, adding clay or silica, or magnesium and lithium fluxes (low CTE materials) will lower glaze CTE. Adding materials rich in high CTE fluxes, such as sodium and potassium, will raise glaze CTE.

Glaze Melt and Seal Point

by Dave Finkelnburg

Defining the Terms

Seal point: The temperature, at a given kiln heating rate, at which a glaze becomes fully melted. This is the point at which the glaze transforms from a dry powder to a molten glass.

Draw trial: A test tile drawn from a kiln during firing to show the progress of maturation of the glaze on the tile at the temperature attained at that point in the firing.

Understanding the complexity of glaze formulation is tough enough, but full knowledge of a glaze is not complete without knowing when it becomes molten (the seal point). This gives us an idea of how long that glaze is molten during the firing, which permits evaluating issues of glaze flow (or lack of it). Whether a glaze melts much before, with, or after densification of the body affects issues such as gas expulsion from the densifying body forming bubbles in the glaze. Without some indication of what is happening when, we cannot truly evaluate the fired result.

Timing Is Everything

It is unusual if any two different glazes, when heated together in a kiln, seal over at precisely the same temperature. Almost always the two glazes can be said to have different seal points. Even if both recipes are intended to produce glazes that mature at a particular cone, or a given peak firing temperature, the temperature at which each glaze becomes completely molten is likely different.

The difference is due to both the individual ingredients and to how those ingredients melt when combined. Individual fluxes tend to melt at different temperatures (lithium melts at a lower temperature than sodium, for example, which melts at a lower temperature than potassium, which melts lower than calcium, which melts—well, you get the idea.) If boron, a glass former in the same way as silicon, is added to the glaze recipe in some form, the recipe will begin melting at a much lower temperature. Boron is dramatically less refractory than silicon. That's why below cone 7 most glaze recipes contain at least some boron, while at cone 10 boron must be used sparingly, if at all, or the glaze may melt too soon, become too fluid, and run off the work.

All glazes that rely on a reduction atmosphere for color development, especially carbon trap glazes and copper reds, as well as crystalline glazes, benefit from one knowing when the glaze becomes molten.

Glaze reduction by kiln atmosphere effectively ceases once a glaze melts. Kiln gases simply do not penetrate more than a few atoms distance into the glaze once it becomes liquid. Thus any reduction of glaze elements that will seriously influence the fired glaze appearance, such as reducing iron in the presence of titanium to produce blue (rutile blues), or reducing iron to make celadons, or reducing copper to achieve copper reds, has to occur before the glaze seals over. Similarly, carbon trapping requires making soot and keeping it on the pot until the glaze seal point is passed. Many a carbon trapper has learned the discouraging lesson that if the kiln drifts even a tiny bit into oxidation before the glaze melts, all trace of carbon is burned away and a mostly clear to translucent glaze results. Once the seal point of a given glaze has been passed, the elements are effectively hidden under the glaze melt from the effects of the reducing atmosphere. At this point in the firing, kiln gases (think vapors here) can no longer penetrate the surface of a liquid. It's like trying to breathe under water—little elements, yearning to be oxidized, just can't breathe from below the a surface of liquid glass. Thus re-oxidizing during a reduction firing will only affect elements at the surface of a molten glaze, and the effect will only penetrate a few angstroms into the glaze.

Crystalline glazers often hold a kiln firing or speed up a firing based on whether they want to soak above the seal point to seed crystals or speed up above that point to reduce crystal seeding. The seal point is used here to exert some control over the number of crystals formed in the glaze.

Everything that can be said about twice firers also applies to single firers. Generally the only difference between once firing and twice firing is in application and one should not use glazes that seal over below their clay's normal bisque temperature.

Plot Your Glaze's Seal Point

It is just as important to test your glaze while it is being fired as it is while formulating it. The seal point of a given glaze is determined by pulling draw trials at different temperatures during a single firing. Tests for drawing from the kiln are made as draw rings or tiles. The draw rings are simply loops formed from flat strips of clay or sliced from extruded tubes, but in either case formed or altered to have one side sufficiently flat so the ring will stand in place during the firing. The draw tiles are tiles capable of standing vertically, of any shape and texture desired, and made with a hole in them that is large enough to pass a metal draw rod through. Multiple tests are made and these are coated with the same glaze. At different times/temperatures during the firing, the draw rod is inserted through the hole in the ring or the hole in the tile and the draw trial is lifted and pulled out of the kiln and carefully set aside to cool. Note: Safety glasses designed for viewing cones (the equivalent of #5 welding glasses) and insulated clothing and gloves should be worn when pulling the draw trials to protect against burns if a hot tile is accidentally dropped.

By carefully plotting a time versus temperature curve for the firing and marking on the curve the progress of glaze maturation revealed by the draw trials, the seal point for a glaze can be estimated quite accurately.

Unfortunately, there is no safe way to pull draw trials from an electric kiln without making significant modifications to the kiln and no one should ever reach into an electric kiln with a metal rod when the power is on to the kiln. The only safe way to take draw trials from an electric kiln is to place the test tiles inside a "shelter" of refractory which can be reached from outside the kiln without any danger of coming in contact with the kiln elements. Since electric kilns are not made with an access to pull draw tiles, it should be no surprise that the development and adoption of electric kilns has coincided with a cessation of the use of draw trials as a means of understanding glaze development by potters.

Carbon Trapping

by Dave Finkelnburg

Defining the Terms

Reduction Firing: A kiln firing in which there is insufficient oxygen (thus not all fuel burns) to fully oxidize all the reactive materials in the kiln.

Oxidation Firing: A kiln firing in which there is enough oxygen (at least 3% in the kiln exhaust) to fully oxidize all the reactive materials.

Methane: CH_4, the principle fuel compound in natural gas.

The late master potter, Malcolm Davis, called the process of carbon trapping, "frustrating and unpredictable." The challenge, Davis once told me, is getting the firing right. Without that, there is little or nothing to show for all the rest of the effort in the process.

A Tricky Process

Carbon trapping uses the presence and absence of carbon, trapped by a glaze, to achieve ceramic decoration. It's a unique process that can be tricky to execute. The chemical reaction that takes place to produce carbon soot is uncomplicated. In a natural-gas kiln, the fuel is a compound of carbon (C) and hydrogen (H) called methane (CH_4). In the presence of heat but limited air (thus limited oxygen) the methane is reduced to carbon and water vapor. The reaction is:

Mild Reduction: $CH_4 + 1.5O_2 \longrightarrow CO + 2H_2O$

The other hydrocarbon fuels commonly used to heat kilns—wood and propane—also yield soot in strong reduction. The chemical reaction involved is similar:

Sooty Reduction: $CH_4 + O_2 \longrightarrow C + 2H_2O$

It can be very frustrating when one is firing a kiln with the temperature climbing nicely only to see the temperature stop climbing or even fall as soon as the kiln is placed into heavy reduction. However, this is exactly what one should expect to happen. Here's why: Full oxidation of fuel in a kiln can be represented by the chemical reaction:

Oxidation: $CH_4 + 2O_2 \longrightarrow CO_2 + 2H_2O$

Oxidation produces considerably more heat than reduction because in reduction, the burning of the fuel is incomplete. As soon as oxidation ends and reduction begins, the amount of heat being produced per unit of fuel drops dramatically. At this point, the person firing may increase the fuel but not the air in an effort to maintain temperature or cause it to rise while still producing soot. An alternative is to decrease the air but not the fuel (or a combination

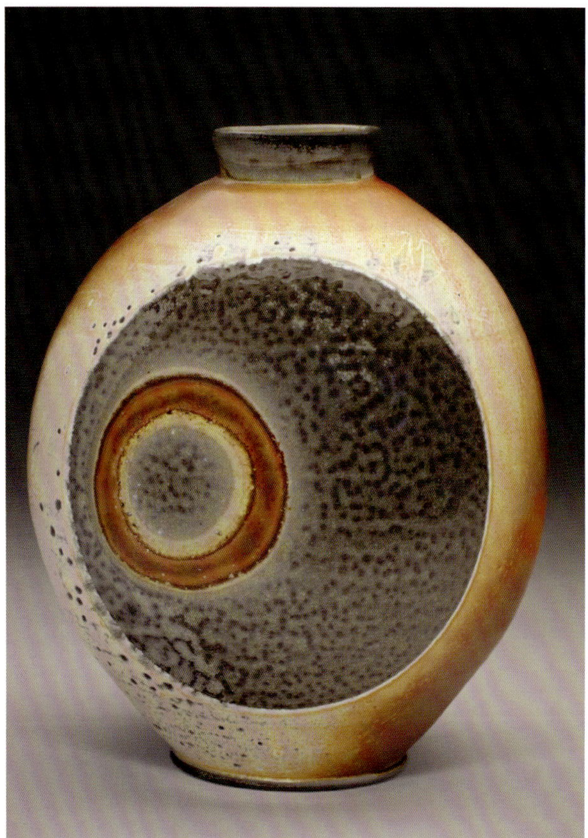

Sam Hoffman's *Orbital*, 12 in. (30 cm) in height, wheel-thrown, soda-fluxed porcelain. *Photo: Bill Bachhuber.*

of these two methods) and suffer the loss of temperature while producing a sooty flame that will generate the carbon needed for the process. The good news is that the carbon will remain, provided further increases in air and fuel still keep the kiln in at least moderate reduction. Judging just how much reduction is sufficient to both keep the carbon and produce enough heat for temperature rise requires experience with the kiln being fired.

Seeking a Sooty Surface

Carbon trapping is just what it says. Pure carbon (soot) is produced from fuel in a kiln and deposits on glazed ware. When the glaze melts, it traps the carbon.

To make soot, a hot, fuel-fired kiln is starved of air so it makes a smoky, sooty flame. The kiln will typically be around 1600°F (870°C) to make soot. However, the temperature must not be so much hotter than this that the glaze has already melted. That would entirely prevent trapping carbon. How hot is too hot depends on the glaze.

Once heavy reduction is achieved and soot is produced, it is critical to the process that the kiln remain in, or at least at some level of, reduction until it reaches the temperature at which the glazes on the ware melt. If the kiln is allowed to go into oxidation at any time between making soot and when the glaze melts, the soot will almost instantly burn off. The result? No carbon will be trapped.

However, as soon as the glazes melt enough to seal over, the carbon is permanently trapped under the glaze. Once the glaze melts, the kiln can be safely placed back into oxidation to finish the firing and any oxygen in the kiln can no longer reach the carbon to burn it away.

Knowing when the glaze has melted requires experience or testing. Pulling a series of draw trials from a kiln during the course of a firing is an excellent method of testing for seal point. The draw trials show the progress of glaze melting at different kiln temperatures. Typically, identical tiles are lined up on a kiln shelf and the one located closest to a peep hole large enough to allow pulling the tile out of it easily is removed. The hole is then closed and later another tile is pulled until a series of draw trials shows how much a particular glaze matures at different temperatures during the firing.

An accurate indication of kiln temperature is very helpful to successful carbon-trap firing.

Glazes for carbon trapping typically have high amounts of low-melting-point fluxes—most often sodium, but sometimes lithium, or a combination of the two. These two fluxes lower the seal point of these glazes. A soluble sodium source, usually soda ash, is also commonly used so that as the water evaporates from the glaze, it leaves a concentration of the dissolved sodium at the glaze surface, even further lowering the melting point there.

Because sodium and lithium melt at relatively low temperatures, as low as 1800°F (980°C), and most carbon trapping is done with porcelain or sometimes stoneware that is ultimately fired to cone 5–10, any glaze used must be stiff (viscous) enough that it will not run. For this reason most carbon-trap glazes have high amounts of alumina, sourced from a significant portion of clay in the recipe.

Firing for Carbon

Firing is the key to successful carbon trapping. Remember that fuel and strong reduction for at least a short period are required. The period of strong reduction must be followed by at least moderate reduction until the glaze reaches its seal point, which is what actually "traps" the carbon.

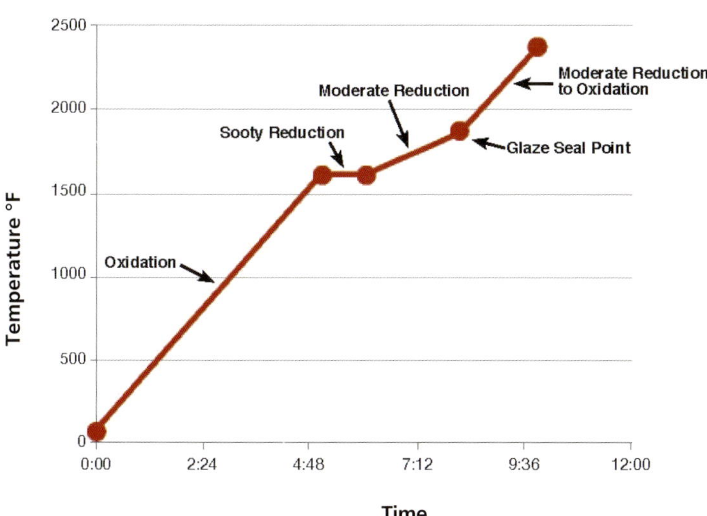

The firing schedule can be oxidation up until reduction begins, then sooty reduction, then at least partial reduction, then moderate to light reduction or even oxidation to peak temperature.

The duration and peak temperature of the sooty reduction portion of the firing is for a period of time and to a temperature judged suitable by the firer. The shift from moderate to light reduction or even oxidation at or near the seal point can emphasize the differences in the location of soluble sodium on the glaze surface. Oxidation will burn off the carbon that has not yet been trapped.

The real sweet spot in carbon-trap firing is to trap some carbon but burn off the rest and also reduce iron present in clay or glaze to produce an array of black, gray, tan, and orange hues on the ware from the single glaze used.

The chart above is a theoretical carbon-trap firing schedule. The important features are that the kiln temperature may stop rising or even fall during sooty reduction, and that the duration of sooty reduction need not be long.

An Alternative Method

SODA-FLUXED PORCELAIN

Cone 8–14

Nepheline Syenite	24 %
SGP Ball Clay	14
Grolleg Kaolin	29
Tile 6 Kaolin	24
Silica	9
	100 %

ORANGE FLASHING SLIP

Cone 8–14

Borax	6 %
OM4 Ball Clay	42
EPK Kaolin	42
Zircopax	10
	100 %

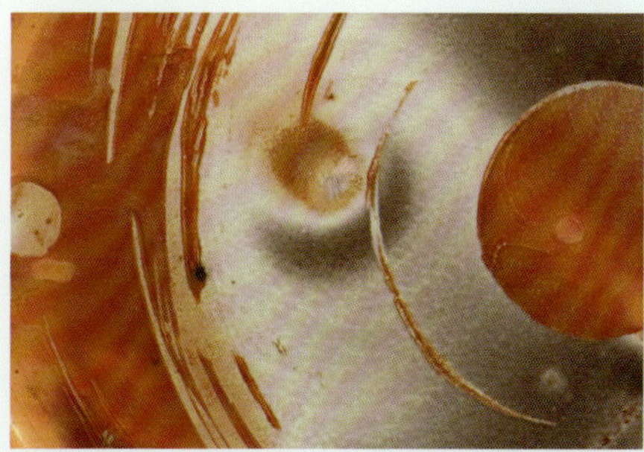

Detail of Sam Hoffman's *Vapor Trails*, with soda-fluxed porcelain and orange flashing slip. *Photo: Bill Bachhuber.*

Both of Sam Hoffman's pieces (facing page and above) were soda-vapor glazed in a wood-burning kiln, with heavy-reduction cooling. The soda feldspar (nepheline syenite) in the porcelain makes it more susceptible to carbon trapping, giving it a black or gray color. The flashing slip tends to resist carbon trapping, remaining orange or red as a point of contrast with the clay body. Refractory wadding placed on the pieces resists the wood ash and soda vapors, creating another layer of color and texture.

36 Find recipes for cone 6 and cone 10 carbon-trap shino glazes.

Matte Glaze

by David Pier

Defining the Terms

Matte: An adjective or noun pertaining to a (glaze) surface that diffusely reflects light.

Glossy: In this context, it is the same as shiny or lustrous. Adjective describing a surface that reflects light in a specular (mirror-like) way.

Gloss: The amount of incoming light that is specularly reflected rather than absorbed or diffusely reflected.

Crystalline: A crystalline material is one in which the constituent atoms, molecules, or ions are arranged in an orderly, repeating pattern extending in all three spatial dimensions.

Microcrystalline: A material in which the individual crystals are so small that the crystals are only visible through microscopic examination.

Amorphous Solid: A solid, such as a glossy glaze, in which there is no long range order in the arrangement of the constituent atoms, molecules, or ions.

Devitrification: The formation of crystals in a melted glass or glaze that happens in the kiln during the cooling phase after the firing.

Specular Reflection: Reflection of light from a surface where the incoming light from a single incoming direction is reflected in a single outgoing direction, as in a mirror.

Diffuse Reflection: Reflection of light from a surface where the incoming light is reflected in many or all directions.

Most people can easily distinguish a matte glaze from a gloss glaze, but the optical phenomenon, as well as the chemistry responsible for these glazes, is much more mysterious. A matte glaze is not simply an underfired glaze and, depending on the formula, the dry or non-gloss surface may actually be a slip or terra sigillata—not a glaze at all. If you're not sure whether matte glazes are appropriate, there are some simple rules to help decide when a matte glaze may be right for your work.

Matte Means Microcrystalline (usually)

First we'll discuss the general physical/optical phenomenon that makes a glaze matte. To understand matte, we need to understand gloss. Glossy glazes are those that reflect light in a "specular," coherent, mirror-like fashion so that you can see reflected images. Glossy glazes are very smooth, smooth on the scale of the wavelength of visible light (390nm–750nm, where a nm is ~1/400,000,000 of an inch). Thus any bumps, pits, or undulations on the glaze surface are smaller than approximately 390nm or 1.5/100,000 inch, so as far as the light is concerned the surface is perfectly smooth. If the light's wavelength is larger than the bump, then you won't be able to see the bump. Conversely, the protruding crystals in matte glazes are larger than this and therefore scatter the light.

Dictionary definitions of matte often use the word "dull," but that isn't very informative for our purposes and it doesn't hint at the many good reasons to use a matte glaze. Matte glazes can be just as "bright" as gloss glazes, if brightness is referring to the amount of light reflected. A more useful definition for us is that a matte glaze is one that isn't glossy because it scatters reflected light in many or all directions. It scatters the light because it doesn't have the super-smooth surface of a gloss glaze. However, since we're talking about smooth on a microscopic scale, a matte glaze can still feel very smooth. In fact, some matte glazes feel smoother than any gloss glaze, because the reduced contact area caused by the tiny, regular bumps actually diminishes the friction-causing attraction forces between the glaze surface and your finger.

By far the most common origin of matte glazes is devitrification, which is the formation of crystals within the glaze during the cooling phase after firing. This type of matte glaze relies on having higher concentrations of certain oxides within the glaze (see next page), and also may require a particular (slower) cooling schedule after the firing. The dependence on cooling rate is why some glazes will end up matte when fired in one kiln and shiny in a different, faster cooling kiln. It is also why some matte glazes come out of some firings feeling smooth, but then come out of other, slower-cooled firings with a rough surface due to larger crystals on the surface of the glaze.

A less common way to make a matte glaze is to incorporate some coarser raw materials into the raw glaze. Since many refractory materials rely on close association with the fluxing oxides in order to melt, some materials that will fully fuse if they are finer will not melt into the glass if they are coarse. These unmelted inclusions can cause microscopic light scattering bumps in the fired glaze. This can happen either where the glaze is applied thinner so the surface tension of the molten glaze is unable to pull the particle below the surface, or all over where the different thermal contraction of the unmelted inclusion causes it to protrude after cooling. Many historic glazes are matte because of coarser materials, but it is unlikely to happen in your studio if you are using standard commercially obtained raw materials, since these are ground very fine.

It is also possible to make a shiny glaze matte after firing by sandblasting or other means of mechanical abrasion. This can be an especially useful method if you desire a transparent or translucent matte glaze, something that is very rare using the other two methods.

Oxides commonly employed to create matte glazes are MgO, CaO, SrO, BaO, Al_2O_3, TiO_2, ZnO, and MnO. Silica is often a component of the crystals, but since it is in all glazes in large amounts, it is not listed. The required amount of any oxide depends on the identity and quantity of other oxides present, the firing temperature, and many other variables such as what clay it is applied to. Matting oxides are often used together. Some crystals grow on the surface of the glaze, and others start at the clay/glaze interface and grow up through the entire thickness of the glaze. The growing crystals have a different oxide composition than the remaining glaze, and the surrounding glaze is now somewhat depleted of the crystal oxides, resulting in two different materials that usually have very different properties. This is why most matte glazes are opaque, and why they are often a very different color than very similarly composed shiny glazes.

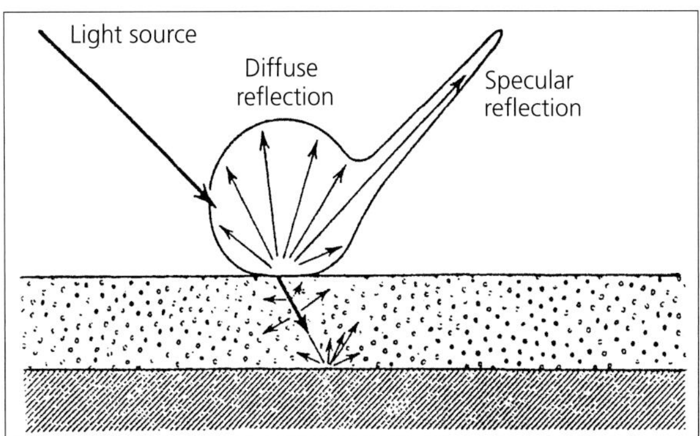

Diffuse and specular reflectance from a coating surface.

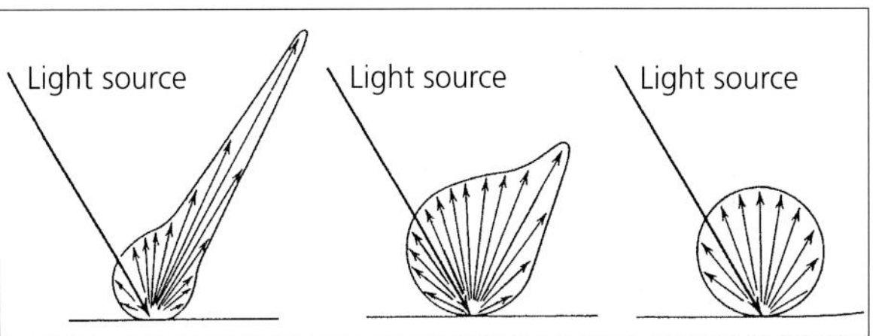

Light reflection from (left to right) high-gloss, satin, and matte coating.

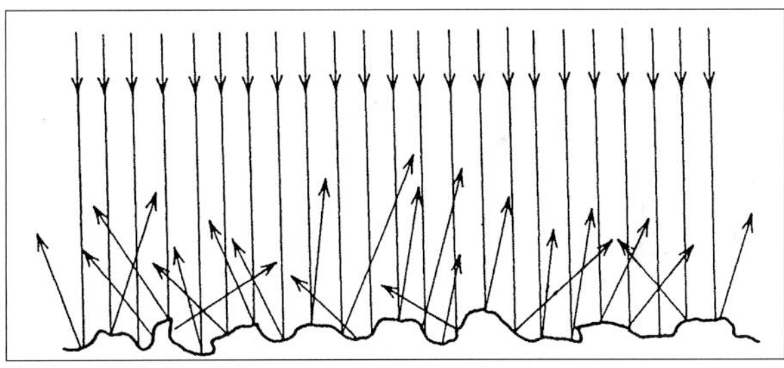

Light reflection from a rough surface. Diagrams excerpted from Understanding Glazes *by Richard A. Eppler with Mimi Obstler, Published by the American Ceramic Society.*

Choosing an Appropriate Surface

At least as important as understanding what makes glazes matte is awareness of important aesthetic and functional considerations involved in deciding between matte and shiny glazes for your work. If your piece has intricate textures or drawings, or a slightly irregular surface, a matte glaze can eliminate distracting reflections that would prevent easy viewing. If your work has simple, precise surfaces, you might want a glossy glaze to show this off.

Keep in mind that there are many different kinds of matte. They all look a little different, and they can be very different to the touch. For instance, magnesium mattes often are described as having a "butterfat" feel, while barium and strontium mattes offer some unique bright colors while being very dry. There are many different degrees of matte, with a "satin" matte about halfway between a dry matte and a gloss glaze. If you look for these subtleties you will be in a better position to make the right glaze choice for your art.

You might be tempted to modify your favorite glossy glaze to turn it into a matte, but remember that any change to a glaze's recipe will affect all of its properties, not just the one you were trying to change. You are probably better off finding a recipe for a glaze that is already matte. Millions of glaze tests have already been run, so you can probably find a recipe that is very close to what you want. Decide what you want in texture and color, then find a recipe that has the appropriate dominant fluxing oxide(s) and appropriate colorant(s). Some testing and alteration may be necessary to adjust the glaze to your exact tastes and your particular combination of clays, firing, and application methods.

Don't take anybody's word on the safety of a particular recipe. Even if it was safe under their circumstances, small change in materials, firing, and clay could result in an unstable glaze. It can be harder to recognize an unstable matte glaze because a heavily leaching surface will not evidence itself with loss of gloss as it would in a glossy glaze. The only way to be sure is to have them lab tested.

Cooling

by Dave Finkelnburg

Defining the Terms

Cristobalite: (inversion @ 428°F) The mineral cristobalite is a high-temperature polymorph of quartz—it has the same chemical composition as quartz but a different crystal structure.

Dunting Point: A crack or fault that can occur during the firing as a result of a thermally induced stress. Dunting is caused when a ware is cooled too quickly past the temperatures at which silica undergoes a shift in crystalline structure from beta back to alpha.

Quartz Inversion: Crystals of alpha-quartz turn to beta-quartz between 1022°–1063°F and the reverse occurs during cooling over the same temperature range. During heating, there's a 2% volume expansion of crystalline quartz between 1070°–1110°F, and an identical 2% contraction on cooling.

Thermal Expansion and Contraction: Thermal expansion is the amount of change in volume in response to a change in temperature. When a substance is heated, atoms within it move more and thus maintain a greater average separation. The degree of expansion divided by the change in temperature is called a material's coefficient of thermal expansion (CTE).

Thermal Shock: Stress in an object caused by a rapid change in temperature. When a ceramic object, which is brittle by nature and also a good insulator, is exposed to a very rapid change in temperature, the thinnest, most exposed parts of the object changes temperature first. These heated parts expand while the cooler parts do not expand as much. The different amounts of expansion in different parts of the piece can create stresses large enough to cause the piece to crack.

An often overlooked part of firing ceramic work is cooling the kiln. Surface, color and integrity of the work are all affected by the rate at which the kiln is cooled.

What Goes Up Must Come Down

A glaze is a glass formed by melting its ingredients on the surface of an object during firing. All glazes are the same while they are molten—they are liquid glass. Some glazes remain glassy when they cool provided they are fully melted during the firing.

Crystals precipitate from a glaze when the glaze is saturated with one or more chemical elements in concentrations too high to remain in the glass as it cools. The effect is crystals in the glaze. Below the saturation temperature, atoms of the elements attempt to move through the molten glass toward points where they can link up with other elements to form crystals. Just as sugar crystals precipitate from a strong syrup over time while the syrup is liquid, glaze crystals can only form while the glaze is molten. Once the glaze sets, atoms within it can no longer rearrange themselves into crystals. These crystals may form anywhere from the glaze surface to the contact layer between the glaze and clay body. The starting point for the crystals is always some seed material (zinc, silica, frit) that is in the glaze or on the body or tiny crystals that nucleate spontaneously from the melt.

Matte glazes composed of crystals that precipitate from the glaze melt require time to develop. Rapid cooling may actually prevent the formation of matte glazes. Cooling a glaze quickly can prevent the elements that would make up crystals from rearranging themselves into the crystals. Cooling a glaze quickly does not guarantee a glossy surface because some glaze compositions just want to crystallize. On the other hand, slow cooling will not guarantee development of a matte glaze. The time necessary for crystal development and the temperature at which the crystals grow is frequently different for each glaze and may even be affected by the clay body.

We have said this before, but it bears repeating; the rate of cooling does not cause crazing. Crazing is a fundamental mismatch between the coefficient of thermal expansion (CTE) of the body and applied glaze. It occurs because the glaze shrinks more than the body during cooling but the rate of cooling has no effect on the CTE of either body or glaze. Thus slow cooling cannot prevent crazing. However, fast cooling may reveal crazing that otherwise might not have been apparent for days, weeks or even months.

So how fast can you cool? As fast as you want, as long as the rate of temperature fall does not dunt the work and the surface results are what you want. If damage is observed due to thermal shock, most often from rapid cooling through quartz inversion (1100°–1000°F), then it is necessary to slow down the rate of cooling. The rate of cooling depends on the amount of quartz in the clay body, the thickness of the ware, and its shape. Cooling fracture is due to a differential in thermal contraction. The first part of the ware to cool to the quartz inversion temperature converts from beta to alpha quartz with a consequent volume shrinkage while the hotter center of the ware has yet to reach that point and shrink. In

Kiln Cooling Chart

TEMP °F (°C)	COLOR	INTERNAL KILN ACTION
2350°F (1288°C)	White	Peak firing temperature and end of glaze reduction
2200°–1800°F (1204–982°C)	Yellow-white to orange	Primary crystal formation range
1800°–1300°F (982°–704°C)	Orange to dull red	Striking range—Molten glazes are still affected by atmosphere and the time held at particular temperatures.
1063°–1022°F (573°–550°C)	Dull red glow	Quartz Inversion—2% contraction
1200°–500°F (649°–260°C)	Dark red to black	Set point of glazes—glazes are no longer molten and are frozen in place.
428°F (220°C)	Black	Cristobalite inversion—3% contraction is possible if cristobalite is present in the clay body.

extreme cases this cracks the ware. Wide, flat rims are prone to radial cracks while tall, small diameter forms are much less sensitive to it.

Cool Work

All glazes, in general, may benefit from a hold or soak at peak firing temperature to help heal glaze flaws such as pinholes and blisters. Glossy glazes, however, are usually not improved by slow cooling. Once the surface of a glossy glaze has fully smoothed out it can be cooled. The first 600°F of cooling of high-fire glossy glazes usually is best if done as rapidly as the kiln and the ware permit.

Mid-range and high-fire matte glazes formed from precipitating crystals seem to develop interesting matte surfaces when held or cooled slowly from somewhat below 2000°F down to about 1500°F.

Most electric kilns cool too fast for maximum crystal development in the glaze, thus requiring some firing down (manual control of the rate of cooling) to achieve the greatest possible surface variation due to crystal growth. Since every kiln load, glaze, and ware combination may be a bit different, experimentation, testing, and record keeping are essential to determining the cooling cycle that produces the best matte glazes under particular circumstances. Holding a high-fire or mid-range matte glaze for two hours at 400°–600°F below peak firing temperature is a good start for such testing.

If you fire a gas-fueled kiln, it is important to note that the cooling cycle is actually a very long period of oxidation. Once the gas is turned off, the kiln atmosphere immediately is oxidizing. When you close the exhaust damper at the theoretical end of the firing, you are actually prolonging a period of oxidation at an extreme temperature by minimizing the kiln's ability to cool. In effect, you are forcing the kiln to cool more slowly. Unless you intentionally create a reduction atmosphere, all gas-kiln cooling is in oxidation. Just closing the damper with the fuel off will not maintain a reducing atmosphere due to secondary air leaks. To circumvent this, fuel firers sometimes cause reduction during the cooling cycle by introducing fuel at a low rate and starving it of air.

This is a cone 10 recipe that also works well at cone 6. It yields yellow "tea dust" crystals particularly when fired in reduction. Here, it has been fired in oxidation, and the iron crystals are a result of thick application and slow cooling.

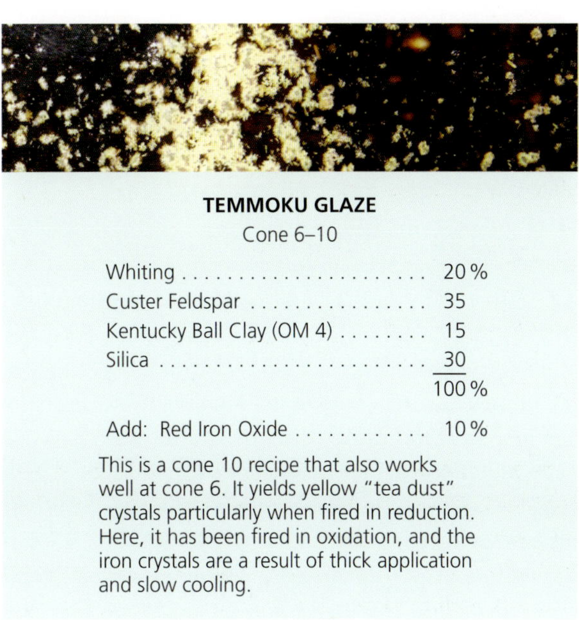

TEMMOKU GLAZE

Cone 6–10

Whiting	20 %
Custer Feldspar	35
Kentucky Ball Clay (OM 4)	15
Silica	30
	100 %
Add: Red Iron Oxide	10 %

This is a cone 10 recipe that also works well at cone 6. It yields yellow "tea dust" crystals particularly when fired in reduction. Here, it has been fired in oxidation, and the iron crystals are a result of thick application and slow cooling.

Faster Firing

by Dave Finkelnburg

The firing cycle for most ceramics consumes hours—if not days—of time. It is the longest single process in almost every ceramic studio. However, many people believe that the firing time is fixed and cannot be changed. This is not true. Over the past several years, ceramic manufacturers have reduced their firing times to one sixth of what used to be normal, simply by changing their thinking about the kiln.

A student once asked me, "what's the best way to fire our kiln?"

"That's easy," I said. "Fire for best results and least cost! "Okay, Okay," he grinned. "What way is that?" "Well," I countered, "It probably won't be as slow a firing as you think. Fast firing saves fuel. It's that simple. Results? That's complicated."

I went on to explain that I occasionally fire to cone 10 in a small gas updraft kiln in just under four hours. The load is functional glazed bisque ware made from a high-quality porcelain and is fired on ½-inch thick mullite shelves. Firing time is from lighting the burners to shutting them off.

Why so fast? Because I like the results and I don't like tending the kiln any longer than I have to. Besides, I don't like paying the gas bill for a firing that uses more fuel than it has to.

I had to confess, the speed is also about three times as fast as I was taught to fire, and about three times as fast as most sources suggest firing, even if only to cone 5 or 6. To achieve a short firing cycle I had to learn about the process and the testing of the kiln, the ware, and the glazes.

What You See and What You Don't

Heat is transferred by conduction and radiation. At low kiln temperatures most heat transfer is by conduction. Hot gas molecules in the kiln touch the ware, shelves, posts, and kiln lining, heating them all. At high kiln temperatures most heat transfer is by radiation. Hot gas molecules give off infrared rays that travel in straight lines in all directions and give up their heat to objects in their path.

In a kiln how do I tell how hot or cool it is inside? That's easy. You can see it! Besides a pyrometer, you can see the kiln temperature, approximately, by the color of the kiln interior. If the kiln interior seen through a peephole is dark or black, little radiant heat is being given off. Once the kiln reaches dull red heat, significant amounts of infrared rays are coming off the kiln interior. As the kiln temperature rises the interior will look more orange, then yellow, and finally approach white, each change indicating a hotter temperature.*

Firing Cycle

How fast is "fast?" A reasonable starting point for most functional ware is on the order of 300°F (167°C) per hour heating and cooling rate. Thick or non-uniform ware may need to be fired more slowly. On the other end of the scale, industry routinely fires tile from room temperature to peak and back to room temperature in well under an hour!

This assumes, of course, that all parts of the ware are dry. It is very reasonable to "candle," or heat a kiln load at a very low rate for an hour or two to ensure it is dry. The energy used is minimal.

Heating Rate Limit

How fast is fast enough to fire? Anyone in the ceramic industry will say "fast enough" is as fast as absolutely possible without increasing the rate of ware losses or unacceptably increasing the rate of wear on the kiln furniture and lining.

What causes loss rates to increase as firing time is shortened? Simply put, greater thermal stresses occur in the ware (and in the kiln furniture and kiln lining, by the way).

The slower ware is heated, the more uniform thermal expansion is between the outside of the ware and the center of the ware. However, when fast firing, the outside may be growing at the rate of the kiln temperature but the center of the ware can be lagging well behind. The greater the temperature difference, the more damage will occur.

Ware

Imagine a kiln loaded with a complex, non-uniform shape. Perhaps a sculpture with sections ranging from one inch thick to ⅛ inch thick. Such a shape will obviously be difficult to fire without cracks. The firing speed will have to be slow enough to allow the thickest section to be heated uniformly.

Next, imagine a kiln loaded only with small, simple, uniform shapes, say tiles of exactly the same size and thickness. These can probably be fired to temperature quite rapidly and successfully.

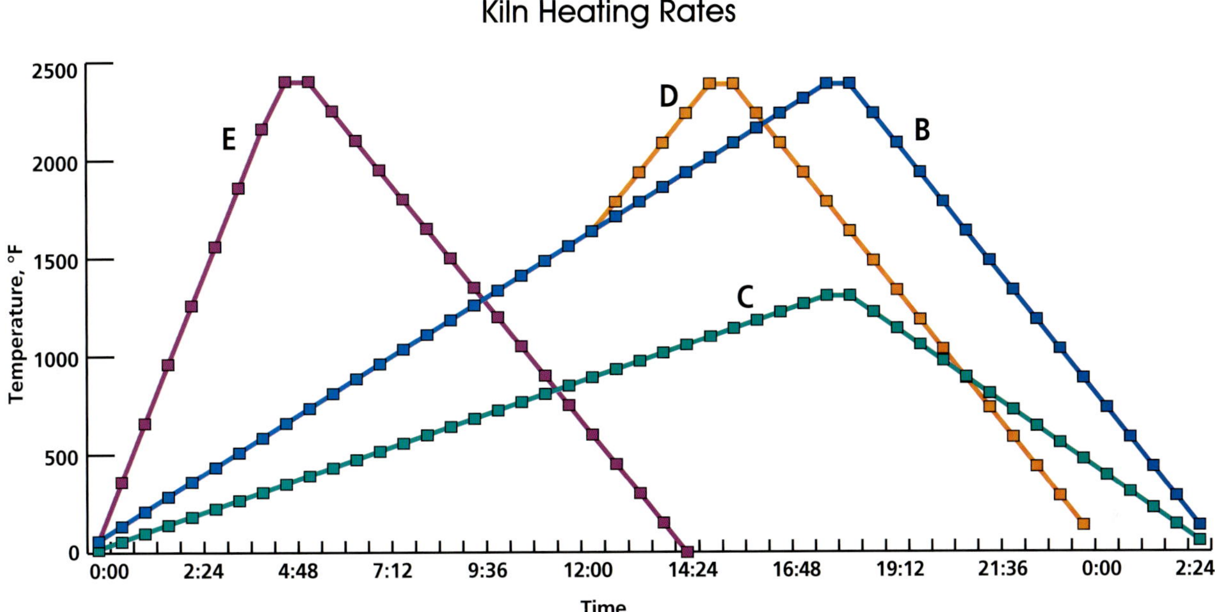

The chart above shows the time versus temperature plots for four firings. **Line B** and **line C** are (theoretical) conservative heating rates suitable for most ceramic work that is less than 1-inch thick, in an open stacked kiln, with a more rapid but still moderate cooling rates. **Line D** is a conservative firing schedule for uniform ware ⅜-inch thick or less, open stacked, with faster firing after organics and sulfur compounds are burned out. Note that just by speeding up the firing after cone 012 the firing is shortened by 2½ hours! **Line E** is a firing schedule only suited to thin ware or open clay bodies with an open stack with kiln furniture and kiln capable of taking the fast firing rate and consequent thermal shock. Note that the firing time is reduced by 9 hours. Fuel consumption will be about half that of the firing in **line D** and ⅓ that of **line B**.

Now imagine a third load which is a mix of the sculpture from the first load and tile from the second load. How fast can that load be fired? No faster than the sculpture can handle, of course. The most difficult piece to fire successfully in the entire load will always determine the firing speed.

Firing Greenware

Whether glaze or bisque firing, if greenware is what you are starting with, the heating cycle should be the same. Heat at a moderate rate until free water and bound water are driven off, and carbon and sulfur compounds are burned off. With relatively light ware, no thicker than ¼-inch, that is pretty much done at full red heat. From that point on, a faster heating rate can be used.

Firing Bisque Ware

If the kiln load is composed of ware that already has free and bound water driven off, and carbon and sulfur burned out of the body, the firing time can be shortened dramatically. The remaining limit to firing speed is presented by the ware's shape, uniformity and thickness, and the glazes being used.

Glazes formulated from frits and clay can usually be fired faster with better results than glazes formulated entirely from raw materials.

The Kiln

When it comes to firing faster, not all kilns are created equal. Kilns insulated with refractory fiber, either board or blanket, at the "hot" face (interior of the kiln) can be fired at very high heating rates without hurting the kiln. Hard brick kilns, however, must be heated slowly or the brick will spall and crack with any but very moderate heating rates.

Insulating fire brick falls between these extremes. I've gotten 40 cycles firing at up to 600°F (333°C) per hour heating rate. I cool at roughly half that rate because I have lost some of my ware to dunting with faster cooling. It's important to test!

Kiln Furniture

Traditional cordierite-mullite kiln furniture is relatively inexpensive, rugged, heavy, and suitable for fast firing. Cordierite has very low thermal expansion so shelves, posts, and setters of approximately 50% cordierite are able to resist thermal shock quite well.

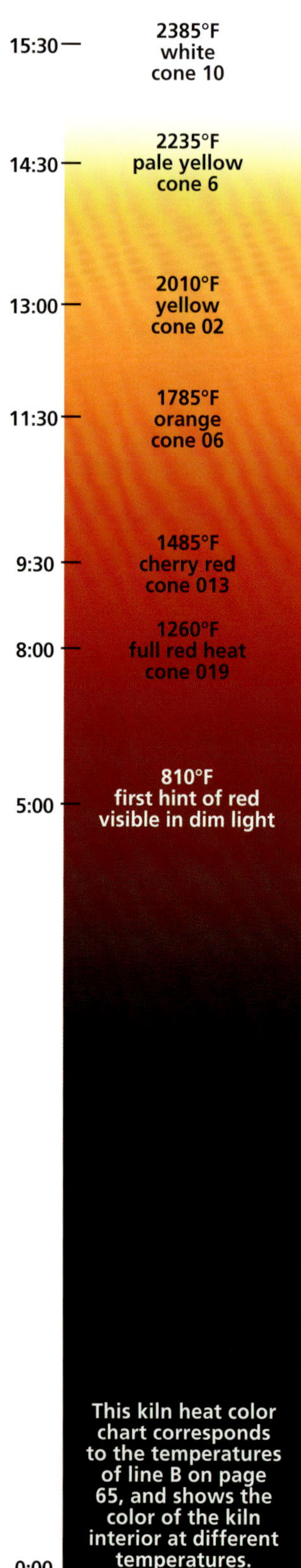

This kiln heat color chart corresponds to the temperatures of line B on page 65, and shows the color of the kiln interior at different temperatures.

Cordierite-mullite kiln furniture with alumina added is suitable at somewhat higher kiln temperatures. Check the manufacturer's heat rating carefully because kiln furniture compositions differ significantly.

Silicon carbide shelves and posts are much lighter and stronger but may be less resistant to the thermal shock that comes with fast firing. At least one US vendor strongly recommends not heating nitride-bonded silicon carbide faster than 275°F (153°C) per hour until 1000°F (556°C) is reached. Thinner silicon carbide shelves are apparently less resistant to thermal shock.

Kiln Loading

A densely loaded kiln can hold a lot of ware, but this sort of loading requires a longer firing schedule. Both conduction and radiation occur readily at the outsides of the kiln shelves, where heat has access to the load. However, kiln gases circulate poorly through a dense stacking and slow heating or an extended soak or both are required to maintain a uniform temperature throughout the kiln.

Can I Fire Too Fast?

If the difference between the temperature of the outside of a piece of ceramic ware in a kiln and the temperature of the center of the piece is too great, it can crack. If this happens during the heating cycle, it's because the outside is expanding faster than the inside of the ware. If the crack occurs during cooling, it's called dunting, and the reverse is the case—the center is hot, the outside is cool.

Dunting should never happen in an adequately insulated kiln. If it's a problem, firing down—running burners, burning fuel, or turning on the heating elements enough to slow the rate of cooling—is necessary. Usually, simply closing up the peep holes, and also vent and burner ports, if any, is sufficient to hold heat in the kiln and allow it to cool slowly. The most common cause of dunting is not poor insulation but opening peeps or vent and burner ports or even a door to cool the kiln faster, and cooling so fast that thermal shock dunts pots.

Whether a crack occurs during heating or cooling is pretty easy to tell by looking closely at the fracture. If the crack has a sharp edge, it occurred in cooling. If it cracked during heating, the edge will be somewhat to very much rounded.

**Protect your eyes! Always use protective glasses or goggles with lenses of #5 welding glass or higher when looking into a kiln. This will protect your eyes from hot kiln gases which may escape from the peep, and from the red heat stage on, to protect your eyes from long wavelength radiation. These rays will penetrate all the way to the back of the inside of the eyeball and cause permanent damage.*

Glaze Unity Formula

by Tina Gebhart

Defining the Terms

Unity Molecular Formula (UMF)—Also known as a Seger Formula. Glaze recipe format based on the number of molecules instead of on weights of raw materials, where the total molecules of flux in a glaze are calculated to total 1.0 (which means they are in unity). The formula shows the ratio between fluxes, but perhaps more importantly, it shows the ratio of combined fluxes to the silica and alumina.

Mole—The base unit of measure for the amount of a substance, which is either atoms (for elements) or molecules (for compounds).

Flux Unity—Unity Molecular Formula expressed as one mole of total flux in proportion to the silica and alumina. A UMF can be arranged to express non-flux components as the unified part in proportion to other parts, but flux unity is the standard format used in ceramics.

Flux System—The arrangement of fluxes in a UMF recipe, showing the internal ratio of fluxes in a given glaze; the common feature in all samples of a UMF grid as shown on pages 68–69.

Batch to Unity— Translation from a standard glaze recipe format (where the raw materials of the base glaze are written as weight percentages) to the UMF format.

Unity to Batch—Translation from a UMF recipe to a raw-materials-oriented, batching-friendly recipe.

Adjusting a Glaze Recipe

There are many approaches to modifying a glaze recipe, and different approaches can meet different needs. Some modifications change the colorant level while others change the colorant type altogether. Some may directly replace one material with another, add a few weight units more (or less) of one of the base ingredients in the recipe, or add an amount of an entirely new ingredient. These strategies we use to alter glazes tend to parallel how we cook and modify recipes in the kitchen, but adjustments to the base glaze using the kitchen method do not always give us the results we want.

If we were using a baking recipe that called for a certain type of readymade baking mix and we added more of it because we wanted a thicker batter, and we had not changed anything else, we may end up with too much leavening (contained in the baking mix) in proportion to the two eggs we had already added. In our glazes, this becomes more complicated because a wide array of our raw materials are similar to baking mixes; they contain more than one glaze component. Many materials that do not say *carbonate*, *oxide*, or *sulfate* at the end of the name (for example) are complex materials similar to a commercial baking or cake mix. Imagine trying to make bread from a cake mix, a cookie mix, a pancake mix, and a biscuit mix. I, frankly, would not know where to start.

The difference is that, in ceramics, we have access to the exact ingredients in each of our raw material mineral mixes. This is the equivalent of knowing how much flour, leavening, salt, etc. is in all baking mixes. Once we know the components of the raw materials, and have these materials reorganized in terms of those components, we are looking at a more standardized, universal recipe.

This universal recipe form is called the *unity molecular formula.* The ingredients in our raw materials are regrouped so that we can see the accumulated amounts of silica (from

AGATE V3 VARIATION

(cone 9–10 oxidation or reduction)

Material	%
Dolomite	13.0 %
Lithium Carbonate	4.0
Whiting	15.2
Custer Feldspar	20.2
Nepheline Syenite	10.3
EPK Kaolin	10.0
Silica	27.3
	100.0 %
Add: Copper Carbonate	2.0 %

UNITY MOLECULAR FORMULA

Oxide	Amount	Total
KNaO	0.13	1.00
Li_2O	0.13	
MgO	0.18	
CaO	0.56	
SiO_2		2.17
Al_2O_3		0.23

our kaolin, feldspar, wollastonite, talc, frits, etc.), alumina (from our kaolin and feldspar), fluxes (from our feldspar, whiting, dolomite, talc, and many of the other white powders), and their proportions to each other.

The unity (one) molecular (molecules) formula (recipe) looks at the *chemical* raw materials in the glaze rather than the *mineral* raw materials used to make that glaze. This version of the recipe reduces the fractions of these chemicals to show us a simple proportional relationship present in the glaze. By unifying the fluxes to equal one, and showing the relationship (ratio) of the silica and alumina to that single amount of flux, we can compare or manipulate glazes very directly. This allows us to make modifications that are quantitative, i.e. modifications that remove the ambiguity and guesswork.

You can certainly learn to make these calculations by hand, but there are several software programs that can do the recipe translations for you. I use HyperGlaze as well as a programmed Excel spreadsheet. There are other commercial programs available, such as Insight, GlazeMaster, Matrix2000, GlazeChem, and even a free version online at www.glazecalc.com.

Creating a Unity Molecular Formula Testing Grid

- Select a glaze recipe to investigate.
- Determine the UMF (with flux unity) of that glaze with the batch-to-unity feature of your software.
- Using the flux system identified there as a constant, and using the unity-to-batch feature of your software, determine four corner recipes. Point A: low silica (2.0), high alumina (0.6). Point B: high silica (6.0), high alumina (0.6). Point C: low silica (2.0), low alumina (0.2). Point D: high silica (6.0), low alumina (0.2). These levels could be expanded to a wider range, but it can become difficult to combine materials to meet those extremes.
- Batch each of these corner recipes as 500g batches in quart containers, making them exactly the same volume in each container. Label each container carefully as you batch.
- Volume blend A with C and B with D to create the side column samples (as volume percents 75:25, 50:50, 25:75 in smaller containers). Note that this does not produce fully even or accurate increments for the UMF grid, due to the volume blending, but this approach is wildly faster than batching each individual sample.
- Volume blend each side sample with its corresponding opposite side to make the horizontal samples (as volume percents 75:25, 50:50, 25:75 in even smaller containers).
- Apply each glaze sample to a well-coded test tile.
- Fire and arrange the grid of glazes, the expanded family of your original glaze.
- Notice glazes near the UMF of your original glaze (the original glaze is near the lower left of the grid below, with levels of 2.17 silica and 0.23 alumina) and note which may look similar but with one changed characteristic. Which samples are crazed? Where does this glaze family change from gloss to satin? From satin to matte? Has one solved a problem for you? Are there substantial color or surface shifts throughout the grid? Which are interesting? Which are undesirable to you?
- Note also where two adjacent samples are extremely different from each other. These may be areas to investigate further (such as a line blend of 1–3 samples in between those two) to discover what surprise glaze might be hiding in between them. These areas also may be ones to avoid if what you want is a very consistent, exacting sameness in your glaze results; these may be the ones that could be somewhat variable depending on mixing/stirring times and glaze settling rates.

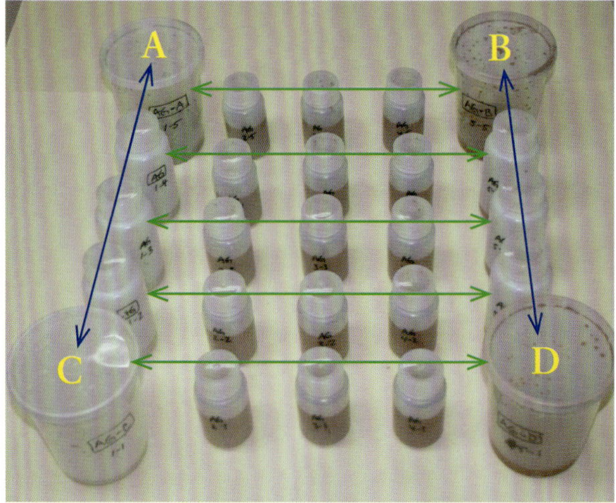

Batch corners first (500g each), then volume blend side columns (200ml each), then volume blend center rows (80ml each).

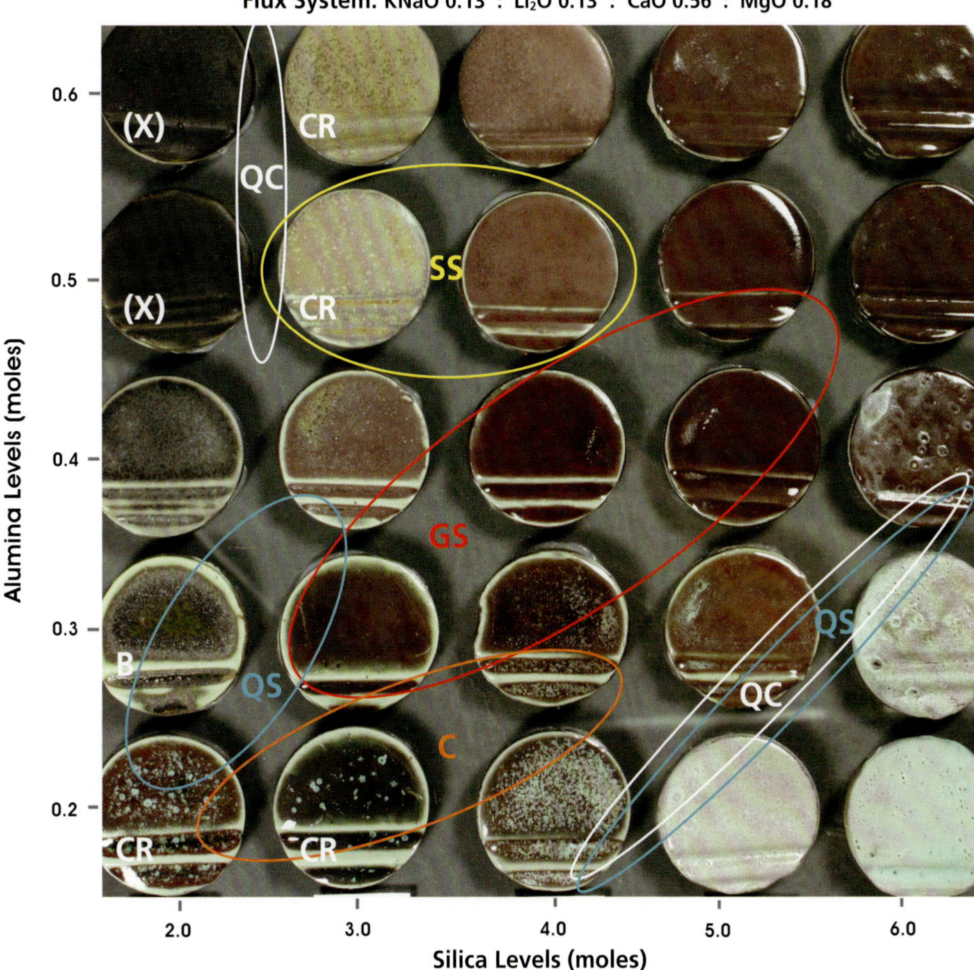

UMF Diagram Coding

QC: Quickly changing color response; area between good for further testing; what color will be between black and beige? Between dark rose and very light green? Potential high-variability.

SS: Good satin surfaces; appear smooth and consistent in this small region.

GS: Good gloss surfaces; ranging from full gloss to semi-gloss in this fairly large region; good potential for consistency in this area.

C: Visible crystals formed; varied frequencies and sizes; good area to explore for additional crystallizing results.

QS: Quickly changing surfaces (gloss to matte); potential high-variability.

B: Blister-puckering in crevices; test toward neighboring samples to remedy.

CR: Crazed sample; can move recipe toward neighboring samples to remedy.

(X): Possibly crazed sample; surface and color interfering with assessment.

This grid method is related to both the Stull Grid (R. T. Stull, *Transactions of The American Ceramic Society, XIV, 1912)*, the Currie Grid Method (Ian Currie, *Revealing Glazes*, 2000), and grid work done with Bill Carty et al, at the former Whitewares Research Center.

Testing Standards

by Dave Finkelnburg

Defining the Tests

Resistance to Acids/Leaching/Glaze Solubility—Glazes can corrode and break down from contact with acidic foods. The breakdown depends on both the glaze and the degree of contact. Studio test: 3-day vinegar immersion.

Resistance to Alkalis (Suitability for Dishwasher Use)—Dishwasher detergents are highly alkaline and can corrode glazes. Studio test: 30-cycle dishwasher test or 6-hour boiling soda ash immersion.

Thermal Shock Resistance (Clay/Glaze Fit)—Clay bodies and glazes that don't expand and contract at the same rate may craze, shiver, and dunt. These faults occur most often during firing but crazing can happen long after. Studio test: Freezer to boiling water 3 times followed by an ink smear test.

Freeze-Thaw Resistance (porosity and absorbency)—Clay bodies not fired to vitrification or open, porous earthenware bodies are prone to absorbing water and can potentially freeze and deteriorate. Studio test: Test for absorption by water immersions and comparison of dry, wet, and boiled weights.

Suitability for Microwave Use—Pots inevitably end up in the microwave. Lusters should not be used on functional ware. Make certain that all pots are fully vitrified. Otherwise the work may heat unevenly, crack, or explode. Studio test: Test for absorption and vitrification.

Metal Marking Resistance—Metal deposits left on ceramic surfaces from utensils or other metal objects (mainly on matte surfaces). Studio test: Drag a metal object over the glazed surface several times. If marks won't wash off, the glaze is not satisfactory.

Abrasion Resistance—Mainly pertaining to the glazed surface but difficult to test. Studio test: Test for Resistance to Acids/Leaching.

Chipping Resistance—Time is the main test but vitrification and clay/glaze fit tests can be helpful indicators of potentially weak materials.

Lead Testing—Home testing kits can be used for an initial investigation and be an indicator of the need for more definitive testing by a certified chemical lab. If you use lead, test for lead leaching.

Strength Compression Testing—Strength and deformation of ceramic materials is tested with uniform compression tests of nonlinear stress behavior developed as a result of cracking, weakened fired structure, clay and glaze misfit, and environmental influences. Definitive testing must be done by a certified lab.

Testing standards are important to both the studio artist and his or her customers. While we may give specific instructions on the care, handling, and durability of our work, the truth is those tips can easily be forgotten and buyers expect our pots to act as well as commercial products. The responsibility falls to us to properly test our ware, accurately read the results, and ultimately sell a safe, durable product.

Standards Science

Standards describe methods for testing specific attributes of fired ceramics. It is important to recognize that the standards are not laws, which define what results testing must produce for products to be sold. Standards simply explain how to do the testing. Standards exist most commonly for functional ware and architectural ceramics. They are intended to measure factors that indicate whether the work is safe to use and whether it will be durable in service.

Standards exist for the very simple reason that without them it would be very difficult to compare the results of testing by different artists or companies. For example, if tile for an installation is described as having a particular strength as measured by a specific standard, say ASTM C1505-01(2007)—*Standard Test Method for Determination of Breaking Strength of Ceramic Tiles by Three-Point Loading*, then it is a simple matter to compare the reported strength to that of a specification for the strength measured using the same test.

Who creates standards? There is an entire alphabet soup of standards organizations around the globe prescribing tests. For ceramic artists in the US and Europe, there are at least six such organizations. The American Society for Testing and Materials (ASTM) is the main one, along with the American National Standards Institute (ANSI). In Europe the British Standards Institution (BSI), the German Institute for Standardization (DIN), the International Organization for Standardization (ISO), and the Committee for European Standardization (CEN), all write ceramic standards.

Standards define ways to measure important indicators of the quality of ceramic art. For example, whether a ceramic sculpture will survive outdoors unchanged by the weather is an element of quality. ASTM C1026-10—*Standard Test Method for Measuring the Resistance of Ceramic Tile to Freeze-Thaw Cycling* can predict whether a sculpture fired from a particular clay body will have that quality.

Professional (Certified) Testing Labs

- **ASTM International (formerly the American Society for Testing and Materials)**—Recognized as the leader in developing and testing standards for product quality and safety. Approximately 12,000 ASTM standards are used around the world. The majority of the standards are designed for use by industry, which employs specific and expensive equipment. Ceramic testing includes: thermal shock resistance of glazed tile, breaking strength, resistance to chemical substances, lead and cadmium leaching, resistance to freeze-thaw cycling, microwave safe reheating, and impact resistance of tableware. www.astm.org.
- **Orton Cone Manufacturing, Materials Testing & Research Center (MTRC)**—A full-service independent, nonprofit research and testing laboratory that specializes in measuring the behavior of refractory ceramic materials. Ceramic tests include: brick and tile structural testing, crazing resistance by thermal shock, chemical resistance, water absorption, porosity, and compression (crushing) strength tests. www.ortonceramic.com/testing.
- **Cutlery & Allied Trades Research Association (CATRA)**—Testing and technical consulting services for cutlery and cookware (among many other things). Dishwasher testing for ceramics. www.catra.org.
- **Professional Service Industries, Inc. (PSI)**—Various testing services. www.psiusa.com
- **Environmental Research, Inc.**—Various testing services. www.eri.us.com

Testing In The Studio

Knowing that your ware, and your glazes in particular, are chemically stable requires that you have answers to several key questions: Is the glaze mature? Is it within acceptable limit amounts? Is your kiln firing consistently and evenly for each firing and throughout the kiln? Is the liner glaze protective enough? Have all instances of shivering and dunting been eliminated?

There are several tests that can be done in the studio requiring only simple equipment and materials. Potters should be aware that these tests are only an indication of possible ceramic instability and they are not technical enough to guarantee that ware is absolutely safe. Accurate testing and analysis is best left to a certified chemical lab.

Absorption testing is useful as an indicator of the maturity, or vitrification of fired clay bodies. Vessels made from adequately vitrified ware do not leak liquids, do not become unsafely hot during microwave heating due to excess internal water, or deteriorate if they absorb water and are placed in freeze/thaw conditions.

TEST: Make a 6-inch-long x 2-inch-wide x ¼-inch-thick tile and fire it to the recommended maturing temperature. Weigh the tile to the nearest 0.01 gram and record that as the **dry weight**. Boil the tile while fully submerged in distilled water for five hours and let it soak in the water and cool for another 24 hours. After soaking overnight, remove the tile, pat dry, and weigh it again. This is the **wet weight**. The **wet weight** minus the **dry weight** divided by the **dry weight,** with the result multiplied by 100, will give the percentage of absorption of the clay body at that temperature. Fire your clay body to several temperatures above and below the maturing temperature and weigh the tests using the same method to determine the range of your clay body.

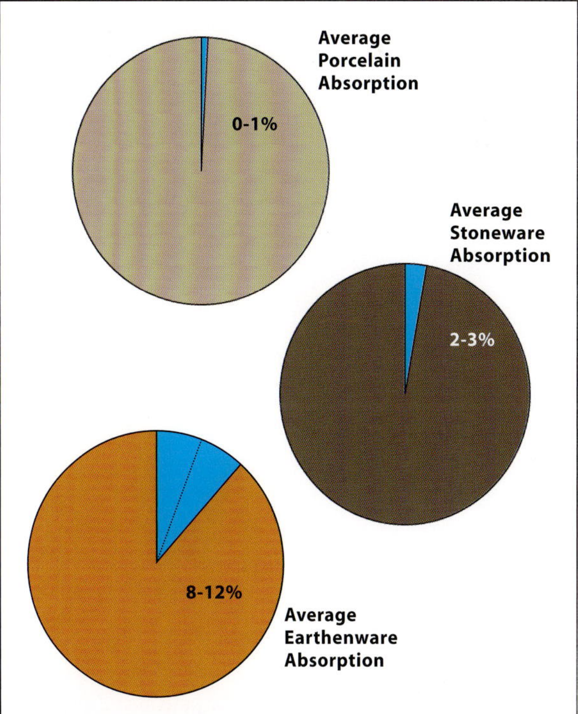

RESULTS: The average absorption for a mature, well vitrified clay body, at any temperature, will be below 5%—porcelains absorb an average of 0–1%, stonewares will absorb 2–3%, and earthenwares will have 8–12% absorption.

Freeze-thaw testing determines if your clay body is safe from deteriorating under freezing and thawing conditions. If water becomes trapped in the pores of an unvitrified clay body and that water freezes and expands, the tremendous force exerted by the ice against the ceramic object will cause it to crack, crumble, and chip the object.

TEST: To determine if your clay body is safe from cracking under freezing and thawing conditions, find the C/B ratio. Take the **dry weight** of your fired clay body sample (remember to always wipe the surface before weighing). Record this weight as **D**. Next immerse this entire sample in water for 24 hours at room temperature (do not boil the water). Remove the sample from the water, pat dry and take the saturated weight. Record this weight as **C**. Now immerse the sample in the water again and boil the water. Leave the sample in boiling water for two hours. After two hours of boiling, remove and pat dry. Weigh the sample. Record the weight as **B**. The math is as follows:

$\frac{C - D}{D}$ = **C** value	Wet weight minus dry weight divided by dry weight equals **C** value
$\frac{B - D}{D}$ = **B** value	Boiled weight minus dry weight divided by dry weight equals **B** value
$\frac{\text{C value}}{\text{B value}}$ = C/B ratio	Wet value divided by the boiled value equals the wet versus boiled ratio
D = dry weight (fired test sample) C = wet weight (sample soaked for 24 hours) B = boiled weight (sample boiled for two hours)	

RESULTS: A proper outdoor clay body will have a C/B ratio of less than 0.78 (approximately)—representing the room for expansion in the fired clay bodies' pores. *Absorption and freeze-thaw testing information courtesy of* Cushing's Handbook *by Val M. Cushing.*

Microwave testing is for ware used for heating and defrosting foods in a microwave. Ceramic wares absorb minimal amounts microwave energy and radiation in a non-uniform manner, which may cause thermal shock and possible cracking or explosions. Do not use lusters on ware intended for microwave use. The main consideration for recommending microwave use should be whether the clay is fully vitrified, and if so, it most likely will not be a problem in the microwave. If it isn't vitrified, it will most likely overheat.

TEST: Absorption Test (same as above).

RESULTS: 2–3% is the maximum recommended absorption allowed for safe microwave oven use. Mature porcelain and stoneware (approximate moisture absorption level is 2–3%) are often safe but earthenware will almost always be a high risk unless it has been totally encased in an excellent glaze.

Leaching/resistance to acids/glaze stability is one of the most important tests you can do to understand the stability of your glazes. Potters should expect that all functional pots will eventually come in contact with acidic foods (i.e. vinegar, citrus juices, tomato sauce, coffee) at varying strengths and for varying lengths of time. Potters should also know that all glazes (glasses) are slowly dissolving, it's just that stable glazes dissolve slower. Unstable glazes are the result of unbalanced formulations (i.e. recipes with 30% or more barium, almost no silica or alumina, or a high metal content) and they must be tested or avoided on food contact surfaces. Other factors influencing glaze stability include impurities, heating and cooling during firing cycles, and fuming from other materials in the kiln (either firing at the same time or in previous firings).

TESTS: Submerge a glaze test half way into a glass container of vinegar (or fill a newly made glazed container half full of vinegar) and leave it for at least three days (1–2). A similar test can also be done with a lemon slice. If your glaze is white, add a small percentage of cobalt to a 100 gram test batch of the glaze and do the vinegar test.

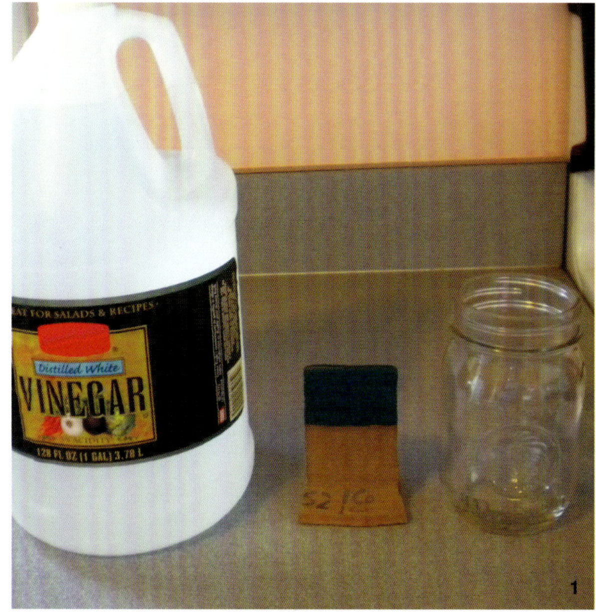

1

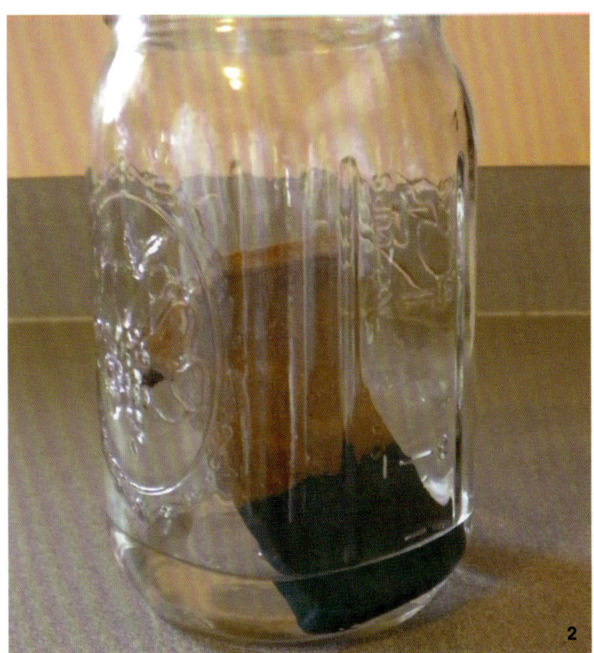

2

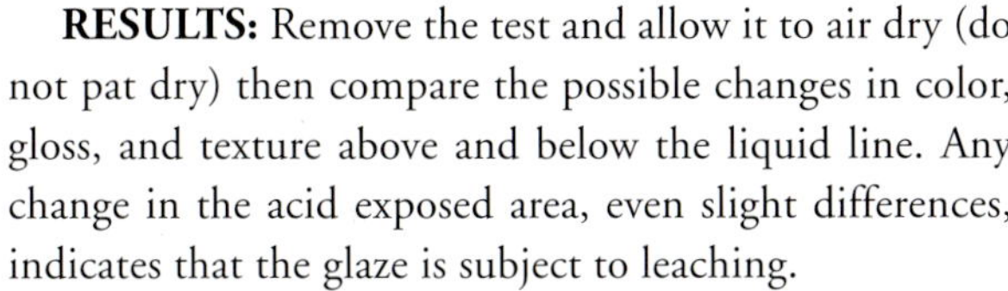

RESULTS: Remove the test and allow it to air dry (do not pat dry) then compare the possible changes in color, gloss, and texture above and below the liquid line. Any change in the acid exposed area, even slight differences, indicates that the glaze is subject to leaching.

Dishwasher testing assess the resistance and suitability of products washed in a standard operating dishwasher. Ceramic wares can be minimally to severely affected by the automated dishwashing process and the alkaline effects of dishwashing detergents. Potters should be fully aware of the possible effects of corrosion, loss of gloss, and cloudiness among other failures.

TEST #1: Take two identical glaze tests and put one on a shelf and one in the dishwasher for two months (or at least 30 cycles). If the glaze is unstable, a comparison of the two test tiles will show evidence of fading and a longer or accelerated test is needed.

TEST #2: The accelerated test simulates the alkaline environment of the dishwasher. Make a 5% soda ash solution (50 grams of soda ash in 1 liter of water.) Put the solution in a stainless-steel pot (a double boiler works best.) Do not use aluminum. Bring the solution to a boil, then reduce the solution to a simmer, submerge a glazed test tile in the solution (make sure to have an identical test set aside to compare afterward), cover the pot, and continue to simmer for six hours (3–4). Check the water levels continuously.

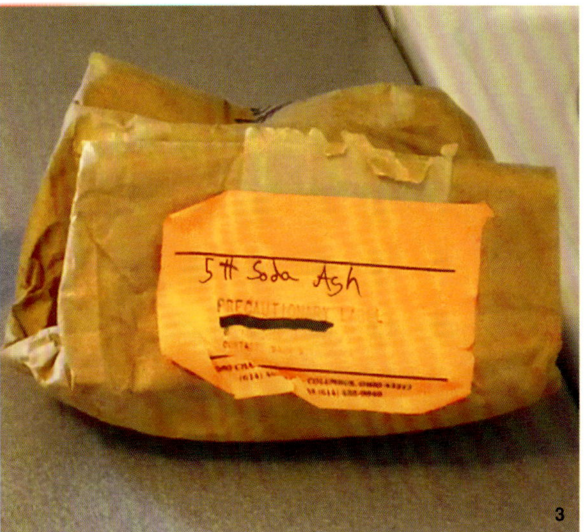

3

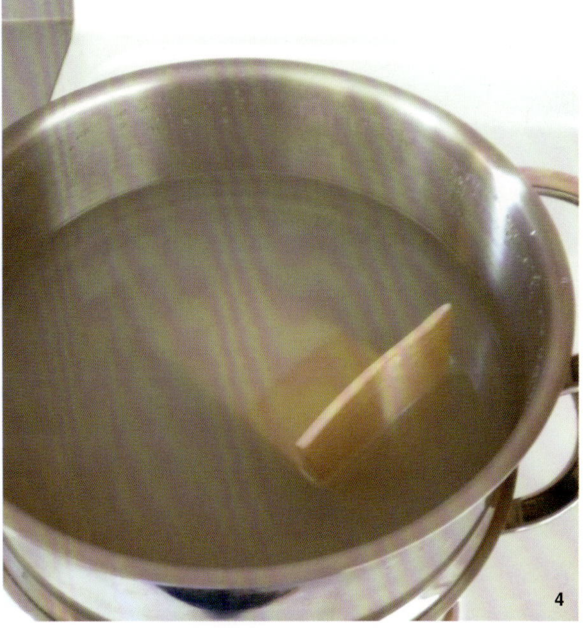

4

RESULTS: Remove and rinse the tile. Look for differences in color, gloss, and texture. Moderately stable glazes show only slight changes in surface sheen and color. Unstable glazes show visible fading of both gloss and color with an etched surface. This test is only an general approximation of the dishwashing environment and not a substitute for an extended cycle test. *Microwave, leaching, and dishwasher testing information courtesy of* Mastering Cone 6 Glazes *by John Hesselberth and Ron Roy.* (www.masteringglazes.com)

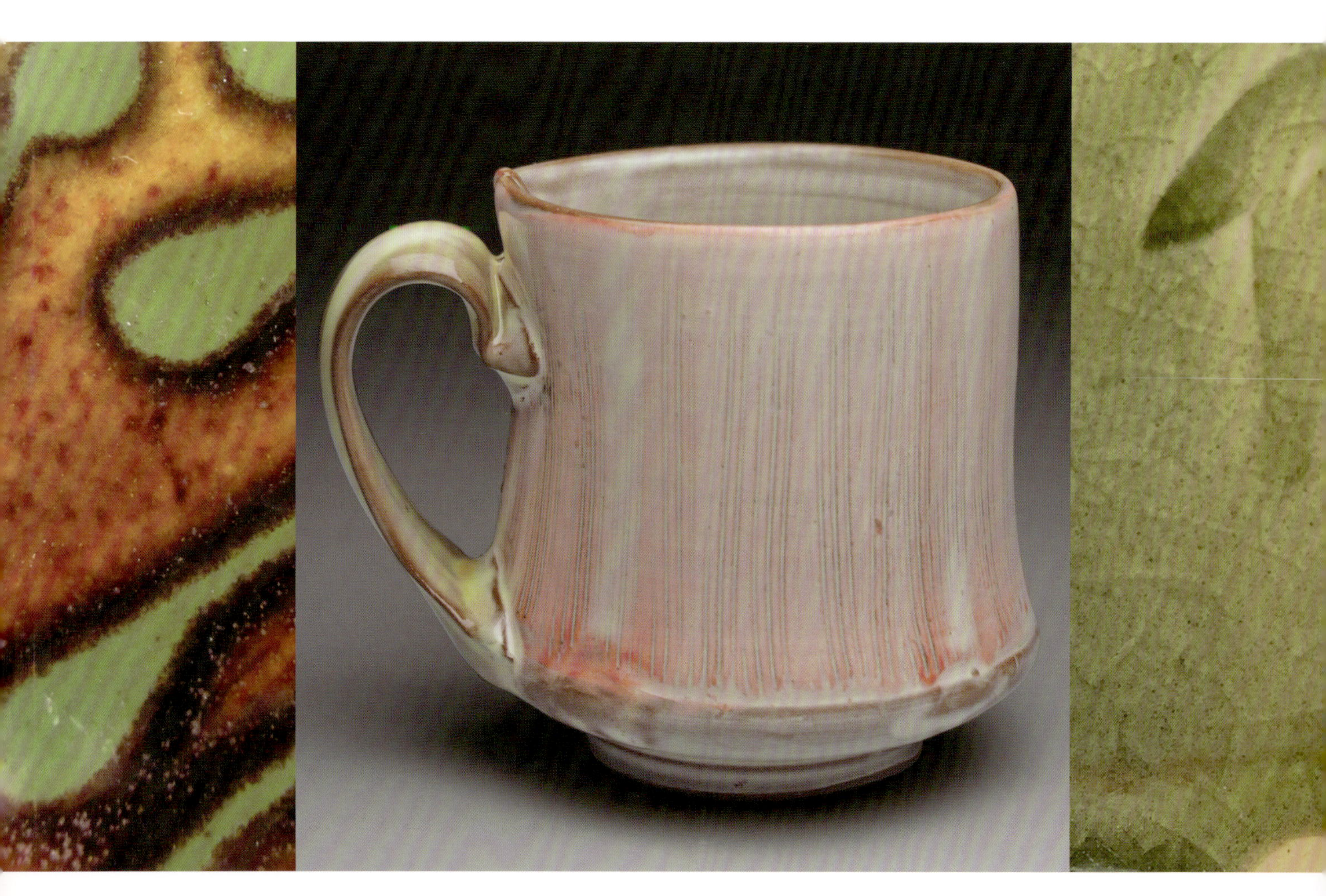

SECTION 3

Recipes, Research, and Techniques

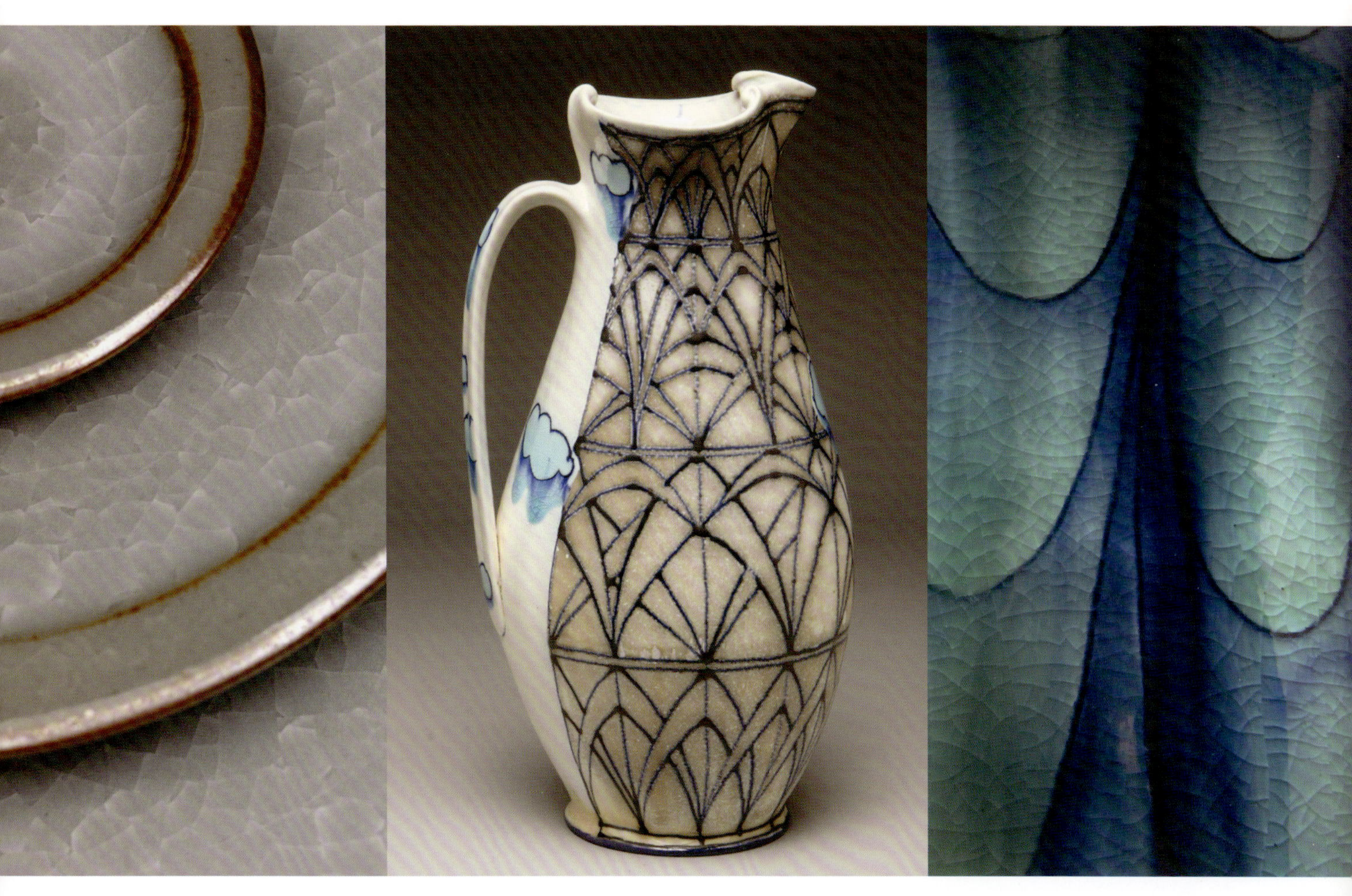

CHAPTER 1

Low Fire

Lusters

by Johanna DeMaine

Defining the Terms

Aromatic Compounds: Organic hydrocarbon chemicals, so called because many have a sweet smell, evaporate rapidly, and contain benzene rings. Typical aromatic compounds are benzene and toluene.

Luster: Extremely thin films of metals fired onto the surface of ware. The effect is due to the interference of incident and reflected light. Precious metal preparations and resinate lusters, in their unfired state, are complex mixtures of up to 40 components with different chemical and toxicological properties. Their toxic and ecological effects vary from product to product.

Noble Metals: As distinct from base metals, these metals do not corrode or oxidize in the presence of moist air or most acids. Most are precious due to their rarity in the earth's crust, and include gold, platinum, palladium, iridium, and silver.

Organic Compound: Any of a large class of chemical compounds in which one or more atoms of carbon are covalently bonded to atoms of other elements, most commonly hydrogen, oxygen, or nitrogen.

Solution: A homogeneous mixture of two or more substances, which may be solids, liquids, gases, or a combination of all.

Suspensions: A heterogeneous mixture of a fluid containing solid particles large enough that they will settle out if left long enough without agitation.

Resinate: A salt of a resin acid (terpenoid acids produced by conifers).

Polymer: A polymer is a chemical compound or mixture of compounds consisting of repeating structural units created through a process of polymerization.

Bismuth oxide: An amphoteric oxide that acts as a flux in ceramic fusions. It is usually introduced in small amounts as a modifier of colorings and is a low-melting-point metal. The nitrate form dissolved in resin and oil deposits a mother-of-pearl luster on glazed ware and is also used as a carrier for other luster colors. The organic materials burn out at 1292°F–1472°F (700°C–800°C), below the melting point of the metal.

Lusters have been described as transmitting the same effect as the light reflected from a thin layer of oil on water. This diffraction of light is produced via the deposition of a very thin film of metal on a ceramic surface—be it glass, earthenware, or porcelain. Knowing what these materials are and how they behave is the key to making them work.

Reduced Lusters vs. Resinate Lusters

Lusters were first in evidence on glass in Egypt in the 4th century. By the 9th century, luster was being used on ceramics. Reduced luster—also known as pigment luster, smoked luster, Arabian or Persian luster—was first used in Iraq in the 9th century. A pigment, based on an iron-bearing clay and containing copper or silver, is brushed onto a fired glaze surface and then refired in a reducing atmosphere. After firing the pigment/clay paste is washed off, leaving behind a thin film of metal, which we call luster. The interactions between the clay paste/pigment, temperature, length of reduction, and base glaze are all important. Most notably the base glaze has to accept and develop the luster from the pigment. The glaze can be either lead- or alkaline-based frits that are non-toxic and non-soluble. They are typically low-temperature glazes as the glaze needs to soften between 1112–1292 °F (600–700 °C) in order to bond with the thin film of metal deposited. Other sources of metallic deposition are possible with luster glazes, resinate lusters, and fuming. The widespread use of electric kilns, together with the increasing interest in and use of overglaze techniques necessitates a focus on resinate lusters.

Resinate lusters are made up of solutions and suspensions of metallic resinates combined with solutions of polymers and thickening agents to aid application by brush and machine. The colors result from metallic oxide films bonded onto the glazed surface by a flux, specifically bismuth oxide, which must be fired to a low temperature otherwise it would burn out. This is the same luster film as produced by *reduced luster*—the main difference being

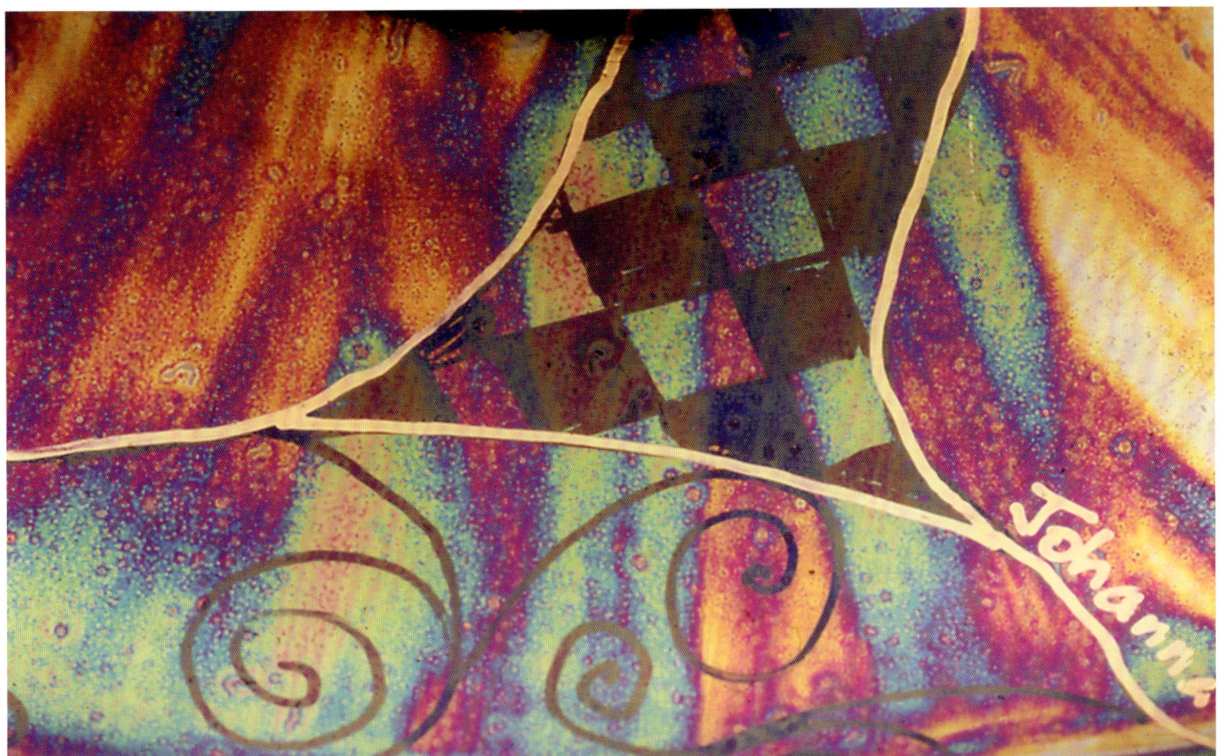

Luster has the appearance of the light reflected from an oil slick on water. The diffraction of light on the ceramic surface is produced by the deposition of a very thin film of metal.

the method of application and firing technique employed. Whereas reduced lusters are either clay paste or water based and fired in a reducing atmosphere, resinate lusters are oil/resin based and are fired in an oxidizing atmosphere. The localized reduction is performed by the carbon produced from the resin (usually pine oil) base. Resinate lusters are a product of the ceramic industry, developed as glaze application and controlled firings were standardized for mass production. Resinate lusters are also known as *oxidation* or *commercial lusters.*

Lusters, then, can be redefined as precious-metal-based organic compounds dissolved in a solvent base and combined with resins. Gold and platinum lusters consist of precious-metal- containing organic compounds combined with other organo-metallic fluxes and resins.

Working with Resinate Luster

Luster takes on the surface qualities of the ware that it is applied to. On surfaces with gloss glazes, luster will be shiny, on matte glazes it will be satin matte, and on

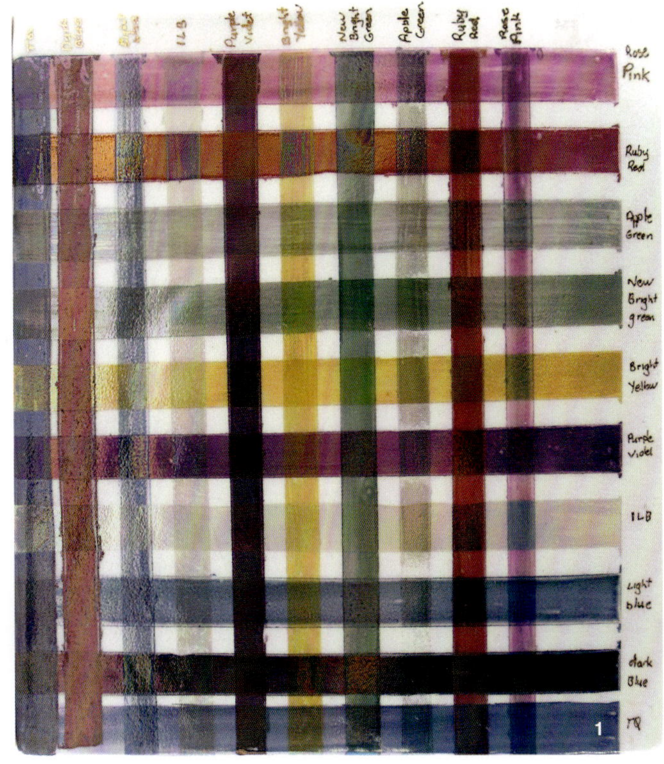

vitrified bisque it will be very matte. As the luster bonds at the softening temperatures of the substrata, there is a wide firing range, which encompasses glass, earthenware, bone China, stoneware, and hard and soft porcelain (this refers to the glaze types used). Lusters can be fired from 1202°F (650°C) for glass through to 1562°F (850°C) for hard-glazed porcelains.

Luster is oil based so that it will adhere to a glossy surface. However, the surface has to be scrupulously clean. Any grease, sweat, and oils from the skin, or lint or dust will repel the adhesion of the luster. The two most common methods used for cleaning the surface of the ware are wiping the surface with an alcohol impregnated cloth or using detergent and very hot water until the water sheets off the pot. It is then dried with a lint free cloth and no further skin contact with the pot is permitted.

Application

When applied, all lusters appear brown and lacquer-like, with their color achieved in the firing process. In order to visualize the end result while working, a permanent color chart can be made for each glaze typically used (1). This is simply a test tile with luster brush strokes applied and labelled, that is fired, then the tile is turned 90 degrees, the brush strokes are repeated, and the tile is fired again. This provides a readout of one and two layers of luster plus many variations of colors when luster is applied over luster. Different color glazes will also influence the luster colors due to their transparent nature.

Lusters can be applied by brush, sponge, and stamping. Some people advocate airbrushing for certain effects, but I do not recommended this as lusters are based on organic solvents. German squirrel hair flat shaders, mainly No. 10 (the old ⅜ inch size) are used for brush application. Broad areas of luster are achieved by laying down the luster in long quick strokes, taking care not to overlap drying areas as otherwise these would be more intense in color. If a very even surface is required, the brushed-on luster can be lightly padded or pounced with a small sponge or cotton ball wrapped in a square of silk held tight with a rubber band. This will even out the brush strokes but will also lighten the luster considerably as excess luster is pulled off. Multiple layers of luster, fired between each layer, can be used to intensify color responses.

Other methods of application are pen work, flow technique, and dipping (2). The batik pen (commonly known as the Tjanting) is used solely for resist. The flow technique is achieved by putting a quantity of luster thinners on the surface and quickly adding drops of luster before manipulating the flow of the luster by positioning/angling the work, causing the luster to flow. A number of resists can be used for specific effects (see below). Other abstract surface effects can be achieved with random application of salt, dispersing agent, glass cleaners, mineral spirits, alcohol, as well as marbleizing fluid. Partial removal with crumpled plastic kitchen wrap, rubber stamps etc. can produce different textures.

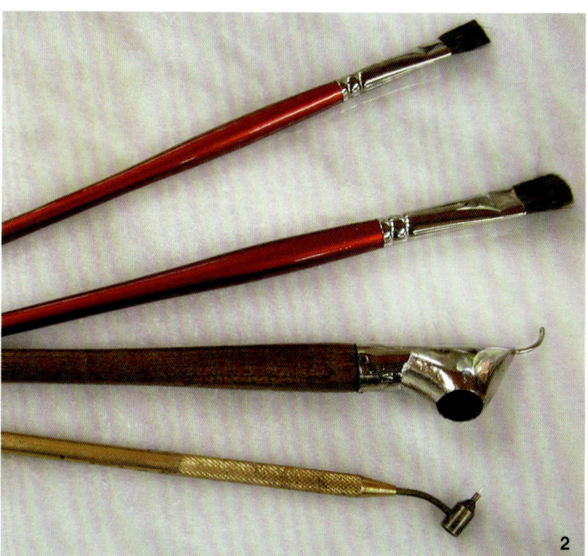

Luster and resist applicators from top to bottom: ¼-inch German squirrel hair flat shader; ⅜-inch, No. 10 German squirrel hair flat shader; Tjanting (batik pen) used for resist detail; Kemper Gold pen/fluid pen used for pen work/writing with luster and gold.

Brush Care

Keep luster brushes for luster use only, as other mediums will contaminate the brushes. To clean brushes, put a small amount of luster essence or citrus solvent into two small glass jars, and fill one jar with a small amount of methylated spirits (denatured alcohol). Swish the brush in the first bottle, blot it on a tissue, then swish it in the second bottle of luster essence, and blot it again. Swish it in the methylated spirits jar and blot it once again. Finally work a detergent into the bristles and rinse the brush exceedingly well under warm running water. Blot it on a tissue and dry it flat.

Working with Resist

My preferred method of working is with resist so as to limit my exposure to luster. I spend a lot of time being precise with the resist, so that 90% of my time is spent in applying inert resist and only 10% in actually applying the luster. This reduces my exposure to the organic solvents in the luster.

Most resists, apart from waxes, will work as luster resist. Latex, white poster paint, adhesive tapes, masking lacquers, stickers, white-out pens, and proprietary luster resists can all be used. I prefer to use Fay Good's black luster resist as this resist can survive several firings without having to be cleaned off and reapplied.

I sketch my drawing onto the glazed surface with a non-permanent, black overhead-projection pen. I then go over this, adding detail with a Tjanting filled with the black luster resist that I have adjusted to flow through the tip. After the resist dries, I apply an even layer of luster in the areas required just the same as for any other painting technique. I then fire to 1472°F (800°C) in approximately 5 hours. I don't subscribe to the fast firing techniques because glaze softening takes time as well as temperature.

After the first firing, I continue adding layers of luster to deepen the color, firing between each layer. I add further resist to help the layering effect that I am after. After the final luster layering, I will either add pen work with a gold pen, or use raised enamel for accent. I remove the resist by gently cleaning the surface with liquid dish soap. Do not use any abrasive cleaners as they will scratch the surface.

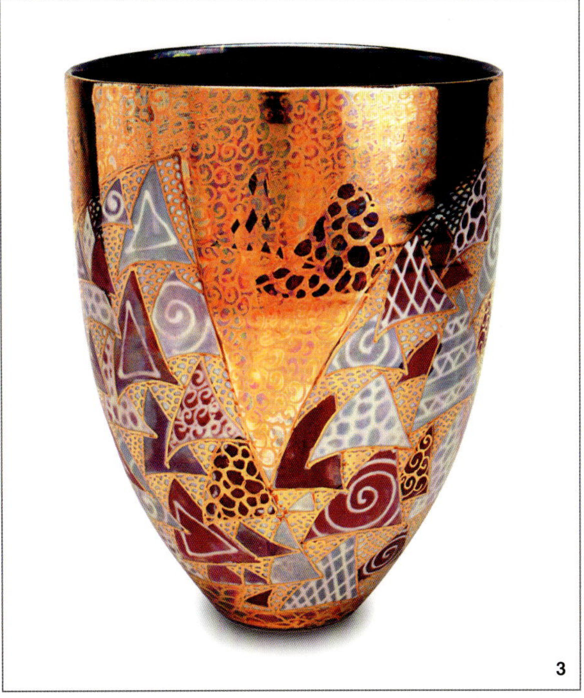

3

Oval vessel, 8½ in. (22 cm) in height, wheel-thrown porcelaneous stoneware, glaze, fired to cone 10, multiple layers of luster and gold with hand-drawn resist patterning, multiple firings to cone 015, gold pen work. Collection of HRH Queen Elizabeth II. *Photo: Errol Larkin.*

Toxicity and Safety

Finding out precisely which of the solvents have been utilized is not easily done, as there is a degree of secrecy within the industry. There are no safe organic solvents. These toxic substances are unstable, poisonous compounds and these toxins can enter the body through skin absorption, ingestion, and inhalation. Though some of the materials that produce these toxins are essential to the creation of ceramics, it is not necessary to stop working with them to remain healthy. However it does mean that a raised awareness and new work habits are essential. So it is best to assume the worst-case scenario. This must take into account the health risks associated with a high concentration of noxious fumes, their flammable nature as well as being irritants to eyes, skin, and respiratory tract. The noxious fumes are present during both application and firing.

Proper ventilation and safe work practices will prevent the inhalation of fumes. Be sure to use either dilution, local, and/or personal ventilation while working with resinate luster. Immediately remove any luster from the skin with methylated spirits or other alcohol and then wash the area with soap and water. Do not bite fingernails, put brushes into your mouth, eat, drink, or smoke while working with lusters. Do not bring food or drink into the decorating workplace. Noxious fumes are present in the firing of lusters as the media burns out. Do not enter a kiln shed/area/room without a respirator while firing lusters—this can be very damaging to the lungs. Under no circumstances should a kiln used to fire lusters be placed inside a dwelling.

Lusters contain all or some of the following toxics in varying proportions (formulas vary per color): Turpentine, O-dichlorobenzene, cyclohexanol, cyclohexanone, methyl cyclohexanol, di-iso-octylphthalate, camphor, white spirit, xyleone, tetrahydronaphthalene, isophorone, tetrahydrofurfuryl alcohol. Classifications for solvents used in commercial luster production: Aromatic hydrocarbons, hydrocarbons with a low content of aromates, hydrotreated aromatic hydrocarbons (tetraline), alcohols and ketones (propanoles, butanoles, butanones, and diacetone alcohol), terpenes (turpentine oil and etheric oils).

For a comprehensive account of Johanna DeMaine's approach to health and safety, read the article in conjunction with "Health and Safety and Overglaze" available at http://overglaze.info. Additional information, bibliography, and recommended reading at http://johanna.demaine.org.

The Colorful World of Majolica

by Linda Arbuckle

The majolica technique is commonly done at low-fire temperatures, although you may work in a similar way on any stiff, opaque glaze at other temperatures with related results. Most of the stain colors used for majolica decorating will fire to mid range (cone 5–6). At cone 10, shino glazes are very viscous and don't move much, but the available palette of colors is different: many of the purples fire out blue; yellows in reduction are often pale and grayish; most of the pinks burn out; and body stains (e.g. Mason Stain 6020 Pink) may be too refractory even at cone 10. Nevertheless, it maybe worth an experiment or two.

History and Name

Majolica (or maiolica) in common contemporary parlance is a white, opaque, glossy glaze that is very viscous to the point that it doesn't move during firing. This allows line quality applied to the raw glaze to be maintained faithfully through the firing process.

Tall Ewer: Grey with Fruit, $12\frac{1}{4}$ in. (31 cm) in height, terra cotta with majolica glazes, fired to cone 04, 2010.

Historically, Middle Eastern potters developed such glazes for use over an earthenware clay at low temperatures. They used tin oxide to make a white, opaque glaze (usually fluxed with lead) that was a good ground for colored decoration. Work from the Middle East made using this method is identified as tin-glazed earthenware. A raw glaze surface was decorated with copper (green), manganese (plum), and iron or antimony (amber/yellow) over a glaze. Cobalt blues were very popular for decoration, and the blue-on-white echoed Asian high-fire ceramics. Metallic reduced lusterware (done in an additional firing) was also developed in the Middle East, often on a tin glaze.

When the Muslims conquered northern Africa, came north across the Strait of Gibraltar, and created a Moorish influence in Spain from the early 8th century until 1492, they brought their pottery technologies and aesthetics with them. This included tin-glazed pottery methods. Spain exported these wares from Majorca, and Italians began calling this tin-glazed ware *majolica.*

There are contemporary disagreements about the spelling, pronunciation, and terminology of *majolica* vs. *maiolica.* I suspect that the origins of the differences reside in what happens when a Spanish *J* is transliterated into another language, and complicated by casual use of terms for things that are not technically related. For instance, in the 19th century, companies produced molded relief wares with bright, jewel-like, transparent, colored lead glazes. The Minton company in England was well known for the production of these wares (teapots in the shape of pineapples and cauliflower, cheese bells in the form of beehives, etc.). The bright low-fire color reminded people of Italian majolica-decorated pottery, and the term *majolica* was used for both, although they are not technically related. I have seen texts that claim that the Minton–style work is done with techniques similar to Della Robbia techniques, but my eyes tell me it's not so. The tin-glazed work is seen spelled either way. The Minton–style work is usually spelled with a *J.* Some revisionists insist this is the only way, but very reputable sources, such as the Metropolitan Museum, have spelled the tin-glaze with a *J*. It seems to be one of those awkward instances where there are variants in spelling and pronunciation, with no one clear "truth." I pronounce the *Maj* in *Majorca* like *my*, and likewise in *majolica*, and spell both with a *J*, but I allow that other spellings and pronunciations are likewise creditable.

Opacifiers

The use of only tin as an opacifier is often modified in contemporary practice. Tin makes a lovely, buttery, very opaque, white glaze. It also increases surface tension in a glaze and may aggravate crawling problems where the glaze is thick (e.g., in corners). Tin in amounts of 5% or above will also cause a color reaction with small amounts of chrome that will cause the tin glaze to turn pink (chrome fuming). This can be delightful if anticipated, but is often not kind to your color plans as a surprise. Many of the green and teal stain colors and some black stains contain chrome, and some rutiles contain small amounts of chrome impurities that can cause chrome-tin pinking in high-tin glazes. For the above reasons, as well as the expense of tin oxide, many artists today use a zirconium opacifier, or a combination of some tin (for denser whiteness) with some zirconium opacifier. This would keep the amount of tin low (say under 4%), yet allow good opacity. Zirconium is weaker than tin in strength, and the usual rule is 1.5% zirconium to replace 1% tin. If chrome-tin pink fuming is a problem, drop the tin a bit, and add that amount multiplied by 1.5 of zirconium opacifier.

Some artists say they enjoy a bit of the terra cotta showing through a translucent white majolica glaze. For me, it darkens the glaze color, damps color response a bit, and makes any thick-thin areas of glaze application more noticeable than a more opaque white. I have always preferred a very white opaque glaze.

Majolica Colorant Suggestions

Gerstley borate production has been erratic, and the material is variable in quality. It pushes decorating colors toward pastel through very fine reticulation (break up) of the glaze surface, and although I used it when I began majolica, I now use frit as a flux (with bentonite added) or commercial majolica decorating colors.

Colorants mixed with only frit settle quickly, have limited brushability, and are very powdery once dry, making wax resist over the color smudge easily. Some artists, like

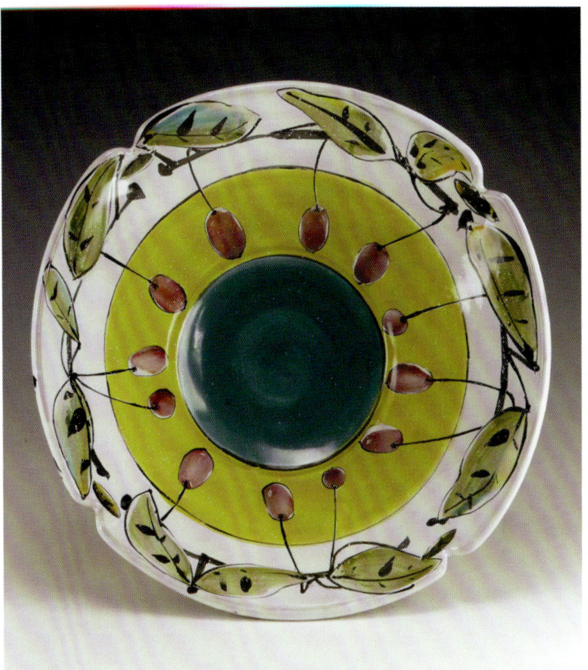

Bowl: Fruits of Our Labor in a Time of Envy, 11 in. (28 cm) in diameter, terra cotta with majolica glazes, fired to cone 04, 2010.

Matthias Ostermann, use this powdery quality to work the movable surface like pastels. The addition of bentonite or CMC gum to the frit and colorant mix aids brushing and hardens the dry surface. Bentonite doesn't mix easily with water, so be sure to mix dry bentonite, frit, and colorant first, then add water. Some people find an immersion blender handy. I mix small amounts and generally use a tiny whisk. If something is really lumpy, I will use a small test sieve (60 mesh) and screen the mixture.

I use Ferro frit 3124. Others will work, with color reactions influenced by the specific chemistry of each frit. To aid brushability, you may add a small amount of glycerin (drug store item), or a few drops liquid CMC gum to the liquid mix. Too much glycerin or gum can make a very slippery color mix that moves well but doesn't apply color in an even thickness.

Colors in studio-mixed oxides or stains and commercial majolica decorating colors will generally mix, but some information about ceramic materials helps. I recommend doing line blends of colors to learn more about mixing and relative strength. Copper melts easily, and will color strongly compared to yellow colors. A nice chartreuse may be four parts yellow by volume to one part mixed copper. With paint, yellow + blue = green. In ceramic colors, blue

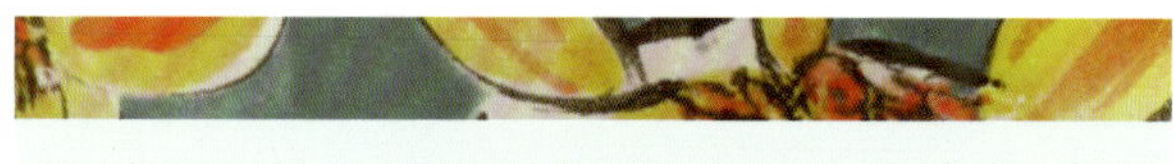

ARBUCKLE MAJOLICA

Cone 03 oxidation

Ferro Frit 3124	65.8 %
F-4 Feldspar (sub Minspar 200)	17.2
Nepheline Syenite	6.2
EPK Kaolin	10.8
	100.0 %
Add: Tin Oxide	4.0 %
Zircopax	9.0 %
Bentonite	2.0 %

ARBUCKLE MAJOLICA

Cone 05 oxidation

Ferro Frit 3124	66.6 %
F-4 Feldspar (sub Minspar 200)	23.0
Nepheline Syenite	8.1
EPK Kaolin	2.3
	100.0 %
Add: Tin Oxide	4.0 %
Zircopax	9.0 %
Bentonite	2.0 %

This is a smooth, white, opaque glaze that does not move during firing. It may crawl if thick in corners or pinhole over rough-trimmed surfaces. Add ½–3 tsp. Epsom salts to 5 gallons of glaze to flocculate if needed (for less settling and better application). Colorants with flux are usually applied in a thin wash to the raw glaze surface. Fire with a small 03 cone in the sitter to provide enough time for a large 04 cone placed in front of a peep hole to bend to about 2–3 o'clock.

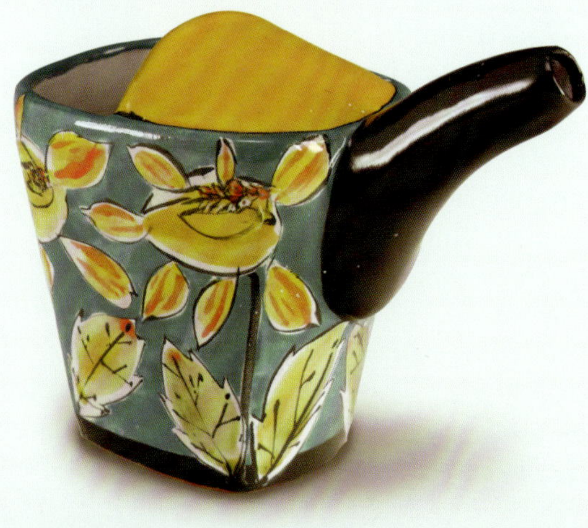

Small Pour: Sunflowers with Black Band, 5 in. (13 cm) in length, terra cotta with majolica glazes, fired to cone 04, 2010.

is made with cobalt, a *very* strong colorant, while yellow may be a stain made with praseodymium or vanadium, which are weaker colorants than cobalt. Equal amounts of mixed yellow and blue decorating colors may still be very blue, due to the strength of cobalt.

Non-refractory Colorants

1 part colorant, 1 part frit, ½–1 part bentonite: copper (blue-green), cobalt (blue), manganese (brown to plum with Ferro frit 3110), iron (brown)

Refractory Colorants

1 part colorant, 3–4 parts frit, ½–1 part bentonite: chrome (grass green), rutile (rusty orange), titanium dioxide (ivory). Most stains are refractory enough to require this ratio. Note that body stains, like Mason 6020 manganese-alumina pink and Mason 6485 titanium yellow are too refractory for use on top of majolica, even with flux added. Refractory colorants that are not adequately fluxed will result in matte surfaces that are bumpy and/or pig-skinned (crinkled). Testing is the only way to really know.

Soluble colorants

Cobalt sulfate (blue), copper sulfate (turquoise), manganese chloride (plummy brown), and chrome chloride (green). All are toxic raw. Do not inhale or ingest. They are also absorption hazards: do not handle these without gloves. Soluble colorants are dissolved, rather than suspended, in water, so they wick into the surface of the ware with the water, making a very uniform ground color with a soft edge. If you want any white areas, or to retain clean edges, areas must be waxed before applying soluble colorants. Over-wetting the glaze when applying solubles may move raw glaze and cause color to migrate through the pot wall and/or cause crawling. Too much water on the raw glaze may also cause crawling in the fired glaze.

Commercial Colorants

Some single-coat commercial underglazes work for decorating on top of a majolica base glaze, while others are too refractory. Testing is the only way to determine which ones work. Several companies now make very nice pre-mixed majolica decorating colors. These colors are generally a combination of stains, flux, and vehicles, and they brush well. I suspect that, unlike underglaze colors, the clay content is kept low for more supple brushability.

Advantages and Disadvantages of Majolica-type Glazes

Advantages	Disadvantages
The viscous glaze does not move when fired. The brushwork stays crisp, with no runny glaze to chip off shelves. Dry-footed areas need less margin on pot bottoms or lid seats.	The viscous glaze does not move when fired, which means any lumps, drips, or pinholes from application remain and do not heal over or smooth out in firing. Thick glaze may crawl.
Because the raw glaze absorbs the color from the brush readily and does not move in the firing, the direction of brush marks, speed of the brush, and loading of the brush show in the fired decoration, adding painterly, expressive qualities to the marks.	Because the raw glaze absorbs the color from the brush readily and does not move in firing, direction of brush marks, speed of the brush, and loading of the brush show in the fired decoration, and may reveal hesitancies, touch-ups, and direction of background when painting around motifs, etc., which may distract from the aesthetic impact.
Thick glaze blankets the piece, which may forgive small handling errors like finger smudges in the surface.	Thick glaze blankets the piece, which may cover small details in clay handling. like carving or incised decoration.
The kiln is a passive tool, resulting in more predictable results from firing to firing. Someone else could fire your work and achieve the same results (easier to share kilns).	The kiln is a passive tool, resulting in uniform color that may look flat or does not describe the form. There are no gifts from the kiln gods.
A bright palette of commercial stains gives easy access to a range of pinks, oranges, yellows, and purples that work well with the blue, green, and rust that are available with oxides.	The bright color may look garish, or the entire palette may look too pastel and therefore lose impact.
Inexpensive color, because it takes less colorant to put a thin wash on the glaze surface than to color a slip or a glaze.	

Application Suggestions

Both the best and worst thing about majolica glaze is that it doesn't move when you fire it. Having a decent base glaze coating goes a long way toward being happy with the final product. Additionally, large bumps and voids in the raw glaze will leave evidence of brush strokes on top of them and emphasize your glaze application issues.

Apply glaze in the thinnest coating that will give you opacity, and attempt an even glaze coat. Dampen pieces slightly before dipping to remove any dust and moisten the ware for better glaze pick up. Dipping is my mode of choice, although I do know potters who spray effectively. I want to have a container that will allow me to do one dip of the bisqueware. If I have a piece that will not fit in my glaze bucket, say a long, oval platter, I use a different container for dipping. Garden stores often carry metal or plastic 5-gallon oval tubs. Oil change pans can be useful. I have flexible plastic tubs from a garden store that are wider than my 5-gallon glaze buckets, and will allow me to flex the bucket for longer-than-wide shapes and to form a spout to pour my glaze back into the bucket. In a pinch, I have used cardboard boxes reinforced with duct tape or dresser drawers double-lined with heavy trash bags to hold glaze for dipping.

For errors in glazing (and there are bound to be some) 400-grit wet-dry sandpaper will sand down lumps, or they may be gently scraped down with a sharp knife. When sanding or shaving glaze, do it over a container of water to trap the dust and prevent it from circulating in your studio environment.

Clay Body, Off-Gassing, and Firing Rates

I am still experimenting with firing rates. Several years ago something in clay materials changed and caused gassing in my clay, resulting in many white gas dots in the fired majolica surface, where the base glaze might seal over, but the colorant layer is so thin that it can't seal and leaves a white spot. Many people maintain that firing slowly is the way to go, and it seems logical that any gas release would be more gentle the slower the firing. On the other hand, I fire many pieces in a small, oval, doll-body test kiln, which cools quickly, and these generally turn out less dotted. The same shapes fired about 200°F per hour in my regular kiln may be more dotted. It's been an infuriating problem that I continue to research. If you have dotting, try bisque firing as high as you can without making the work too dense to accept glaze. This may drive off gassy materials before glaze application and firing. Bisque at a slower rate, vent your kiln, and glaze thinner if possible. Thinner glaze is less likely to trap the gas bubbles and cause dotting.

the author *Linda Arbuckle is a member of the CM Editorial Advisory Board, and is a professor of art at the University of Florida, Gainesville. For more majolica glaze recipes, including a cone 6 version, and additional resources, see her handouts page on her website at http://lindaarbuckle.com/arbuckle_handouts.html.*

Polychrome Glazes

by Joan Bruneau

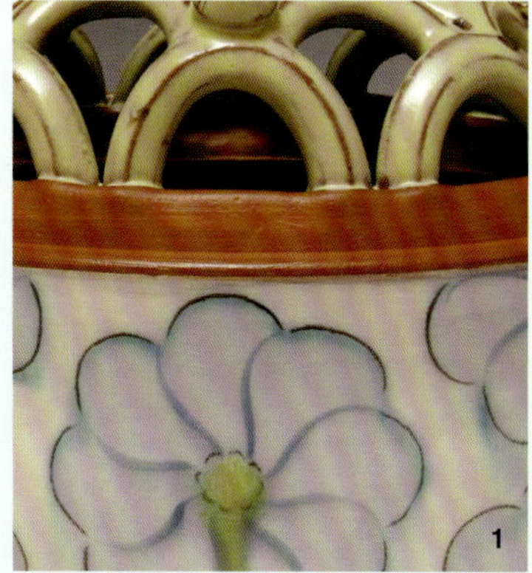

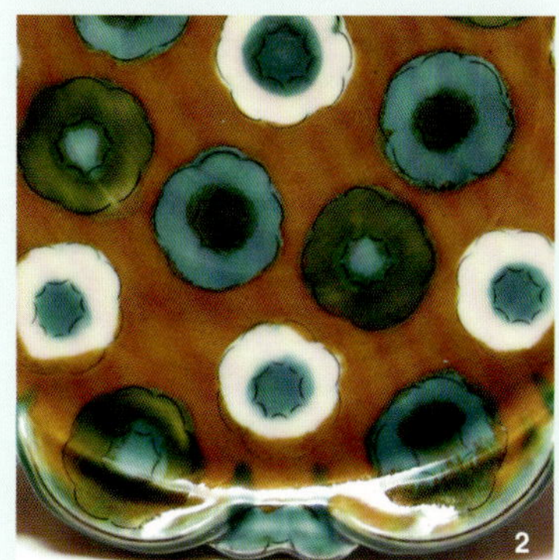

JACKIE'S SATIN MATTE

Cone 04 oxidation

Gerstley Borate	36.84 %
Lithium Carbonate	8.42
Nepheline Syenite	5.26
EPK Kaolin	5.26
Silica	44.22
	100.00 %
Add: Tin Oxide	5.26 %
(OR Zircopax	10.53%)

Colorant Additions:

Blue: Copper Carbonate	0.25 %
Cobalt Carbonate	2.50 %
Turquoise: Copper Carbonate	3.00 %
Mottled Tan: Black Iron Oxide	7.00 %
Mottled Peach: Rutile	12.00 %
Yellow: Vanadium Stain	8.00 %
Chartreuse:	
Chartreuse Mason Stain	8.00 %
Whiting	10.00 %

This glaze is not safe for surfaces that come into contact with food. Add 5–10% whiting along with stains that need the presence of calcium to enhance color, ie: Victoria Green Mason stain, Chartreuse Mason stain, or chrome-tin pinks.

DEB'S CLEAR BASE

Cone 04 oxidation

Ferro Frit 3195	45.00 %
Ferro Frit 3134	30.00
EPK Kaolin	25.00
	100.00 %

Colorant Additions:

Butter Yellow to Bright Yellow:	
Mason Zirconium Yellow Stain	2–6 %
Honey: Burnt Umber Stain	6.00 %
Moss: Copper Carbonate	2.50 %
Burnt Umber	4.00 %
Turquoise: Copper Carbonate	2.50 %
Blue: Copper Carbonate	2.50 %
Cobalt Carbonate	0.25 %
Teal: Copper Carbonate	3.00 %
Chrome Oxide	0.25 %

This glaze is transparent, shiny, and very responsive to stains and oxides. To achieve a transparent clear, apply thin. Use a thicker application with colorants for a rich, translucent glaze.

COPPER CARBONATE WASH

Cone 04 oxidation

Ferro Frit 3124	60 %
Copper Carbonate	40
	100 %

Add a mixture of CMC gum and water to form a wash.

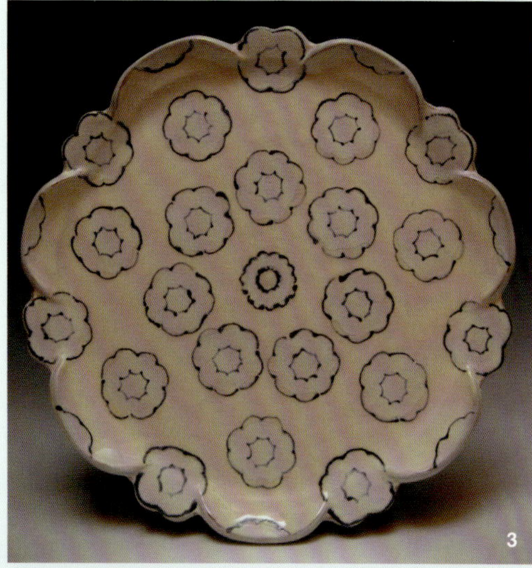

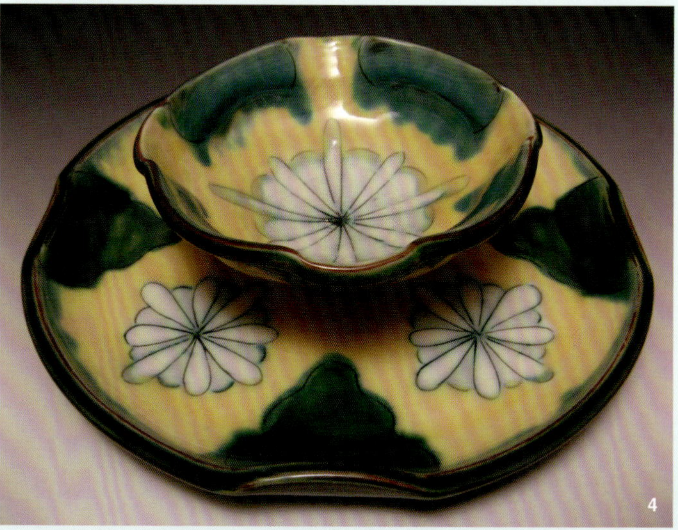

1 Flower brick detail, 8½ in. (22 cm) in length, base: Deb's Clear Base over cobalt sulfate underglaze, lid: Jackie's Satin Matte Chartreuse. **2** *Savory Platter* detail, 17¼ in. (44 cm) in diameter, glazed with Deb's Clear Base in Honey, Teal, and Moss. **3** *Salty Platter*, 17¼ in. (44 cm) in diameter, glazed with Deb's Clear Base and Jackie's Satin Matte over black underglaze. **4** *Crocus Bowl and Plate Set*, glazed with Deb's Yellow, Teal and Clear over copper sulfate underglaze. All pieces are wheel-thrown and assembled Lantz (Nova Scotia) earthenware with slip, polychrome glazes, terra sigillata, 2012–14.

Low-fire Slip and Glaze

by Martina Lantin

The following recipes are for a low-fire slip and a great base glaze for making both transparent and opaque surfaces. After making a form, I add the surface decoration, starting with incising patterns into the clay before or after the white slip is applied. I also introduce lines into the compositions through a combination of wet applications such as toner-resist transfer, slip trailing, and mono printing. I fire a slow bisque to cone 05 and a fast glaze (both set kiln programs) to a hot cone 03.

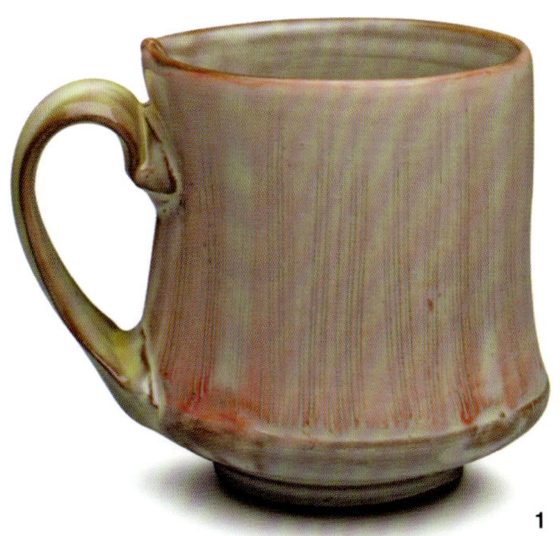

1

WHITE SLIP FOR EARTHENWARE

Cone 06–02 oxidation

Nepheline Syenite	15%
Talc	15
Ferro Frit 3124	10
Ball Clay	40
EPK Kaolin	20
	100 %

Colorant additions vary, altering in intensity depending on the desired color, and are often mixed by eye rather than by percentage. Add powdered stains or coloring oxides into the wet slip mixture.

WOODY HUGHES BASE GLAZE

Cone 04–03 oxidation

Gerstley Borate	26.0 %
Lithium Carbonate	4.0
Nepheline Syenite	20.0
Ferro Frit 3124	30.0
EPK Kaolin	10.0
Silica	10.0
	100.0 %
Add:	
Dark Green: Copper Carbonate	4.0%
Pink: Red Stain	1.5%
Opaque: Titanium Dioxide	7.5%

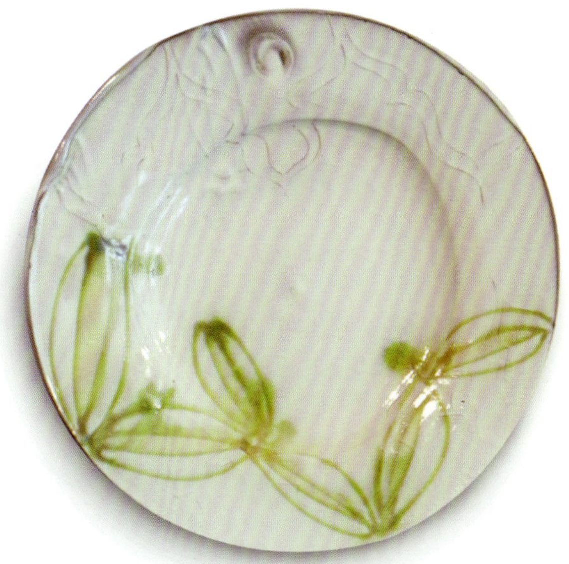

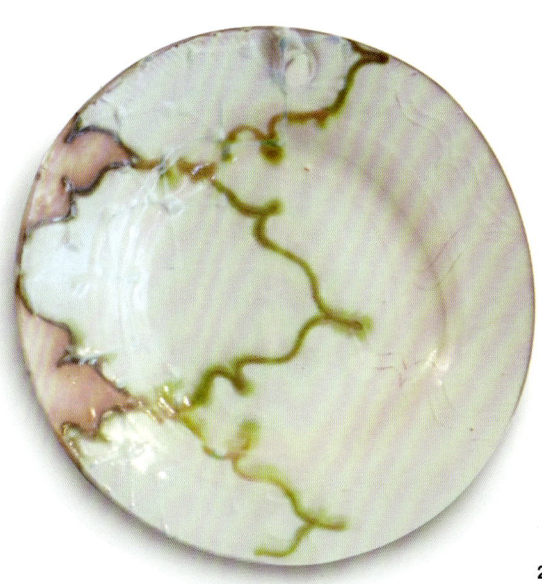

2

1 Yellow-handled mug, 4 in. (10 cm) in height, wheel-thrown and altered earthenware, slip, glaze, 2011. **2** *Installation of Plates* (detail), 3 ft. 6 in. (1.1 m) in height overall, earthenware, slips, glazes, 2013. *Photo: Kathryn Gremley.*

Low-fire Red Glaze

by Dave Finkelnburg

Selenium/Cadmium Red

The easiest, most reliable path to red is to use relatively recently developed cadmium inclusion stains. These stains also contain selenium combined with sulfur, and they will produce the full range of colors in the red spectrum from yellow through orange to brilliant red. They work in both translucent and opaque glazes, in oxidation and reduction firings, and at all firing temperatures.

Historically, cadmium and selenium have produced glamorous red glazes but only at low temperatures. The colorants burned out at higher kiln temperatures and the resulting red glazes were pale. The discovery of the encapsulation process (the of melting the colorants into a zirconium silicate glass at high temperatures) has now made the many hues of yellow through red reliable at temperatures through cone 10 in both oxidation and reduction atmospheres and made working with and achieving these colors at lower temperatures more predictable. These stains are refractory at pottery temperatures and do not melt much, if at all. However, the manufacturers recommend that the stain not be ball milled.

As with lead, cadmium stains can produce food-safe colors. However as with lead, cadmium under certain circumstances can be leached from the fired glaze. A sample of any cadmium stain-tinted glaze used on potential food surfaces should be tested for leaching by a qualified laboratory.

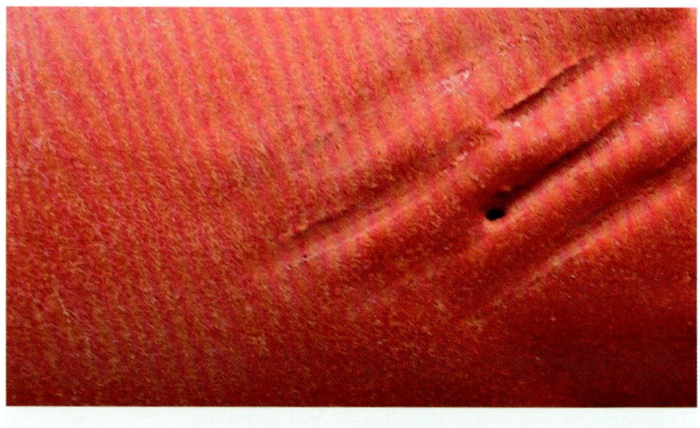

LOW-FIRE SATIN GLAZE

Cone 04 oxidation

Ferro Frit 3195	50 %
Dolomite	30
EPK Kaolin	20
	100 %
Add: Encapsulated Mason Stain #6025 Coral Red	15 %

Inclusion stains are suitable for use in a wide variety of base glazes. The amount of stain to use must be determined by testing, because the base glaze and application thickness will influence the fired results. Reds produced with these stains, while very reliable, tend to be flat and lack the variation produced when using oxides and/or atmospheric kilns.

CHAPTER 2

Mid Range

Chrome Red/Green Glazes

by John Britt

Chrome produces a wide range of greens, from a transparent glossy lime green to the more iconic, opaque, satin kelly green. The strong green color can often be modified by very small amounts of other oxides, like cobalt oxide, copper oxide, iron oxide, manganese dioxide, rutile, tin oxide, etc. In addition to green, chrome oxide also produces gray, brown, red, pink, and orange colors. It is also used in black glazes and stains to give a strong, true black color.

Because chrome produces such strong opaque greens, even when used at less than 1%, it is often used as a decorator color rather than a single glaze for the piece (see Temmoku Gold and Odyssey green glaze (p. 89)). Other techniques may include using a dark clay body, glazing with a chrome green, and after firing, sandblasting the piece to give it visual interest.

Because chrome oxide is volatile, placing a chrome green glaze next to a tin white glaze will often produce pink flashes on the tin white glaze. A good kiln vent can help to pull out the chrome fumes before they have time to latch onto the tin whites. But chrome flashing is best avoided by not mixing the two glazes in the same firing. Alternatively, if you like the pink flashing, this can be encouraged by mixing chrome greens and tin whites in a firing or even firing pieces in a partially closed saggar with a chrome green glaze painted on the inside wall of the saggar.

Chrome oxide gives a burgundy/red when combined with tin oxide at cone 6 in oxidation (see Raspberry and Cranberry (below) or Chrome Red glaze (p. 88)). These iconic cone 6 glazes need a specific formulation to be successful. First, there

RASPBERRY AND CRANBERRY
(FROM *MASTERING CONE 6 GLAZES* BY JOHN HESSELBERTH AND RON ROY)

Cone 6 oxidation

Whiting	20 %
Ferro Frit 3134	14
Nepheline Syenite	18
Kentucky Ball Clay	18
Silica	30
	100 %

For Raspberry		
Add:	Tin Oxide	7.50 %
	Chrome Oxide	0.20 %
For Cranberry		
Add:	Tin Oxide	3.8 %
	Chrome Oxide	0.2 %

Raspberry base

Raspberry base with 0.25% cobalt carbonate

Raspberry base with 8% Mason 6006 Stain

needs to be a specific ratio of tin oxide to chrome oxide. Start with 0.1–0.5% chrome oxide and 7.5–9.0% tin oxide. Remember that these are targets that should help you, but you can get red colors to develop with less amounts of tin oxide (for example, by adding 3.5% tin oxide to the Raspberry and Cranberry glaze on page 87). Varying the amounts will give a variety of pinks to deep burgundy colors. The calcium content of the glaze should be high (10–15% or 0.7–0.9 moles). It is also important to have no zinc in the recipe or the glaze will turn brown. Alumina is also best if kept low. Some recommend no magnesium oxide (talc, dolomite, or magnesium carbonate) in the base recipe while others use a small amount of magnesium oxide to achieve interesting red/burgundy colors (see Burgundy/Red glaze below). A thin application is best as a thicker coating may produce a gray glaze.

You can also get chrome/tin reds at low-fire temperatures but they don't work well above cone 8. If you don't want to mess with the ratio of tin to chrome, an easy way to get cone 6 burgundy reds is to simply add 5–8% stain, such as Mason Deep Crimson 6006, (which contains calcium, chrome, tin, and silica), to a high-calcium base glaze (see Raspberry and Cranberry glaze (p. 87)).

Adding cobalt carbonate to a chrome/tin or burgundy red glaze can push the color toward purple but adding too much will overpower the red (just 0.25% cobalt carbonate will have a noticeable effect. See Raspberry and Cranberry and Chrome Red glaze tiles with added cobalt carbonate). You can also alter the tone of the burgundy/red glaze with small additions of iron oxide, rutile, or manganese dioxide. Test several options to find the percentage that yields the desired color.

BURGUNDY/RED

Cone 6 oxidation

Gerstley Borate	8 %
Talc	4
Whiting	21
Ferro Frit 3134	9
Custer Feldspar	31
EPK Kaolin	9
Silica	18
	100 %
Add: Tin Oxide	5.00 %
Chrome Oxide	0.20 %

Burgundy Red

CHROME RED

Cone 6 oxidation

Gerstley Borate	21 %
Whiting	20
Nepheline Syenite	16
EPK Kaolin	11
Silica	32
	100 %
Add: Tin Oxide	5.00 %
Chrome Oxide	0.15 %

Chrome Red with 0.25% cobalt carbonate

CHUN BASE

Cone 6 oxidation

Whiting	14 %
Zinc Oxide	12
F-4 Feldspar	38
Kentucky Ball Clay	6
Silica	30
	100 %

A great cone 6 electric base that is a nice clear and gives excellent colors except with chrome because it contains zinc, which turns brown.

Chun Base with 0.15% chrome

Chun Base with 0.5% chrome

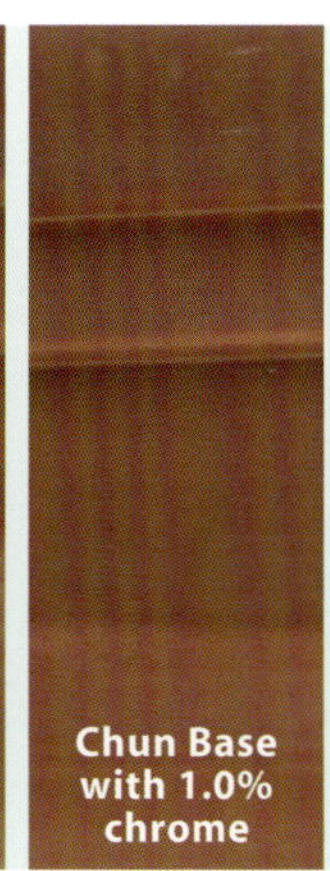

Chun Base with 1.0% chrome

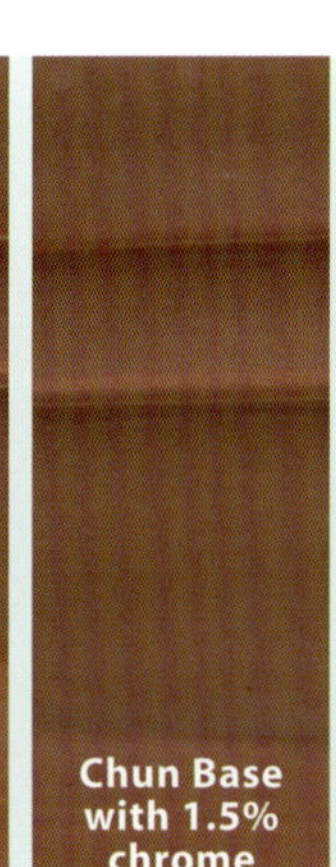

Chun Base with 1.5% chrome

Chun Base with 2.0% chrome

ODYSSEY BASE
Cone 6 oxidation

Material	%
Gerstley Borate	20 %
Whiting	10
Nepheline Syenite	30
EPK Kaolin	10
Silica	30
	100 %

A standard base from the Odyssey Center in Asheville, North Carolina. Contains high boron, calcium, and sodium, gives bright, glossy, transparent colors.

Odyssey Base with 0.15% chrome

Odyssey Base with 0.5% chrome

Odyssey Base with 1.0% chrome

Odyssey Base with 2.0% chrome

RANDY'S BASE
Cone 6 oxidation

Material	%
Gerstley Borate	31.7 %
Talc	13.8
Minspar 200	19.8
EPK Kaolin	5.0
Silica	29.7
	100.0 %

An excellent and popular base (originally from Randy's Red). Contains a lot of boron and low alumina, gives bright, glossy, transparent colors.

Randy's Base with 0.15% chrome

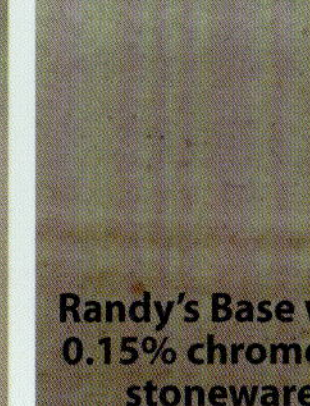
Randy's Base with 0.15% chrome on stoneware

Randy's Base with 0.5% chrome

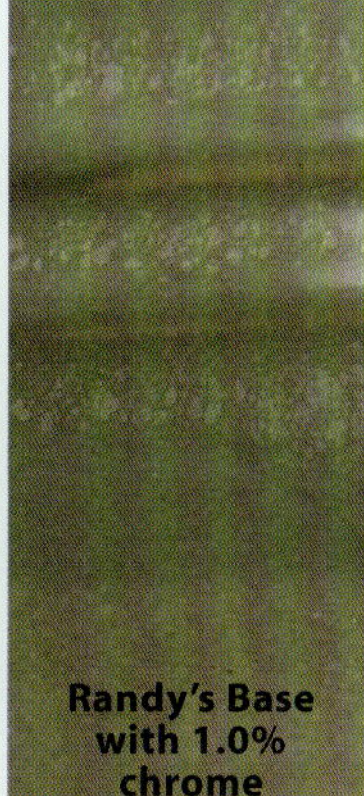
Randy's Base with 1.0% chrome

TEMMOKU GOLD
Cone 6 reduction

Material	%
Cornish Stone	67.4 %
Dolomite	7.9
Gerstley Borate	3.4
Lithium Carbonate	6.2
Whiting	8.9
Silica	6.2
	100.0 %
Add: Red Iron Oxide	11.2 %

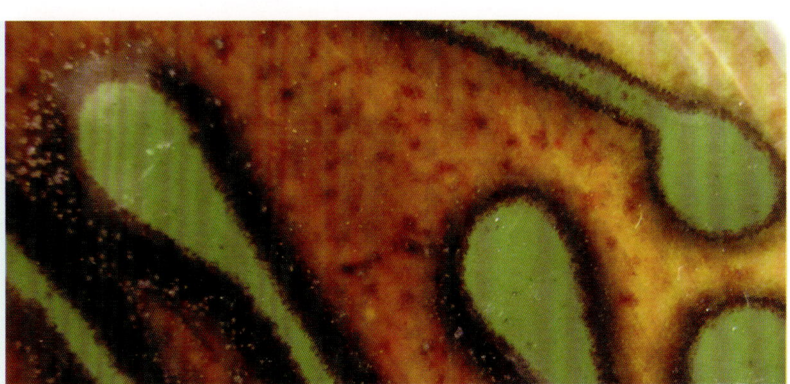

All glazes shown here were fired on porcelain except where otherwise noted.

Learn more about chrome's properties and the ways it can affect glazes.

Glazes with Iron

by John Britt

Iron is everywhere in many different forms, but that doesn't mean it has to be boring—or even brown. It would be impossible to show all of the types of iron glazes here, but highlighting a few will give you a glimpse of the wide variety.

19 See "All About Iron" for more information

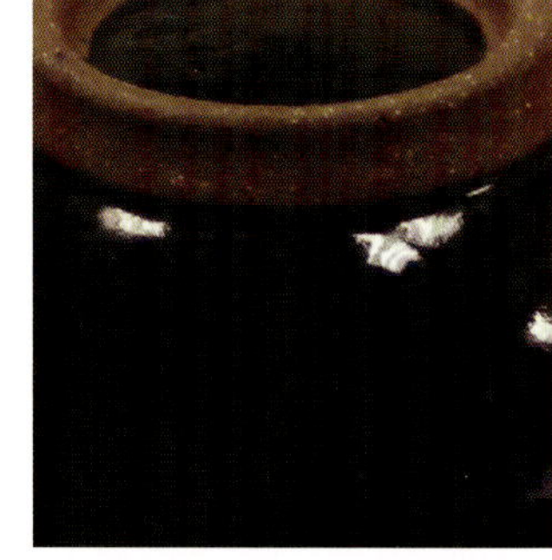

RON ROY BLACK

Cone 6 oxidation or reduction

Talc	3 %
Whiting	6
Ferro Frit 3134	26
Minspar 200 Feldspar	21
EPK Kaolin	17
Silica	27
	100 %
Add: Cobalt Carbonate	1 %
Red Iron Oxide	9 %

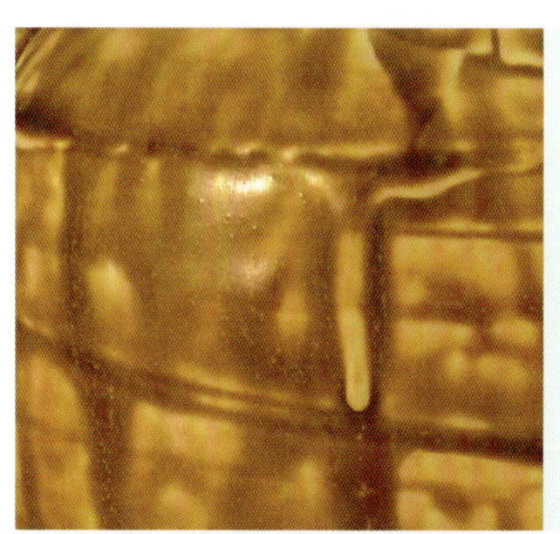

FAKE ASH

Cone 6 reduction

Bone Ash	5.0 %
Dolomite	24.5
Gerstley Borate	10.0
Lithium Carbonate	2.0
Strontium Carbonate	9.5
Ball Clay	21.0
Cedar Heights Red Art	28.0
	100.0 %

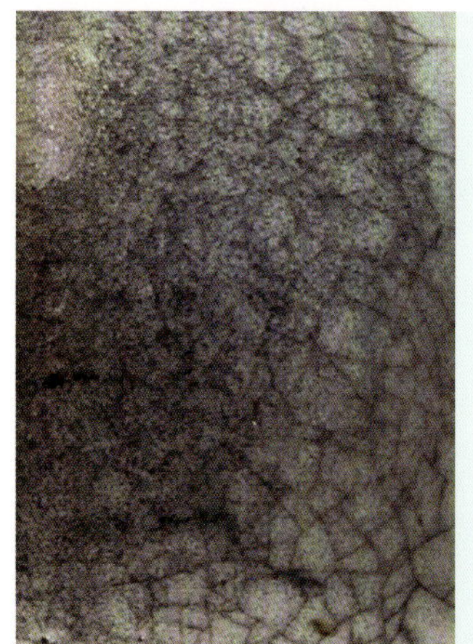

CHINESE CRACKLE (KUAN)

Cone 10 reduction

Custer Feldspar	83 %
Whiting	9
Silica	8
	100 %
Add: Zircopax (optional)	10 %

Adding small amounts of red iron oxide to this feldspathic base and firing in reduction will result in the following:

Blue Celadon: 0.5%–1.0%
Blue–Green: 1–2%
Olive to Amber: 3–4%
Tenmoku: 5–9%
Iron Saturate: 10–20%

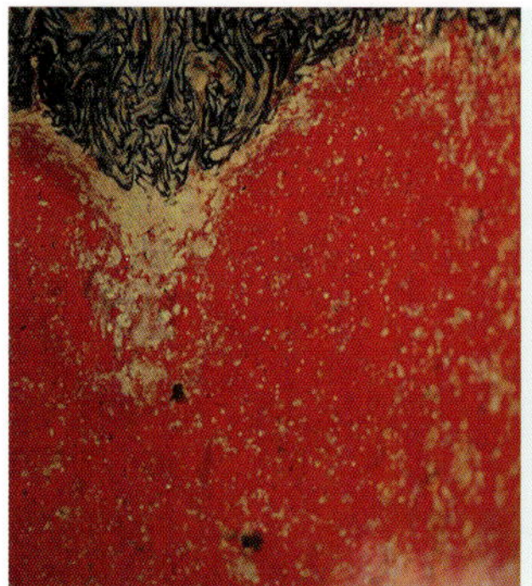

KETCHUP RED (JAYNE SHATZ)

Cone 6 oxidation

Gerstly Borate	31 %
Talc	14
Custer Feldspar	20
EPK Kaolin	5
Silica	30
	100 %
Add: Spanish Red Iron Oxide	15 %

Works best on dark colored stoneware. If used on a buff clay body, the red is less intense.

Celadons at Six

by John Britt

Celadon glazes are some of the most popular glazes in ceramics. In particular, transparent blue celadons have a very delicate, beautiful color that shows carving very nicely. But celadons aren't just blue; they can range from blue to blue-green to gray-blue to gray-green to green to amber, and even to white. They often have distinctive crackle patterns that are sought after but can also be craze-free.

Celadons originated in China thousands of years ago and were meant to mimic jade. The Lung-chuan (Longquan) satin green celadons were important Chinese exports for over 500 years. The term "Celadon" is a European name thought to have derived from a character in a French play who wore gray-green ribbons over his cloak. However, there are several competing theories of its origin.

Technically, celadons are feldspathic transparent high-fire glazes that are colored with iron and fired in reduction. This differentiates them from transparent copper greens known as Oribe, but both glaze names denote a type of ware as well as a color of glaze. Celadons were thought to have been made from the local clay body and ash, but as the glaze traveled to Korea and Japan, potters began using porcelain stone (a naturally occurring decomposed feldspathic rock) in the glaze.

Purists would say that a cone 6 celadon is impossible, since, by definition, it is high fired, but if we take a more practical approach and widen our definition of celadon to a transparent blue-green glaze colored with iron or other oxides, then we can include cone 6 celadons in reduction or oxidation.

Since I have worked extensively with cone 10 blue celadons, and know the principles necessary to produce that glaze, I assumed that those same principles could be used to make a cone 6 celadon. The idea is to select a glaze with high potassium (better chances for blue), high silica, small amounts of iron, and low titanium (to prevent opacifying the glaze and to prevent the iron from going green to brown). Also, a small amount of tin oxide and barium carbonate improve the blue color. Apply it thickly (two to three coats; ⅛–3⁄16 inches or 3–5mm) on a clay body also low in titanium. This means that you should use Grolleg kaolin in both the clay body and the glaze recipe. Fire in an early reduction cycle, using heavy reduction (0.75–0.80 oxygen probe reading) beginning at cone 012–010 (1582–1657°F; 861–903°C), then hold moderate reduction (0.70–0.75 oxygen probe reading) to the end of the firing. Theoretically, this should be simple, but in order to melt a glaze at cone 6 (2232°F, 1222°C), you need to add different fluxes, all of which have different color responses. Boron oxide is an active flux at cone 6, as are sodium, lithium, and zinc oxide, but each have their own characteristics that have to be taken to consideration. For example, zinc oxide is an excellent flux in oxidation, but if fired in reduction it will volatilize, leaving the glaze unmelted. Boron is an excellent flux in oxidation and reduction but can make the glaze cloudy. Because you have to add so much flux, sometimes up to 30% frit or Gerstley borate, it is sometimes necessary to start reduction a bit earlier when firing to cone 6 or the glaze might seal over and the atmosphere will not be able to act on the iron.

1%

2%

3%

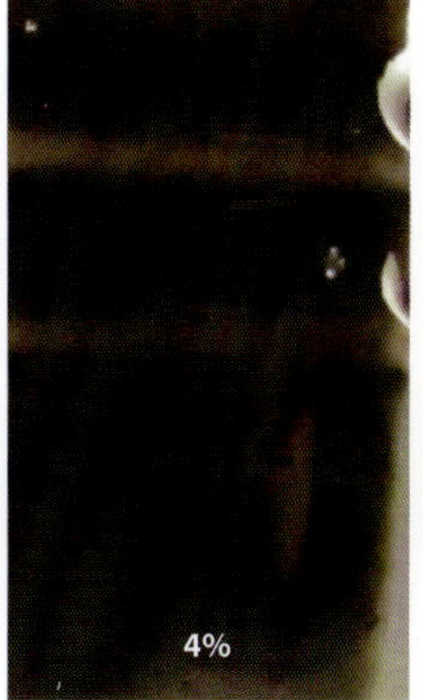
4%

5%

The shift from green or blue toward brown or black can happen with a very small change in the amount of iron.

So, with these considerations in mind, there are several ways to make a cone 6 blue/green celadon: move a cone 10 reduction celadon down to cone 6 reduction; test existing cone 6 bases with varying amounts of iron; or use stains to make blue/green celadons in an electric oxidation firing.

Adjusting a Cone 10 Celadon to Cone 6

Blue celadon is the most difficult color to obtain with iron, so if we start with one of those recipes, then getting a green celadon should be easy. Taking Pinnell Celadon, which is a cone 10 glaze, and substituting nepheline syenite for the Custer feldspar should help bring the melting temperature closer to cone 6. (Nepheline syenite is a feldspathoid that melts at cone 6, while most feldspar starts melting at about cone 9.) If a straight substitution doesn't cause the glaze to sufficiently melt at cone 6, which it does not in this case, start adding additional cone 6 fluxes, like frits, Gerstley borate, lithium carbonate, or zinc oxide (for oxidation only, which we'll cover later), running progressions from 1–10%. In this case, 10% Gerstley borate worked well. Alternatively, finding the proper glaze melt can be aided by glaze software, in which you get the unity molecular formula of the glaze into acceptable limits for cone 6. You will need to recalculate the total for the recipe to 100 if you add additional fluxes. After you find the surface you like, run iron oxide colorant addition progressions, varying the iron from 1–6% to get a celadon color you like (see tiles on page 91).

PINNELL CELADON
Cone 10 reduction

Whiting		20.0 %
Custer Feldspar		25.0
Grolleg Kaolin		20.0
Silica		35.0
		100.0 %
Add:	Tin Oxide	1.0 %
	Synthetic Red Iron Oxide	0.5 %
	Barium Carbonate* (optional)	2.0 %

Note: Synthetic red iron oxide is 96–99% pure red iron, made by calcining black iron oxide in oxidation. It is then milled to 325 mesh, which makes it ideal for celadons, because it will enter the melt more quickly and thoroughly. For more, see "All About Iron," on page 19.

PINNELL CELADON REVISED
Cone 6 reduction

Gerstley Borate (or substitute)		9.09 %
Whiting		18.18
Nepheline Syenite		22.73
Grolleg Kaolin		18.18
Silica		31.82
		100.00 %
Add:	Tin Oxide	1.00 %
	Synthetic Red Iron Oxide	0.50 %
	Barium Carbonate* (optional)	2.00 %

Use the same firing cycle as for cone 10 gas reduction, but simply stop it at cone 6/7.

* You can substitute 1.5% strontium carbonate for the barium carbonate if you prefer.

Pinnell Celadon Revised with 0.5% synthetic red iron oxide on Grolleg porcelain.

Use an Existing Cone 6 Recipe as a Celadon Base

Since you have to do a lot of experimenting and testing to move a cone 10 glaze down to cone 6, I find that you can make an iron celadon pretty easily by just taking one of the hundreds of workable cone 6 glazes already in use with a surface you like and then, after taking out the colorants and opacifiers, running an iron progression. This will take you through a range of iron colors from blue to blue green to green to amber to tenmoku to iron saturate. Remember, always use Grolleg kaolin as the clay to keep the titanium as low as possible. The tone of the colors is dictated by the oxides that predominate in the base and the amount of iron. So a high calcium base will give different colors than a high sodium base, regardless of firing temperature.

Use Stains to Imitate a Celadon

Using stains in a cone 6 base allows you to fire in oxidation (particularly useful for all of the folks out there firing electric kilns) even though some stains work in reduction as well. As I said earlier, zinc oxide in oxidation makes a wonderful cone 6 flux and can produce some nice colors with both oxides and stains.

Many stain manufacturers recommend using 8% stain, but that makes the glaze flat and uninteresting to me, so I use very small amounts (1–3%) to keep the color delicate and transparent.

JOHN'S SATIN BLUE CELADON
Cone 6 reduction

Whiting	20.69 %
Ferro Frit 3195	17.24
Nepheline Syenite	6.90
Grolleg Kaolin	25.86
Silica	29.31
	100.00 %
Add: Tin Oxide	1.00 %
Synthetic Red Iron Oxide	0.50 %
For Lung Chuan (on white stoneware):	
Synthetic Red Iron Oxide	3.00 %

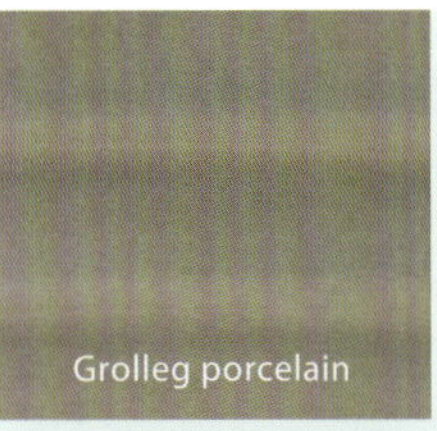
Grolleg porcelain

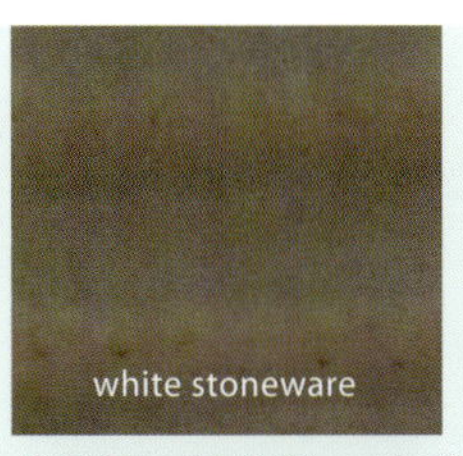
white stoneware

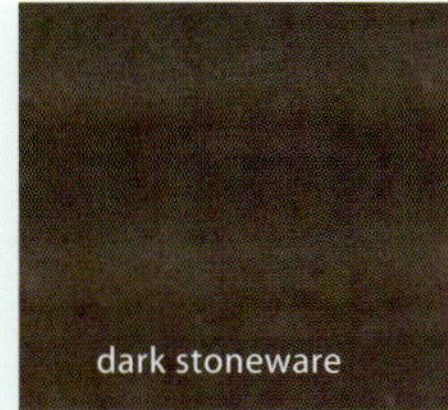
dark stoneware

John's Satin Blue Celadon with 0.5% synthetic red iron oxide.

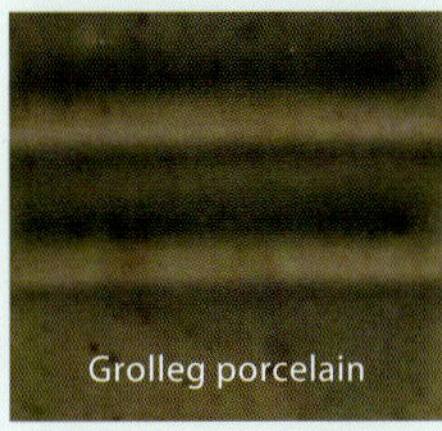
Grolleg porcelain

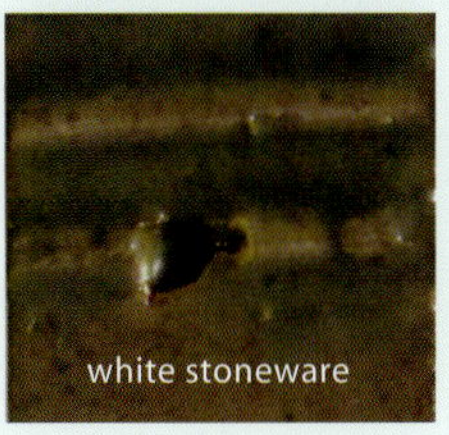
white stoneware

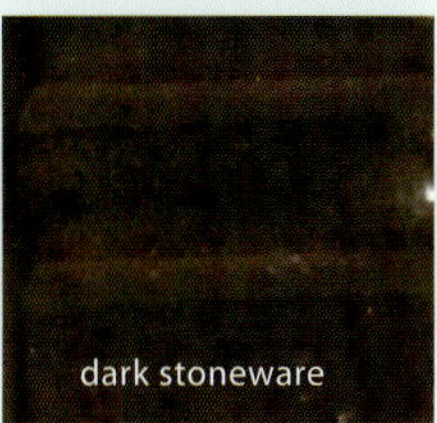
dark stoneware

John's Satin Blue Celadon with 3% synthetic red iron oxide.

Grolleg porcelain

white stoneware

dark stoneware

TONY HANSEN 20 X 5
Cone 6 reduction

Whiting	20.00 %
Ferro Frit 3134	20.00
Custer Feldspar	20.00
Grolleg Kaolin	20.00
Silica	20.00
	100.00 %
Add: Tin Oxide	1.00 %
Synthetic Red Iron Oxide	0.75 %
Barium Carbonate (optional)	0.75 %

Tony Hansen 20x5 with 0.75% synthetic red iron oxide.

V. C. 71
Cone 6/7 reduction

Talc	9.0
Whiting	16.0
Ferro Frit 3124	9.0
Custer Feldspar	40.0
Grolleg Kaolin	10.0
Silica	16.0
	100.0 %
Add: Red Iron Oxide	0.5 %

V. C. 71 with 0.5% synthetic red iron oxide.

Grolleg porcelain

white stoneware

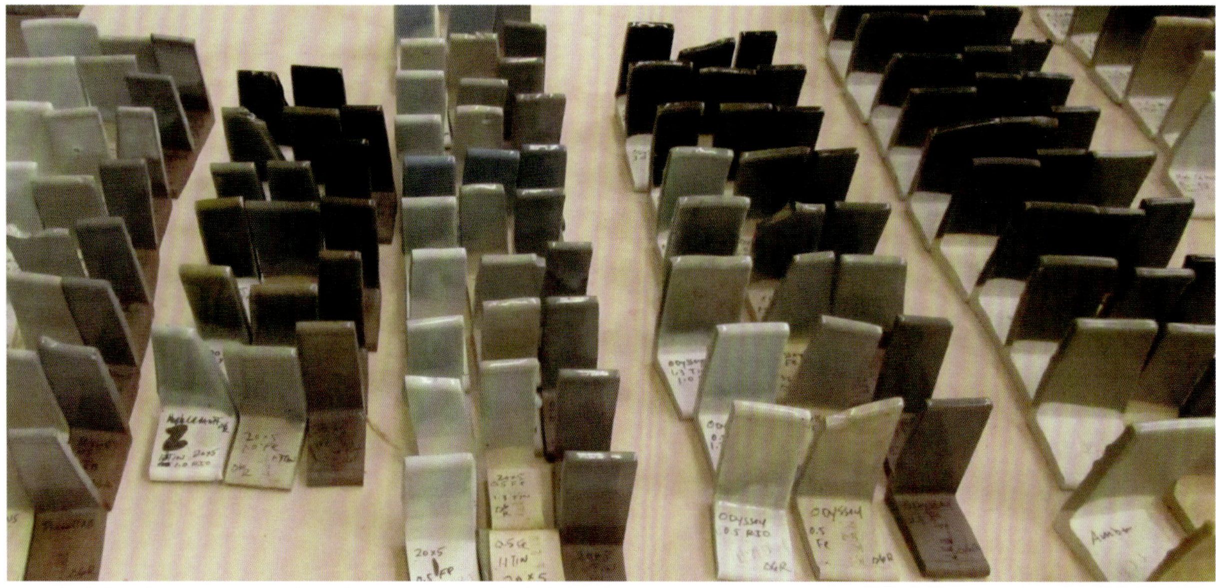

Cone 6 celadon glaze tests on porcelain, white stoneware, and a dark stoneware clay.

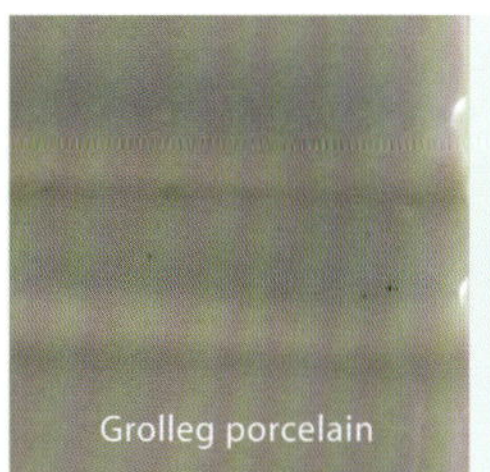

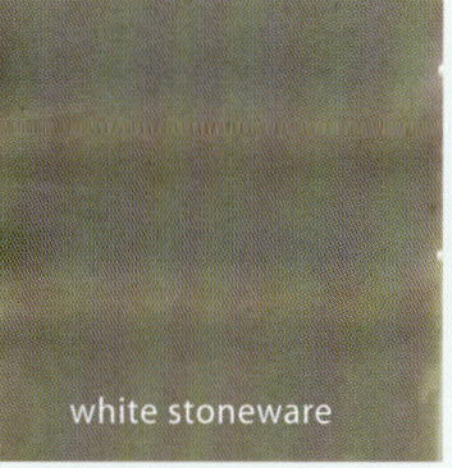

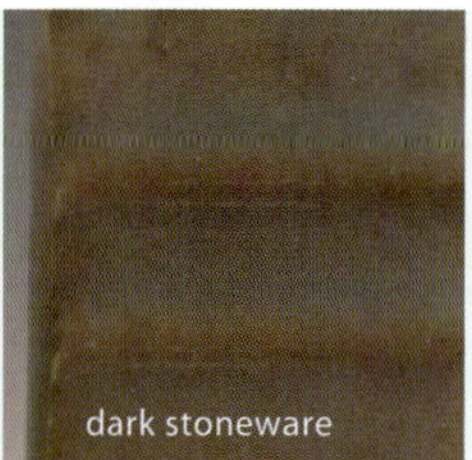

Chun Clear with 2% Turquoise Mason Stain 6393.

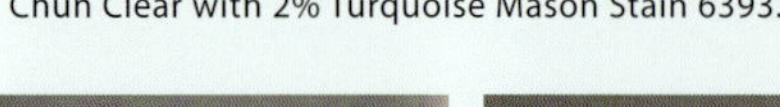

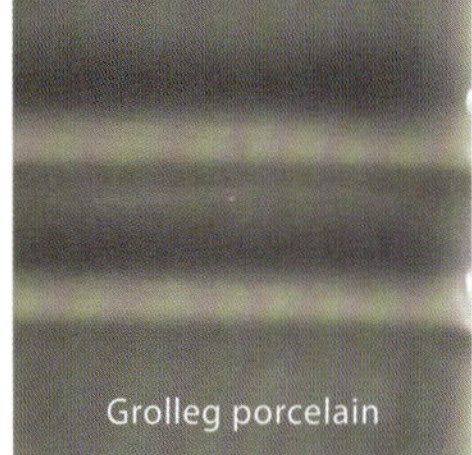

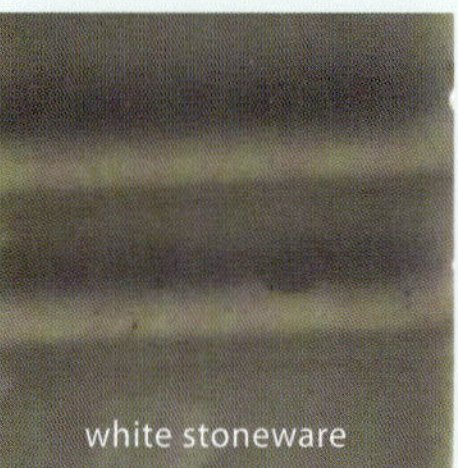

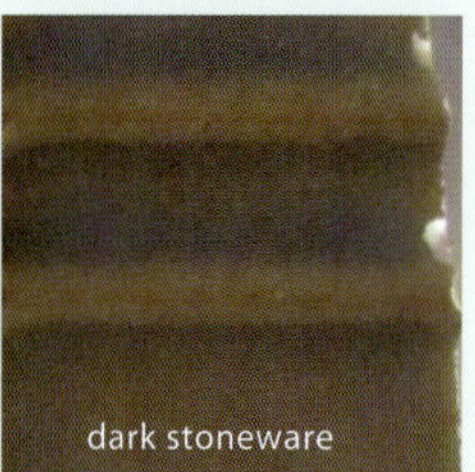

Chun Clear with 2% Cadet Blue Mason Stain 6302

CHUN CLEAR

Cone 6 oxidation

Whiting		14.00 %
Zinc Oxide		12.00
F-4 Feldspar (sub Minspar 200)		38.00
Kentucky Ball Clay		6.00
Silica		30.00
		100.00 %
Add:	Barium Carbonate (optional)	0.75 %
	Stains	2–3.00 %
Or:	Cobalt Carbonate	0.10 %

Clay Body Considerations

Finally, clay body must be considered when making cone 6 celadons. To get delicate iron blue celadons you will need to use a Grolleg clay body. Some suppliers only produce cone 10 Grolleg clay bodies, which only start to mature (less than 1% absorption) at cone 7, so you may need to fire them to cone 7. If you want a blue/green celadon, there are many cone 6 domestic porcelains that will work, as well as light and dark stonewares. It is important to mention that different clay bodies have different CTE (coefficients of thermal expansion) and that will affect the crazing or the crackle pattern. Also, expansion and contraction is affected by firing temperature, and mid-range firing (cone 5–7) spans a large temperature range (2167– 2262°F; 1186–1239°C) so maintaining consistent firings is essential.

Firing at cone 6 is a great way to both save energy and still get outstanding celadons. You can knock about three hours off of a typical cone 10 firing time, and save about a third of the fuel by firing celadons to cone 6. No one will know unless you tell them!

Mid-Range Reduction: It's Not Just Cooler, It's Cool

by John Britt

With all the current discussion about global warming and conservation, I thought I should relate a workshop I taught at MudFire Clayworks and Gallery, a community ceramic art center in Decatur, Georgia, just outside of Atlanta. They offer studio space, monthly workshops and a beautiful gallery of contemporary ceramics artists. They also fire to cone 6 in reduction. Erik Haagensen and Luba Sharapan, the owners of MudFire, had started to fire cone 6 reduction because of a defect in the kiln they'd purchased, but after seeing the results they had no reason to change back, even after the kiln was repaired. Firing to cone 6 was cheaper, faster, and the results were almost indistinguishable from high fire.

The Project

Although they fire to mid-range reduction, Erik and Luba had read my book, "The Complete Guide to High-Fire Glazes," and wanted me to give a workshop on the cost and time benefits of cone 6 reduction firing, as well as to explain the reasoning behind glaze recipes, firing cycles and to show them how to bring glazes from cone 10 down to cone 6.

I normally work with, and teach about, high-fire glazes (cone 9–11), approximately 2350°F (1288°C), while mid-range, (cone 5–7), is about 2200°F (1204°C). Although this is only about a 150°F (66°C) temperature difference, raising the temperature 150°F at the peak of the firing takes quite a bit more energy and puts a lot of extra wear and tear on the kiln. It could easily take two to four more hours of firing to go from cone 6 to cone 10 with the gas on high, so firing to mid-range reduction would save considerable fuel if comparable glazes could be found.

At that time, I didn't have a lot of experience with mid-range reduction and I found it hard to believe that the results were "almost indistinguishable." I did have a good bit of experience firing mid-range oxidation in an electric kiln and the results are far from the look of cone 10 reduction. But the idea intrigued me, and the more I thought about it, the more I realized that the same principles of high fire reduction should apply to mid-range reduction. The key question would be if the oxides and materials needed to melt the glazes at a lower temperature would negatively affect the glaze colors. So I took the challenge, reasoning that I could use the same research methods I used for the high-fire glazes to explore these mid-range glazes.

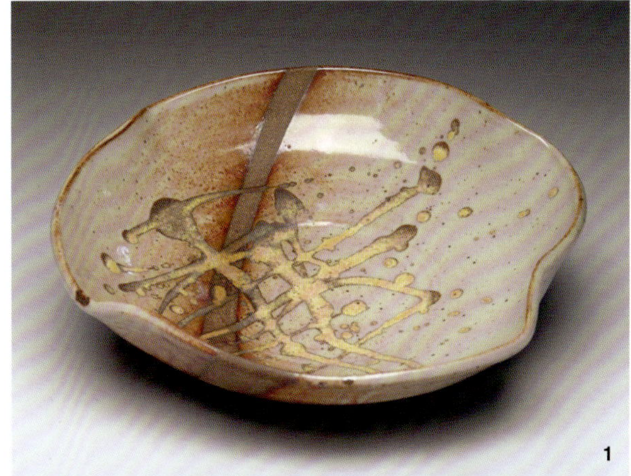

1

Thrown and altered platter, 12 in. (30 cm) in diameter, stoneware with Cherry Blossom Shino and Woo Yellow glaze, fired in reduction to cone 6, by Barbara Morgenbesser. See recipes on page 100.

Mid-range firing in both oxidation and reduction is a well researched area dating back before the energy crisis of the 1970s. There are also several college clay programs that use mid-range reduction and have published their glazes. One notable example is Diana Pancioli, at the University of Eastern Michigan, who started her "Glaze Forward" program. (For a small shipping fee, you could send for a list of cone 6 reduction recipes and test tiles of those glazes.) There are also organizations like the Clay Studio in Philadelphia that fire cone 6 reduction and have developed a wonderful palette.

The Research

My first step is always completing an exhaustive survey of known glazes from books, internet and workshop handouts. Luba and Erik generously sent me all their recipes from MudFire [see selected recipes on page 100], and I pulled out my cone 6 glaze notebooks and began assembling recipe lists and firing instructions.

There is so much information available today that it is almost paralyzing; you don't know what to do with it all. So in order to make it usable, I organized the recipes into types, like iron glazes (celadon, temmoku, kaki, iron saturate, etc.), shino, copper red, oribe (copper green), magnesium matt,

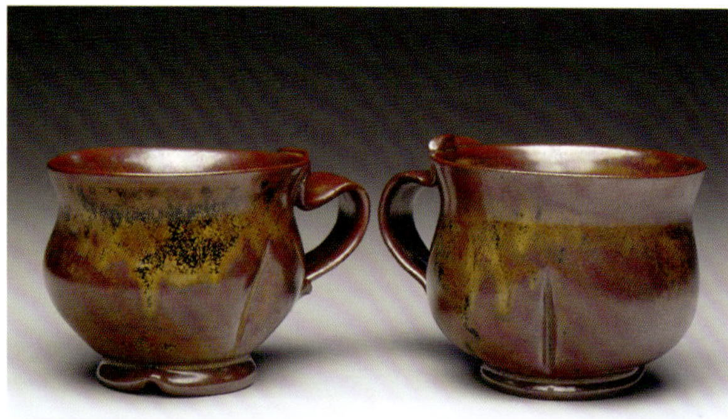

2

Mugs, 4 in. (10 cm) in height, stoneware with Temmoku Gold, gas fired in reduction to cone 6, by Luba Sharapan. See recipe on page 100.

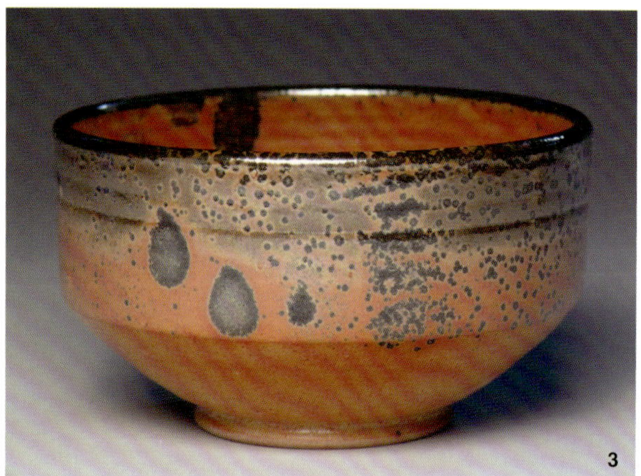

3

Noodle bowl, 4 in. (10 cm) in height, stoneware with Malcolm Davis Shino Glaze, gas fired in reduction to cone 6, by Erik Haagensen. Recipe: page 100.

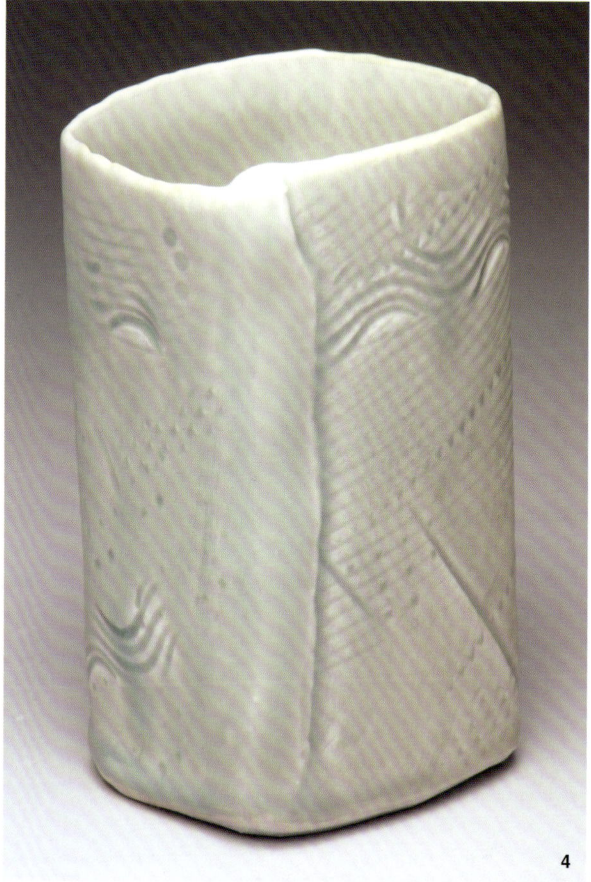

4

Handbuilt vase. 8 in. (20 cm) in height, porcelain with Mint Julep Glaze, gas fired in reduction to cone 6, by Melissa Keen-Boggan. See recipe on page 100.

etc. Then, after eliminating all the duplicates, I looked for similarities and differences, and from those, selected enough glaze recipes to test that would show a broad range of possibilities within a type. Then I test those recipes in a variety of firing cycles, like heavy reduction, light reduction, early reduction, late reduction and oxidation. This way, I can reveal a glaze's full potential.

Iron glazes are a great type to start with because you can see a wide range of colors by incrementally adding one colorant; iron oxide. For example, when firing in reduction using the same base glaze, adding 1% red iron creates a blue celadon, adding 2–4% iron oxide will give green to amber celadons, adding 5–10% iron oxide makes temmokus, and 10–20% iron oxide gives iron saturates. Teadust temmokus result from additions of magnesium carbonate to temmokus with cooling soaks. Kakis, which are also part of the iron glaze type, are obtained with additions of bone ash and magnesium carbonate. Finally, oil spots result from stiff oxidized temmokus with magnesium oxide. So you can see how one glaze type can show you a world of glaze colors.

Copper red glazes are generally low alumina and high alkaline bases with small amounts of copper carbonate (0.3%) and tin oxide (1%). Oribe glazes use copper to get greens while magnesium matt glazes yield satin whites and purples with cobalt oxide. You can try to reproduce these "types" at various cones and, as always, you may then have to make adjustments after you see the results.

The final type I concentrated on was shino glazes. Shinos are generally made with varying amounts of feldspar and clay. For example, you may have somewhere between 60–90% feldspar and 10–40% clay. A typical recipe would be 70% feldspar and 30% clay. This is the most difficult glaze type to reproduce at mid-range because most feldspars melt around cone 9 and then with the added clay it is hard to melt much lower than cone 10. I started by using nepheline syenite, which is not a true feldspar but rather a feldspathoid (containing less silica than a true feldspar). It melts around cone 6. Because it is high in sodium oxide and lower in silica, the effects are not identical, but it was a good starting point and worth a try.

Firing

I loaded the kiln with these various glaze types and then filled the remainder with line blends within these glaze types and a variety of other recipes, like blues, greens, yellows, blacks, etc., to see the overall effect of varying firing cycles across the board of glaze colors.

For first firing, I started reduction at cone 010 and kept it heavy (0.65–0.72 on the oxygen probe) to cone 6 at 3 o'clock (cone melting position, not time of day). I had pretty good copper reds and iron glazes but the shinos were dull and washed out. For the next firings, I increased the firing temperature to cone 7 at 3 o'clock, which gave me about 25°F more and brightened up the glazes. I ran five more firings to this cone, including full oxidation, light reduction, medium reduction, heavy reduction and oxidation with reduction at peak temperature. I also tested glazes with flux variations too numerous to mention, exploring mid-range fluxes like boron oxide, sodium oxide, lithium oxide, calcium oxide and zinc oxide [see sidebar on page 98]. Adding fluxes and reducing alumina and silica affects the response of coloring oxides in glazes, so the trick was finding suitable colors in properly melted glazes.

Results

The results were great for copper reds and iron glazes, as well as greens, blacks, blues and carbon-trap shinos, which were very nice in heavy reduction. The carbon trap

Side By Side

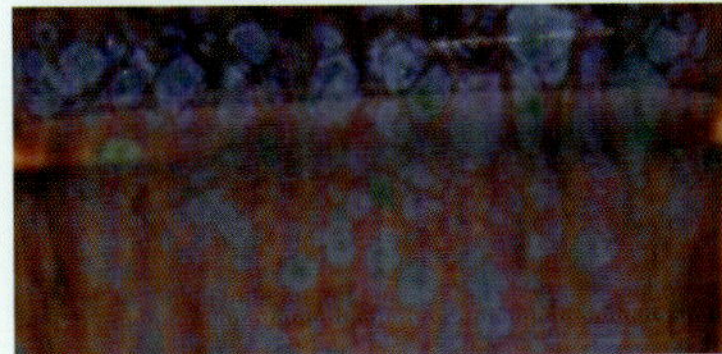

JEFF'S RED
Cone 10 Reduction

Barium Carbonate	4.4 %
Dolomite	8.7
Whiting	8.4
Zinc Oxide	1.7
Frit 3134 (Ferro)	8.7
Custer Feldspar	41.9
Silica	26.2
	100.0 %
Add: Tin Oxide	2.6 %
Copper Carbonate	0.5 %
Bentonite	1.0 %

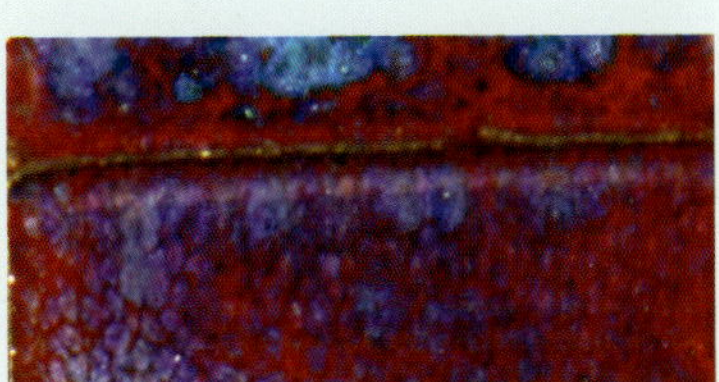

PANAMA RED
Cone 6 Reduction

Dolomite	8.0 %
Gerstley Borate	11.0
Strontium Carbonate	4.3
Whiting	2.7
Zinc Oxide	2.7
Custer Feldspar	45.5
Frit 3110 (Ferro)	10.0
EPK Kaolin	2.7
Silica	16.3
	100.0 %
Add: Tin Oxide	2.7 %
Copper Carbonate	1.8 %

SHANER ORIBE
Cone 10

Bone Ash	1.1 %
Talc	7.9
Whiting	22.1
Custer Feldspar	31.0
Kaolin	12.6
Silica	25.3
	100.0 %
Add: Copper Carbonate	5.2 %

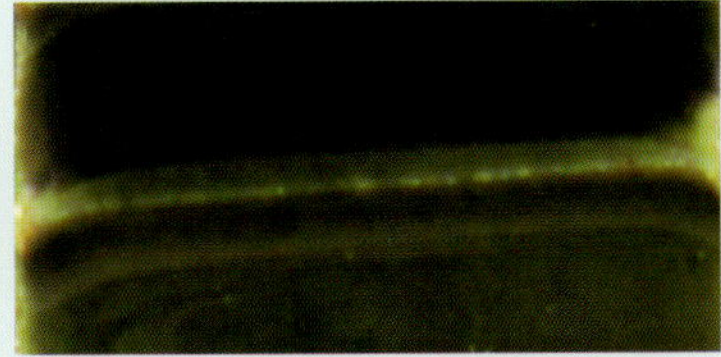

SELSOR ORIBE
Cone 6

Gerstley Borate	12.50 %
Whiting	10.41
Nepheline Syenite	56.25
Silica	20.83
	100.00 %
Add: Copper Carbonate	5.00 %

This is a test I made with Selsor Copper Red and I removed the colorants and added copper carbonate, so I called it Selsor Oribe.

COLEMAN TEADUST TEMMOKU
Cone 10

Talc	7 %
Whiting	16
Custer Feldspar	40
Ball Clay	12
Silica	25
	100 %
Add: Red Iron Oxide	10 %

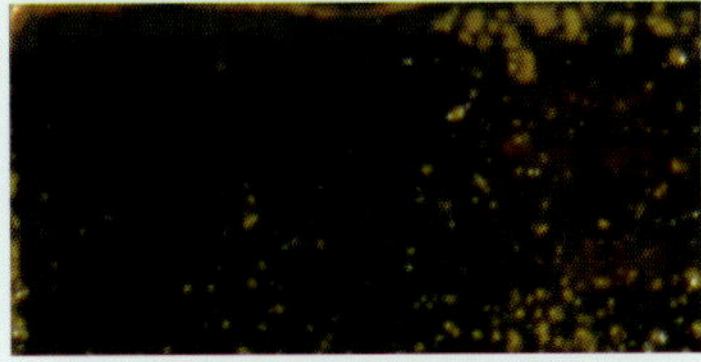

TEADUST TEMMOKU
Cone 6

Whiting	10.5 %
Frit P-25 (Pemco)	26.3
Alberta Slip	63.2
	100.0 %
Add: Red Iron Oxide	5.0 %

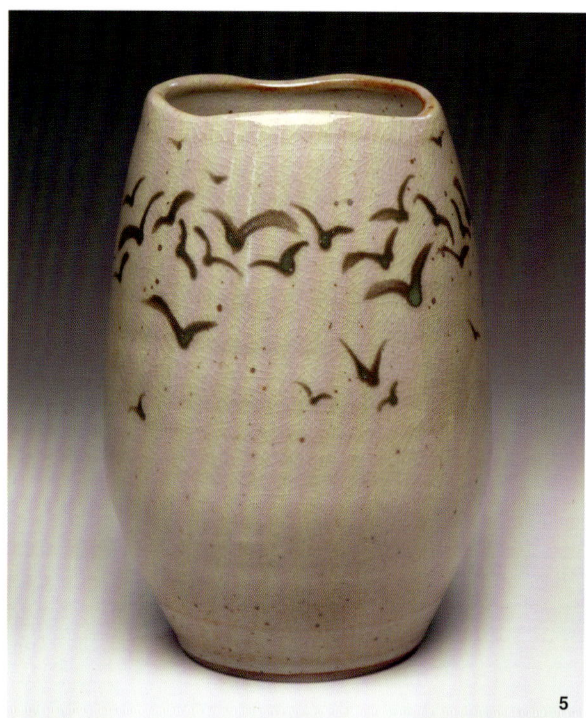

5

Eggy Vase, 15 in. (38 cm) in height, John's Shino with decoration using Amaco Velvet underglaze, gas fired in reduction to cone 6, by Erik Haagensen. See recipe on page 100.

shinos worked because they contain soda ash, which melts very early, and with early reduction the carbon is already "trapped" below the soda layer so the peak temperature is not a factor. The only glaze type I could not achieve was traditional shinos, as I had expected. And I only had limited success with oil spots in the gas oxidation trials. This was also to be expected as iron oxide only starts to self reduce at 2250°F (1232°C) and that is about the peak temperature we reached. Soaking at cone 7 helped, but they were not as spectacular as a cone 13 oil-spot firing. Nevertheless, we did get spotting and some promising oil-spot recipes.

From all this testing, I came to the inescapable conclusion that Erik and Luba were correct. Ninety percent of the mid-range glazes were indistinguishable from their high-fire twins. This leads us to ask, why don't more potters fire to cone 6/7 in reduction?

Making the Switch

There seem to be a few obstacles in getting potters to convert to the idea of mid-range firing. First, there is the inertia of their current practice. Change is hard in spite of the obvious benefits, especially if you have been doing the same thing for 20 years and it is working.

Mid-Range Fluxes

Glazes contain alumina and silica, which both melt at very high temperatures, so getting them to melt at mid-range temperatures requires different fluxes than those used at high-fire temperatures:

Sodium Oxide ($Na_2$0) is a strong alkaline flux and creates brightly colored glazes. It has a melting point of 1652°F (900°C) and a high expansion/contraction rate, which will often cause crazing in glazes. It is often found in association with potassium oxide in feldspars. Common mid-range sources include sodium feldspars (nepheline syenite—actually a feldspathoid—is the lowest melting feldspar and so it is often used at midrange because it is high in sodium and lower in silica than other feldspars and melts around cone 6), soda ash, wood ash, borax, frits and Gerstley borate or its substitutes.

Lithium Oxide (Li_2O) is the lightest weight, smallest particle size and most powerful of the alkaline fluxes with a strong color response similar to sodium and potassium oxides. It has a melting point of 1472°F (800°C) and has a low expansion/contraction rate, which can cause shivering in glazes. Sources include lithium feldspars and lithium carbonate.

Zinc Oxide (ZnO) is an auxiliary flux in oxidizing atmospheres. It has a dramatic color response, both good and bad, depending on the colorant. It can heighten colors with copper and cobalt oxides, but produces dull colors with chrome oxide. It has a melting point of 3587°F (1975°C), but if it is fired in reduction it will change to the metal zinc and volatilize at 1742°F (950°C). It has a low expansion/contraction rate, so it can help to reduce crazing. Sources include zinc oxide and calcined zinc oxide.

Boron Oxide (B_2O_3) is a glass former and a flux with a molecular structure similar to alumina. It melts at 1292°F (700°C) but begins melting at 572°F (300°C). It has a low expansion/contraction rate and produces good color response in glazes, with characteristic bluish, milky streaks and cloudy effects. Sources include Gerstley borate (or its substitutes like Gillespie Borate, Murray's Borate, Laguna Borate, etc.), borax, and frits.

Note: Frits come in a wide range of types. They are used by industry as reliable and consistent sources of fluxing oxides in relatively insoluble form. They are relatively low in alumina and silica and are active melters, but they can settle rapidly.

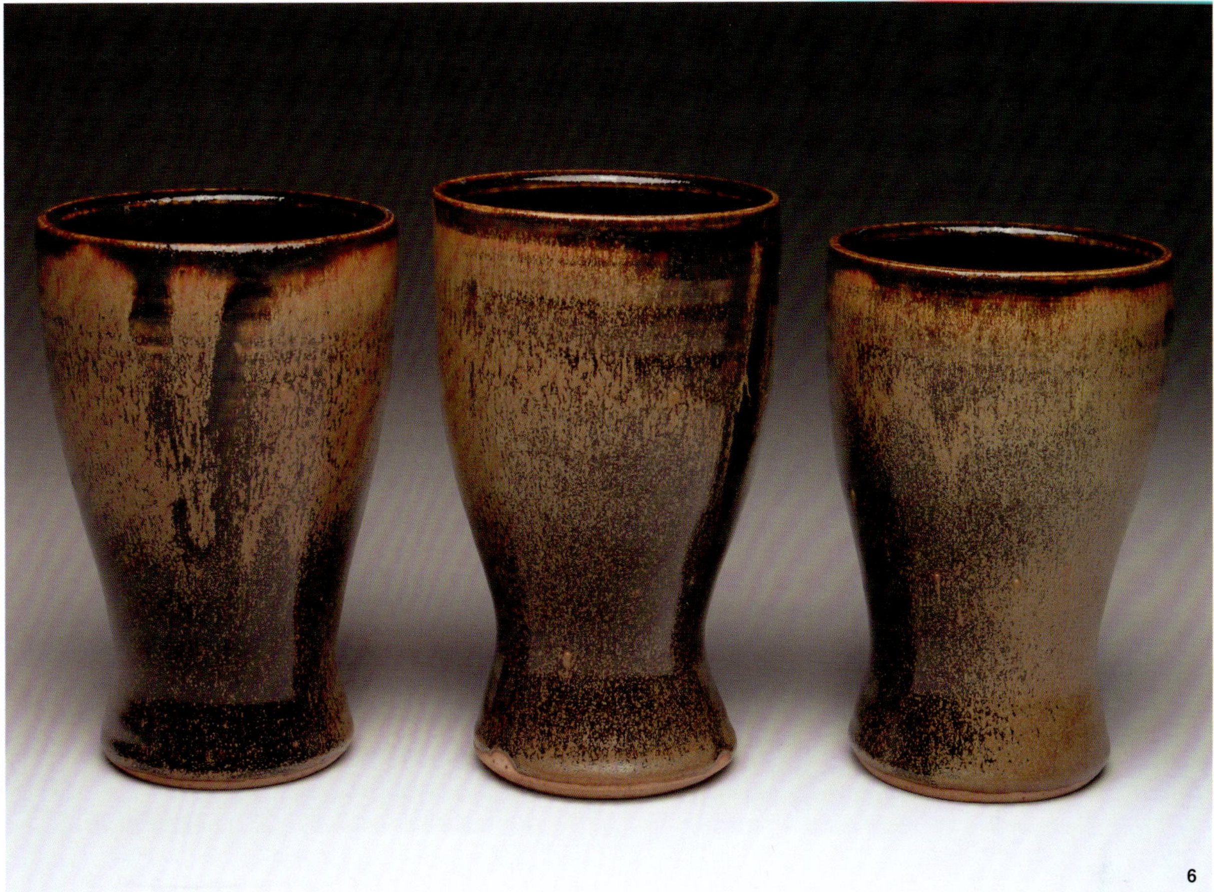

Tumblers, 7 in. (18 cm) in height, stoneware, Temmoku Gold liner, Raw Sienna exterior glaze, gas reduction fired to cone 6, by Erik Haagensen. See recipes on page 100.

Also, there is an underlying belief, although it is completely incorrect, that cone 10 is superior to mid-range or low-fire, and changing this mind set is an educational challenge. I think that this comes from the long historical European search to imitate Chinese high-fire porcelain. The goal was always to achieve high fire, so it gained the psychological high ground.

When you mention mid-range, potters immediately think, as I initially did, of mid-range electric oxidation. But this is not the only way to fire mid-range. Mid-range reduction has a completely different look, as does mid-range oxidation soda firing or mid-range reduction soda firing.

And finally, when you mention firing to mid-range, potters immediately want to change or convert their cone 10 glazes to this lower temperature. This is perceived as a significant challenge because it means that they will have to learn a glaze calculation software and unity molecular formulation. Most just want recipes that work. They know it will take time and effort to learn to convert all these recipes and they just don't want to spend their time doing that.

I don't recommend converting glazes to the lower temperature, because when you lower the firing temperature of a glaze you are using different fluxing oxides that have different color responses. So although it is possible to convert your glaze to the lower temperature, you will end up with a different glaze anyway. It is better to use the many tried and true mid-range glazes already in use and test them in your cycle. This is the same way potters find high-fire glazes; they get glaze recipes from books or from friends and then vary the colorants and opacifiers.

Although change is hard, potters should focus on the benefits of firing mid-range reduction. First, as stated above, it saves fuel, reduces your carbon footprint and costs less. Second, it saves time. It may take 2–4 hours to

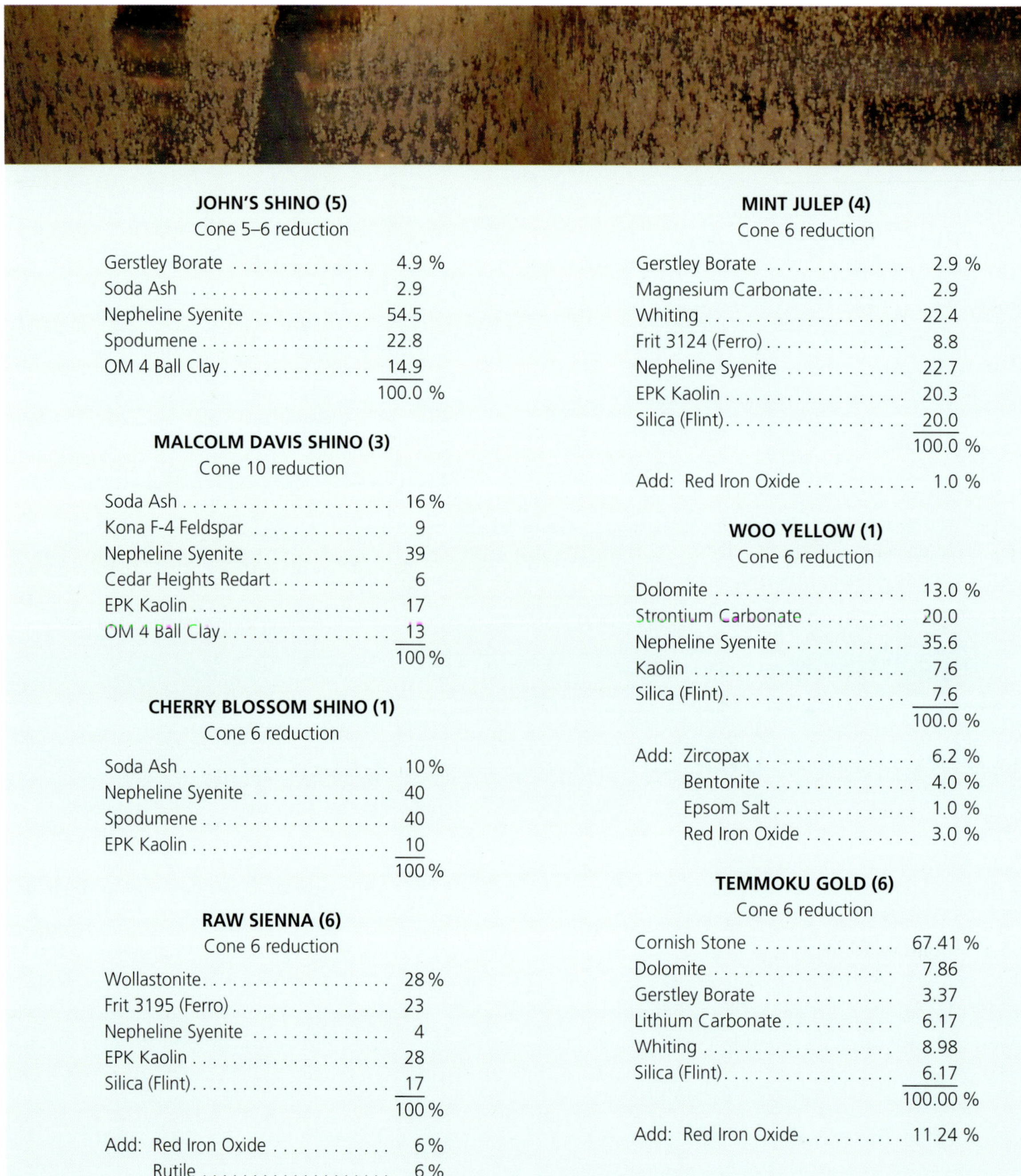

JOHN'S SHINO (5)
Cone 5–6 reduction

Gerstley Borate	4.9 %
Soda Ash	2.9
Nepheline Syenite	54.5
Spodumene	22.8
OM 4 Ball Clay	14.9
	100.0 %

MALCOLM DAVIS SHINO (3)
Cone 10 reduction

Soda Ash	16 %
Kona F-4 Feldspar	9
Nepheline Syenite	39
Cedar Heights Redart	6
EPK Kaolin	17
OM 4 Ball Clay	13
	100 %

CHERRY BLOSSOM SHINO (1)
Cone 6 reduction

Soda Ash	10 %
Nepheline Syenite	40
Spodumene	40
EPK Kaolin	10
	100 %

RAW SIENNA (6)
Cone 6 reduction

Wollastonite	28 %
Frit 3195 (Ferro)	23
Nepheline Syenite	4
EPK Kaolin	28
Silica (Flint)	17
	100 %
Add: Red Iron Oxide	6 %
Rutile	6 %

MINT JULEP (4)
Cone 6 reduction

Gerstley Borate	2.9 %
Magnesium Carbonate	2.9
Whiting	22.4
Frit 3124 (Ferro)	8.8
Nepheline Syenite	22.7
EPK Kaolin	20.3
Silica (Flint)	20.0
	100.0 %
Add: Red Iron Oxide	1.0 %

WOO YELLOW (1)
Cone 6 reduction

Dolomite	13.0 %
Strontium Carbonate	20.0
Nepheline Syenite	35.6
Kaolin	7.6
Silica (Flint)	7.6
	100.0 %
Add: Zircopax	6.2 %
Bentonite	4.0 %
Epsom Salt	1.0 %
Red Iron Oxide	3.0 %

TEMMOKU GOLD (6)
Cone 6 reduction

Cornish Stone	67.41 %
Dolomite	7.86
Gerstley Borate	3.37
Lithium Carbonate	6.17
Whiting	8.98
Silica (Flint)	6.17
	100.00 %
Add: Red Iron Oxide	11.24 %

get the extra temperature of cone 10 and maybe longer depending on the size of the kiln. So rather than firing for 10–12 hours you will be out in 8–10 hours. Firing to mid-range also reduces the wear and tear on your kiln, which means that it lasts longer. Finally, and most importantly, you get great results!

After all this testing, we discovered that the methods used to test high-fire glaze types also apply to mid-range types and, as a result, we found some very nice glazes. Erik, Luba and the potters of MudFire Clayworks are proof of that. Hopefully, this will help other potters get started firing to mid-range reduction.

Atmospheric-like Effects for Electric Firing

by Steven Hill

It can be a daunting experience for the novice to build and fire a fuel-burning kiln. Compared to their "fire-breathing brethren," electric kilns are safe, affordable, and predictable. Installing and firing an electric kiln is not much more complicated than an electric clothes drier. Because of this, many feel like they make the choice out of necessity, but the typical cone 6 electric-fired pot, with its shiny and rather flat glazes, leaves many potters wanting more. Firing to cone 10 opens up some possibilities, but many electric kilns are limited to cone 6.

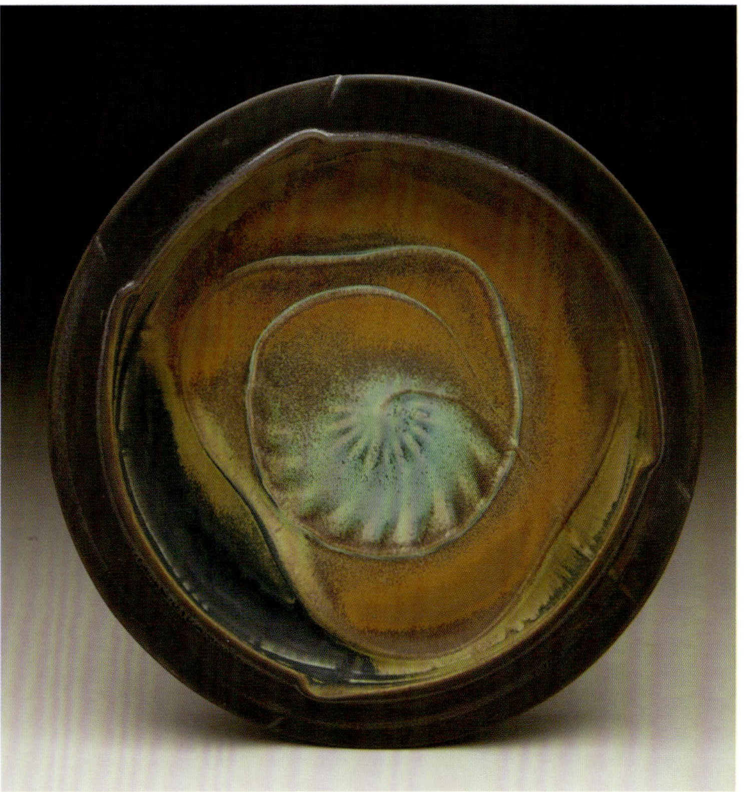

Platter, 16 in. (41 cm) in diameter, thrown and altered porcelain, with ribbed and trailed slip, multiple sprayed glazes, single-fired to cone 6 in an electric kiln, 2011.

My goal is to dispel the myth that electric firing has to involve compromise. I would also like to encourage potters to take additional responsibility for their surfaces rather than blaming or crediting the kiln gods. Gradually, over the course of my career, I have learned that kiln atmosphere has less impact on the surface of my pottery than I once thought. This is based on my techniques of layering multiple glazes. I want to help potters who are seeking the soft, textured, and varied surfaces traditionally associated with reduction and atmospheric firings to achieve those surfaces regardless of the firing process. After a little rethinking and adjusting of firing cycles and glazing techniques, you just might be able to free yourself of the alleged limitations of electric firing.

Firing

Fuel-burning kilns tend to be much larger than electric kilns. Because of their size, they usually have a slower heat rise, a soak at the top temperature, and slower cooling cycles. If you want similar results from an electric kiln, especially when firing to cone 6, one of the most important things you can do is emulate the heating and the cooling cycles of larger kilns. This means slowing the temperature gain to about 100°F (38°F) an hour during the last several hours of the firing, soaking the kiln at the top temperature, and then down-firing to slow the cooling cycle. Electric kilns are built with thinner insulation and legs (to allow for air circulation), and they cool very quickly, especially at higher temperatures. If you are seeking buttery, matte surfaces but have trouble achieving them in the electric kiln, it is most likely due to fast cooling. Matte surfaces are usually caused by microcrystal growth during cooling, and, if the cooling cycle is too steep, there isn't enough time for crystals to develop. In extreme cases, I've even seen matte glazes go glossy and transparent.

I came to electric firing with a basic understanding of the significance of the cooling cycle but had my eyes further opened after reading *The Many Faces of Iron* by Dr. Carol Marians in *Glazes and Glazing: Finishing Techniques.* Originally published in the June 2007 issue of CM, the article describes a controlled experiment in which one application method, one clay body, one forming process, one firing cycle, and seven different cooling cycles were applied to one cone 6 iron saturate glaze. Amazingly, the results looked like seven different glazes.

I fired cone 10 gas reduction for 38 years, but, when I began electric firing, I knew it was time to drop my firing temperature in order to preserve elements and electricity. My first experiments were at cone 8, but, to make the final transition to cone 6, I needed to reformulate glazes. With the help of my science/art-major assistant, Mike Stumbras, and Digitalfire's glaze calculation program Insight, I was able to make the transition rather smoothly. It's beyond the scope of this article, but I have found the journey from cone 10 to cone 6 inspiring, and it has revitalized my sense of experimentation.

Glazing

In electric firing—and especially at cone 6— it is natural to achieve flat, solid colors that look more paint-like than glazes in reduction firing. If you are seeking a softer effect with more variation and atmospheric qualities, it is up to you to achieve it through glaze application. Remember, the atmosphere is static in an electric kiln, and it's not going to happen naturally!

Throughout my career, there have been occasional "Ah-ha!" moments, backed up with lots of hard work. The latest revelation came through a conversation with Pete Pinnell, in which he helped me understand how I made the transition from gas reduction to electric oxidation as easily as I did. According to Pete, "In reduction firing, glazes can stratify into layers during the course of the firing. Longer firings and slower cooling cycles, along with the effects of reduction, can result in the creation of complex structures that can result in a variety of beautiful visual effects. Even seemingly opaque glazes can have enough translucency for one layer to subtly affect the next, creating variation and softness in surface color. In oxidation, shorter firing cycles, faster cooling, and an oxidizing atmosphere can result in less layering, simpler structures and less interesting visual qualities." It just so happens I have been spraying multiple, undulating layers

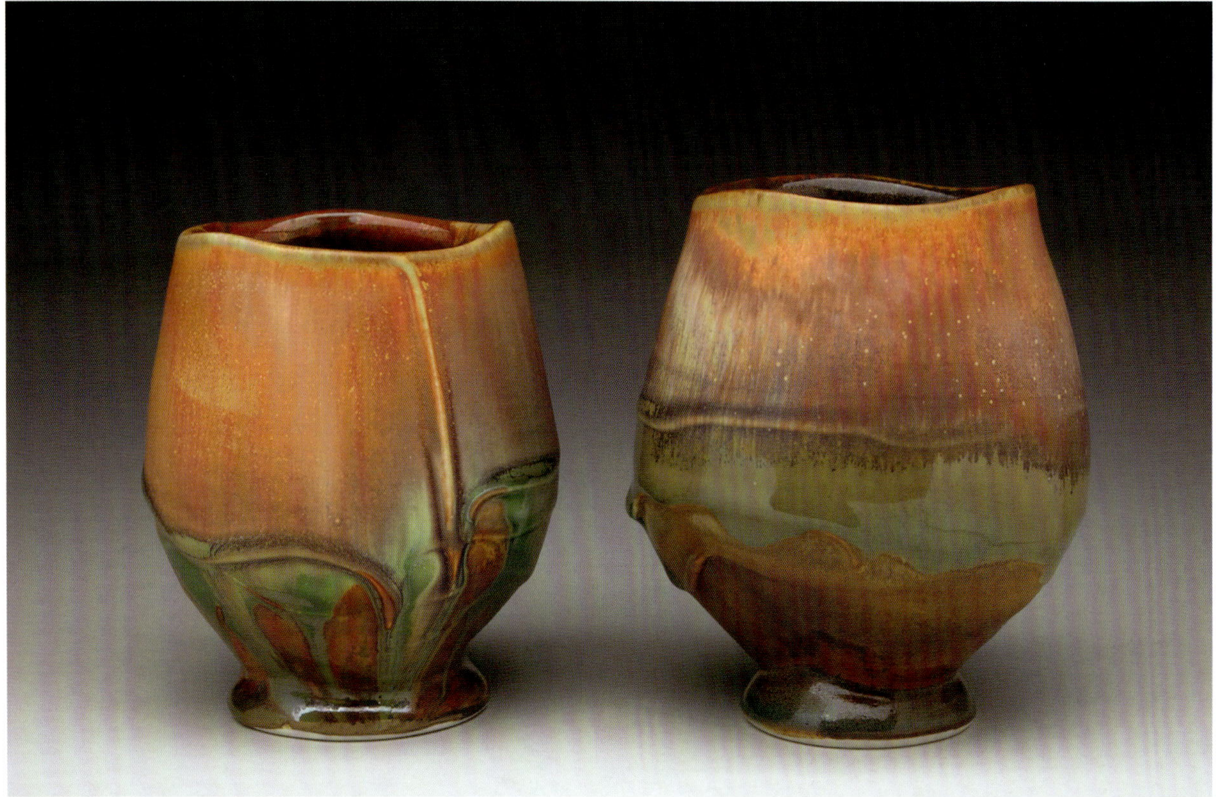

Pair of yunomis, to 4 in. (10 cm) in height, thrown and altered porcelain, applied slip design (either ribbed or slip trailing), multiple sprayed glazes, single-fired to cone 6 in an electric kiln, 2011.

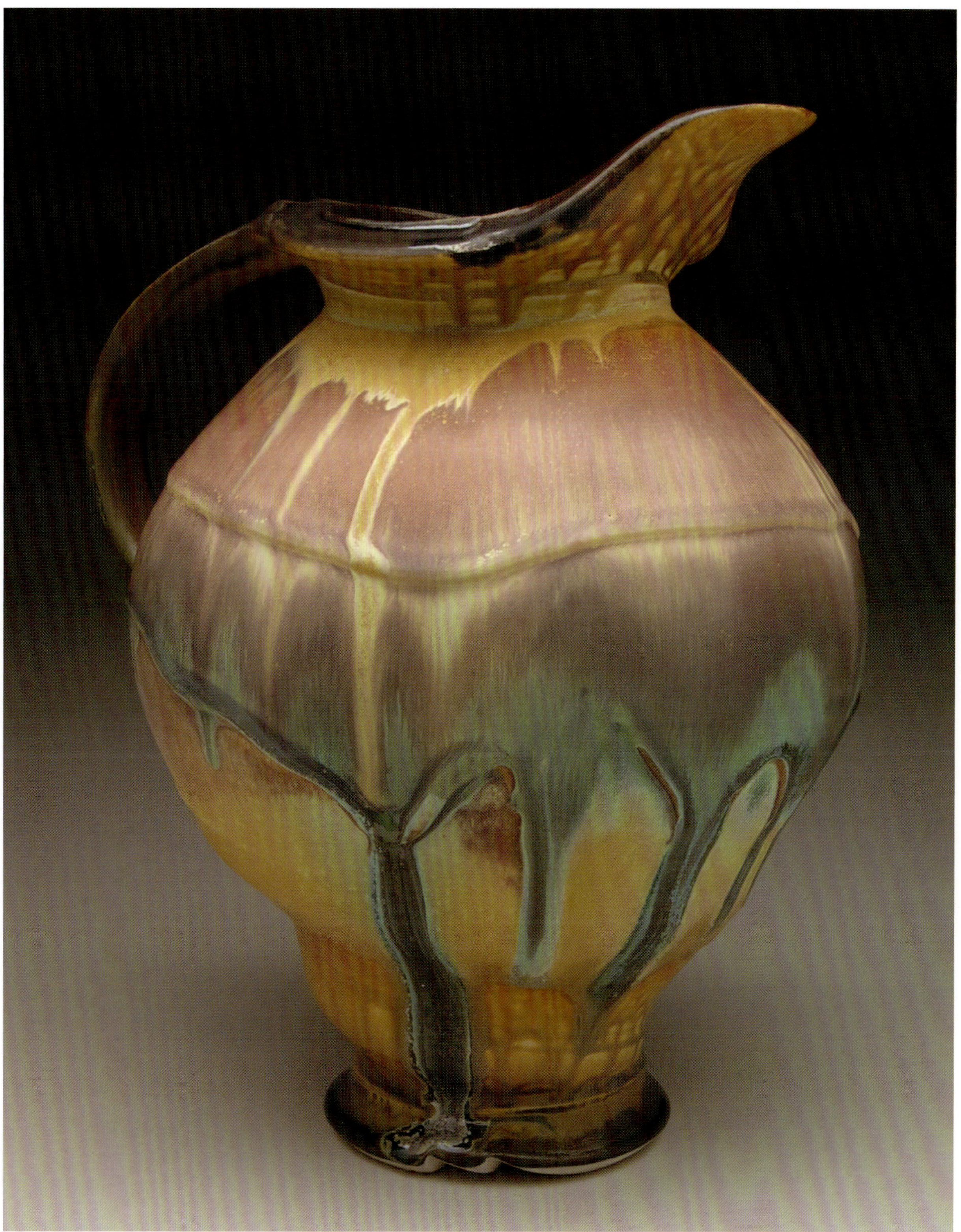

Melon Pitcher, 13 in. (33 cm) in height, thrown and altered porcelain, applied slip design (either ribbed or slip trailing), multiple sprayed glazes, single-fired to cone 6 in an electric kiln, 2011.

Glaze Spraying Tips

• I work with the same general glaze consistency for spraying as I do for dipping.

• Any glaze is suitable for spraying as long as you use an appropriate spray gun. If the glaze is particularly coarse, such as a chunky ash glaze, you can use a gun made for spraying textured ceilings.

• I use guns with an air adjustment, but no gauge, and set the line pressure for 50 or 60 lbs. While spraying, I adjust each gun down while watching the spray pattern.

– If you have too little air pressure the glaze will splatter.

– If it atomizes well, but is not too forceful of a spray, your gun is adjusted properly.

Gravity HVLP (high volume, low pressure) guns with stainless steel inner parts work well with glazes. They are available in both full size and detail guns. If I am aiming for broad coverage, I use a full size gun, but if I am highlighting small areas I use a detail gun.

• I always test the gun by spraying into the side of the booth before I spray the pot. This is to make sure the gun is adjusted and not clogged. Then I spray towards the area on the pot I want to glaze. Experienced sprayers often want to start spraying off the piece and move across it, this is fine as long as you are going for general coverage, but it doesn't give you enough control to highlight specific details.

• The most important spraying technique to know is feathering. This can be generally defined as applying the glaze sensitively and it can be accomplished with three different methods:

1. Spray short, overlapping, wispy strokes either back and forth or up and down. Use this technique to highlight details and on smaller pieces.

2. Hold the trigger down, keep the gun moving in a circular motion, and apply overlapping strokes, while slowly rotating the piece on a banding wheel. This gives you faster coverage, but less control over details.

3. For even application on symmetrical pots with no appendages, hold the trigger down as you spin the pot on a banding wheel, slowly making your way either up or down the side. This works well for evenly applying one glaze or blending horizontal bands of color.

• One of the challenges of spraying is to know when enough glaze has been applied. Watch for the sprayed glaze turning to liquid on the surface and you will be close. There is no substitute for the intuition gained through repeated practice.

• I always use an underlying base glaze and think of glazes layered over it as modifiers. The base establishes the general character and also helps insure that the final result is more cohesive. The modifiers are used to enliven the surface and introduce color and/or texture change.

• Keep in mind that you don't want the total glaze thickness to be much thicker than when dipping or pouring. You might want to layer 4 glazes, but you should never apply 4 full layers of glaze. One of the advantages of spraying is that you have the ability to apply anything from a dusting to a full coat. If I am layering, I just spray less of each glaze. The only way to make effective decisions about blending and thickness is through experimentation.

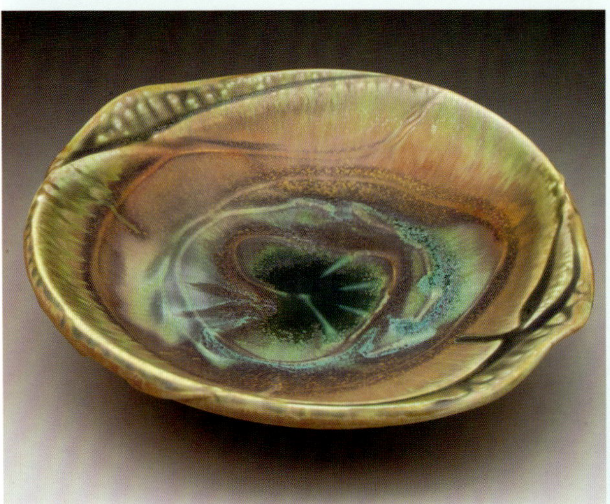

Plate, 11 in. (28 cm) in diameter, thrown and altered porcelain, ribbed slip design, multiple sprayed glazes, single-fired to cone 6 in an electric kiln, 2011.

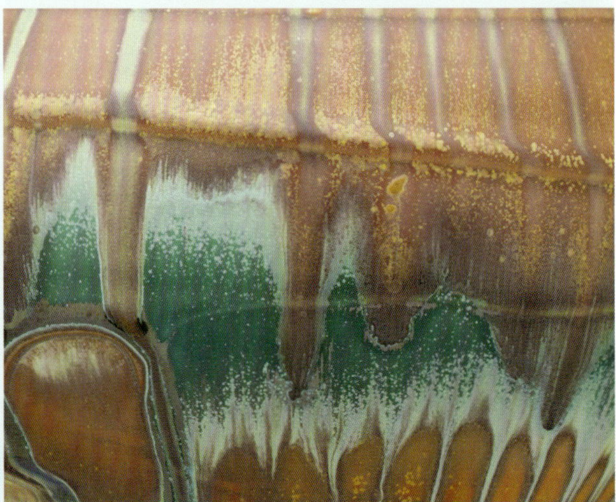

Detail of glaze surface created by spraying layers of different glazes over one another to achieve an atmospheric-like effect.

Recipes

I am constantly searching for new glazes that will stir my soul and inspire previously inaccessible colors or textures. I both formulate and collect glazes from other sources, but I am constantly experimenting with new combinations. The base glaze that underlies many of the surfaces and encourages crystal formation on my pots is Strontium Crystal Magic (SCM), which began as a Tom Coleman glaze, Yellow Crystal Matte. Through an extended series of experiments and the shift from barium to strontium, it ended up far enough afield to warrant renaming. It is rather dull by itself, but it brings glazes layered over it to life.

SCM—Warm loves iron-saturated glazes sprayed over it for rich earth tones. SCM-Cool can develop icy colors with cobalt or copper glazes sprayed over it. Shiny transparent glazes can break from matt to glossy depending on the thickness used. I have never sprayed a workable cone 6 glaze over SCM that didn't show some potential. If you have any interesting cone 6 glazes, I would love to add them to my ongoing glaze experiment.

STRONTIUM CRYSTAL MAGIC—WARM

Cone 6 oxidation

Ingredient	%
Lithium Carbonate	4.5 %
Strontium Carbonate	12.6
Whiting	17.3
Ferro Frit 3124	4.5
Custer Feldspar	45.9
EPK Kaolin	15.2
	100.0 %
Add: Titanium Dioxide	13.8 %
Yellow Iron Oxide	2.8 %
Bentonite	2.3 %

Combine with iron-saturated glazes for rich earth tones.

STRONTIUM CRYSTAL MAGIC—COOL

Cone 6 oxidation

Ingredient	%
Lithium Carbonate	5.7 %
Strontium Carbonate	12.4
Whiting	16.8
Ferro Frit 3124	5.7
Custer Feldspar	22.5
Nepheline Syenite	22.5
EPK Kaolin	14.4
	100.0 %
Add: Titanium Dioxide	13.5 %
Bentonite	2.0 %

Combine with glazes containing either copper or cobalt to develop icy colors.

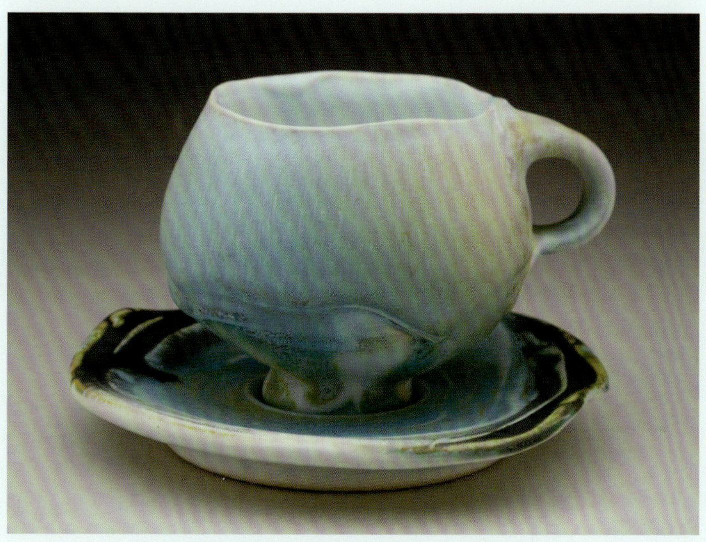

Mug and saucer, 4½ in. (12 cm) in height, thrown and altered porcelain, applied slip, sprayed glazes, single-fired to cone 6 in an electric kiln, 2011.

of contrasting glaze on my pieces for most of my career in an effort to achieve a more atmospheric look. In effect, my sprayed layers are accomplishing what happens naturally in reduction firing, and these layers give my surfaces the softness and variation commonly associated with reduction firing.

If you apply thin coats of two or more contrasting glazes, they will intermingle as they melt, but the layers never mix thoroughly. The result shows up as soft and subtle surface variation. You can apply multiple layers by any number of methods—dipping, pouring, brushing, splattering, sponging, etc.—but spraying gives you the opportunity to subtly modulate the thickness of each layer, varying glaze surface and color in a way that has the potential to look natural and organic.

A totally separate issue in the oxidation vs. reduction debate is color development. Some coloring oxides change color when fired in reduction. The most dramatic of these is copper, which changes from green to red. So, I'm not trying to say that my oxidation-fired pots look just like they would in reduction, but rather that they have all of the subtleness and variation that they once had when fired in reduction and that many of them show no appreciable difference.

Certainly, not all glazes will create inspired surfaces when layered. In my never-ending quest to find new and magical combinations, there are enormous benefits from experimenting with many different types of glazes. Layering similar glazes will create subtle variations, while using highly contrasting glazes can lead to more drama. If you alternate matte and glossy glazes in layers, it will encourage surfaces to break. If you layer light and dark colors, you will get variation in both color and value.

Geoffrey Wheeler uses stains to color his glazes, and he will often color both matte and transparent glazes similarly. When spraying these two glazes, he blends the matte glaze gradually into the transparent glaze, creating a surface that, while uniform in color, gradually breaks from matte to glossy.

Most of my pots have four to eight glazes applied in overlapping layers, and my biggest challenge is making everything look cohesive. Some glazes are sprayed with techniques that isolate one from the other others, like the black or white glazes I apply on the rim of a bowl or the rim, handle, and foot of a pitcher, but most are layered and blended. My intention is for the whole pot to look as if it is one rich and varied surface, much like agate, marble, or layers of metamorphic rock. I want my glazes to ebb and flow (but not run too much!) with color and surface texture gently emphasizing changes in the form. I work with microcrystalline glazes, which can resemble a snowstorm or falling leaves, and use ash-like glazes to encourage streaking, leaving vivid traces of interaction as they melt. Most of my glaze combinations are rather unstable to work with, but, at their best, they have an amazing ability to allure and captivate. One thing is certain: They are never boringly predictable—just as unstable people are often more captivating, enticing, and provocative than those we regard as pillars of the community.

If you think about the flame, ash, salt, or soda responsible for the soft surface variations we characterize as atmospheric effects, the common denominator is that they travel through the kiln via the kiln's draft. When you spray glazes, the spray has the potential to wrap around the piece and move past it in much the same way as the draft moves past a pot in a fuel-burning kiln. Spraying layers of overlapping glazes gives you the ability to create surfaces that naturally flow across a piece, softly highlighting its form. As sublime as this can be at its best, insensitive use of a spray gun can lead to surfaces characterized by obvious spray patterns and blotchy color. With experience, however, spraying glazes has the potential to integrate seamlessly with the form.

Think about how clumsy and uncoordinated your hands felt when you first attempted to throw on the potters' wheel, and compare your experience to how naturally and intuitively a seasoned potter's hands move across the form, applying pressure just where it is needed. The results achieved as a beginning sprayer are not too dissimilar, but, fortunately, the learning curve is much quicker when learning to spray than it is for throwing!

Spraying has the potential to be every bit as painterly as decorating with brush in hand. As with any painting, you will benefit from both a clear vision of what you are trying to create and the flexibility to let the process lead you in directions you never imagined.

The journey into spraying as my main method of glazing began more than 35 years ago. For most of that time, my goal was simply to create atmospheric surfaces on pottery fired in a gas reduction kiln. When I made the transition to electric firing in December 2008, I was lucky—I had already laid the groundwork for success, or, as Pinnell says, "Luck favors the prepared mind."

48 Learn more about how to raw glaze and single fire work.

Opaque Glazes

by John Britt

In addition to the base glaze tests with Zircopax, tin oxide, and titanium dioxide opacifiers on page 110, John Britt shares several additional recipes and line blends using opacifiers and various clay bodies.

SELSOR RED (1–2)

Cone 6 Reduction

Gerstley Borate	12.50 %
Whiting	10.41
Nepheline Syenite	56.26
Silica	20.83
	100.00 %
Add: Copper Carbonate	0.80 %
Tin Oxide	1.50 %

1 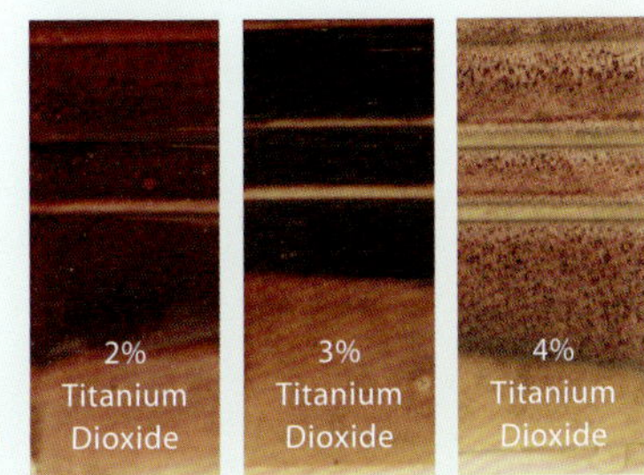

Selsor Red with additions of titanium dioxide on Frost porcelain, fired to cone 6 in reduction.

2 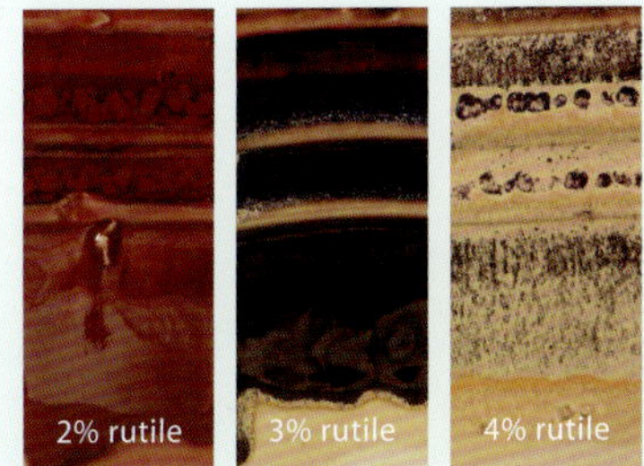

Selsor Red with additions of rutile on Frost porcelain, fired to cone 6 in reduction.

3 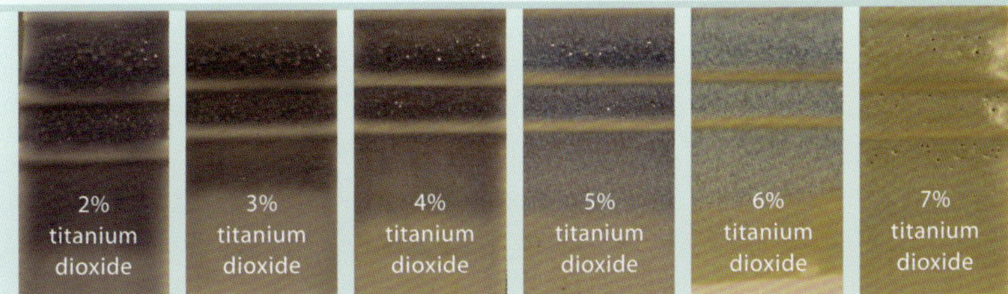

John's 10x Series #11 Blue Glaze with titanium dioxide variations on Frost porcelain.

4 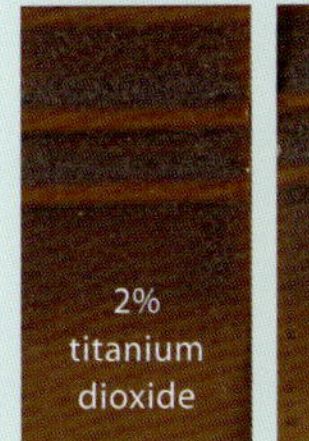

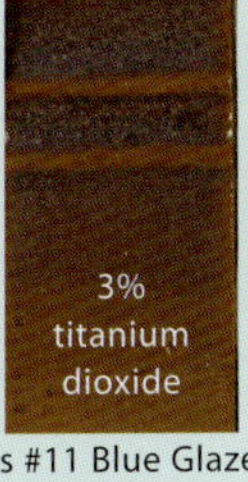

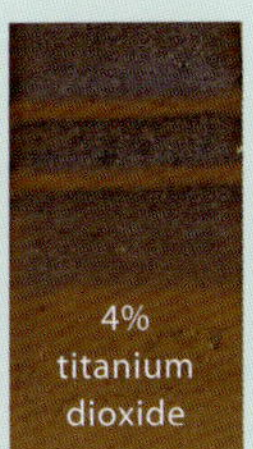

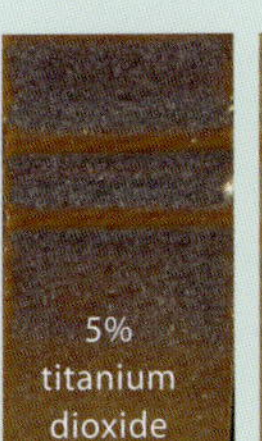

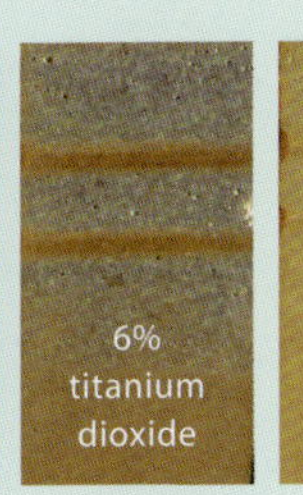

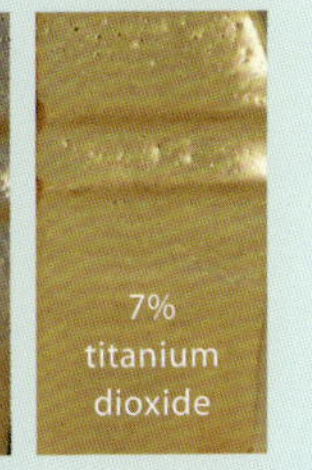

John's 10x Series #11 Blue Glaze with titanium dioxide variations on stoneware.

5 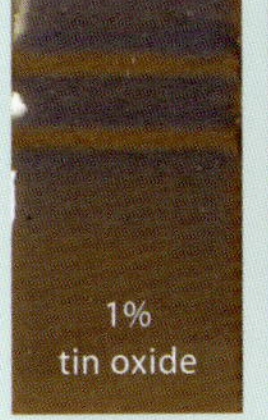

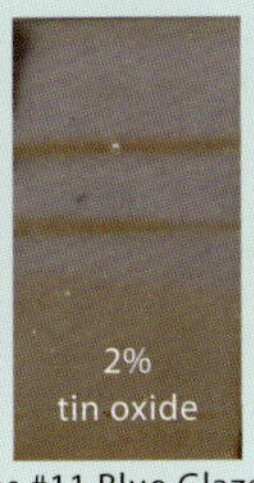

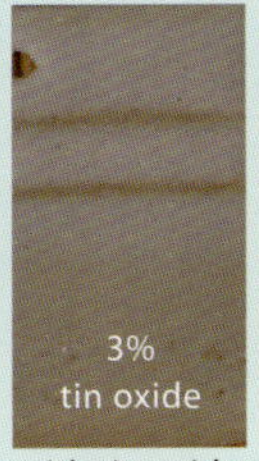

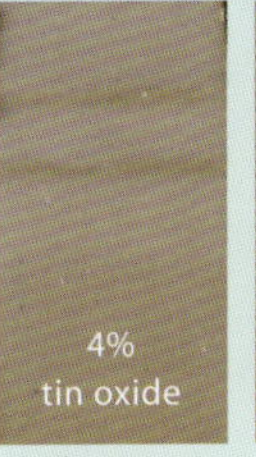

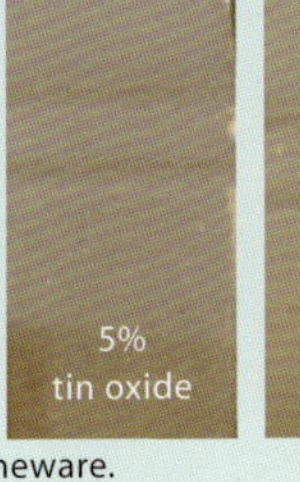

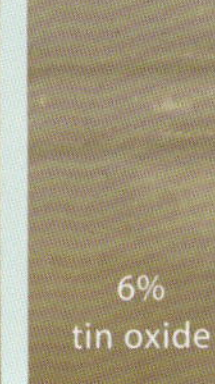

John's 10x Series #11 Blue Glaze with tin oxide variations on stoneware.

6 2% tin oxide
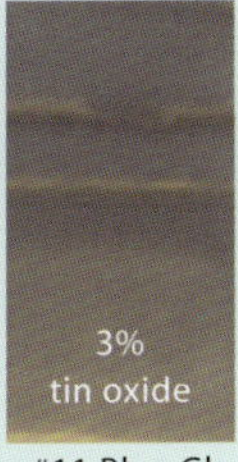

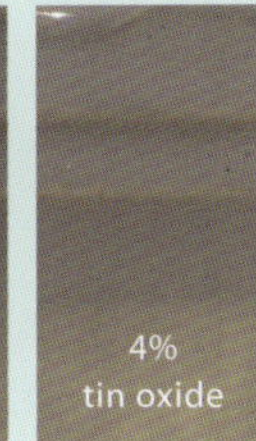

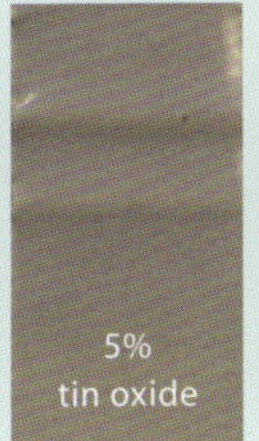

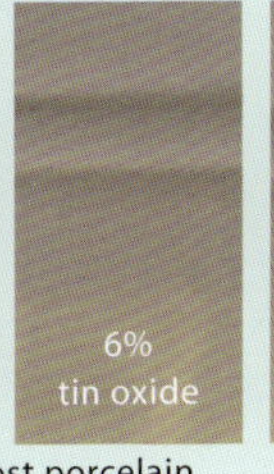

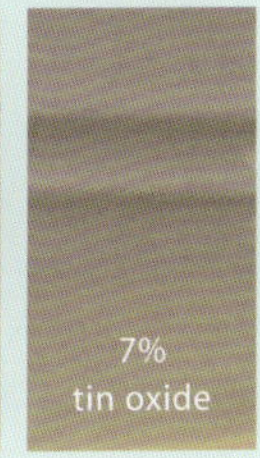

John's 10x Series #11 Blue Glaze with tin oxide variations on Frost porcelain.

JOHN'S 10x SERIES #11 BLUE GLAZE (3–6)

Cone 6 oxidation or reduction

Talc	10 %
Wollastonite	10
Ferro Frit 3134	10
Ferro Frit 3195	10
Custer Feldspar	10
Spodumene	10
Ball Clay	10
Kaolin	10
Silica (200 mesh)	10
Silica (325 mesh)	10
	100 %
Add: Cobalt Carbonate	0.25 %

The color of this blue glaze changes depending on the amount of opacifier added.

The John's 10x Series #11 Blue Glaze tiles were fired in an electric kiln.

23 Read about the characteristics of different opacifiers.

Versatile Cone 6 Glazes

by Julia Galloway

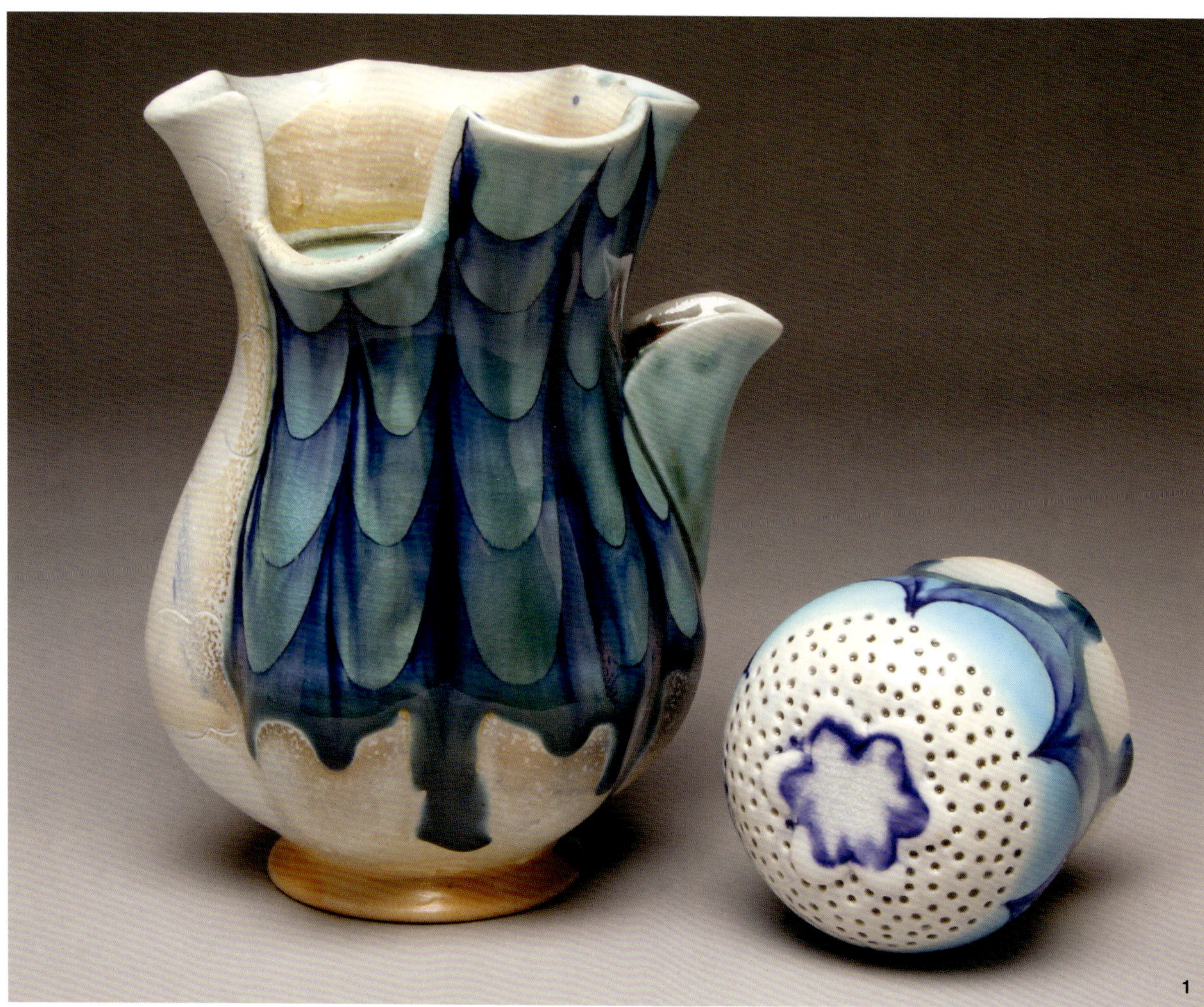
1

I layer glazes over and next to each other to create depth and support the ideas in my work. Putting glazes into a few different categories helps me to better understand color and surface to develop ideas for surface decoration. First is a paint-chip glaze: a glaze of straight color. It's extremely reliable and what you see is what you get, over and over again. The Karros Base that I use is a great example of this. Second is a historical glaze: a glaze with strong historical ties. The glaze itself can influence the content in the work. The Water Blue Glaze I work with mimics the high-alkaline glazes from early Iranian pots. Third is the phenomena glaze: a glaze that changes when it is fired. From this type of glaze, you gain a sense that the material has had an experience of firing or time passage. When it fumes and develops crystal growth, Some Bright Green is an example of this kind of glaze. Often a glaze will fit into two of these categories.

I fire to a soft cone 6 in a soda kiln. During the glaze firing, I introduce very little soda. My kiln is two shelves deep (12×24-inch shelves) and I spray the soda solution into the kiln when cone 5 gets soft. I use about 2 pounds of soda ash mixed with two gallons of hot water. I fire in as clean an atmosphere as possible; however, I always get a little reduction when I spray in the soda.

HAMADA BASE (REVISED FOR CONE 6) (2,3)

Cone 6 oxidation or Reduction

Barium Carbonate	16.49 %
Whiting	9.28
Zinc Oxide	9.28
Custer Feldspar	54.64
Minspar 200 Feldspar	8.25
Ball Clay	2.06
	100.00 %
Add: Bentonite	2.06 %
For Dark Green	
Add: Copper Carbonate:	3.09 %
Red Iron Oxide	3.09 %
Rutile Oxide:	2.06 %
For Light Blue	
Add: Copper Oxide:	2.06 %
For Blue	
Add: Cobalt Carbonate:	0.26 %
Rutile:	3.09 %

The original recipe for this glaze came from Kim Dickey, and it was a cone 10 glaze. This is a high-barium, satin glaze. I do not use it in any areas that come in contact with food. It produces beautiful blues and greens with copper, iron, and rutile.

I often use many variations of coloring oxides in this base together. In addition, I put spots or lines of Chartreuse Base glaze on top of this glaze to make it run like crazy. I fire it to cone 6 in a soda kiln.

KARROS BASE REVISED (1)

Cone 5 Oxidation or Reduction

Gerstley Borate	10.71 %
Whiting	3.57
Wollastonite	7.14
Ferro Frit 3124	5.36
Minspar 200 Feldspar	9.82
Nepheline Syenite	18.75
EPK Kaolin	8.94
Silica	35.71
	100.00 %
Add: Bentonite	1.79 %
For Red	
Add: Encapsulated Red Stain	8.93 %
Rutile	1.79 %
For Orange	
Add: Degussa Orange Stain	7.14 %
Rutile	3.57 %

This is an older variation of Karros Base. It is a reliable and consistent glaze. I use this base glaze both as a clear glaze and with a variety of metallic oxide colorants and stains to get strong colors.

In general I add 5–10% commercial stain, with an additional 2–4% metallic oxides to get different colors.

I fire this glaze to cone 5 in a soda kiln.

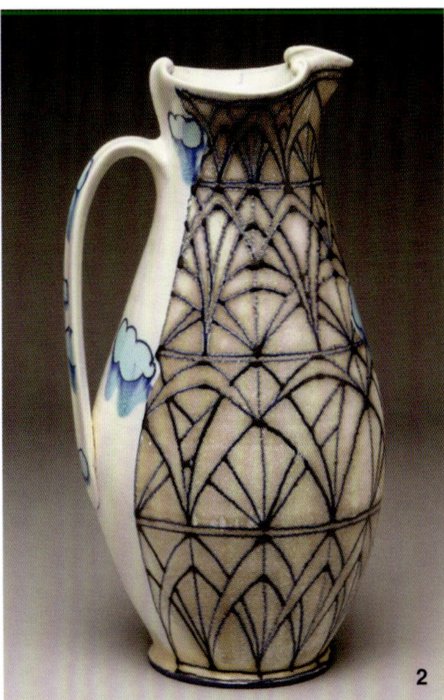

2

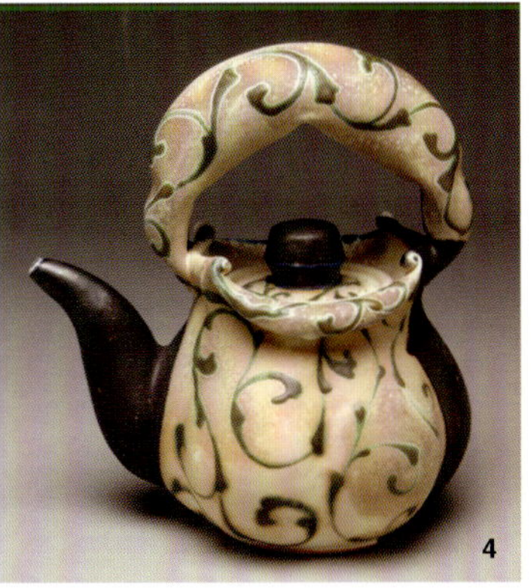

4

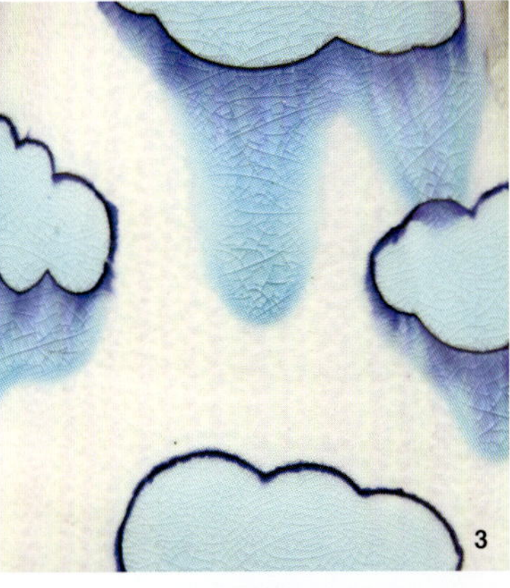

3

1, 5 Water ewer with blue inlay slip, water blue glaze on the outside and Karros base with 8% Degussa orange stain and 2% rutile oxide on the foot. The cup is pierced and the holes are filled with Karros Base with no colorant. Chartreuse Base (clear) is brushed on top of the cloud on the very top of the cup.
2, 3 Pitcher with blue slip inlaid cloud pattern on one side. After the bisque firing, Chartreuse Base (clear) was applied with a slip-trailing bottle over the incised slip lines, and a layer of Hamada Base with 2% copper carbonate was painted inside of the cloud lines. The Chartreuse Base pulled the cobalt from the slip and the copper from the Hamada Base glaze. The other side of the pitcher has flashing slip as the base layer with Metallic Black glaze applied using a slip trailer to create the arch pattern. It is not as matte as on the teapot (4), because it was exposed to more soda during the firing.
4 Teapot, dipped in flashing slip at a stiff leather-hard stage before bisque firing. It has Some Bright Green glaze slip trailed on the sides, handle, and lid, and Metallic Black glaze on the knob, spout, and back of pot.

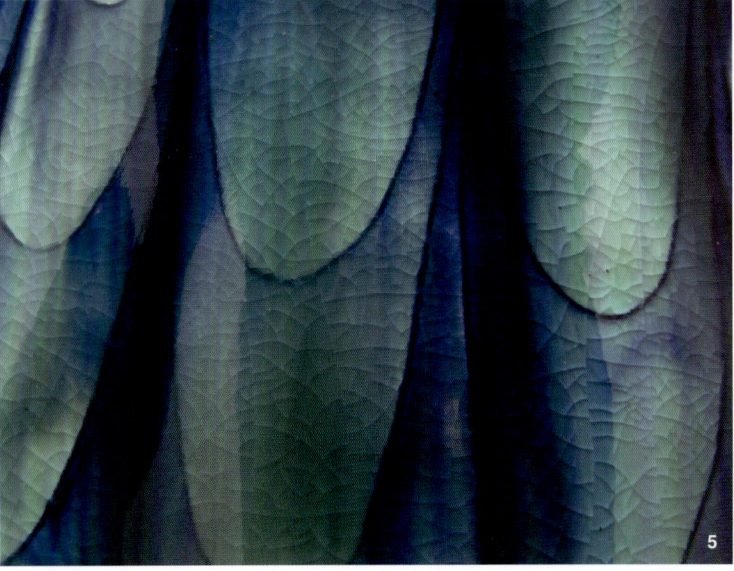

5

CHARTREUSE BASE (2,3)

Cone 04 Oxidation

Barium Carbonate	15.53 %
Lithium Carbonate	12.62
Whiting	4.85
Ferro Frit 3124	7.77
Nepheline Syenite	24.27
Ball Clay	2.92
Silica	32.04
	100.00 %

For Chartreuse

Add:	Chrome Oxide	0.24 %
	Bentonite	1.94 %

This is a low-fire, cone 04 glaze. I only use it on top of other glazes. When I put it on top of Hamada Base or Some Bright Green and fire to cone 6, it helps the glazes run beautifully. This glaze will bubble if fired alone to cone 6. In addition, I use this glaze applied lightly over slip inlay to encourage a streaky blue running glaze.

FLASHING SLIP (2,4)

Cone 6 Oxidation or Reduction

Whiting	10 %
6 Tile Kaolin	70
Grolleg Kaolin	20
	100 %

I dip my pots in this slip when the clay is a stiff leather hard.

WATER BLUE GLAZE (1,5)

Cone 04 Oxidation

Gerstley Borate	6 %
Ferro Frit 3110	77
EPK Kaolin	7
Silica	10
	100 %

Add:	Copper Carbonate	4 %
	Bentonite	3 %

This is a low-fire glaze that is not food safe due to extensive crazing. Generally I use it in small amounts to accent knobs, spouts, and handles. I apply it thin with a brush, and over fire it to cone 6 in a soda kiln. This glaze bubbles if fired to cone 6 in an electric kiln, and I only use it in a soda kiln, as the extra flux from the soda smooths out the glaze. It also turns out better if I do a quicker firing.

SOME BRIGHT GREEN (REVISED) (4)

Cone 6 Oxidation or Reduction

Strontium Carbonate	28.18 %
Whiting	6.36
Zinc Oxide	9.09
Ferro Frit 3134	3.64
Custer Feldspar	40.91
Ball Clay	11.82
	100.00 %

Add:	Copper Carbonate	2.73 %
	Red Iron Oxide	1.82 %
	Rutile	2.73 %
	Bentonite	1.82 %

This recipe came from Jeff Oestreich. It's a deep satin emerald green that fumes beautifully when you add Epsom salts to it and fire it in a soda kiln. I mix the glaze thick and apply it with a slip-trailing bottle. This glaze is very sensitive to the atmosphere in the kiln. I do not use this glaze in areas that come in contact with food.

METALLIC BLACK (2,4)

Cone 6 Oxidation

Gerstley Borate	16.67 %
Whiting	5.56
Minspar 200 Feldspar	73.33
EPK Kaolin	4.44
	100.00 %

Add:	Cobalt Oxide	2.22 %
	Copper Oxide	4.44 %
	Manganese Dioxide	4.44 %
	Bentonite	2.00 %

This is a flat matte black glaze that is very heavy looking and not food safe. It is excellent for slip-trailing decoration. I add the manganese dioxide after I sieve the glaze, so it's a little clumpy. I like the unevenness of the glaze. I fire it to cone 6 in a soda kiln, and depending on placement in the kiln and the amount of soda it is exposed to, the surface can become slightly shiny during the glaze firing.

Expanding Your Palette in Mid-range Firing

by Yoko Sekino-Bové

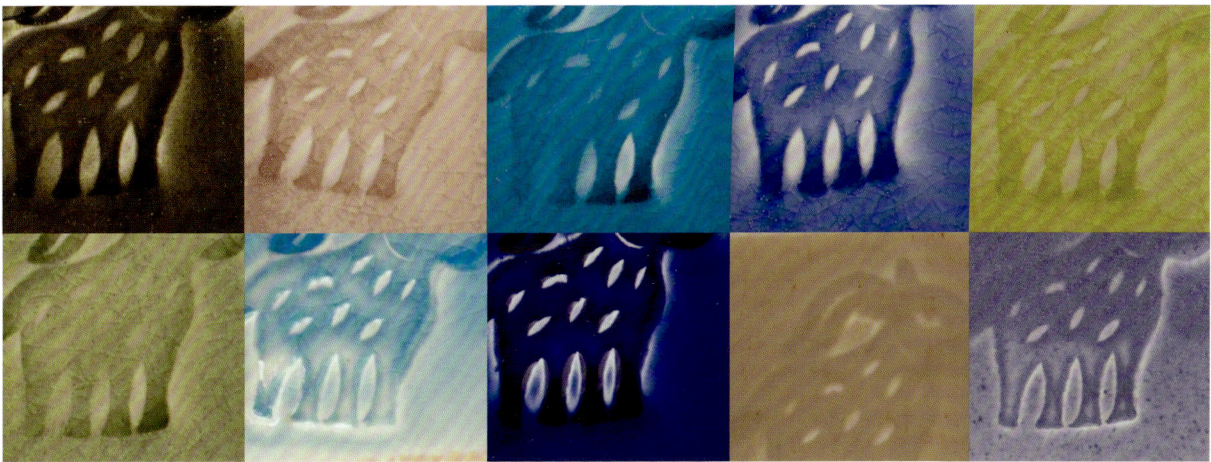

There are so many wonderful books, websites and even software that feature spectacular glaze formulas. Keeping that in mind, the focus of my glaze palette research was to establish a comprehensive visual library for everyone. Rather than just providing the reader with a few promising glaze formulas, this reference is a guideline. Because it is a guide, there are some test tiles that do not provide immediate use other than the suggestion of what to avoid, or the percentages of certain chemicals that exceed the safe food-serving level, etc., but I believe that this research will be a good tool for those who wish to experiment with, and push the boundaries of, mid-range firing.

Many people may be thinking about switching their firing method from high-fire to mid-range. For instance, students who recently graduated and lost access to school gas kilns, people with a day job and those who work in their garage studios who want to spend less time kiln sitting, or production potters who are concerned about fuel conservation and energy savings. This reference is intended as a tool for those people to start glaze experimentations at mid-range that can be accomplished with minimal resources.

There is no guarantee that this chart will work for everyone everywhere, since the variety between the different resources overwhelmingly affects the results, but by examining a few glazes in this chart you can speculate and make informed adjustments with your materials. This is why all the base glazes for this research use only simple materials that are widely available in the US.

Five years ago, when I was forced to switch to mid-range oxidation firing with an electric kiln, from gas-fueled reduction firing at high temperatures, most of my hard-earned knowledge in high-fire glazes had to be re-examined. Much to my frustration, many earth metal colorants exhibited completely different behaviors in oxidation firing. Also, problems in adhesion were prominent compared to high-fire glazes.

The role of oxides and carbonates used for texturing and opacifying were different as well. But compiling the available glazes and analyzing them were not enough. I felt there should be a simple chart with visual results that explained how the oxides and carbonates behave within this firing range. This motivated me to write a proposal for mid-range glaze research to the McKnight Foundation, which generously sponsors a three-month artist-in-residence program at the Northern Clay Center in Minneapolis, Minnesota.

Most of the tests presented in these experiments were executed at the Northern Clay Center from October to December in 2009 using clay and dry materials available at Continental Clay Co. The rest of the tests were completed after my residency at my home studio in Washington, Pennsylvania. For those tests, I used dry materials available from Standard Ceramics Supply Co.

N501 TRANSPARENT, GLOSSY, AND CRACKLES
Cone 5

Ingredient	%
Ferro Frit 3110	90 %
EPK Kaolin	10
	100 %

N502 TRANSPARENT AND GLOSSY
Cone 5

Ingredient	%
Gillespie Borate	30 %
Minspar 200 Feldspar	46
EPK Kaolin	13
Silica	11
	100 %

See chart on page 113 for test results. See page 114 for examples of this glaze base with added opacifiers.

N503 OPAQUE, GLOSSY, AND TEXTURED
Cone 5

Ingredient	%
Gillespie Borate	52.6 %
EPK Kaolin	21.0
Silica	26.4
	100.0 %
Add: Zircopax	10.0 %

N504 SEMI-OPAQUE, SEMI-SATIN WITH TEXTURES
Cone 5

Ingredient	%
Whiting	9.5 %
Ferro Frit 3124	44.5
F-4 Feldspar	20.0
Zinc Oxide	5.5
Bentonite*	7.5
EPK Kaolin	5.0
Silica	8.0
	100.0 %
Add: Zircopax	9.0 %

See chart on page 113 for test results.

* Bentonite is typically listed as an addition to recipes, but in larger amounts it contributes appreciably to the amount of alumina and silica in the recipe and is therefore included along with the clays in the list of the main ingredients.

N505 SATIN, OPAQUE WITH TEXTURES
Cone 5

Ingredient	%
Dolomite	12 %
Gillespie Borate	14
Wollastonite	10
Ferro Frit 3124	8
Cornwall Stone	46
EPK Kaolin	10
	100 %
Add: Magnesium Carbonate	6 %

Test Conditions

Clay body: Super White (cone 5–9) a white stoneware body for mid-range, commercially available from Continental Clay Co.

Bisque firing temperatures: Cone 05 (1910°F, 1043°C), fired in a manual electric kiln for approximately 10 hours.

Glaze firing temperatures: The coloring metals increment tests (page 50) were fired to cone 5 (2210°F, 1210°C) in a manual electric kiln for approximately 8 hours. The opacifier/texture metals increment tests (page 51) were fired to cone 5 in an automatic electric kiln for 8 hours.

Glaze batch: Each test was 300g, with a tablespoon of Epsom salts added as a flocculant.

Glazing method: Hand dipping. First dip (bottom half): 3 seconds. Second dip (top half) additional 4 seconds on top of the first layer, total 7 seconds.

Coloring Metals Increment Chart

The following colorants were tested: black nickel oxide, cobalt oxide, copper carbonate, chrome oxide, iron chromate, manganese dioxide, red iron oxide, rutile, and yellow ochre. You should note that tests with cobalt oxide and chrome oxide in high percentages were not executed due to the color predictability. Other blank tiles on the chart are because either the predictability or the percentages of oxides are too insignificant to affect the base glazes.

Depending on firing atmospheres, manganese dioxide exhibits a wide variety of colors. When fired in a tightly sealed electric kiln with small peepholes, the glaze color tends toward brown, compared to purple when fired in a kiln with many and/or large peepholes.

Please note that some of the oxides and carbonates in this test exceed the safety standard for use as tableware that comes in contact with food. Check safety standards before

Glaze base N502 with coloring oxides and carbonates

Glaze base N504 with coloring oxides and carbonates

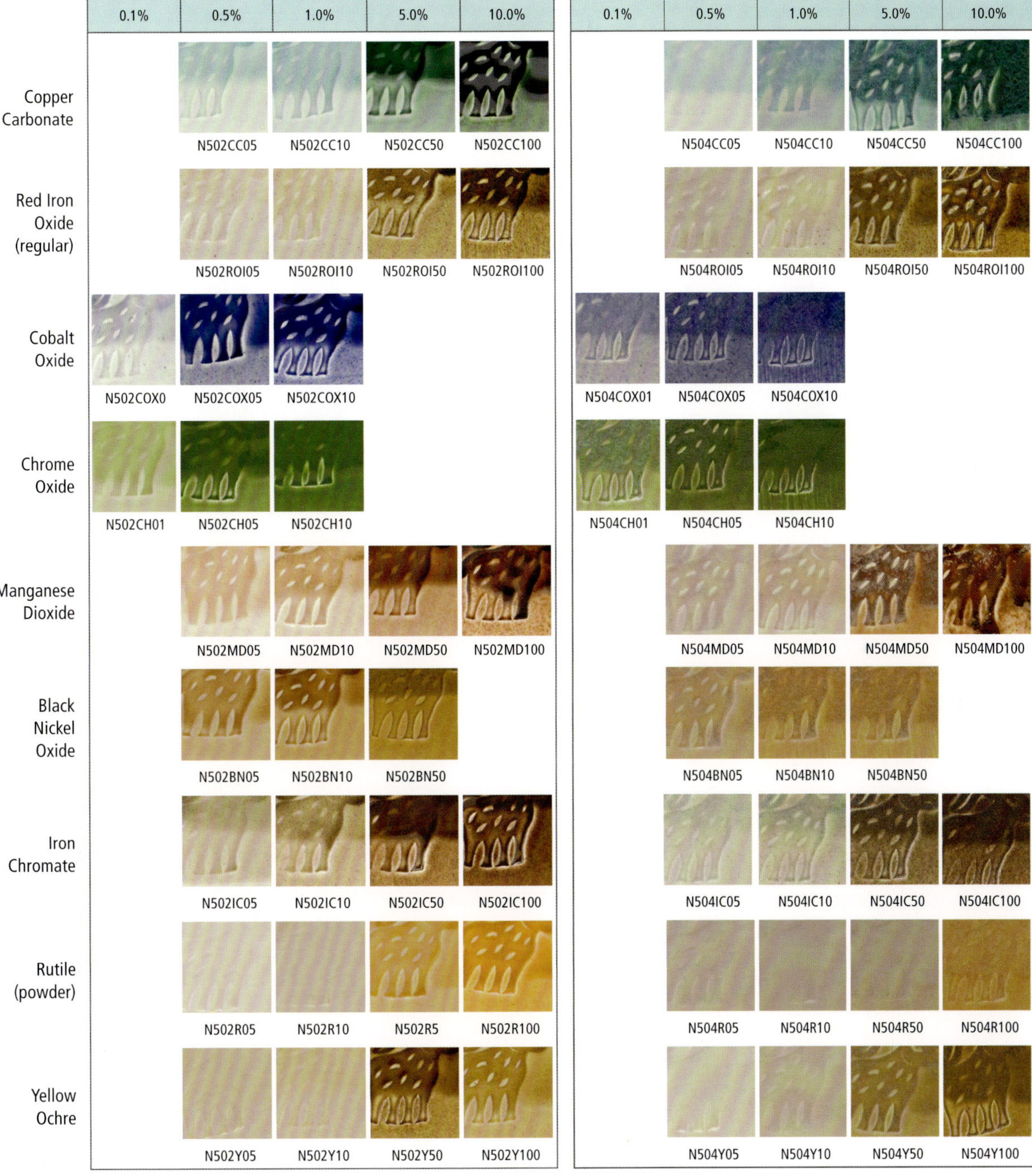

Test tile numbering system: The glaze name is the first part of the identification number, followed by an abbreviation or code that stands for the colorant name. The last part is a two or three digit number referring to the percentage of colorant added. For example if a test was mixed with glaze base N501, and 1% cobalt oxide was added, the test tile marking would be: N501COX10.

Colorant abbreviations: CC=copper carbonate, RIO=red iron oxide, COX=cobalt oxide, CH=chrome oxide, MD=manganese dioxide, BN=black nickel oxide, IC=iron chromate, R=rutile, Y=yellow ochre.

Glaze Base N502 with Opacifiers

	1.0%	5.0%	10.0%
Tin Oxide	N502CT10	N502CT50	N502CT100
Titanium Dioxide	N502CTD10	N502CTD50	N502CTD100
Zircopax	N502CZ10	N502CZ50	N502CZ100

Opacifiers were added to glaze base N502 in increments. The chart at left shows which materials were added for this purpose, and the percentages tested. All glazes in this test batch also had 1% copper carbonate added to increase the visual effect of the chemicals on the glaze.

Note: Some of the oxides and carbonates did not exhibit a significant visual effect by themselves. However, sometimes a combination of more than one chemical can change the glaze characteristics and create spectacular visual effects.

applying a glaze with a high percentage of metal oxides to food ware and test the finished ware for leaching.

Conclusion

This group of tests has been a great opportunity for me to study the characteristics of oxides and carbonates and how they behave at mid-range temperatures. There are scientific methods for calculating glazes and proven theories, but there are many small pieces of information that can only be picked up when you actually go through the physical experiments. It is important for us to become familiar with a glaze's behavior so that we can better utilize it. Key to that is learning both the theory and application. It is my hope that these tests will benefit many potters by helping them to expand their palette and inspire them to test the possibilities.

Ceramic Stains in Glaze

by John Britt

Stains are a mixture of ceramic oxides and coloring metal oxides that are melted in kilns, quenched, ground to specific mesh size (some are acid washed), and colored with organic dyes to simulate the fired color. Essentially they are fritted colorants.

Washes

Washes made with commercial stains can be used both over and under many glazes. Mason Color Works recommends mixing 85% stain and 15% Ferro frit 3124 as a starting point, but many potters us a 50% stain and 50% frit ratio with good success. When used under a glaze, cover with a transparent or semi-transparent glaze. When used over a glaze, be sure to have sufficient flux in the mix because if the stain or wash is too thick, it can turn into a crusty surface after the firing.

A very popular use of washes is on majolica-glazed work. Potters using majolica often mix 50% stain with 50% frit or Gerstley borate to brush designs on top of the white majolica-base glaze. If the stains are refractory, as listed by the manufacturer, increase the flux—use 1 part stain and 4 parts frit or Gerstley borate.

5 X 20 BASE GLAZE

Cone 6 oxidation or reduction

Ingredient	%
Wollastonite	20 %
Custer Feldspar	20
Ferro Frit 3134	20
EPK Kaolin	20
Silica	20
	100 %

Note: Add stains at 2–14%. Fire in oxidation or electric for best results with most stains.

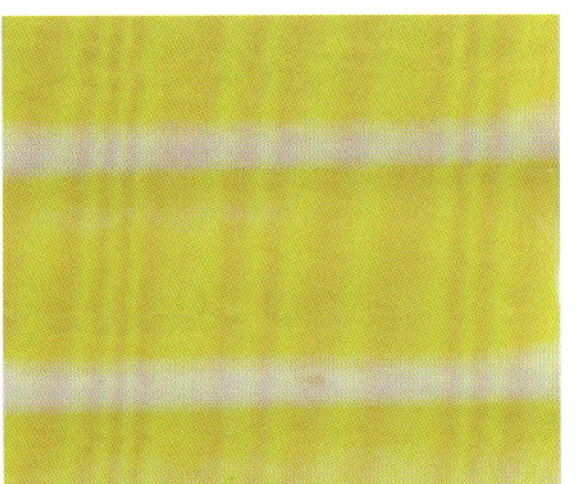

Degussa Yellow 239496 stain 4% in 5 × 20 Base Glaze on porcelain, fired to cone 6 in an electric kiln.

Degussa Yellow 239496 stain 8% in 5 × 20 Base Glaze on porcelain, fired to cone 6 in an electric kiln.

Praseodymium Yellow 6433 stain 4% in 5 × 20 Base Glaze on porcelain, fired to cone 6 in an electric kiln.

Praseodymium Yellow 6433 stain 8% in 5 × 20 Base Glaze on porcelain, fired to cone 6 in an electric kiln.

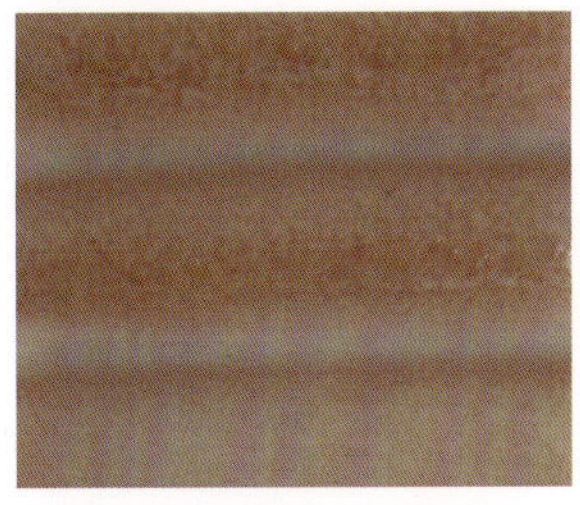

Degussa Intensive Red 279496 stain, 4% in 5 × 20 Base Glaze on porcelain, fired to cone 6 in an electric kiln.

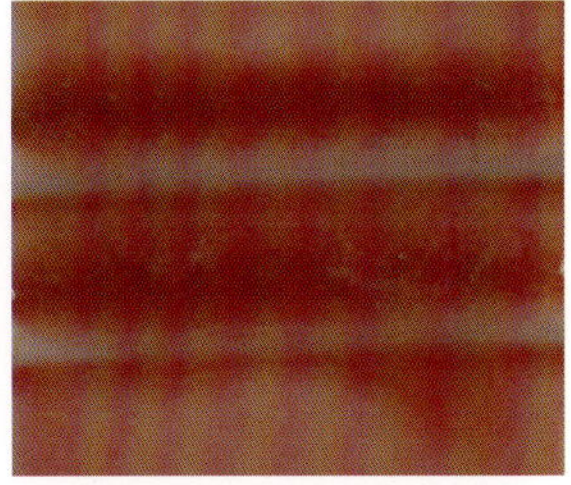

Degussa Intensive Red 279496 stain, 8% in 5 × 20 Base Glaze on porcelain, fired to cone 6 in an electric kiln.

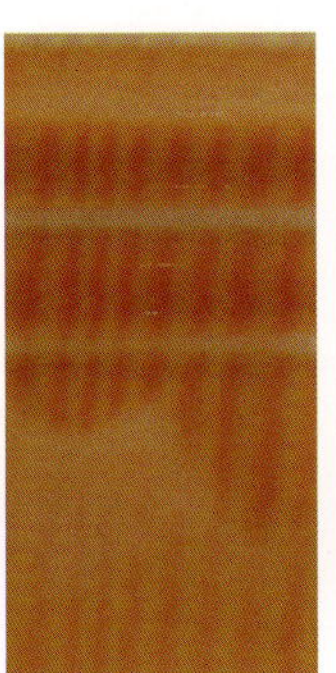
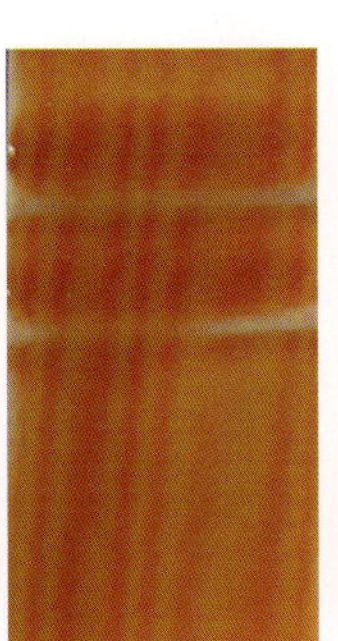
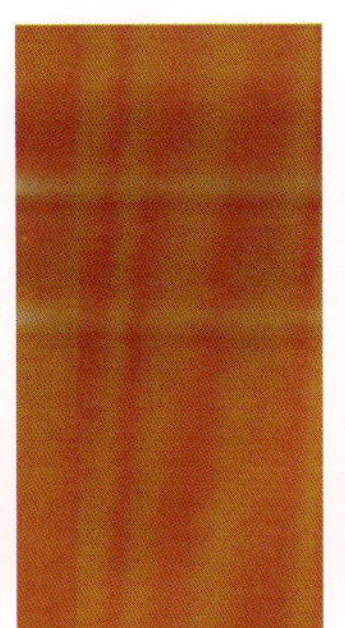

Progression blend of Degussa Orange 239616 stain in 5 × 20 Base Glaze on porcelain, fired to cone 6 in an electric kiln, showing a transparent glaze with only 2% stain and an opaque glaze with 14% stain.

Discovering New Colors

A triaxial blend is a method of testing three ingredients on a three-axis system similar to a two-ingredient line blend.

Often triaxial blends are used to test the primary ingredients in a glaze base, (for example, feldspar, whiting, and kaolin). It is often employed when you don't have a percent analysis to reference. If you have a percent analysis, you can use a glaze software program to predict glaze surfaces, but if you don't, a triaxial blend is the empirical method to see how they melt.

Another use of the triaxial system is color blending. In this method, you keep the base glaze the same and vary the colorants (oxides or stains or even opacifiers). In this triaxial color blend, I tested various stains to develop different colors. Since we do not know the exact amounts of oxides in commercial stains, blending them in a triaxial can reveal surprising and unusual colors.

A 21-point triaxial is a systematic blending of three variables with 100% of each variable at the three corners. So in this case, Mason Deep Crimson #6006 is corner **A** at 100%, Mason Sky Blue #6363 is corner **B** at 100% and Mason Praseodymium Yellow #6433 is corner **C** at 100%. The flow along the vertices is then 80/20, 60/40, 40/60, 20/80. Instead of using the numbers directly from the triaxial chart, I used 4 grams of stain at each corner. So 100% = 4 grams and then I figured out that 80% of 4 grams was 3.4 grams, 60% was 2.4 grams, and 20% was 0.8 grams. Then I substituted those numbers into the triaxial mixtures. For the triaxial glaze chart shown at the right, I used the 5 × 20 Base Glaze as shown on page 115.

For additional testing you can also add metallic oxides to stains to change the colors or add visual textures; add 3% Zircopax to brighten a color; add 3% titanium dioxide to make colors slightly more variegated; add 1% copper carbonate to any stain to push it toward green. The list can go on and on.

21 Learn more about ceramic stains.

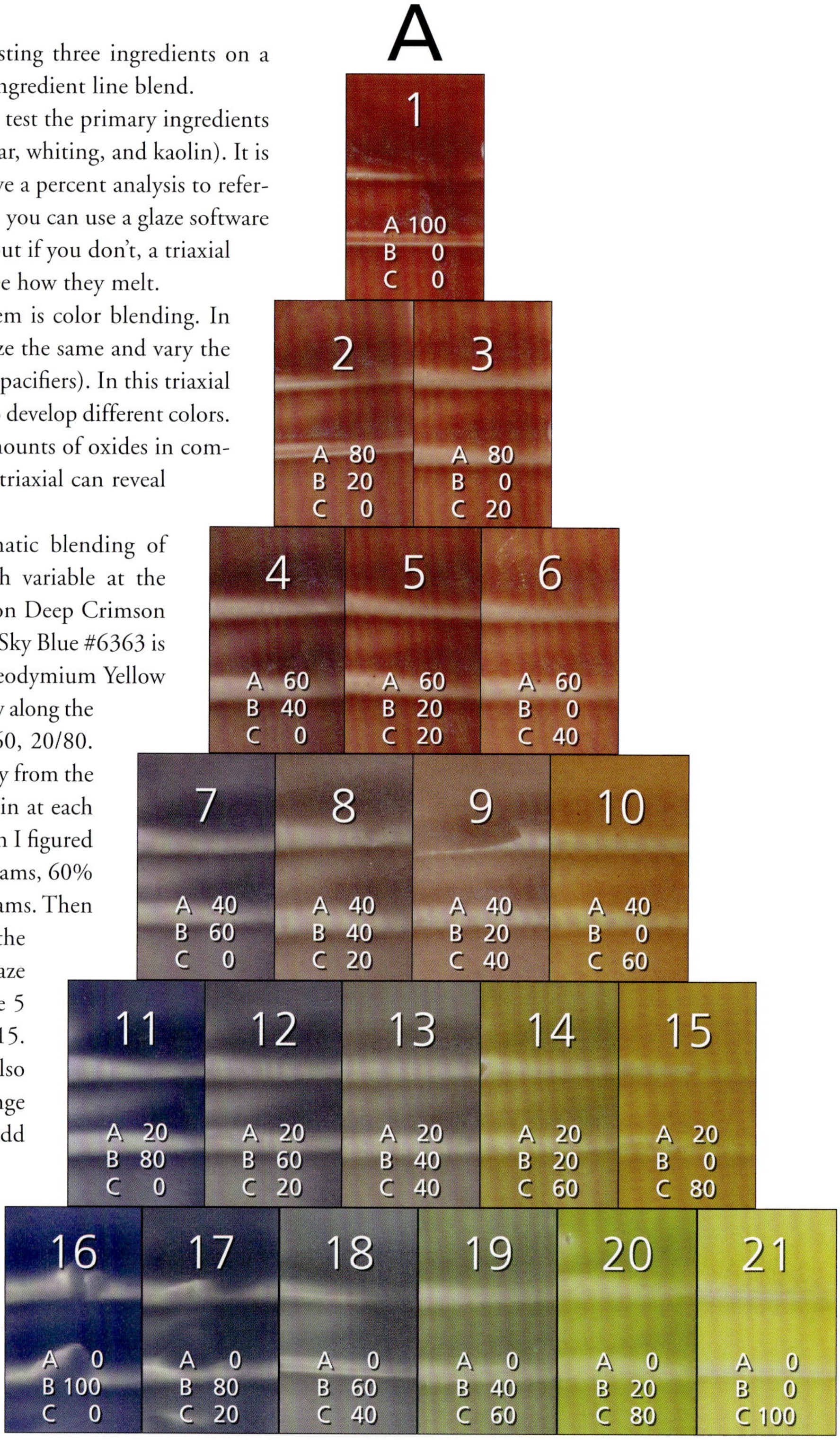

A

Tile	A	B	C
1	100	0	0
2	80	20	0
3	80	0	20
4	60	40	0
5	60	20	20
6	60	0	40
7	40	60	0
8	40	40	20
9	40	20	40
10	40	0	60
11	20	80	0
12	20	60	20
13	20	40	40
14	20	20	60
15	20	0	80
16	0	100	0
17	0	80	20
18	0	60	40
19	0	40	60
20	0	20	80
21	0	0	100

B C

21-Point Triaxial Blend Grid: Hansen 5 × 20 Clear Glaze mixed with **A**–Mason stain Deep Crimson 6006 (Cr, Sn), **B**–Mason stain Sky Blue 6363 (Co, Al, Si), and **C**–Mason stain Praseodymium Yellow 6433 (Pr, Zr, Si,) dipped on porcelain, fired to cone 6 in an electric kiln.

Crater Glazes

by Mark Chatterley

If 20–30% silicon carbide is added to any shiny glaze at any temperature, the result will be a bubble reaction. You don't have to read any further—that is all you need to know to get started.

In my work, I didn't want to use the traditional surface—shiny or matte. I was interested in the effect that I got from under-fired raku glazes (rough and pitted), but the process left the work too fragile. I also like the gnarly surface that results from some wood-fired work but wanted a firing process that was not so labor intensive. After seeing the pitted and craterd surfaces on some of the pots made by Gertrude and Otto Natzler, I suspected that they used silicon carbide to get the surface and tested it.

In larger amounts, silicon carbide creates bubbles in the form of carbon gas coming

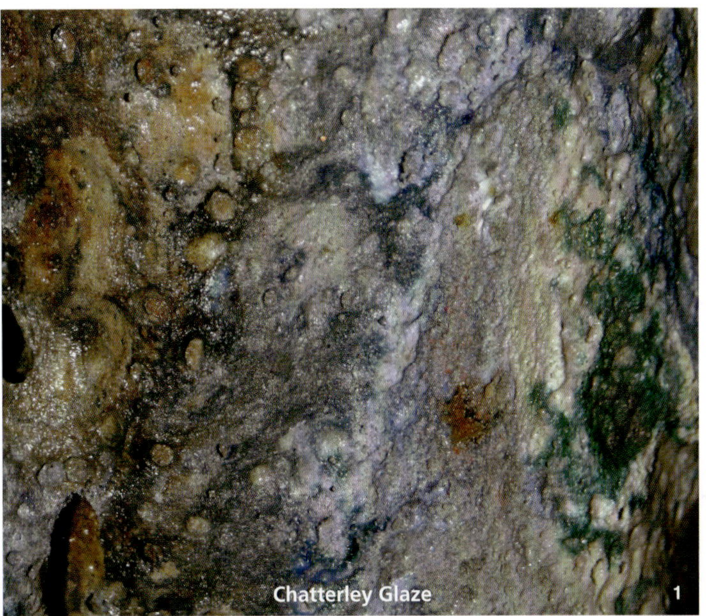
Chatterley Glaze 1

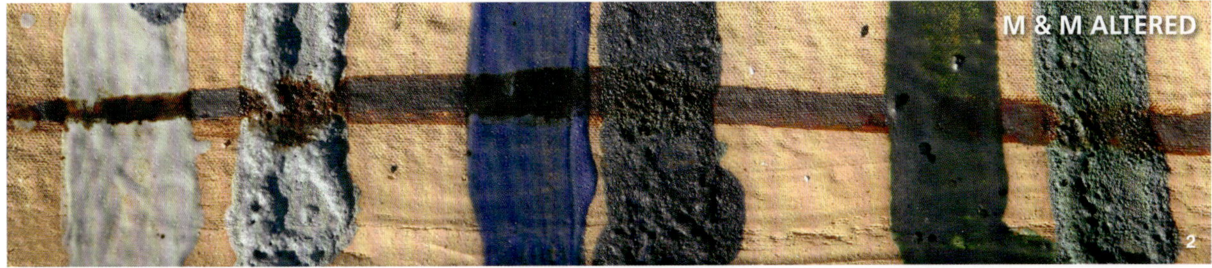

Control (no additions)	20% Silicon Carbide	1.5% Cobalt Oxide	20% Silicon Carbide 1.5% Cobalt Oxide	10.5% Copper Oxide	10.5% Copper Oxide 20% Silicon Carbide

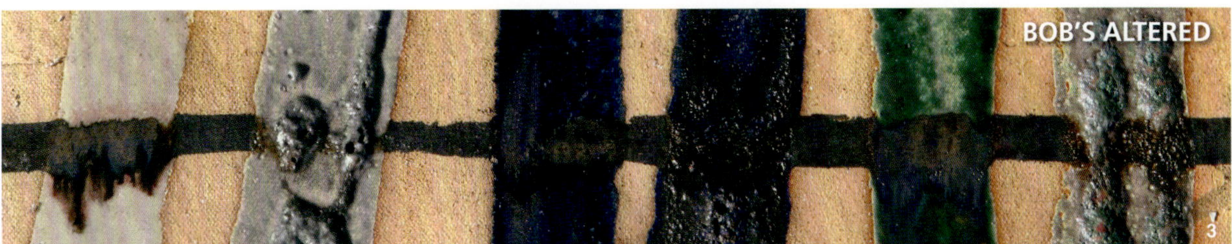

As you can see, there are two different results. The M & M Altered glaze (2) created bumps, while Bob's Altered (3) made small holes. Both have potential for a working glaze. It just takes time to experiment on actual work.

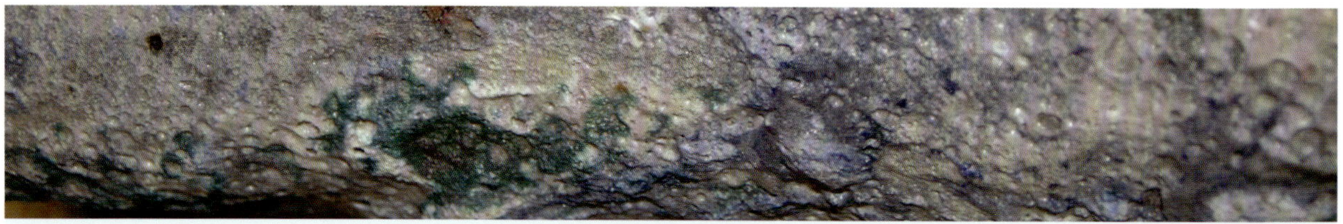

CHATTERLEY GLAZE (1)
cone 6 oxidation

Gillespie Borate	50.0 %
Kaolin	17.5
Silica	32.5
	100.0 %
Add: Silicon Carbide	20.0 %
Sand	12.0 %

The image above shows a detail of the surface on one of Mark Chatterley's sculptures. The surface varies in color from green to purples and browns, while the texture also varies from low- to high-relief craters.

To prove my beginning statement that silicon carbide works with any glaze, I took two recipes not originally intended to be used with silicon carbide, made some minor changes, and ran some tests with silicon carbide and colorants added (see page 117):

M & M ALTERED (2)
cone 5–6 oxidation

Gerstley Borate (sub Gillespie Borate)	18.0 %
Whiting	16.0
Custer Feldspar	40.0
EPK Kaolin	10.0
Silica	16.0
	100.0 %

BOB'S ALTERED (3)
cone 6 oxidation

Bone Ash	9.09 %
Dolomite	9.09
Gerstley Borate (sub Gillespie Borate)	9.09
Talc	9.09
Nepheline Syenite	18.18
EPK Kaolin	18,18
Silica	27.28
	100.00 %

through the glaze. The larger the grit size, the bigger the craters will be. Conversely, the smaller the grit or mesh size, the finer the patterns of bubbles on the fired surface. I use 180 grit in my glaze.

If used in large amounts, silicon carbide cause the glaze to spit onto kiln shelves and the walls of the kiln. I found that placing a layer of sand down makes it easy to clean the shelves. If you fire an electric kiln, you will need to put slicon carbide glazed work in an unsealed saggar to protect the elements (and other work, for that matter).

It only takes one coat of cream consistency glaze covering the work to get a bubbly, crusty surface. If you apply more than one coat, larger reactions happen. The cooling of the kiln will also affect how your glaze looks. I cool mine down for three days before opening it. The faster you cool, the more you "freeze" the bubble effect. Long cooling allows for more gas to dissipate, but it is also hard on the kiln and kiln furniture.

These glazes are not food safe. They can also have sharp edges on the ends of the craters so caution should be used when handling the work.

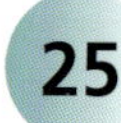

See "Silicon Carbide" to learn more about this material.

Snowflake Crackle

by John Britt

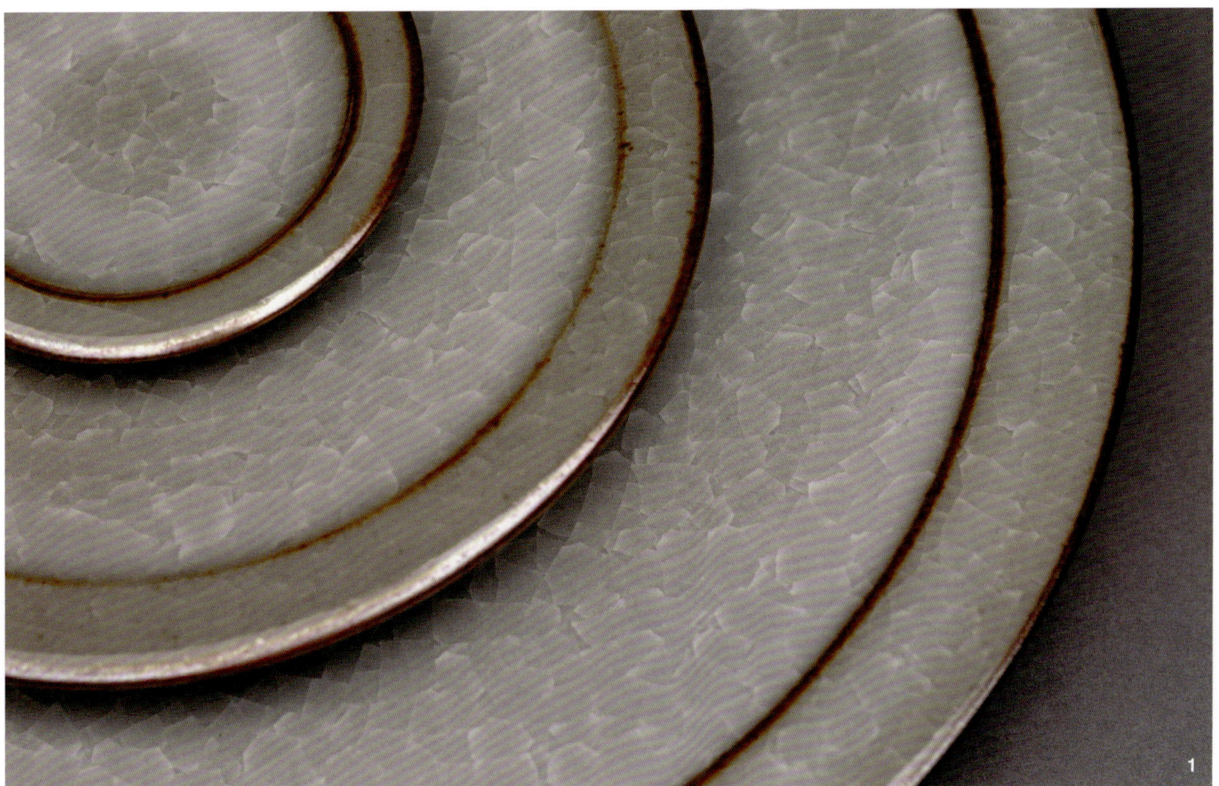

Plates by Matt Fiske with Fiske Ice Crackle Glaze.

I only had a brief glimpse of this glaze some fifteen years ago in a museum gift shop. It was on a little sake set in a traditional Japanese wooden box. It was glazed with the most beautiful crackle glaze—not the usual crackle glaze that is common in raku. It had a conchoidal fracture, with the crazes layered on themselves like a stack of books that had slid over.

Only later did I find out that this glaze was called Snowflake Crackle; actually, it has many names (Snowflake Crackle, Fish Scale Crackle, Ice Crackle, Ice-like Crazing, and Tortoise Shell Crackle), which is generally a sign of how much people like something.

Regardless of what you call it, it's a crazed glaze that is applied so thick that the fractures run not just vertically but horizontally. These crackle patterns can be large or small, and they are distinct hexagonal shapes. When they are large, it is easy to see why it is sometimes called tortoise shell crackle.

Crazing

It is often said that, if you don't like it, you call it crazing; if you like it, you call it crackle. Crazing is often thought of as a glaze defect, but as Nigel Wood describes in his book *Chinese Glazes: Their Origins, Chemistry, and Recreation*, the Song dynasty potters are thought to be the first to treat crazing as a decorative effect. Commonly called Guan (Kuan) Crackle, the Ru, Guan and Ge ware were all beautiful examples of crazing as a decorative technique. In a specifically beautiful type called "iron wire and golden threads," or "golden floss and iron threads," the larger cracks, or primary cracks, were stained black while the pots were still hot. The smaller, secondary cracks developed over months or years as the delayed crazing occurred, leaving them brown.

Almost everything (except rubber and ice) will expand when heated and contract when cooled. When a clay body and a glaze are fired on a pot, they fuse together. As they cool, if the glaze contracts more than the clay body, it cracks or crazes. If the opposite occurs and the clay body contracts more than the glaze, the result is shivering, where the glaze actually pops off of the pot. But if there is just the right amount of compression between a clay body and a glaze, it adds strength to the piece.

Crazing is usually thought of as a glaze defect because a crazed piece can be approximately 75% weaker than its uncrazed counterpart. It is also thought that the craze lines can harbor bacteria and viruses. For these reasons, dinnerware suppliers like to provide uncrazed ware.

Snowflake crackle is the most extreme kind of crazing, where the glaze is applied so thick and the fit with the body is just right so that the crackles appear to lay on top of one other. The glaze can be twice as thick as the body, just like during the Song dynasty. According to Wood, in order to get the glaze thick enough, Song Dynasty potters often bisque fired pieces between glaze coats.

A crazing pattern is always the result of the relationship/marriage between the expansion and subsequent contraction (governed by the coefficient of thermal expansion, or CTE) of a clay body and a glaze. By knowing a little about the CTE of oxides, you can easily control the crackle pattern in glazes to create any range of crazing from very small to very large crackles. Since a glaze is a mixture of oxides with a variety of CTEs, knowing that sodium oxide has a high CTE and magnesium oxide has a low CTE allows you to control the overall CTE of the glaze by adding one or the other.

As a glass, silica has a low CTE (it is amorphous), but as a crystal, it has a high CTE. So adding silica to a glaze can lower its CTE, because the silica melts to its glassy state. However, adding silica to the clay body (where it remains a crystal) can increase its CTE. It is important to keep the firing cone consistent as heating the piece a cone higher will result in melting more of the silica in the body to glass, thus lowering its CTE. Similarly, firing to a lower cone will melt less of the silica in the body giving it a higher CTE. The time and temperature of the firing is extremely important to the CTE of the clay body and thus to the crazing pattern.

Testing

Since seeing this glaze in the museum store, I tried many potential recipes with only moderate success. Since I couldn't get anyone to share their recipe with me, and I had no understanding of the principles of how to achieve this effect, I postponed my search, but in the back of my mind I remembered this beautiful glaze.

Fast forward about fifteen years to a workshop I was giving last year. I had assigned a student a series of tests to improve a magnesium crawling (reticulated) glaze that she was working on in cone 6 oxidation:

SDSU CRAWL/BEADS
Cone 6

Ingredient	%
Magnesium Carbonate	25 %
Nepheline Syenite	70
OM-4 Ball Clay	5
	100 %

Note: This is not a Snowflake Crackle glaze.

I had her make up the glaze (above) without the magnesium carbonate and then add it back in 5% increments up to 40%. She then dipped tiles of stoneware, dark stoneware, and porcelain. Fortunately, one of the clay bodies she was using was a very dark low-fire Redart body that she liked to fire to cone 6 (it is rated from cone 05–6). When the tiles came out of the firing, my eye went immediately to the 5% magnesium carbonate test on the dark body; it was Snowflake Crackle! What a stroke of luck. Unfortunately, I didn't care about her reticulated surface anymore, as I was so excited about this crackle pattern.

When I returned home, I tried the glaze on a variety of store-bought cone 6 clays. The best, in terms of CTE, were Highwater's Earthen Red and Brownstone at cone 6, and Orangestone at cone 10. There very well may be others that work, but these were the best of those I tested.

Since potters today generally buy premixed clay bodies rather than making their own, changes in CTE are usually made to the glaze rather than the clay body. This glaze crawled a bit, so I decided to remove the magnesium carbonate (because it has such a high shrinkage) and substituted talc (which is magnesium silicate).

While I was analyzing the glaze in the glaze calculation software program Insight (www.digitalfire.com), I decided to look at the CTE numbers, which were around 8.59 (Insight CTE). I then constructed about four more glazes with similar CTEs, between 8.59 and 8.70. I came up with several nice glazes this way, but I also tested the original

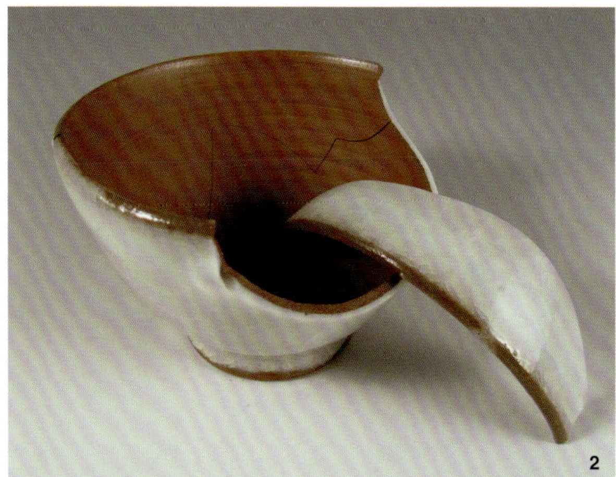

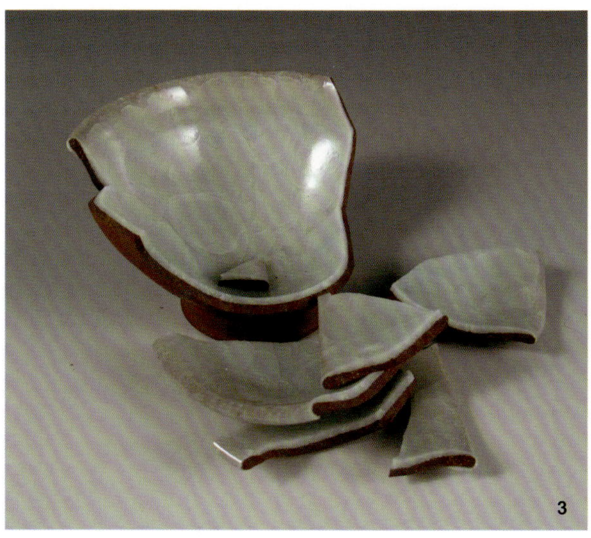

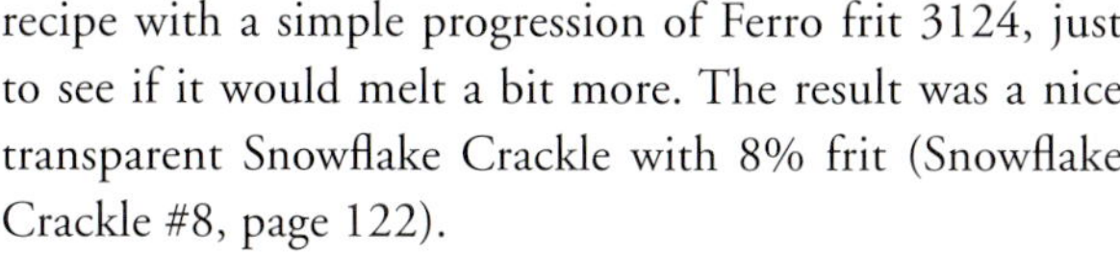

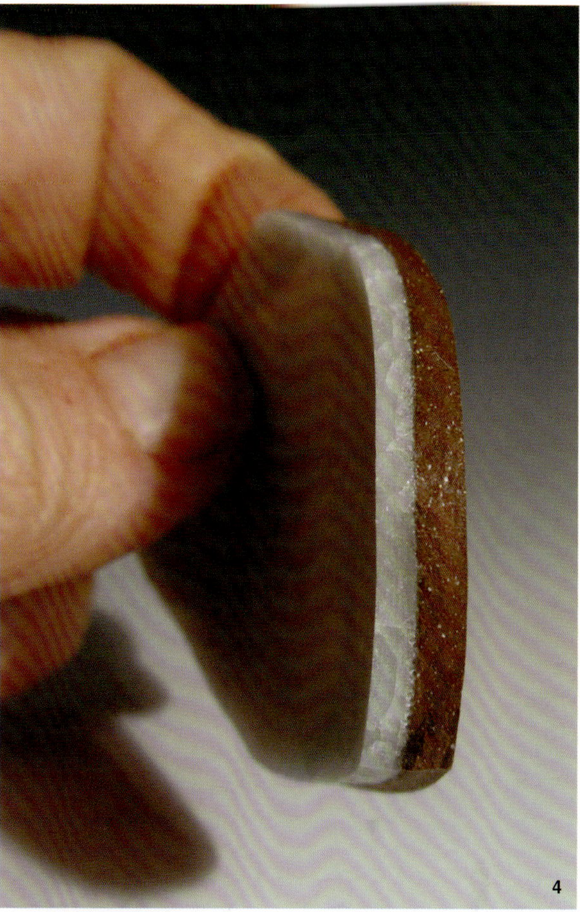

2–3 The uneven stress of glazing only the inside or only the outside of a piece can cause it to shatter from unequal tension. **4** Side view of a cracked bowl showing thickness of fired snowflake crackle glaze versus the thickness of the clay body. The glaze thickness is $^{1}/_{8}$–$^{3}/_{16}$ of an inch thick after being fired.

recipe with a simple progression of Ferro frit 3124, just to see if it would melt a bit more. The result was a nice transparent Snowflake Crackle with 8% frit (Snowflake Crackle #8, page 122).

Color

The first thing I noticed when I did color tests with the usual colorants and opacifiers (copper carbonate, red iron oxide, chrome oxide, stains, Zircopax Plus, etc.) was that, as the color improved, the crazing ceased. This was because all oxides have expansion/contraction rates and adding them changed the CTE of the glaze enough to stop the crackle effect. I ran more tests with very low levels of colorants (under 1%), which kept the crazing yet still produced a nice color.

Mixing and Application Notes

• These glazes contain high amounts of nepheline syenite, which is partially soluble, so the glaze slop can easily deflocculate affecting application thickness. Adding Epsom salts corrects the problem. Mix to a specific gravity of approximately 1.55–1.60.

• These glazes must be applied thick, between an eighth and a quarter of an inch (3–6 mm).

• Snowflake crackle is not limited to cone 6; that is just the first temperature where I discovered it. In the cone 10 versions, watch for the flocculating effect of bone ash. You may need to add a deflocculant (sodium silicate), otherwise the glazes can flake off before you get the pots into the kiln. If they don't flake off, they usually crawl badly during the firing.

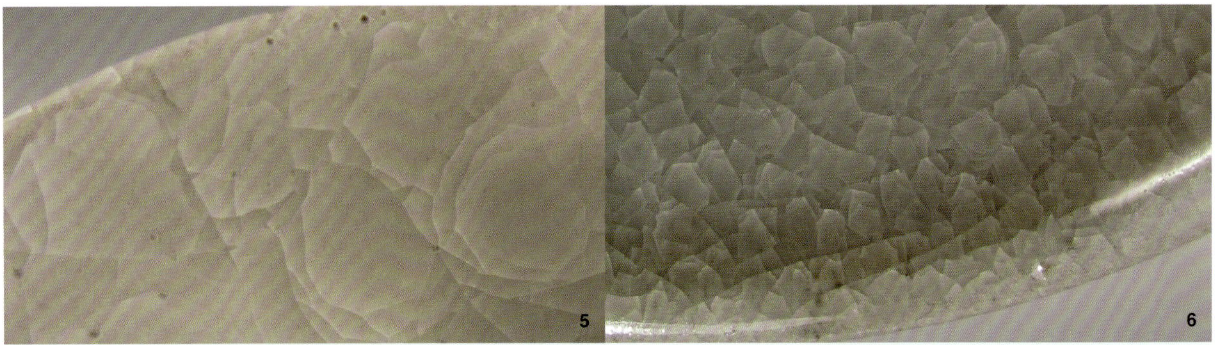

ORIGINAL SNOWFLAKE CRACKLE (5)
Cone 6/7 electric

Magnesium Carbonate	4.26 %
Nepheline Syenite	89.36
OM-4 Ball Clay	6.38
	100.00 %
Add: Bentonite	2.00 %

SNOWFLAKE CRACKLE #8 (7)
Cone 6/7 electric

Magnesium Carbonate	3.94 %
Ferro Frit 3124	7.41
Nepheline Syenite	82.74
OM-4 Ball Clay	5.91
	100.00 %
Add: Bentonite	2.00 %
Turquoise: Copper Carbonate	0.20 %
White: Superpax	0.50 %
Blue: Cobalt Carbonate	0.07 %
Yellow: Degussa Stain 239416	0.50 %
Rust: Red Iron Oxide	0.50 %

SNOWFLAKE CRACKLE #4 (8)
Cone 6/7 electric

Talc	7.86 %
Ferro Frit 3124	5.77
Nepheline Syenite	86.37
	100.00 %
Add: Bentonite	2.00 %
Turquoise: Copper Carbonate	0.20 %

FISKE ICE CRACKLE GLAZE (1)
Cone 10 reduction

Bone Ash	5.00
Ferro Frit 3134	3.00
Nepheline Syenite	91.00
EPK Kaolin	1.00
	100.00 %
Add: Bentonite	2.00 %

This is the glaze used on Matt Fiske's plates shown on page 121.

ICE, ICE BABY
Cone 10 reduction

Bone Ash	4.32 %
Talc	4.98
Ferro Frit 3134	1.99
Custer Feldspar	29.90
Nepheline Syenite	54.82
EPK Kaolin	3.99
	100.00 %

SNOWFLAKE CRACKLE 13
Cone 10 reduction

Bone Ash	3.96 %
Talc	7.43
Ferro Frit 3134	1.49
Nepheline Syenite	81.67
EPK Kaolin	5.45
	100.00 %

SNOWFLAKE CRACKLE 1234 (6)
Cone 10 reduction

Bone Ash	3.24 %
Talc	4.99
Ferro Frit 3134	3.99
Custer Feldspar	43.64
Nepheline Syenite	41.15
EPK Kaolin	2.99
	100.00 %

Notes: 1) Add a deflocculant (sodium silicate) to counter the flocculating effects of bone ash in the cone 10 glazes. This will prevent glaze from either flaking off prior to firing or crawling during the firing.

2) Add Epsom salts to the glazes containing high percentages of nepheline syenite, which is slightly soluble, to counter the deflocculating effects.

5 Detail of Original Snowflake Crackle Glaze fired to cone 6 in an electric kiln. **6** Detail of a bowl with Snowflake Crackle 1234 on Orangestone clay, fired to cone 10 in reduction.

Testing Serendipity

After arriving at the cone 6 recipes, I started testing for cone 10. I took four separate recipes and tested each on four clay bodies. But before I threw them out, I poured each cup into another to get a blended test. I poured cup 1 into cup 3 (Snowflake Crackle 13—1+3, get it?), then I poured in cup 2, which became Ice, Ice Baby (more fun that 123) and finally I combined all four glazes together to make the glaze named Snowflake Crackle 1234 (1+2+3+4). As it turned out, none of the original four recipes worked very well, but the three blends were great! (That is a super secret way to get more mileage out of your tests!)

Snowflake Bowl, 5 in. (13 cm) in diameter, wheel-thrown Brownstone Clay, with Snowflake Crackle Glaze #8, fired to cone 6 in an electric kiln.

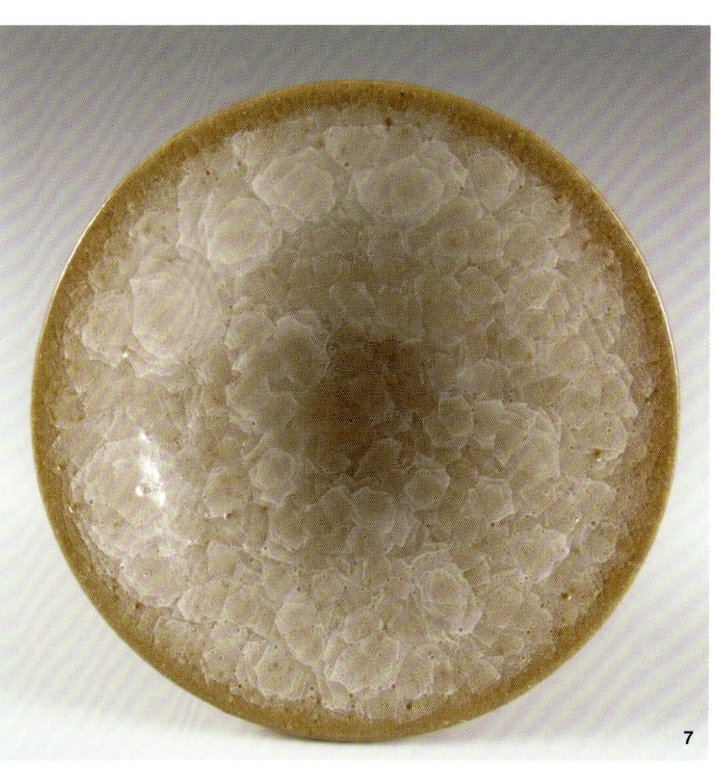

7

8

Test tile of Snowflake Crackle #4 with 0.2% copper carbonate on Brownstone clay, fired to cone 6 in an electric kiln.

- Be sure to wait a couple of days after firing for the crazing to finish forming enough to see it (this is called delayed crazing.) One load came out and I thought they were unsuccessful, with no crazing. I went away for a long weekend and, to my surprise, when I came back they were all crazed nicely with the snowflake crackle effect.
- These glazes are not recommended for functional work as you can often feel the crazing patterns with your hand.
- Glazing only one side of a bowl, either inside only or outside only, will cause the bowl to shatter from unequal tension.
- After the pots are fired, the glaze sometimes thins on the rim and you can see the brown clay body. This is called "brown mouth" or "purple rim and iron foot" (the glazed rim will reoxidize differently from the unglazed foot).
- The crackle works best on the inside of bowls as the concave interior accentuates the crackle effect.

CHAPTER 3
High Fire

Copper Glazes

by John Britt

Copper Glaze Tips

• Oribe pieces are decorated on one side with an iron oxide design over a transparent glaze while the other side is decorated with a transparent copper green glaze. Then they are fired in oxidation. Oribes can get a scummed layer on top that dulls the color. The traditional method for getting a clearer copper Oribe is to soak chestnut husks in water and then soak the pots in this acidic solution. But today potters just use a weak muriatic acid (hydrochloric acid) solution. (This is toxic so use in a well-ventilated area with safety glasses and a mask.)

• Copper volatilizes above 1877°F (1025°C) and becomes increasingly volatile, making it a fume hazard. The volatilization can affect adjacent pots, particularly those with tin whites or celadons, resulting in a pink blush. This property can also be used to decorate a pot. Glazing the inside of a saggar with an Oribe glaze and then placing a tin white glazed tea bowl in the saggar will give a delicately blushed pink tea bowl.

• Copper glazes are often used in soda and salt firings because the introduction of volatile sodium during the firing turns copper glazes various shades of blue/turquoise/green. Sometimes potters use high amounts of copper (10%) in a green salt glaze, which turns black, but when the salt fumes hit that part of the pot, the area turns deep green on one side with the other side of the pot fading to black.

• Raku: With sufficient post-firing reduction, the copper oxide/carbonate can be reduced to metallic copper finishes. These copper lusters are only microns thick so they can reoxidize to produce green colors (much like a penny oxidizes) if the pots aren't coated with a polyurethane sealant.

Copper is also used in Islamic luster firing techniques as well as Egyptian Paste (ancient Faience), which is a self-glazing, low-fire clay body that goes back 7000 years. It was probably discovered by firing sand, clay, and salt or soda ash. Then colorants were added to make colorful beads and ornaments.

Toxicity

While there is no legal limit set for safe leaching of copper in glazes, potters should be aware that the legal level of allowable copper deemed safe for drinking water is 1.3 mg/L (based more on its effects on taste than toxicity). Levels of above 5% can create black metallic surfaces and should not be used in functional ware.*

Excessive amounts in a glaze can be leached with prolonged or repeated contact with acidic foods or beverages. The extremely basic conditions in dishwashers can attack a glaze surface, causing erosion of the surface and resulting in increased leaching over time.

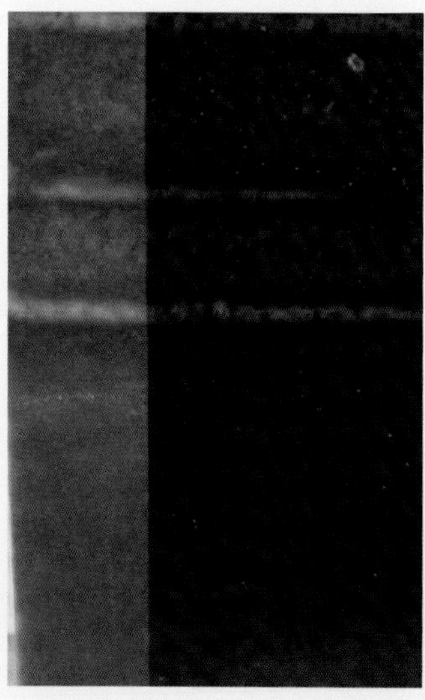

WILLIE HELIX

Cone 10 Ox. or Red.

Nepheline Syenite	40.0 %
Whiting	19.0
Kaolin	11.0
Silica	30.0
	100.0 %
Add: Copper Carbonate	1.2 %
Black Copper Oxide	5.0 %

The tile to the left, glazed with Willie Helix, was soaked in muriatic acid for 48 hours to simulate an acidic environment and show possible leaching, which has occurred and is noticeable on the left side.

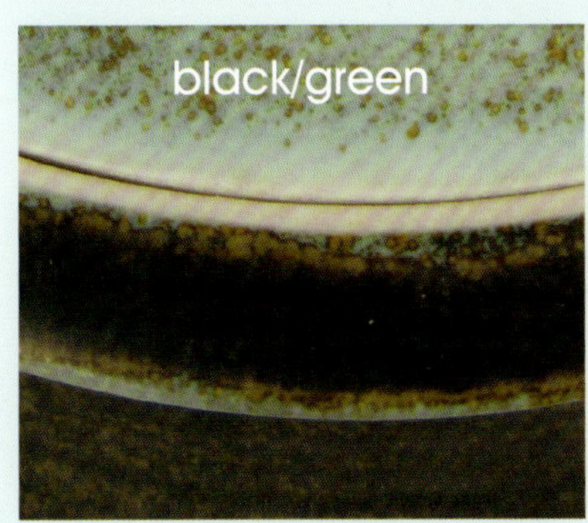

V.C.A.A. COPPER
Cone 10 reduction

Cornwall Stone	46 %
Whiting	34
Silica	20
	100 %
Add: Tin Oxide	4 %
Copper Carbonate	4 %

Apply thin for a speckled green or thicker for a mottled black. Both applications shown here on porcelain.

PATSY'S GREEN (ORIBE)
Cone 10 oxidation

Gerstley Borate	13.4 %
Dolomite	5.9
Whiting	8.3
Zinc Oxide	4.0
Minspar 200 Feldspar	46.2
EPK Kaolin	2.4
Silica	19.8
	100.0 %
Add: Black Copper Oxide	4.0 %

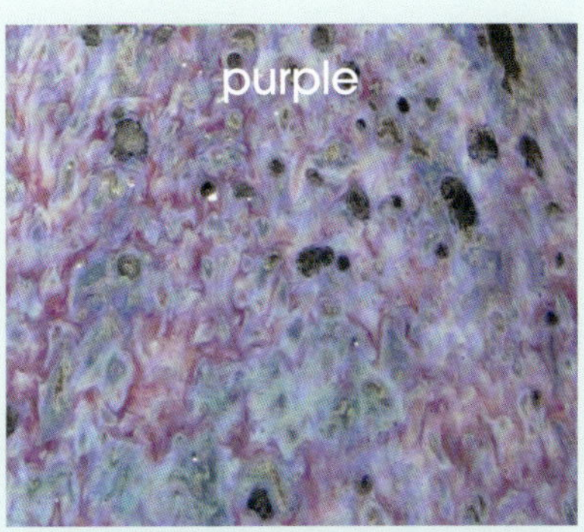

JEFF'S RED (UNDER ORIBE GLAZE)
Cone 10 reduction

Barium Carbonate	4.4 %
Dolomite	8.7
Whiting	8.4
Ferro Frit 3134	8.7
Custer Feldspar	41.9
Zinc Oxide	1.7
Silica	26.2
	100.0 %
Add: Bentonite	1.0 %
Copper Carbonate	0.5 %
Tin Oxide	2.6 %

Jeff's red is fired once then reglazed with an Oribe glaze and fired again.

JOHN'S RED
Cone 10 oxidation

Talc	3.64 %
Whiting	13.64
Zinc Oxide	4.55
Ferro Frit 3134	9.09
Custer Feldspar	48.18
EPK Kaolin	5.45
Silica	15.45
	100.00 %
Add: Tin Oxide	1.20 %
Copper Carbonate	0.80 %

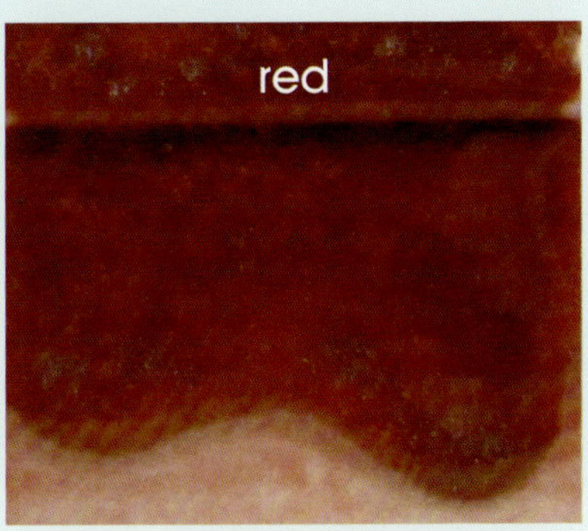

JOHN'S RED
Cone 10 reduction

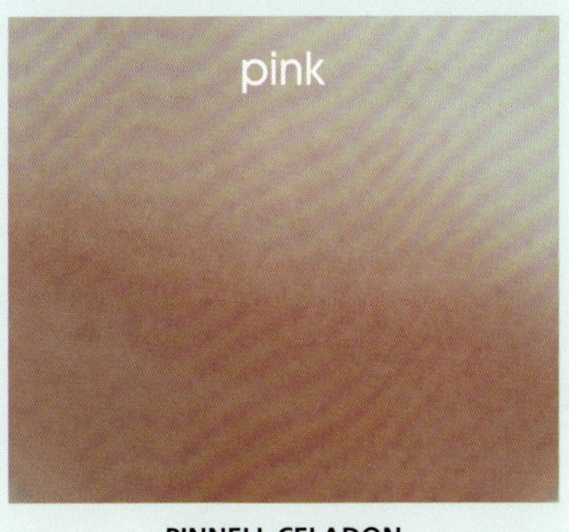

PINNELL CELADON
Cone 10 reduction

Barium Carbonate	1.9 %
Whiting	19.6
Custer Feldspar	24.5
Grolleg Porcelain	19.6
Silica	34.3
	100.0 %
Add: Tin Oxide	1.0 %
Yellow Iron Oxide	0.5 %

Celadon glaze with tin oxide, pink flashing of copper from Oribe glazed pieces next to it in the kiln.

18 Learn more about copper oxide.

Experiments in Peach Bloom

by John Britt

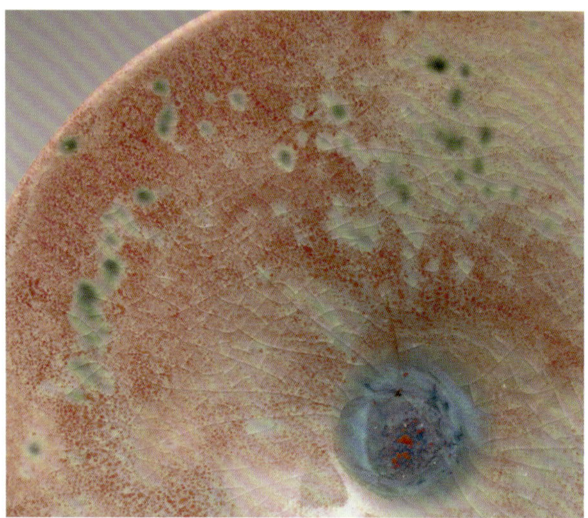

TOM TURNER FLAMBÉ 2

Cone 10 reduction

Barium Carbonate	3.89 %
Dolomite	5.56
Gerstley Borate	11.12
Whiting	8.34
Wood Ash (soft wood)	1.00
Zinc Oxide	1.67
Minspar 200 Feldspar	41.72
EPK Kaolin	1.67
Silica	25.03
	100.00 %
Add: Tin Oxide	0.83 %
Copper Carbonate	0.42 %

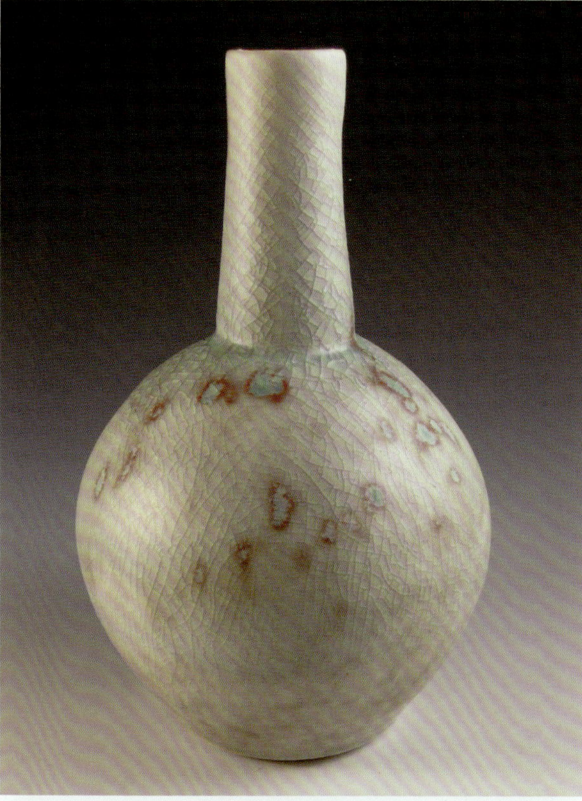

Vase, 11 in. (28 cm) in height, wheel-thrown porcelain, with Tom Turner Flambé 2 Glaze, black copper oxide sprinkled on when wet, bisque fired to cone 06, gas oxidation fired cone 10, striking for 2 hours at 1500°F, refired in electric bisque to cone 06 along with greenware pots made of dark stoneware.

Peach Bloom glazes are some of the most delicate, beautiful, and elusive glazes known. They were used in China during the Qing dynasty (1644–1911) to decorate objects for the emperor's writing table, like water pots and ink wells, as well as decorative vases and bowls. In his definitive book *Chinese Glazes,* Nigel Wood lists many names for Peach Bloom glazes, like "apple red," "bean red," or "drunken beauty" for a category of glazes with various shades and a mottled surface, while "beauty's blush," "baby's face," and "peach blossom" are reserved for those with lighter tones. The number of names given to describe these glazes shows the wide variety in this magnificent glaze.

What is most intriguing is that the secrets of this glaze and firing technique have remained a mystery for centuries. However, at its core, Peach Bloom is a copper-based glaze that gives the impression of ripening fruit. So it may be a transparent green that blushes pink or a pinkish background with green or red speckling.

I have long been interested in this glaze but had never had an opportunity to pursue it fully. Then, Lindsey Elsey, a studio arts major at Appalachian State University in Boone, North Carolina, approached me with an interest in studying copper red glazes for her senior internship, which would end with her giving a presentation as well as an exhibition at the Crimson Laurel Gallery in Bakersville. She said that, for her, copper reds were the first truly satisfying glazes she experienced in her work. She felt that, beyond their vibrant color, successful copper reds embodied the idea that if everything came together just right—the clay body, the glaze mix, application, form, firing, and cooling—then magic could happen. Although she understood that struggling with so many variables could be a frustrating process, she believed that, in the end, producing one successful pot would be worth the entire struggle.

I suggested that rather than working with the entire category of copper reds, we focus on Peach Blooms, which are the most difficult to achieve. Since the project seemed interesting and challenging to both of us, we agreed to work together and began by designing a testing program.

Current Literature

We found very little written on the subject of Peach Blooms. However, several books did have small sections: *Copper Red Glazes* by Robert Tichane, *Stoneware Glazes* by Ian Currie, *Chinese Glazes* by Nigel Wood and my book, *The Complete Guide to High-Fire Glaze: Glazing and Firing at Cone 10*. While none of these books have a definitive method, from these sources we set up a group of tests to see if we could achieve something close to ancient Peach Bloom glazes.

Testing Methods

- Aging glazes to allow crystallization (Currie)
- Spraying copper/tin over a celadon glaze (Britt)
- Layering copper pigment and clear glaze (Wood)
- Sprinkling black copper oxide over glazed pots, using coarse flaked copper oxide (Tichane)
- Using Oribe glazes in oxidation firing (Britt)
- Placing pieces in saggars coated with Oribe (Britt)
- Underfiring (Britt)
- Starting reduction later, around cone 011–08 (Britt)
- Strike firing (Britt)

Due to time constraints, we knew we could not pursue all these methods, and we decided the most promising were strike firing (reduction period during the cooling) aging glazes (because I had five "old" buckets of copper reds) and

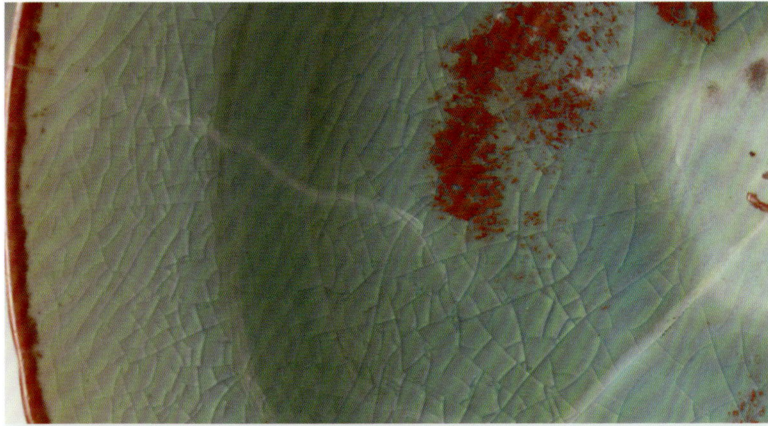

DALY RED TITANIUM

Cone 10 reduction

Bone Ash	1.0 %
Talc	3.0
Whiting	15.0
Zinc Oxide	2.0
Ferro Frit 3110	17.0
Nepheline Syenite	35.0
Silica	27.0
	100.0 %
Add: Tin Oxide	1.5 %
Titanium Dioxide	3.0 %
Copper Carbonate	1.5 %

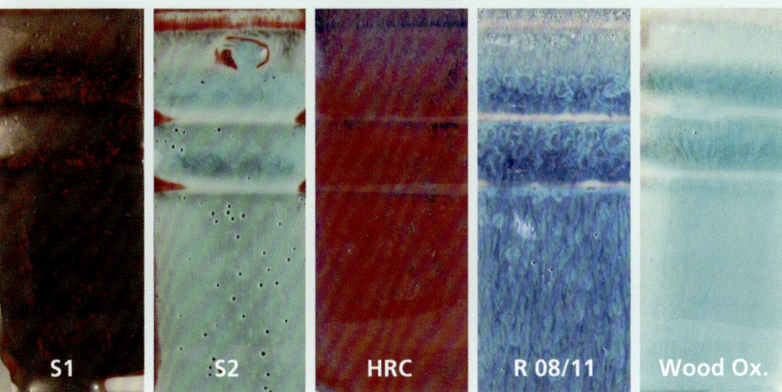

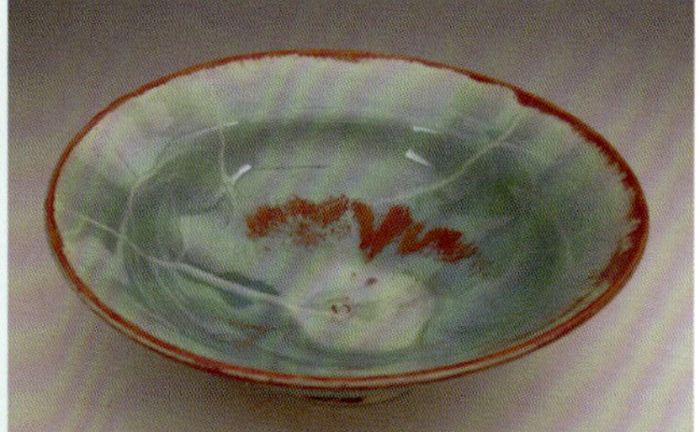

Bowl, 6 in. (15 cm) in diameter, wheel-thrown porcelain, with Daly Red Glaze (w/titanium dioxide), gas-oxidation fired cone 10, very quick cooling to 1500°F, then strike firing for 2 hours.

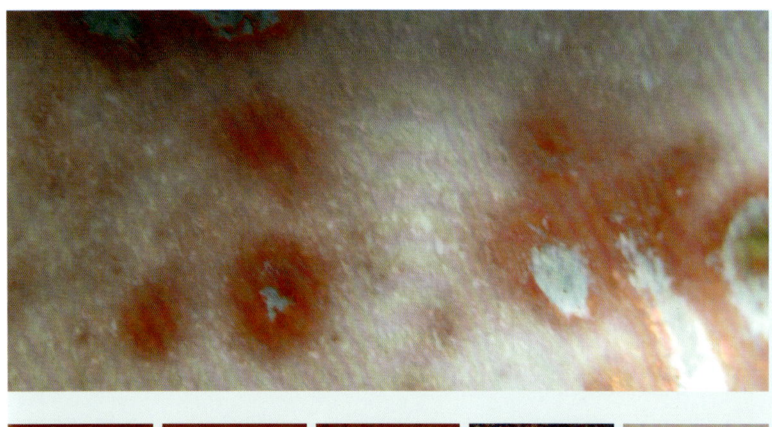

SPLOTCHY LAVENDER
Cone 10 reduction

Barium Carbonate	2.0 %
Lithium Carbonate	2.0
Whiting	15.0
Zinc Oxide	4.0
Hommel Frit 14	7.0
Custer Feldspar	50.0
Silica	20.0
	100.0 %
Add: Tin Oxide	1.0 %
Copper Carbonate	0.6 %
Bentonite	1.0 %

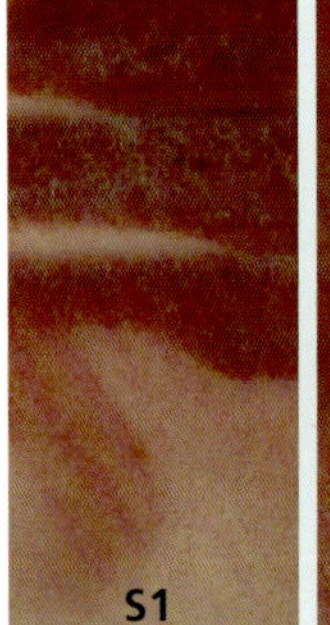

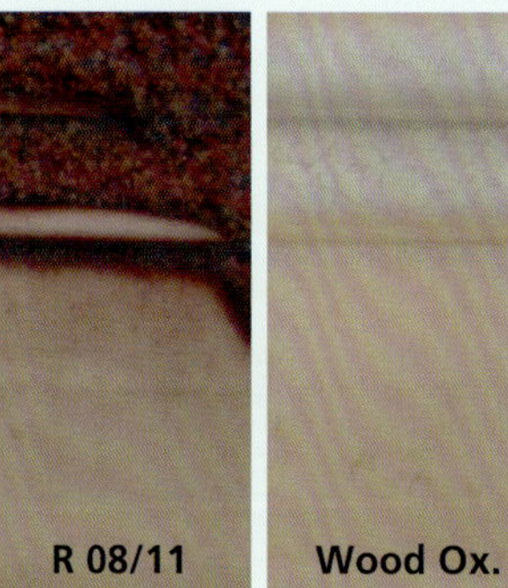

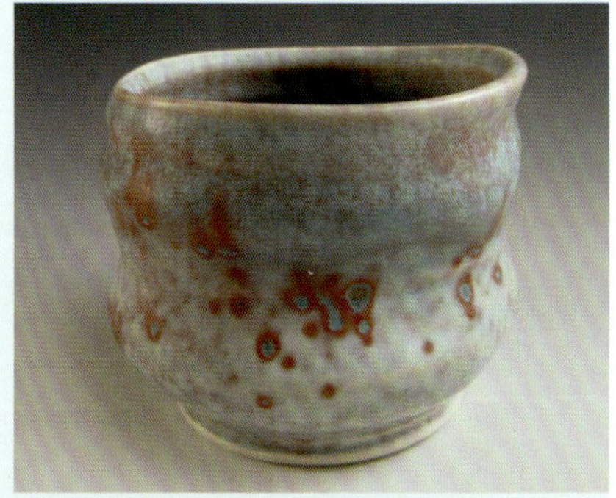

Teabowl, 5 in. (13 cm) in height, wheel-thrown porcelain, with Splotchy Lavender Glaze, black copper oxide sprinkled on when wet, gas-oxidation fired to cone 10, striking for 2 hours at 1500°F, refired in electric bisque to cone 06 along with greenware pots made of dark stoneware.

sprinkling coarse copper oxide on wet glazes. While our main focus was on these avenues, we could also sample some of the other ideas without fully investigating them to see if there were some areas for future study.

We then set out to collect as many copper red recipes as we could, eventually ending up with 80 distinct recipes. As we collected recipes, we searched for as wide a variation as possible. That way, even if we did not find the perfect recipe, we would at least get something in the ball park that would hopefully lead us in the right direction.

We made 600 tiles of Helios, a Grolleg porcelain, and also threw several dozen test pieces that we would use after the initial test firings. We then made 300 gram batches of each test glaze, dipping five tiles in each glaze. Each of these was then fired in one of five different firing cycles.

Firing Cycles

Strike Firing 1 (S1) oxidized to cone 10 (2345°F or 1285°C) in a gas kiln, cooled to 1550°F, then restarted and put into reduction (0.80 on the oxyprobe) for two hours, then shut off. Missing the initial glaze reduction period on the way up causes the glaze to seal over and then the striking (reduction period during the cooling) causes only the glaze surface to reduce to reds or spotty reds. The results from this firing cycle were so good that we did another (S2) to see if we could duplicate it, but this time with even heavier reduction.

Strike Firing 2 (S2) was similar to S1, but with slightly heavier reduction (0.85 on the oxyprobe). Some of the pieces in this cycle came out of the kiln too dark or a flat monochrome red. This was caused by excessive reduction and meant we needed to lighten up reduction for the next trial. But in order salvage the pieces we wanted to reintroduce the spots and blue-green color, so we put them into an electric bisque kiln firing and refired them to cone 06, this was basically an oxidation soak that re-oxidized some of the copper and caused the pieces to become more visually interesting.

We did another strike firing with a very a quick cool to 1550°F (843°C). This made no difference with our color but it did cause an interesting "earthworm" or "tear" mark effect. These appear to be cracks in the glaze or piece but, in fact, are the glaze surfaces cooling rapidly while the glaze under it is still molten, causing it to shift and tear (see bowl on page 127).

Coarse copper oxide was also applied to some of the fresh raw glazed pots in these strike firings with the hope that we could better recreate the green or red spotting we saw in pictures. We made a shaker (similar to a pepper shaker) and just after we glazed our pots, but while they were still wet, sprinkled them with black copper oxide. Black copper is coarser than copper carbonate and we thought that it may not completely melt, thereby producing some green spots.

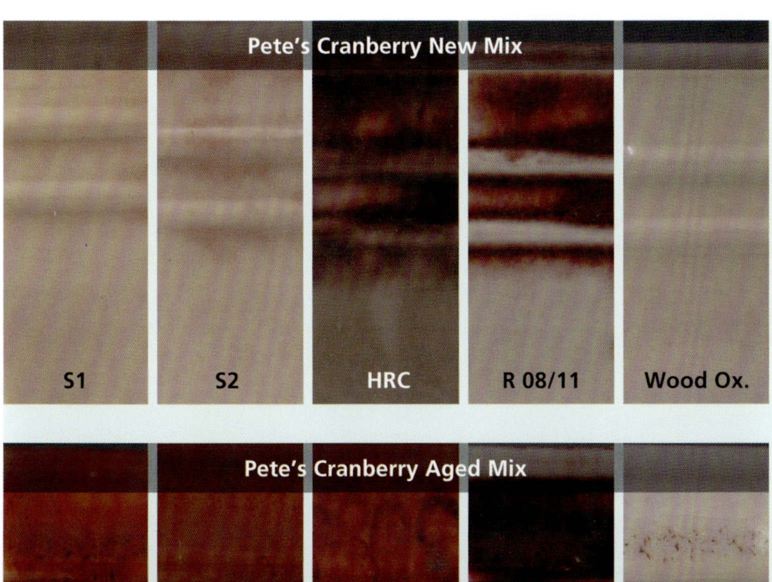

PETE'S CRANBERRY

Cone 10 reduction

Ingredient	%
Gerstley Borate	10.20 %
Whiting	11.10
Custer Feldspar	73.80
Silica	4.90
	100.00 %
Add: Copper Carbonate	0.35 %
Tin Oxide	1.00 %

SAM'S SATIN CELADON

Cone 10 reduction

Ingredient	%
Barium Carbonate	4.0 %
Dolomite	6.0
Whiting	15.5
Custer Feldspar	40.0
Silica	34.5
	100.0 %
Add: Synthetic Yellow Iron Oxide	0.5 %

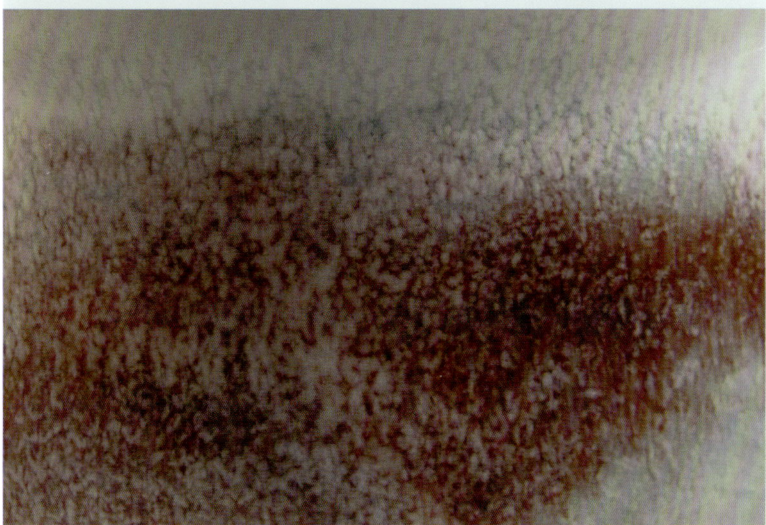

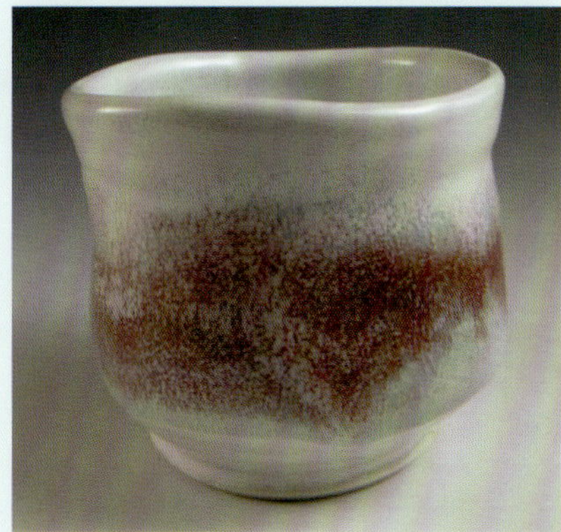

Teabowl, 5 in. (13 cm) in height, wheel-thrown porcelain, with Pete's Cranberry Red Glaze sandwiched between Sam's Satin Celadon Glaze, gas-oxidation fired cone 10, striking for 2 hours at 1500°F.

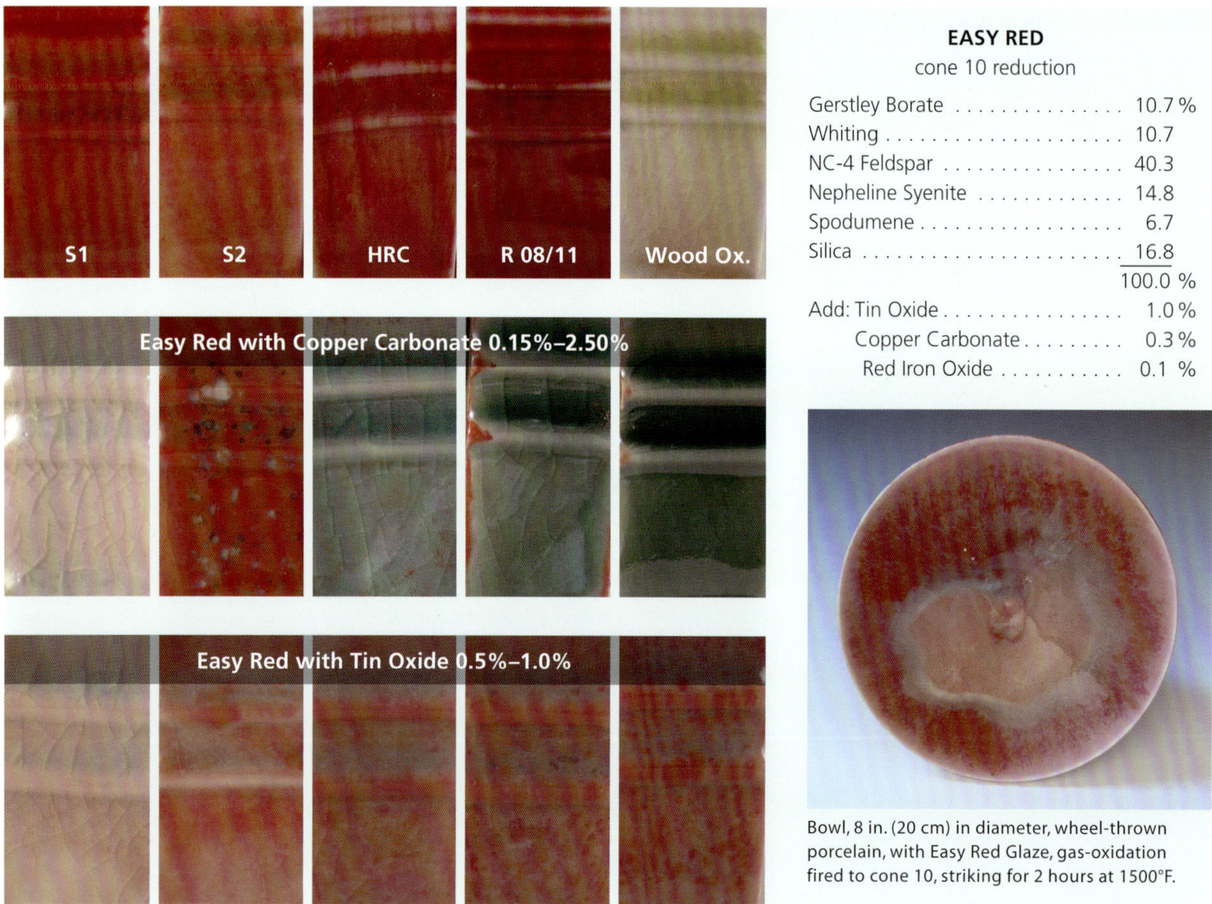

EASY RED

cone 10 reduction

Gerstley Borate	10.7 %
Whiting	10.7
NC-4 Feldspar	40.3
Nepheline Syenite	14.8
Spodumene	6.7
Silica	16.8
	100.0 %
Add: Tin Oxide	1.0 %
Copper Carbonate	0.3 %
Red Iron Oxide	0.1 %

Bowl, 8 in. (20 cm) in diameter, wheel-thrown porcelain, with Easy Red Glaze, gas-oxidation fired to cone 10, striking for 2 hours at 1500°F.

We reasoned that, since our grinding technology has greatly improved, the materials used today are much finer than those of the Qing dynasty, which may explain why you don't see much green spotting in glazes. Just as we had hypothesized, the black copper oxide produced green and black spots with green or red halos around them (see examples on pp. 126 and 128).

Heavy Reduction Cycle (HRC) was fired to cone 022 (1100°F or 593°C), which is the beginning of dull red heat, and then put into heavy reduction (>0.80 on our oxyprobe). This was continued until cone 10 was bent to the 3 o'clock position and then the kiln was closed up and allowed to naturally cool. The results were nothing in the Peach Bloom range but rather the standard copper reds with very dark red to black to purple with some mottled surfaces.

R 08/11 Reduction Cycle started reduction at cone 08 and held to cone 11 (0.72 on the oxyprobe). This is a little later than the standard reduction cycle, where you start reducing copper reds at cone 010 and we also went a little hotter, to cone 11.

Wood Oxidation Firing was attempted because we had the offer of space in a firing and we thought we might learn something since the Chinese potters of the Qing dynasty fired with wood. Unfortunately, the firing was mainly oxidizing and so there were no Peach Blooms acquired in this firing.

Results

- The crystallization of the aged glazes showed a great difference in the outcome of the tiles. See Jeff's Red (page 131) and Pete's Cranberry (page 129). The aged Splotchy Lavender (page 128) also produced some very interesting mottled results.
- Layering a blue celadon glaze with a copper red over it, as well as sandwiching the red between two blue celadon coats, gave wonderful mottled blue reds (Pete's Cranberry, page 129).

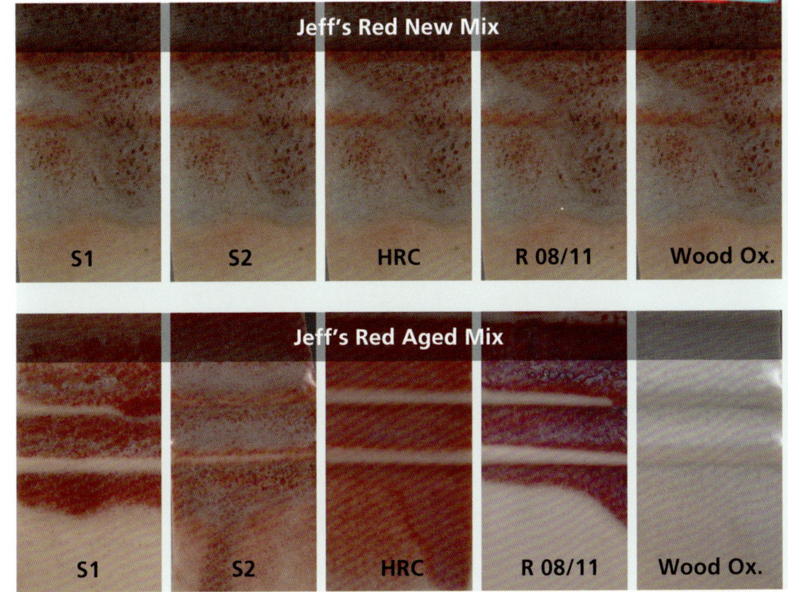

JEFF'S RED
cone 10 reduction

Barium Carbonate	4.4 %
Dolomite	8.7
Whiting	8.4
Zinc Oxide	1.7
Ferro Frit 3134	8.7
Custer Feldspar	41.9
Silica	26.2
	100.0 %
Add: Tin Oxide	2.6 %
Copper Carbonate	0.5 %
Bentonite	1.0 %

NORTON RED
cone 10 reduction

Whiting	14.1 %
Nepheline Syenite	44.4
Ferro Frit 3134	13.1
Kaolin	3.0
Silica	25.3
	100.0 %
Add: Copper Carbonate	0.2%
Tin Oxide	1.0%

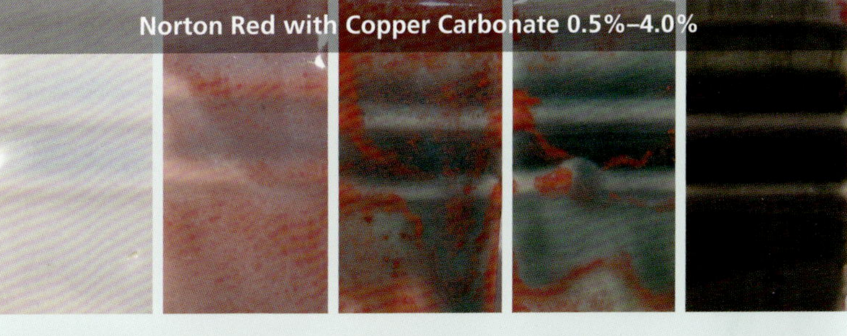

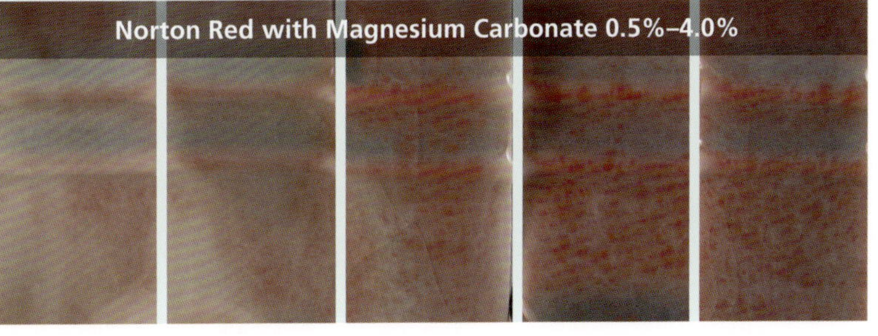

- Higher amounts of tin oxide in the glaze (0.15%–2.5%) did make the glaze more milky and mottled (Easy Red, page 130).
- Higher amounts of magnesium carbonate appeared to produce more pinks (Norton Red, page 131).
- Using black copper oxide as the source of copper and/or sprinkling it on while glazing produced green and red patches (Tom Turner Flambe 2, page 126, and Splotchy Lavender, page 128).
- Additions of copper carbonate (1%–3%) in the base recipe pushed it toward green and yet still retained some red highlights (Easy Red, page 130, and Norton Red, page 131).
- Refiring the over-reduced peach blooms (the ones we fired in the sooty S2 strike firings) in electric bisque with other greenware pieces of dark stoneware or earthenware gave the glazes a wonderful satin surface while re-oxidizing the red to blue with spots. This satin surface was caused by the gases (sulfur) being released from the earthenware clay. This will often happen if you mix dark greenware pieces

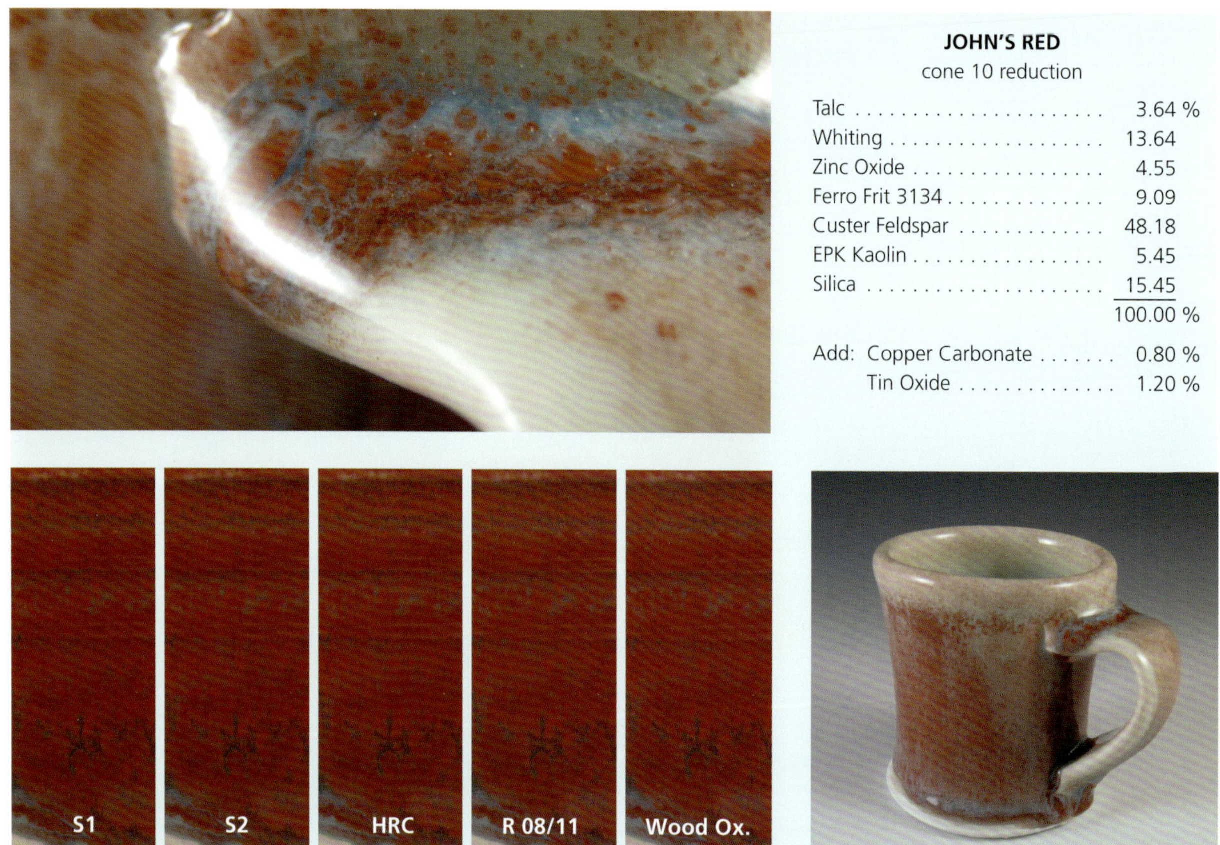

JOHN'S RED

cone 10 reduction

Talc	3.64 %
Whiting	13.64
Zinc Oxide	4.55
Ferro Frit 3134	9.09
Custer Feldspar	48.18
EPK Kaolin	5.45
Silica	15.45
	100.00 %
Add: Copper Carbonate	0.80 %
Tin Oxide	1.20 %

Cup, 5 in. (13 cm) in height, wheel-thrown porcelain, with John's Red Glaze outside, Pinnell Celadon inside, gas-oxidation fired cone 10, striking for 2 hours at 1500°F.

in a majolica glaze firing (Tom Turner Flambe 2, page 126 and Splotchy Lavender, page 128).

For Further Testing

Although we did achieve our goal of reproducing some beautiful Peach Bloom glazes, there is still a lot more to be learned about this elusive and beautiful glaze. Our testing led us to new and unusual methods of glazing and firing and opened many new roads for further testing. Layering two different copper reds and strike firing gave some more varied surfaces. Lower flux amounts made flat pink, as did under firing copper reds to cone 9 rather than cone 10. We did not get definitive results from saggar firing with Oribe or copper wash on the inside of the saggar. We also got no definitive results from spraying tin and copper over a celadon or under firing celadons, but that is not to say we have eliminated them from testing.

Through it all, it turns out that Lindsey was right: Occasionally, if everything comes together just right, magic can happen!

Cobalt Glaze Recipes for Purple and Green

by Dave Finkelnburg

If we use lots of talc, dolomite, or another source of magnesium in a cobalt glaze, a beautiful bubble-gum purple glaze can be the result! Magnesium oxide (MgO) shifts the wavelengths of light emitted from our fired cobalt glaze from blue to purple. Every mole of flux should include more than 0.2 moles of MgO to get purple. Make a line blend varying MgO content to test for the shade of purple desired. Lesser amounts of MgO will produce lavender, larger amounts combined with an opacifier will produce a strong grape purple.

Alumina and titania in a cobalt glaze will shift the fired glaze color from blue to green. Because a significant amount of alumina can be dissolved from the clay body by the glaze during firing, glaze thickness can cause the same glaze to turn blue (where thick) and green (where thin) on the same piece. Glaze layering can have a similar effect with layering of the cobalt glaze over a white glaze firing blue but the cobalt glaze alone firing green. Cobalt greens are invariably satin to matte rather than glossy glazes. These glazes are typically flux saturated and the matteness comes from precipitating crystals of the flux in combination with aluminum and silicon. The amount of titanium oxide used, either as rutile or titanium dioxide, influences the green color. While cobalt greens have been reported using as much as 7.5% rutile in a cone 9 glaze, 2% rutile is far more typical. Less rutile also helps avoid pinholes in the glaze. The two glaze examples given here, Reitz Green Glaze and Emily's Purple, are both cone 9–10, but cobalt's spectrum of effects can be seen at all temperatures.

Black glazes are typically achieved using cobalt oxide or cobalt carbonate plus a blend of iron and other metallic oxides. Typical cobalt levels are between 1 and 3% and iron levels up to 9%. The total of all the colorant oxides need not be more than 10 or 11%. Cobalt should be used with care—it is expensive, and in thick applications, too much cobalt can make a glaze fluid enough to flow off the ware. Iron is not required to make a black glaze, but as an alternative, it is inexpensive, readily available, and nontoxic. One or more of the oxides of copper, manganese, and chrome are added in many black glazes. Glazes high in iron black tend to fade brown and glazes with high amounts of cobalt tend to fade blue over a white glazes. A simple black glaze can be made with 9% red iron oxide plus 2% cobalt. If other oxides are used, a good starting point is 4% iron, 2% cobalt, 2% manganese dioxide, and 2% copper oxide.

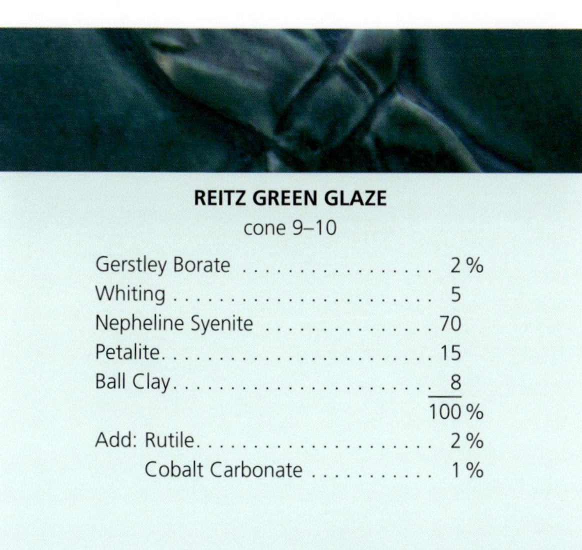

REITZ GREEN GLAZE
cone 9–10

Gerstley Borate	2 %
Whiting	5
Nepheline Syenite	70
Petalite	15
Ball Clay	8
	100 %
Add: Rutile	2 %
Cobalt Carbonate	1 %

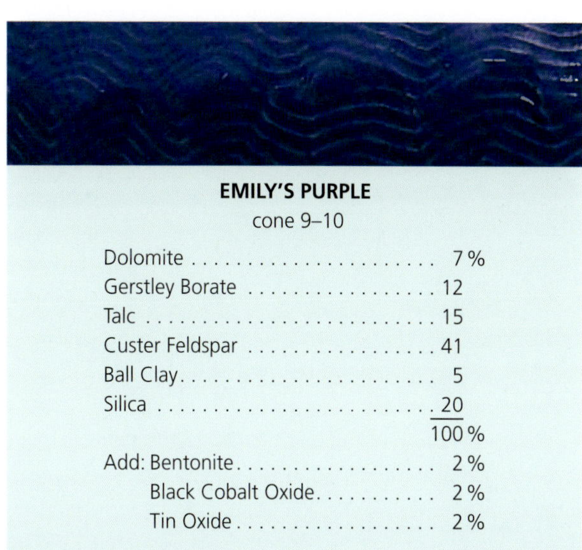

EMILY'S PURPLE
cone 9–10

Dolomite	7 %
Gerstley Borate	12
Talc	15
Custer Feldspar	41
Ball Clay	5
Silica	20
	100 %
Add: Bentonite	2 %
Black Cobalt Oxide	2 %
Tin Oxide	2 %

17 Learn more about cobalt's role as a powerful colorant

High-fire Red Glazes

by Dave Finkelnburg

Iron Red

Iron red glazes often have vibrant names like Tomato Red or Ketchup Red, and they are generally warm reds. The true reds are produced in oxidation around cone 5. By cone 10, they tend to turn toward orange or persimmon. High-iron glazes fired in heavy reduction will turn maroon to black.

Iron reds are mainly iron saturated, which means they contain between 5 and 10% iron oxide in the glaze recipe (most recipes use 7% or more). Iron reds with bone ash (calcium phosphate) as a source of phosphorous (phosphorous in general causes opalescence and brighter colors) typically contain on the order of 10%.

Even considering the above specifications, there is wide variation in iron red recipes. Traditional persimmon or kaki recipes, for example, are very high in both alumina and silica but contain no phosphorous.

The source of iron oxide is important to the color produced and is possibly the most variable colorant used in glazes. The percentage of iron, particle size, and amount of clay, silica or other contaminants may be dramatically different from one source of iron oxide to another.

Copper Red

Copper reds are achieved between cones 5 and 11 by reducing the copper (either copper oxide or copper carbonate) in the glaze. Only a small quantity of copper is necessary for this; 0.25% copper carbonate is sufficient, though more is often used. The red color is aided by the presence of a limited amount of tin. Iron can also help produce a red color in copper red glazes, but too much iron will lead to muddy reds.

The various hues of copper red are influenced by the amount of alumina, magnesium, and boron present in the glaze. High alumina tends to produce cooler reds, as does magnesium, while high boron produces warmer reds.

Copper red glazes tend to be somewhat fluid, so glaze runs should be guarded against in glaze application. Boron particularly enhances the fluidity at cone 10. Where copper reds flow off of rims or high points, they tend to turn white.

Oxidation copper reds in electric kilns are achieved by mixing a reducing agent, silicon carbide, with the copper in the glaze. Because silicon carbide can be a source of glaze blisters and pinholing, its use presents its own set of problems in the studio.

At cone 10, any combination of glaze ingredients that contains, in terms of flux (molar) unity, 0.3 moles of alkalis, 0.7 moles of alkaline earths (preferably most or all as CaO), 0.4 moles of alumina, 3.5 moles of silica, 0.15 moles of B2O3, 1% tin, and 0.5 % copper carbonate can produce a fine copper red if properly fired.

Understanding and controlling the reduction atmosphere in a kiln to achieve copper reds is usually by far the most difficult part of working with this family of glazes. The glaze above is best if the kiln is placed in moderate reduction at cone 010 and held there until cone 9 drops. The kiln can then be soaked in oxidation until cone 10 is down. A smoky fire, as used with carbon trap glazes, is never necessary to achieve copper reds. In fact, a sooty atmosphere in the kiln is likely to produce gray, dingy copper reds due to carbon trapping.

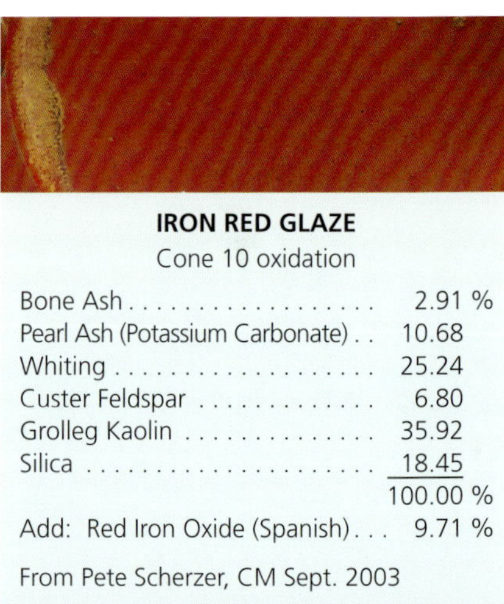

IRON RED GLAZE

Cone 10 oxidation

Ingredient	%
Bone Ash	2.91 %
Pearl Ash (Potassium Carbonate)	10.68
Whiting	25.24
Custer Feldspar	6.80
Grolleg Kaolin	35.92
Silica	18.45
	100.00 %
Add: Red Iron Oxide (Spanish)	9.71 %

From Pete Scherzer, CM Sept. 2003

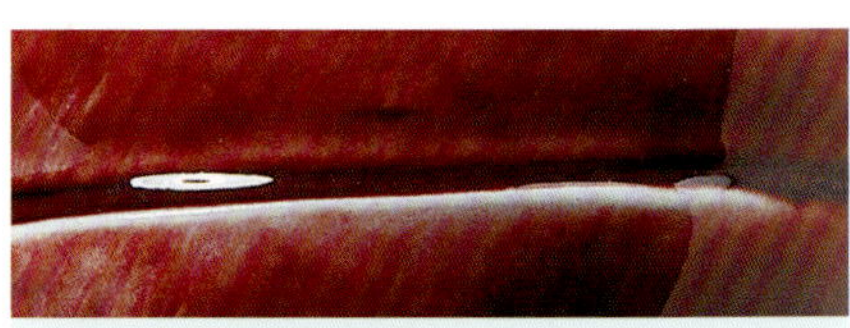

COPPER RED #11 GLAZE

Cone 10 reduction

Ingredient	%
Colemanite	10.80 %
Whiting	15.73
Kona F-4 (sub Minspar 200)	15.57
Nepheline Syenite	20.43
English China Clay	1.48
Silica	35.99
	100.00 %
Add: Tin Oxide	1.72 %
Copper Carbonate	0.42 %

A vibrant red that may turn blue, green, or purple where thick; runs when thick. From Andy Cantrell, CM May 2000.

5 Find more information on alkaline and alkaline earth fluxes.

The New World of Crystalline Glazes

by Diane Creber

Before exploring the possibilities of crystalline glazes, the potter needs to understand the basics. The process of creating a crystalline glaze is more involved than working with a regular glaze as it has a tendency to run off the pot and the firing cycle is very dependent on accurate temperature measurements.

For the purpose of growing crystals, the kiln is taken up in temperature to around 300°F beyond the melting temperature of the glaze, (typically cone 6 to 12), which allows some of the zinc-silicate nuclei, or seed crystals, to dissolve. The crystals will grow from the few remaining nuclei.

After reaching top temperature, the kiln is cooled either by shutting it off or using a predetermined cooling rate, until it reaches the temperature where the crystals will grow. This is usually somewhere around 2100°F–1900°F. When the glaze is molten, all these ingredients float around in a liquid matrix. By holding the temperature at the point where the glaze is still slightly molten but just beginning to stiffen, the crystals form, with their size being determined by the amount of time they remain in this state (typically 3–5 hours). The kiln is then shut off and cooled naturally.

Making a Crystalline Glaze

There are three main ingredients in a crystalline glaze. Zinc oxide and silica make up approximately 25 parts each of the glaze and these are the crystal formers. They come together to form zinc silicate. The remaining 50 parts are the various ingredients that form or flux the glass melt, which can include boron, magnesium, calcium, lithium, sodium, and potassium. However, some of these ingredients are soluble in a glaze. Therefore, it is to the potter's advantage to use a frit. When using a frit, a crystalline glaze could consist of only three ingredients: frit, zinc oxide, and silica. This combination, in the right proportions, will produce a crystalline glaze.

The most commonly used colorants are cobalt, copper, iron, manganese, nickel, and rutile. Less common are gold, silver, uranium, and some rare earth metals. These can be used alone or in combination with each other.

Let's look at these ingredients individually. Most crystalline glaze recipes will call for calcined zinc oxide. Almost all

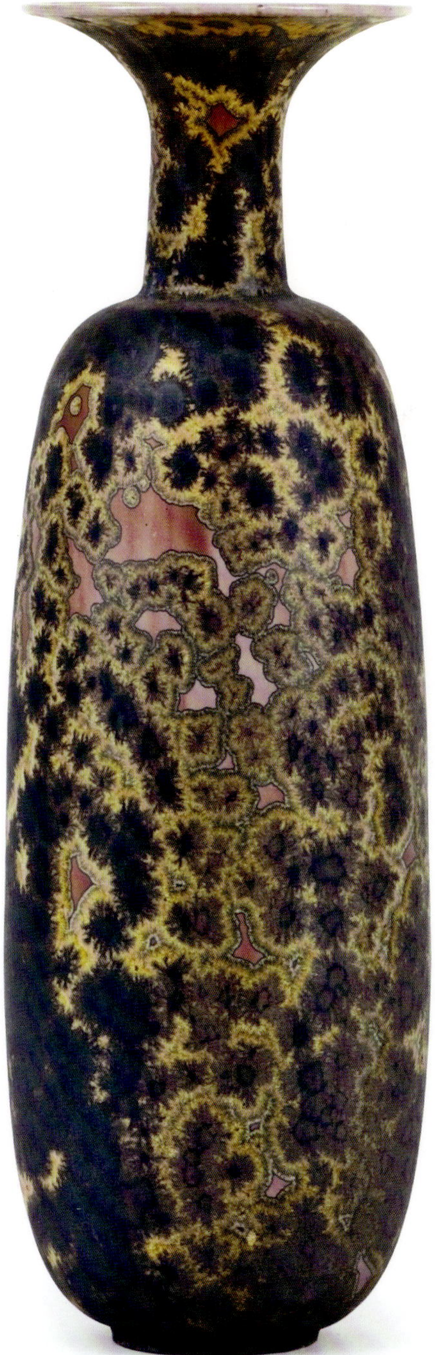

Bottle with glaze containing copper and iron, initially fired in oxidation to develop crystals, then refired to 1500°F and reduced down to 1250°F using a vegetable-oil drip, by Diane Creber, Wilton, Ontario.

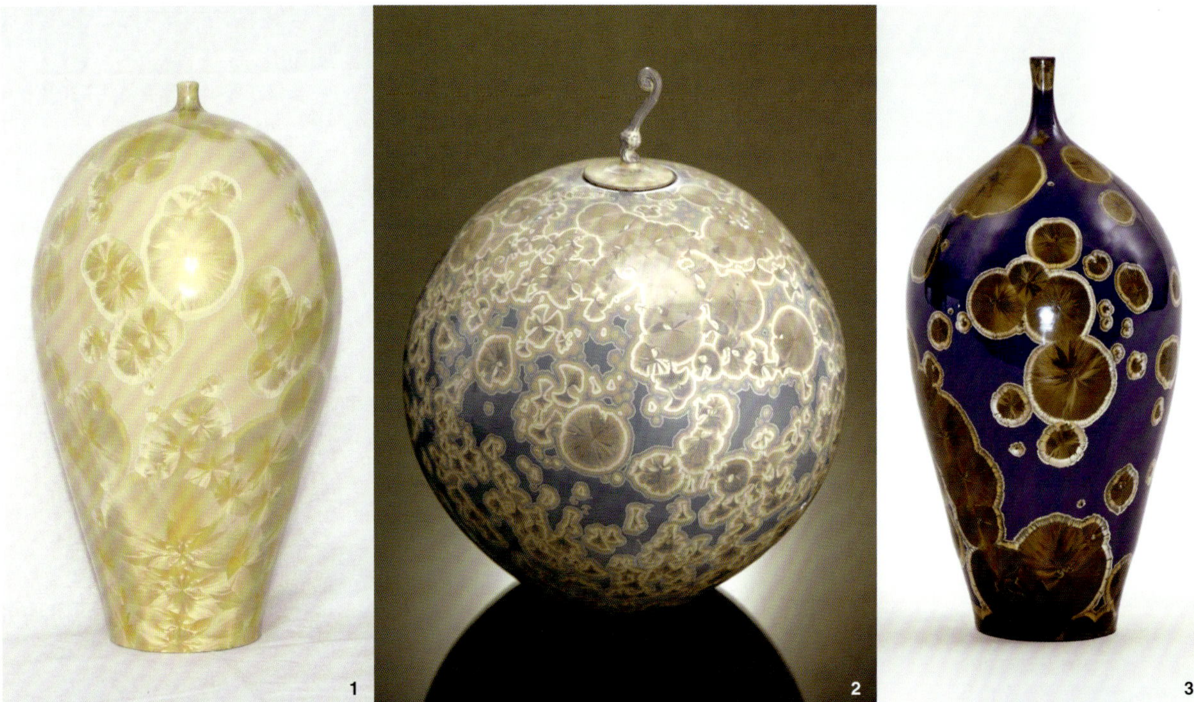

1 Bottle with Gold Stuff Glaze (see recipe on page 140) fired in oxidation, by Diane Creber, Wilton, Ontario, Canada. **2** Covered jar with Gold Stuff Glaze, fired in oxidation to grow crystals, then reduced from 2000°F to 1850°F, by John Tilton, Alachua, Florida. **3** Bottle with Gold Stuff Glaze, first fired in oxidation, then refired to 1500°F and reduced until the kiln cooled to 1250°F, by Diane Creber. Cooking oil was introduced into the kiln via a tube, at approximately one drop per second. For a 7-cubic-foot kiln, less than 8 oz. of oil is used per firing for light reduction. If there is heavy black smoke, reduce the amount of oil entering the kiln. In half an hour, the temperature should be around 1250°F, the tube removed, the peep replaced, and the kiln allowed to cool.

of the zinc oxide you buy today is calcined, so there is no need to calcine it yourself. Check with your glaze supplier to ensure your zinc is calcined. If not, calcining is not a difficult procedure; place the zinc in a bisque bowl and heat it to cone 06–04, which means essentially putting it through a bisque firing. This will drive off any absorbed moisture. Zinc oxide absorbs moisture from the air so it must be stored in an airtight container. Calcined zinc oxide weighs less than uncalcined so make sure you are using calcined as recipes are based on the calcined weight. The silica should be 400 mesh (used for most glazes—but double check), because this particle size makes it easier to get a complete melt and no nucleation (the beginning of crystal growth, based around an unmelted zinc-silicate crystal).

There are many frit manufacturers on the market, which becomes confusing as frits are primarily made for industrial applications, and manufacturer names change. The most common frit used by crystalline potters is readily available and is called Fusion-75. It was formerly called Ferro 3110. If you ask your supplier for Ferro 3110 they usually know what you are asking for but sell you Fusion-75 (the same thing). I suggest using one frit and getting to know it well before trying another. Although different frits can give slightly different effects on the glaze, the greater variety comes from the minerals used. If using another frit, the glaze must be altered accordingly. You cannot substitute one frit for another without making adjustments based on the chemical composition of the frit.

Very small amounts of alumina or bentonite are often added to a glaze to help keep the materials in suspension (1–2%). These ingredients must be in very small quantities or the glaze will opacify and become a matte glaze. Adding a small amount (1%) of Epsom salts to the glaze keeps the glaze flocculated.

Experimentation should be done first with the colorant. These are easier to adjust than other ingredients and can give the most dramatic results. Start with one colorant and add it to the base glaze in gradual increments. Also try mixing two or more colorants together. Final glaze slurries should be passed through an 80-mesh sieve.

The glaze should be thickly applied by pouring, dipping, or spraying, with a thicker application at the top of the pot, thinning towards the bottom. Once the pot is glazed, it is placed in the collection dish and put in the kiln ready for firing (see "Planning for Glaze Overflow" on page 138).

Suitable Clays and Forms

These glazes are translucent, and the color of the clay will show through and affect the color of the glaze. Porcelain is the preferred clay, but white stoneware can be used as long as it is free of grog or large-grained silica, which could become nucleation sites for crystals. This would result in far more crystals than usually desired. When there is a large number of crystals, they butt up against each other and become a mass of crystals. This has the potential to make the glaze matte.

Porcelain that is slightly immature at cone 10 is preferred. Translucent clay is not ideal for crystalline glazes, though some use it. Most forms do not allow for translucency and making a super thin pot might cause it to crack because of the thick application of the glaze. These glazes are corrosive and can absorb alumina from the clay body if the clay starts to flux, which is what happens in a translucent body. Alumina affects crystal growth, and can also make the glazes go matte.

Not all shapes work well with crystalline glaze, either aesthetically or practically. Some consider these glazes to

Strike Firing

Striking is a glassblowing term that merely means re-heating a piece. Crystalline glaze potters have been using the term to apply to a firing procedure that also involves re-heating the piece in order to achieve different color effects. How great the change depends on the colorant. Some colorants react dramatically and others hardly change at all.

Once the pots are selected to be re-fired, the kiln temperature is taken up to cone 018 in a neutral or oxidizing atmosphere and shut off.

After the initial glaze firing, a cobalt glaze with 3.5% titanium dioxide results in dark blue crystals and a lighter blue to green background (4). After the cone 018 refiring, the glaze has changed to a yellow/orange background with dark blue crystals and might also have an interesting smoky effect where the glaze is thicker (5). Glazes with at least 3.5% titanium dioxide, along with any of the usual colorants like iron, copper, and cobalt, will respond well to a cone 018 refiring. The background gets darker and the crystals show more contrast with deeper colors.

Copper is very sensitive, so a glaze with as little as 3% copper carbonate and very little titanium changes dramatically. The first glaze firing results in silver/green crystals on a green background. Refiring to cone 018 results in a deep silvery dark green color with a mirror finish.

A glaze containing 5% titanium and 2.5% iron oxide appears an overall yellow and is rather bland looking after the initial crystalline firing. When re-fired to 018, it results in more contrast and a darker background. A yellow halo is produced around areas where the glaze pools, which isn't there after the first firing.

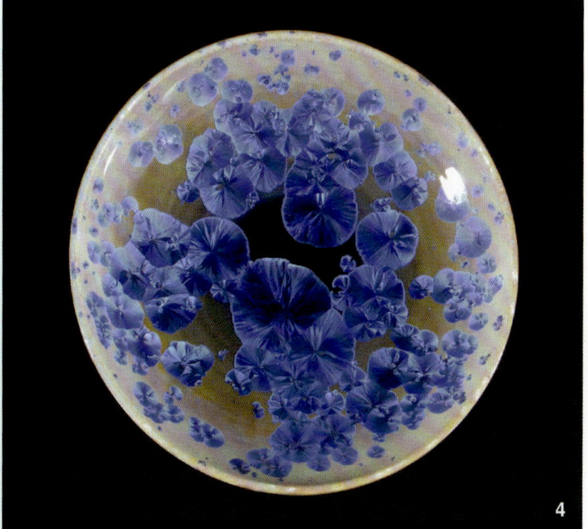
4

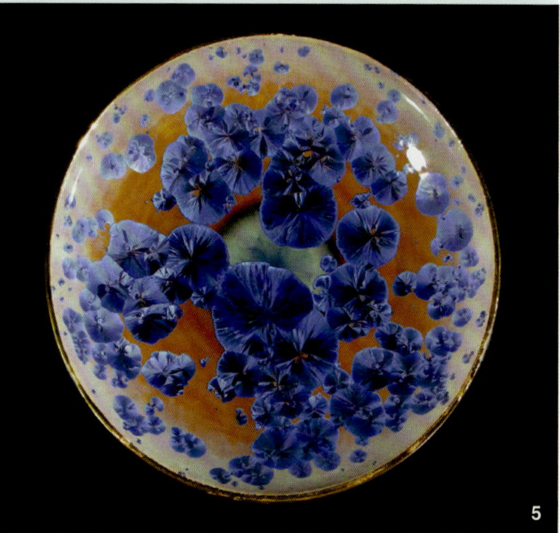
5

Before (4) and after (5) shots of a plate with glaze containing titanium and cobalt, strike fired to cone 018, by Bill Boyd, Galliano Island, British Columbia, Canada.

be rather glitzy so a pot with a simple but elegant form is usually most suitable. The glaze can collect on the inside of bowls and containers often creating unattractive matte areas that can be rough to the touch. However, with experimentation, the correct glaze thickness can be achieved in the bottom of plates and bowls and give pleasing results.

Interiors of vases or jars are sometimes glazed with a liner glaze, with the crystalline glaze applied only to the outside. When glazing the interior of a bowl, the glaze should be applied thickly to the rim area, becoming thinner on the sides and thinnest on the bottom.

Planning for Glaze Overflow

Precautions must be taken to protect kiln shelves from running glaze. The most typical method is to make either a one- or two-piece pedestal with a dish under it so that the top of the pedestal is the same diameter as the foot ring of the pot. The pot is glued to the pedestal and the excess glaze runs down the pedestal and into the collection dish. The glue may be a mixture of 50% kaolin and 50% alumina or it could be just kaolin mixed with a little water and Bondfast glue. The kaolin and alumina help separate the pot from the pedestal after the firing so the glue mixture should be applied thickly. I glue my pots to their pedestals before they are glazed.

Firing Crystalline Glazes

Most crystalline glaze firings take place in an electric kiln. It is possible to fire in a fuel kiln and that will be discussed later. The kiln must be capable of going to cone 10 or 11 without difficulty. A temperature controller is an asset. Kilns may be purchased with factory-installed controllers or a controller can be purchased separately and installed by an electrician. The controller must interface between the power source and the kiln's main switching panel.

There are two types of temperature probes on the market: the *S* type and the *K* type. The *S* is more accurate, particularly for cone 9 or above, and is preferred by crystalline potters, although it is more expensive than the *K*.

Most new kilns come with three temperature probes so a potter can see what is happening in three different locations in the kiln. A laptop computer can be plugged into a jack provided by the manufacturer on some controllers. It can be attached directly to the processor and connected to a computer with KISS. (Kiln Interfacing Software System). This allows one to see graphically what is and has happened in three different areas of the kiln at the same time, and to make any necessary adjustments. During the firing, the actual time and temperature profile can be displayed, logged on the printer, and saved electronically, giving a complete picture of the entire firing sequence. Several kilns can be fired at the same time, and using a remote, the potter can monitor, graph and program firings while away from location. Another advantage is that firings can be repeated exactly, and the programs stored in the computer.

It is possible to fire without a temperature programmer by carefully watching the pyrometer and monitoring the

Crystalline Firing Program for a Digital Controller

Every kiln is different, and what measures 2350°F on one kiln may be out by several degrees on another. Experimentation is necessary to find out the firing temperatures that work best. Cones should be used to measure total heatwork, and the rate of temperature climb to reach top temperature should be noted. (see pp. 49–52 for more information on heatwork and cones). Once the target cone temperature has been reached and the kiln is cooling, to measure temperature drop and soaking temperature, a pyrometer or temperature controller is used.

The following is a very simple guide for programming a temperature controller for a crystalline firing:

- 150°F/hr to 250°F. No hold (slow climb initially to dry the glazes)
- 300°F/hr to 2200°F. No hold
- 108°F/hr to 2345°F. No hold (The rate of climb is slowed to allow for less wear on the elements. This should get to cone 10 at 2345°F. Some potters hold at peak temperature for a few minutes.
- 325°F/hr to ~2000°F*. Hold for 4 hours. Often potters set "9999°F to 2000°F" on their temperature controller, which tells the controller to lower the temperature as fast as possible.
- Kiln off.

*2000°F is a temperature in the middle of the crystal growing range. Crystals can be grown a little hotter or cooler than this temperature (+/- 100°F). If held at the hotter temperature range, the crystals may be more bar shaped or double-axe-head shaped. At the cooler end, they tend to round out and more resemble flowers. Raising and lowering the temperature within the crystal growing phase results in growth rings in the crystals.

kiln visually, but it requires the potter being present from the time the kiln reaches peak temperature throughout the crystal growing phase.

When the kiln has cooled to the point that the pots can be handled, they can be removed from the kiln. Lifting them by their collection dishes avoids the possibility of the pot separating from the dish and the dish falling back into the kiln.

Take a small hammer and tap around the collection dish to separate the pot from the dish. Usually the pot will separate. If not, use a glass cutter and score around the seam where the foot rim of the pot meets the top of the pedestal. Then take a small chisel and gently tap around this seam with a hammer.

Another method for removal is to use a propane torch, either the type used for spot welding or a crème brulée torch. The flame is aimed at the join line as the pot turns on a banding wheel. The pot quickly breaks away from its base. In both methods, it is necessary to wear safety goggles to protect the eyes from flying glass particles.

The bottom of the pot may have sharp edges of glass that can cut the hands. A silicon carbide grinding wheel can be used to remove the pieces of glass and smooth the bottom, and that may be all that is needed. To get a really smooth bottom, a diamond grinding pad is helpful. Whatever grinding method is used, wear a dust mask to protect your lungs from the dust.

Reduction Firing Crystalline Glazes

Safety is always a factor when firing all kilns, but especially when fuel is introduced. These are flammable materials and one must never leave a kiln unattended throughout the reduction period. Good ventilation is a necessity and reduction should not be attempted unless one has a kiln hood to extract fumes, or the firing is conducted outdoors.

Crystalline glazes contain a large proportion of zinc oxide compared to standard glazes, sometimes comprising as much as 30% of the glaze. Zinc oxide is easily reduced to the metal at temperatures above 1742°F and the metal alone melts at 786°F and boils at 1697°F. Even slight reduction is sufficient to extract the oxygen which results in the loss of the zinc. Therefore any reduction at these temperatures or above will take away the oxygen, leaving a boiling metal. The boiling metal volatilizes and is lost. It is widely advised that zinc oxide be used only in fully oxidized or neutral firings. Because of this, it was long believed that crystals could not be grown in a reduction atmosphere.

Before electric kilns were available, crystals were grown in a neutral-to-oxidizing atmosphere in gas kilns. The crystalline glazed pots would be placed in saggars to protect them from any reduction that might occur. However crystalline glaze potters have been recently experimenting using reduction to enhance the pre-formed crystals, or introducing reduction during the final stages of the crystal growing phase, to completely alter the glaze.

The preference has been for electric kilns for firing crystalline glazes. Once potters realized that reduction can alter the glaze and create many more exciting effects, they started looking for ways to introduce reduction. With electricity, the ability to reduce is somewhat limited, although possible. But firing crystals in a gas kiln and using reduction as part of the process is also possible, using specific firing schedules.

At a recent workshop (Hamling studio, Warwick, New York), reducing in standard and custom-made electric kilns was demonstrated at two different temperatures (1500°F down to 1250°F and 2000°F down to 1850°F), and there were several firings with variations of these methods.

When reduction takes place after the crystals are grown and at temperatures below 1900°F, the zinc oxide is unaffected. This is sometimes done at the end of the initial glaze firing.

Crystalline glazes containing minerals that are affected by reduction (rutile, copper and iron) can be fired in oxidation and then refired in reduction. They no longer need their protective dishes and pedestals, which may be removed before firing. Before loading the kiln, a small fired dish is placed under the bottom peep hole inside the kiln to catch the fuel used to create the reduction atmosphere. The kiln is fired to 1500°F and then is either shut off and reduction started as the kiln cools naturally down to 1250°F, or reduction can be introduced while the temperature drops to 1250°F using a temperature controller.

Reduction requires a fuel, and there are various ways the fuel can be introduced. One method of introducing fuel is to use an IV bag filled with the fuel (oil or denatured alcohol), available from some drug stores or a hospital supply store. When the kiln has reached the temperature to start reduction (1500°F), the bag is suspended above the kiln and the end of the tube is inserted into a protective ceramic sheath that goes into the kiln above the ceramic dish. The point of entry into the peep hole

TYPICAL CRYSTALLINE GLAZE

(cone 10)

Lithium Carbonate	00.1 %
Zinc oxide (calcined)	30.0
Fusion Frit 75 (Ferro frit 3110)	44.9
Silica	25.0
	100.0 %
Add: Bentonite	1.0 %
Color Variations:	
Blue: Cobalt Carbonate	0.5–2 %
Green: Copper Carbonate	1–5 %
Pink/Tan: Manganese Dioxide	1–5 %
Yellow/Green: Red Iron Oxide	1–4 %
Green: Nickel Oxide	1–2 %
Yellow: Rutile	1–4 %

These colorants can be combined, but when doing so use less of each ingredient.

GOLD STUFF GLAZE (1–3)

(cone 10)

Fusion Frit F644	45.1 %
Zinc Oxide (calcined)	25.3
Bentonite	0.7
Molochite	0.4
Silica	28.5
	100.0 %
Add: Rutile	5.0 %
Illmenite	3.0 %

See examples of Gold Stuff Glaze fired three different ways on page 136.

should be sealed with clay or fiber blanket to make the area airtight and to keep the sheath in place. Just below the bag on the tube is a small dial that regulates the rate of flow from the bag.

The difference between reducing at the higher and lower temperatures are obvious in the finished results. For instance, Gold Stuff Glaze (see recipe above and images on page 136), when fired in oxidation produces cream-colored crystals on a white background. When reduced at the higher temperature, the results are a blue background with gold colored crystals ringed in white. The same glaze reduced at the lower temperatures produces a deep purple background with olive green to gold crystals ringed in gold.

It is the firing that gives the diversity of glaze results, and using only one or two glazes gives the potter a whole palette of amazing colors.

Oil Spot and Hare's Fur Glazes

by John Britt

As a category, oil spot glazes are sometimes called Black and Brown ceramics. They include a wide variety of iron glaze effects like black/brown tenmoku, oil spot, iridescent oil spot (Yohen), hare's fur (Yuteki), tortoiseshell, and partridge feathers. A complete discussion of this category would be too lengthy so I will discuss oil spot and hare's fur glazes, which operate in the same way. For an exhaustive academic account of these elusive glazes, read Robert Mowry's acclaimed *Hare's Fur, Tortoiseshell, and Partridge Feathers; Chinese Brown and Black-Glazed Ceramics, 400–1400 A.D.*

The term Tenmoku is thought to derive from the Chinese characters for Mt. Tianmu (Mountain Eye of Heaven). Japanese monks regularly traveled to China during the Song Dynasty to study Buddhism. This is where they first encountered some of these black glazed tea bowls. By the 13th century, Chinese Jian oil-spot tea bowls became highly prized and large quantities were imported to Japan for use in the tea ceremony. White tea was dried, ground to a fine powder, and whipped in a bowl to produce a frothy white drink (matcha tea) that the monks thought looked better in the black glazed tea bowls.

Today, most potters are familiar with tenmoku glaze in a reduction firing. But to get oil spot effects, stiff tenmokus need to be fired in oxidation. This relies on a very simple chemical principle that, once understood, can lead to many successful firings. Red iron oxide (Fe_2O_3) acts as a refractory in oxidation but it can easily be changed to a flux in the form of black iron oxide (FeO), in reduction. Most potters are familiar with this property, but for oil spots we are interested in iron's ability to self-reduce. At approximately cone 7

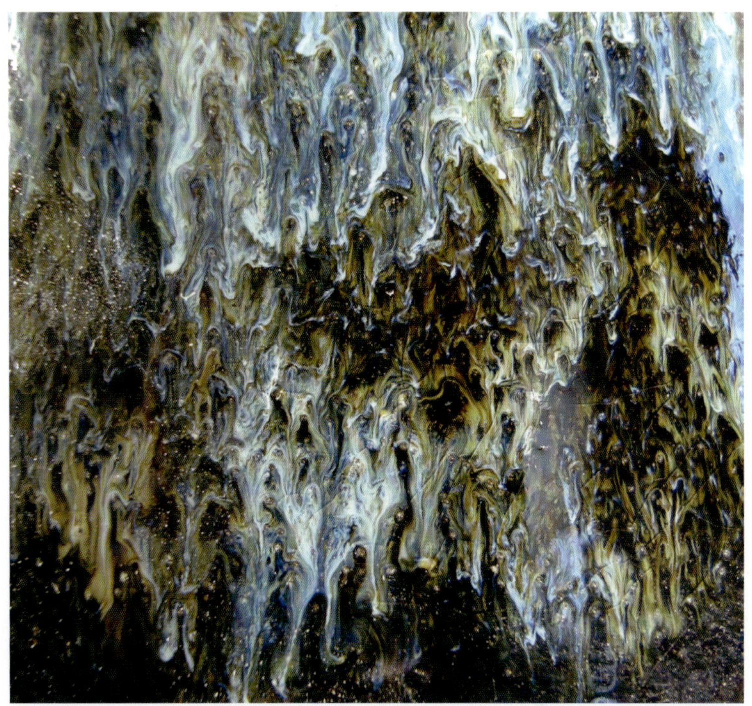

Vase (detail), porcelain with Nuka Glaze over Hamada Rust, fired to cone 10 oxidation. While this is not a true oil spot hare's fur glaze, it produces a similar pattern, and is often referred to as hare's fur for this reason.

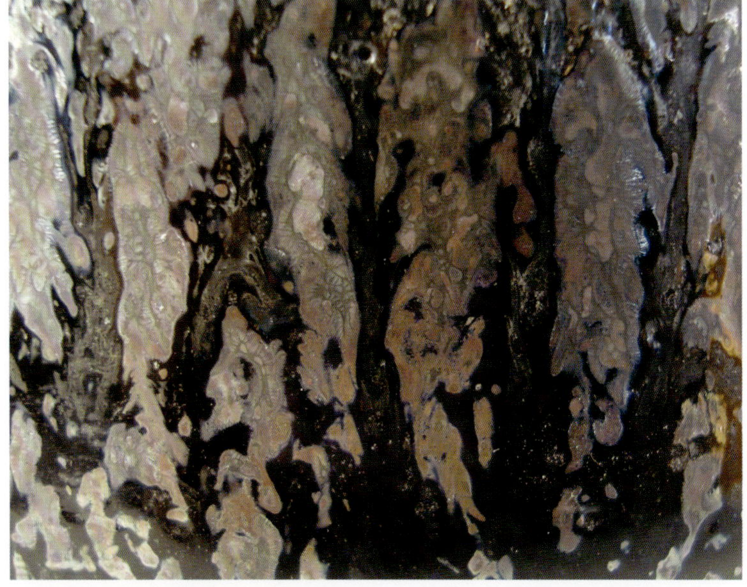

Silver iron cup (detail), porcelain with a hare's fur combination glaze composed of two coats of John's SG-12, one coat Candace Black, and one coat of Hamada Rust, fired to cone 10 in oxidation.

(2250°F or 1232°C), ferric iron (Fe_2O_3) cannot maintain its trigonal crystalline structure and rearranges to a cubic structure, magnetite (Fe_3O_4), which further reduces to become ferrous (FeO). This is called thermal reduction, and what this means in layman's terms is that, when it is sufficiently heated, the red iron oxide used in the glaze recipe will naturally let go of an oxygen atom. As the liberated oxygen bubbles rise to the surface of the glaze, they drag a bit of the magnetite with them and deposit it on the surface. A rough black spot is left on the glaze surface that is a different color than the surrounding glaze, due to the larger concentration of iron oxide in that small area and its subsequent re-oxidization during cooling.

To achieve the oil spot effect you must first apply the glaze very thick (¼–⅜ in.) and then fire it in oxidation to cone 10 or higher (though it can be done at cone 6, which we'll get to shortly). The glaze will bubble vigorously as the iron thermally reduces. A soaking period is helpful at the end of the firing to allow the bubbles to smooth over. This can be done in multiple ways, each resulting in subtle changes to the final look of the glaze. For example, some firing cycles slow the final climb from 2250°F to 2350°F

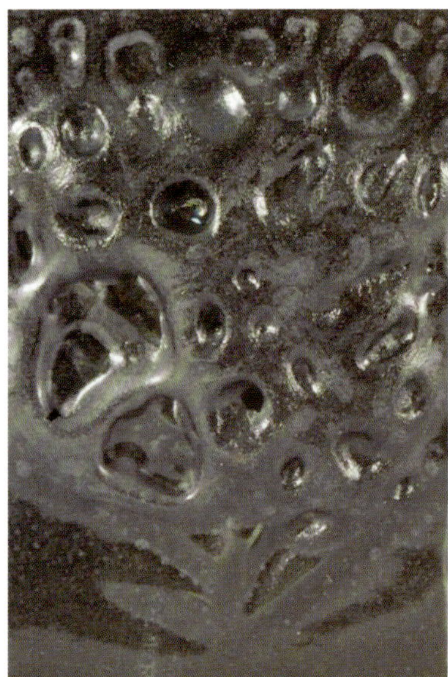

Above: This test tile shows the bubbling of an immature oil spot glaze. As CO_2 bubbles rise through the glaze, they deposit iron on the surface, which forms the spots after the bubble holes seal over.

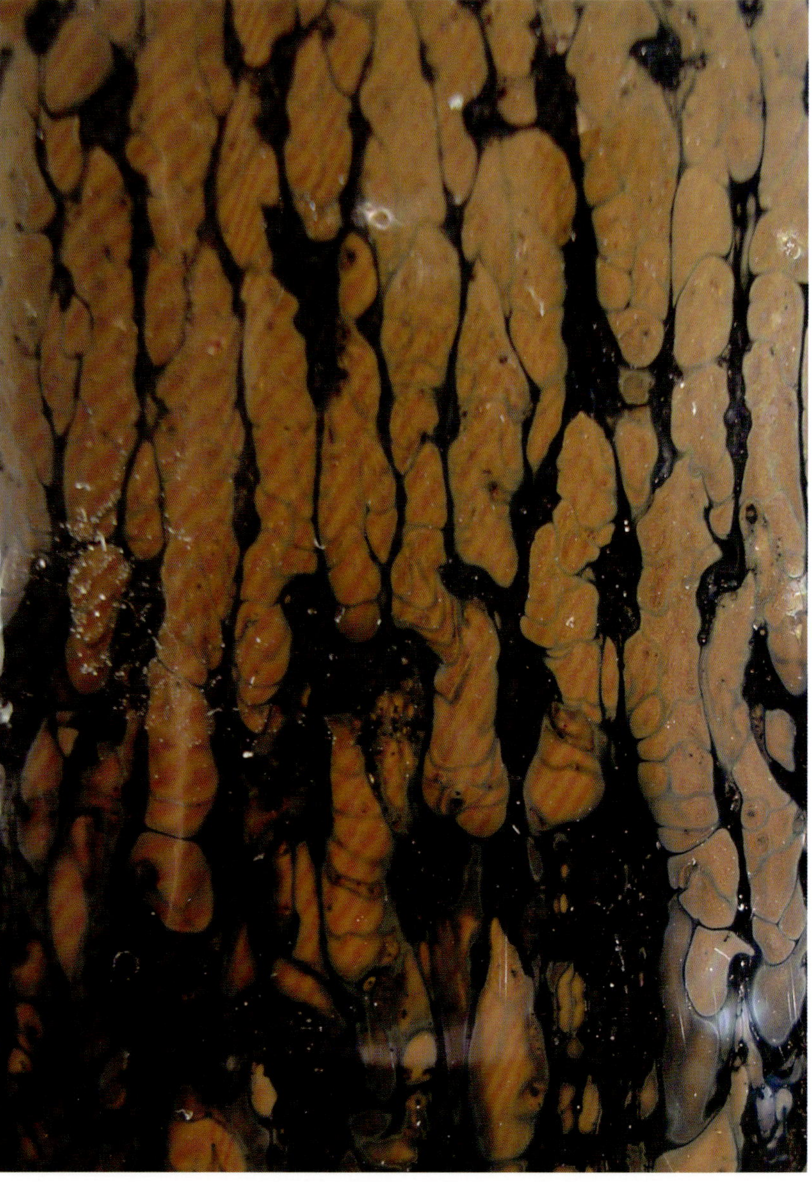

Right: Espresso cup (detail), porcelain with John's SG-12, then Hamada Rust over it, fired to cone 10 in oxidation, 2011. Variations in pattern can be achieved by adjusting the thickness of the undercoat (SG-12) and overcoat (Hamada Rust).

CANDACE BLACK (2)
Cone 10 oxidation

Dolomite	5 %
Whiting	5
F-4 Soda Feldspar	65
Kaolin	5
Silica	20
	100 %
Add: Red Iron Oxide	8 %
Cobalt Carbonate	2 %

JOHN'S SG-12 (2, 3)
Cone 10/11 oxidation

Bone Ash	2.06 %
Dolomite	5.53
Talc	3.08
Whiting	1.73
Custer Feldspar	38.03
Red Art Clay	40.12
Kentucky Ball Clay	9.46
	100.00 %
Add: Red Iron Oxide	4.50 %
Rutile	1.00 %

215 COVER GLAZE
Cone 10/11 oxidation

Whiting	13 %
Custer Feldspar	45
EPK Kaolin	11
Silica	28
	100 %
Add: Red Iron Oxide	8 %

HAMADA RUST (1–3)
Cone 10 oxidation

Gerstley Borate	12.40 %
Whiting	6.20
Custer Feldspar	77.00
EPK Kaolin	4.20
Silica	0.20
	100.00 %
Add: Synthetic Red Iron Oxide	8.70 %

NUKA (1)
Cone 10 oxidation

Bone Ash	2 %
Talc	2
Whiting	22
Wood Ash (unwashed) or Frit 3134	3
Custer Feldspar	36
OM-4 Ball clay	6
Silica	30
	100 %

OIL SPOT COMBO #1
Cone 6 oxidation

Whiting	17.39 %
G-200 Feldspar*	47.83
EPK Kaolin	10.87
Silica	23.91
	100.00 %
Add: Red Iron Oxide	9.78 %

*For G-200 Feldspar, mix 70% G-200HP (the new G-200) and 30% Minspar 200.

OIL SPOT COMBO #2 COVER GLAZE (APPLY OVER #1)
Cone 6 oxidation

Gerstley Borate	33 %
Custer Feldspar	33
EPK Kaolin	6
Silica	28
	100 %
Add: Zircopax	11 %

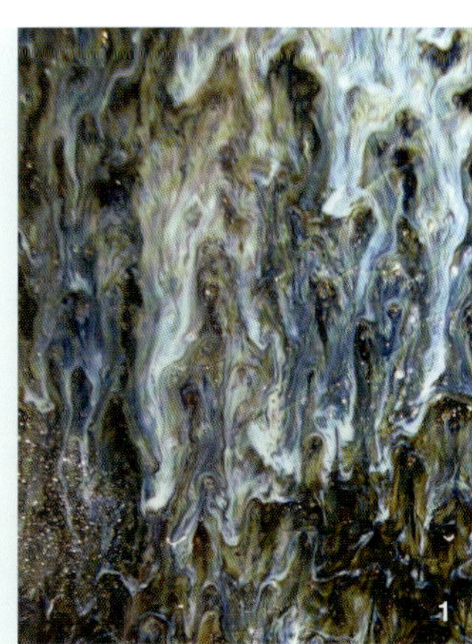
1

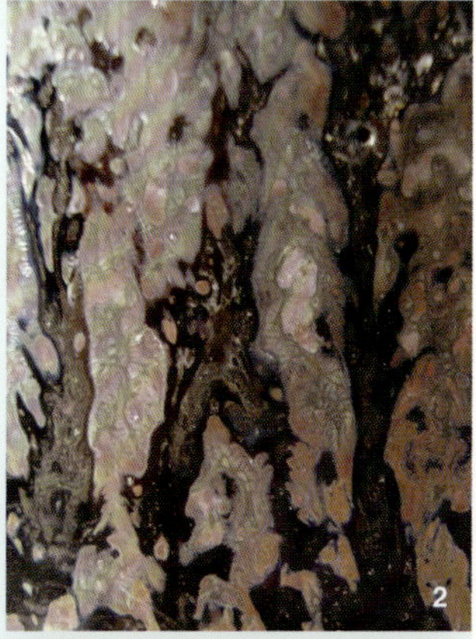
2

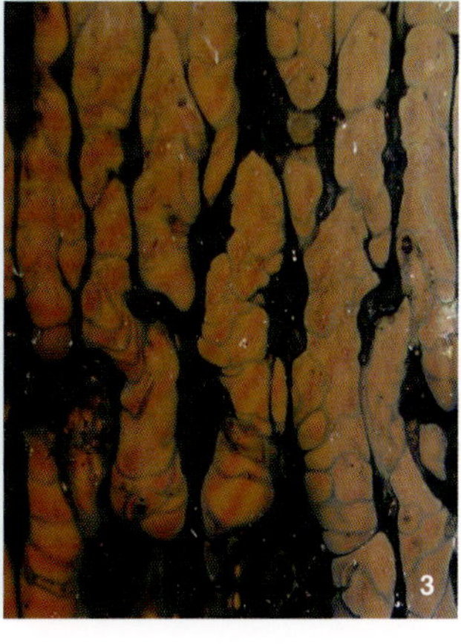
3

(1230–1290°C) to 50 degrees per hour or less, while others hold the top temperature for an hour or so, until draw tiles reveal the maturation of the glaze. Still others fire to cone 12 or 13.

There are several glaze types used to achieve oil spots. Most are stiff feldspathic bases with 5–8% red iron oxide. This will produce brown-on-brown oil spotting. Adding cobalt carbonate at approximately 2–5% produces a glazed surface with silver spots floating in a black field (see above).

Another popular option involves a multi-layered glaze approach. Oil spots can be achieved using an iron slip under a tenmoku glaze. This should be more accurately described as an "iron slip glaze" under a tenmoku glaze. John's SG-12, which is called a "slip glaze" because it contains a high quantity of slip clay (like Albany, Alberta, Redart, shale, etc.), is applied first. A cover glaze is then applied over it. In this case, the 215 Cover Glaze is used. The John's SG-12 is still applied thickly (three coats) and then the cover glaze is applied in one or two coats.

Hare's fur is named because it is said to resemble the fur of a hare. It is a specific type of oil spot glaze that is black with delicate brown streaks. Another form has silvery streaks floating in a black/brown base (also called Yuteki). An even more difficult form to achieve has iridescent streaks, which is why it is highly prized and commands a high price. (Also called Yohen, which means color-changeable.)

One way to achieve the hare's fur effect is to fire the glazes very hot and have a long soak to allow the glaze to run down the side of the pot, causing the oil spots to run and melt together on vertical surfaces, but an easier way is to use a more fluid cover glaze, like Hamada Rust, over the slip based glaze (John's SG-12). This causes the oil spots to run down the pot forming delicate streaks rather than stiffly holding the oil spotting. This running and streaking can be varied by using different cover coat glazes. You can use a kaki cover glaze to achieve more orange colors, or an iron saturate to give more iron spangles.

There is some confusion in describing hare's fur glazes because some potters refer to all streaky, milky, runny glazes as hare's fur (e.g., blue hare's fur). Technically this is incorrect. Streaky, milky, runny glazes could be caused by rutile or a nuka glaze over another glaze, creating an effect similar to oxidation oil spot streaking. One example is a Nuka Glaze over Hamada Rust.

Oil spots can also be achieved at cone 6 but since the process starts somewhere around (2250° F) the spots may be small. To improve the look you can soak the kiln beginning at cone 6, until cone 7 drops.

Strontium/Barium Matte Glazes

by Dave Finkelnburg

Barium can contribute to remarkable copper blues, beautiful satin matte surfaces, brighter glossy glazes and somewhat lower glaze expansion compared to calcium.

Strontium can be used to make exceptional satin to matte glazes, also lowers glaze expansion compared to calcium, and brightens glossy glazes.

Are there disadvantages to using barium or strontium? Safety is certainly a problem with barium carbonate as a raw material, and barium leaching from glazes is widely reported. Both fluxes are relatively expensive.

Barium carbonate decomposes at a relatively high temperature. Where pinholing and blistering are problematic a barium frit may be a better way to introduce this flux.

Strontium is not toxic in any form so it has none of the safety issues associated with barium. Strontium carbonate decomposition, though, can occur at a high enough temperature to cause pinholing in mid- to high-fire glazes. Thus, the lower the firing temperature, the more likely a strontium frit should be used instead of strontium carbonate. If you do not have access to a strontium frit, at the

SG-259 OPAQUE BLUE MATTE WITH BARIUM

Cone 10

Barium Carbonate	38.4 %
Nepheline Syenite	48.0
Ball Clay	6.1
Silica	7.5
	100.0 %
Add: Copper Carbonate	4.0 %
Bentonite	1.0 %

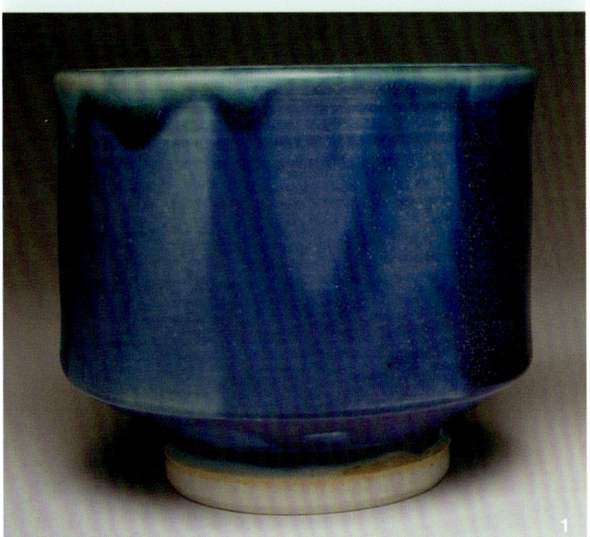

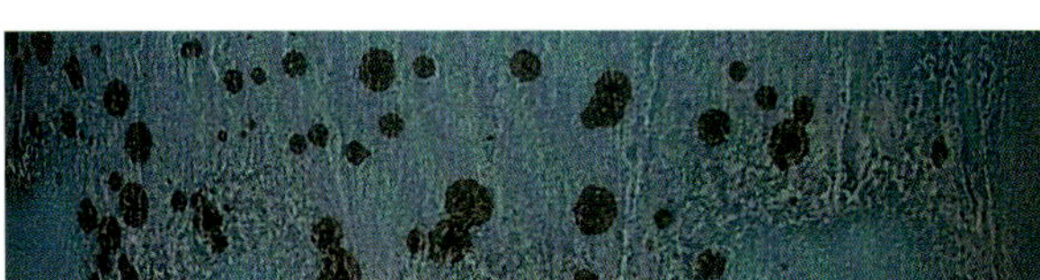

SG-259 OPAQUE BLUE MATTE WITH STRONTIUM

Cone 10

Strontium Carbonate	31.9 %
Nepheline Syenite	53.1
Ball Clay	6.7
Silica	8.3
	100.0 %
Add: Copper Carbonate	4.0 %
Bentonite	1.0 %

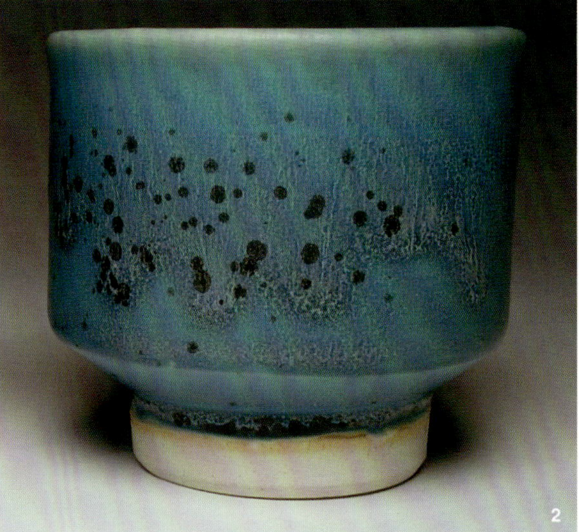

1 A perfect example of the difficulty in replacing barium carbonate in a glaze is SG-259, a silky matte barium copper blue. SG-259 is a completely different color when strontium carbonate (**2**) is used. The surface feel is similar, but slightly smoother in the strontium glaze.

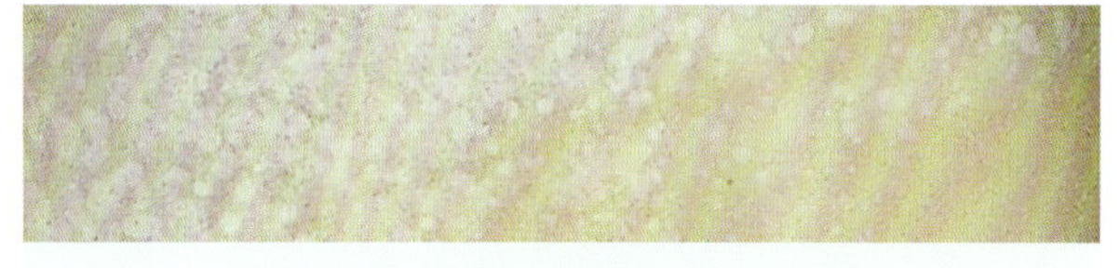

SG-302 OPAQUE GRAY-TAN MATTE WITH BARIUM

Cone 10

Barium Carbonate	23.26 %
Whiting	9.80
Custer Feldspar	55.96
Ball Clay (OM 4)	10.98
	100.00 %
Add: Rutile	9.20 %
Ultrox (Sub. Zirconium)	7.70 %
Bentonite	1.20 %

SG-302 OPAQUE GRAY-TAN MATTE WITH STRONTIUM

Cone 10

Strontium Carbonate	18.52 %
Whiting	10.40
Custer Feldspar	59.42
Ball Clay (OM 4)	11.66
	100.00 %
Add: Rutile	9.20 %
Ultrox (Sub. Zirconium)	7.70 %
Bentonite	1.20 %

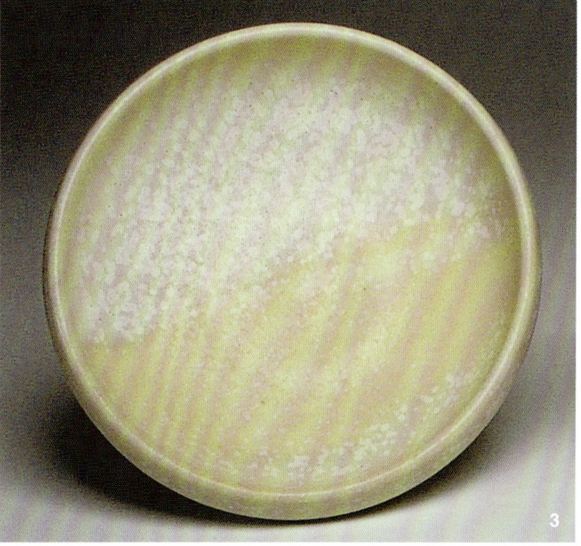

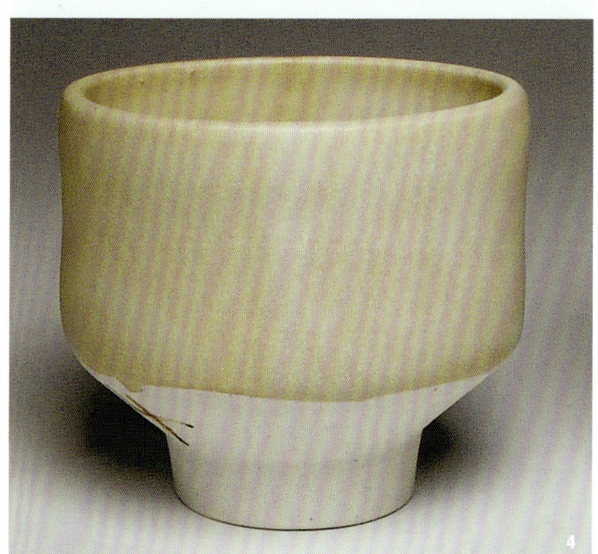

SG-302 is a satin matte glaze with nearly 10% rutile added to the base glaze. The barium matte (**3**) has a buttery feel, which is entirely gone in the strontium glaze (**4**), which is very dry. The color varies between thin and thick applications, and the speckling in the barium glaze where it's thickest is not repeated in the thicker application of the strontium glaze. Additionally, some strontium mattes may be drier than barium mattes with the same molar concentration of flux, and there may be some pitting in such glazes. *Recipes and images in figures 1–4 originally appeared in "Leaving Bariumville" by Daniel Semler,* Ceramics Monthly, *October 2007, pp. 43–47.*

least, a relatively slow firing rate near the peak temperature may be necessary to smooth glaze flaws.

Because both barium and strontium are available in frits, a form suitable for use at much lower firing temperatures, excellent low-fire barium or strontium matte glazes have become possible.

A glaze containing several alkaline earth fluxes can be less likely to produce the tiny crystals that form satin and matte surfaces than a glaze with only one. Barium tends to produce very small crystals, thus beautiful satin glazes, followed next by strontium, with calcium likely to produce more matte surfaces.

Of course, the kiln cooling cycle is a variable that must also be considered. Formation of even tiny crystals from the glaze melt takes time. Matte glazes thus require a somewhat slower cooling cycle than glossy glazes.

When using different fluxes, the fired surface is not the only glaze feature affected. Glaze expansion, color response, and glaze melting temperature may all change, too. Only testing will show whether the combination of glaze recipe, application, body, and firing will produce desired results.

5 Learn more about these and other fluxes

Soda Surfaces

by Nolan Baumgartner

Using a mix of glazes along with commercial and homemade underglazes, Baumgartner sometimes breaks the rules on how hot to fire certain products, which can lead to great discoveries.

Materials

I use two different commercial porcelains, depending on my needs. One throws really well and is stable for tall forms, but it moves if you fire it too hot. The other doesn't throw that well, but it is really stable and forgiving for wider forms and altering.

I use a fine-tipped slip trailer and low-fire majolica-type underglazes for the black lines. So far, I have tried Duncan Concepts and Mayco Stroke And Coat. I really like how the low-fire underglazes react with the high-fire glazes and how they keep their intense black color, but I have found that in my specific situation, they tend to be unstable and blister when fired to cone 10 in a soda kiln. So, I am currently testing other brands, as well as formulating my own.

These low-fire underglazes are applied to greenware underneath the flashing slips. I have found that they like to shiver if they are bisque-fired on over the slips. When applying a design, I map everything out with a ruler and Crayola magic markers. After bisque-firing, I use a water-based wax that is dyed with food coloring to help me to relate the pre- and post-firing colors.

Firing

I fire to cone 10–11 in our 26-foot soda kiln. I reduce pretty heavily at cone 010, taper it off a little, and adjust the atmosphere occasionally to keep the atmosphere slightly reducing and the cones even. When cone 9 is down, I close the damper, open the passive damper, and spray in the soda. I am in a heavy, smelly reduction during soda spraying. My solution is 3 pounds washing soda (sodium carbonate) and 1 pound of baking soda (sodium bicarbonate) added to 3 gallons of water. I spray this in three series, between each series, I open the damper up (neutral/oxidation) to get back to temperature, then returning to the smelly reduction for the spray. I always use draw rings, and I don't always use all of the solution. I open the damper up at the end to clear the glazes up for about 20 to 30 minutes. When I'm at a solid cone 10–11, I turn the kiln off and do a 10-minute crash-cool by opening the ports to set the glazes and keep them glassy (I discovered this at the Clay Studio of Missoula).

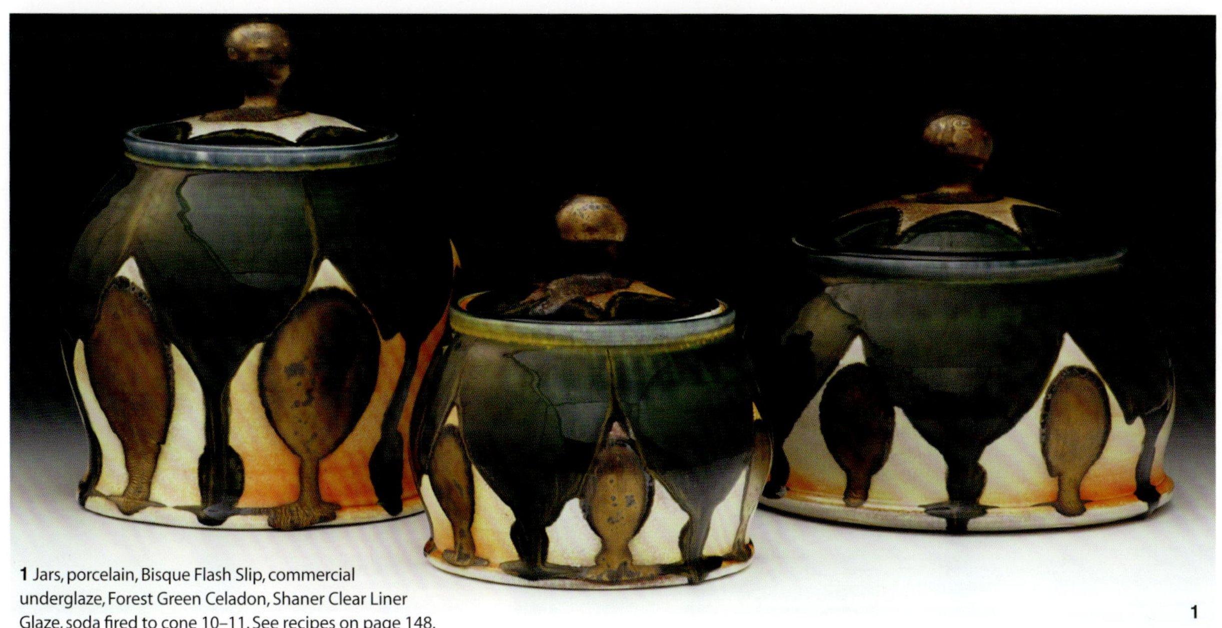

1 Jars, porcelain, Bisque Flash Slip, commercial underglaze, Forest Green Celadon, Shaner Clear Liner Glaze, soda fired to cone 10–11. See recipes on page 148.

1

SHANER CLEAR LINER GLAZE (1–3)
Cone 10 Reduction

Dolomite	5 %
Whiting	16
Zinc Oxide	5
Kona F4 Feldspar*	30
EPK Kaolin	14
Silica	30
	100 %

FOREST GREEN CELADON* (1)
Cone 10 Reduction

Gerstley Borate	7 %
Strontium Carbonate	8
Talc	3
Zinc Oxide	1
Whiting	12
EPK Kaolin	4
Kona F-4 Feldspar*	39
Silica	26
	100 %
Add: Red Iron Oxide	6 %
Cobalt Carbonate	1 %
Bentonite	2 %

ORIBE GREEN (2)
Cone 10 Reduction

Bone Ash	1.05 %
Talc	7.81
Whiting	22.36
Custer Feldspar	30.91
EPK Kaolin	12.55
Silica	25.32
	100.00 %
Add: Bentonite	2.50 %
Copper Carbonate	5.50 %

BISQUE FLASH SLIP (1)
Cone 10

EPK Kaolin	10 %
Grolleg Kaolin	50
Newman Red Clay	10
Nepheline Syenite	30
	100 %

BAUER ORANGE FLASHING SLIP (2–3)
Cone 10

Borax	6.36 %
EPK Kaolin	46.82 %
OM4 Ball Clay	46.82 %
	100.00 %
Add: Zircopax	11.73 %

My washes and flashing slips are mixed very, very thin (think skim milk), which measures between 1.1 and 1.2 on my DIY hydrometer (available on ceramicartsdaily.org). I apply them to bone-dry greenware then bisque fire them prior to glazing.

*Substitute Minspar 200 Feldspar.

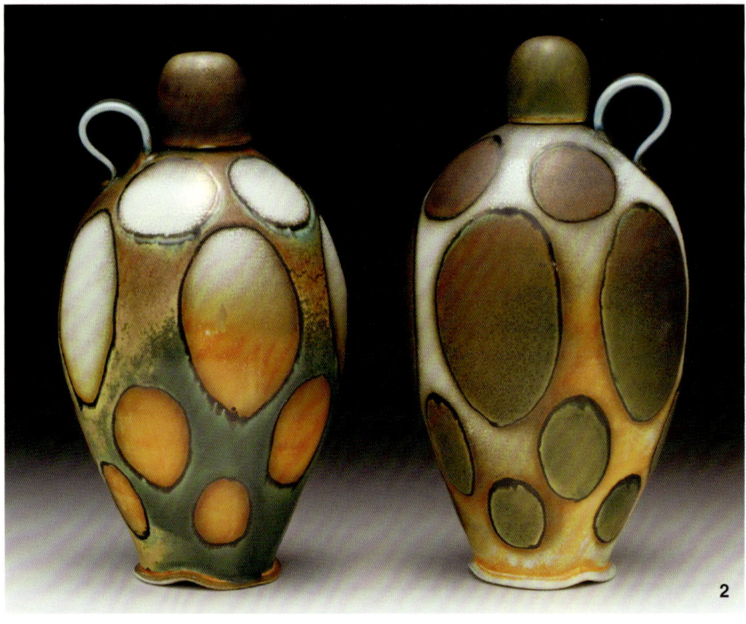

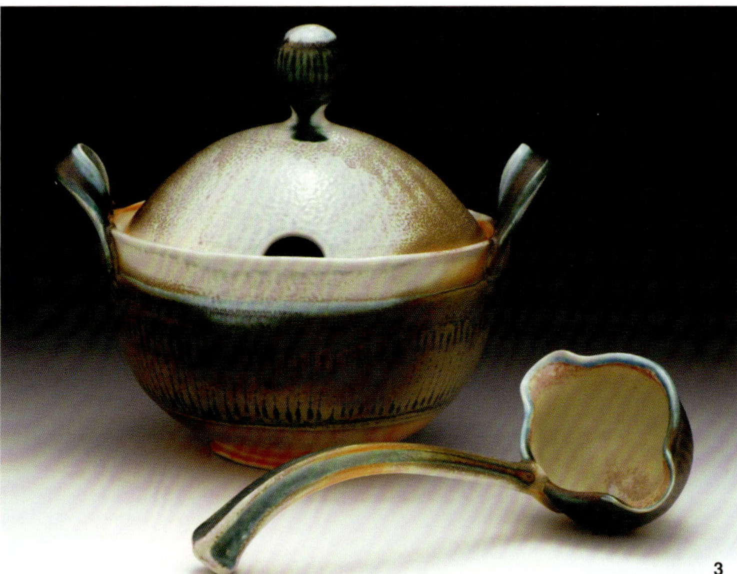

2 Two bottles, porcelain, Bauer Flashing Slip, commercial underglaze, Oribe Green, soda fired to cone 10–11. **3** Tureen and ladle, porcelain, Bauer Flashing Slip, commercial underglaze, Shaner Clear Liner Glaze, Oribe Green, soda fired to cone 10–11.

Woodfire Glazes

by Matt Schiemann

Schiemann shares recipes for his clay body, a flashing slip, and a liner glaze he uses on his wood-fired functional work.

MATT SCHIEMANN'S CLAY BODY
Cone 10

NC 4 Feldspar	12 %
Hawthorne Fireclay	20
XX Saggar Ball Clay	16
Cedar Heights Goldart	26
Helmar Kaolin	12
Alumina	6
Silica	8
	100%

GLASS TO FLASH FLASHING SLIP (1–2)
Cone 10

Nepheline Syenite	33 %
XX Saggar Ball Clay	33
Helmar Kaolin	34
	100%

LEACH TEMMOKU (1–3)
Cone 10

Custer Feldspar	40
Whiting	20
Kaolin	10
Silica	30
	100%

I use this glaze mainly as a liner glaze and then dip the rims of pots in it so it starts to move with the ash at higher temperatures.

I usually take this glaze up to around cone 11–13 to encourage it to run more.

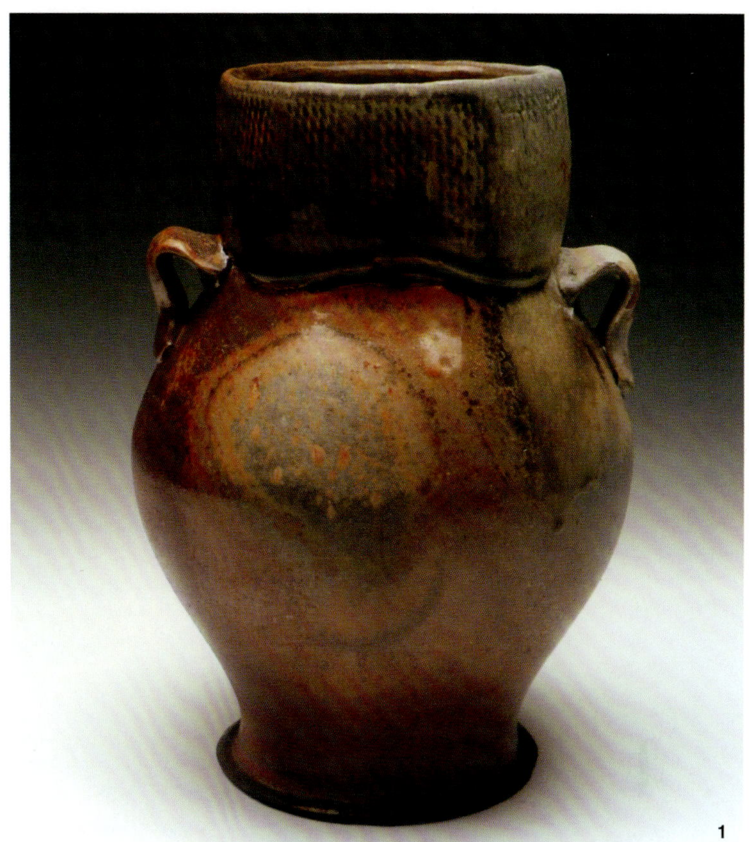

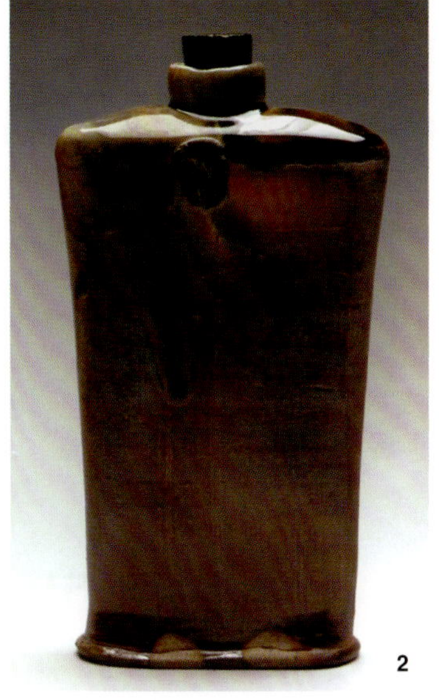

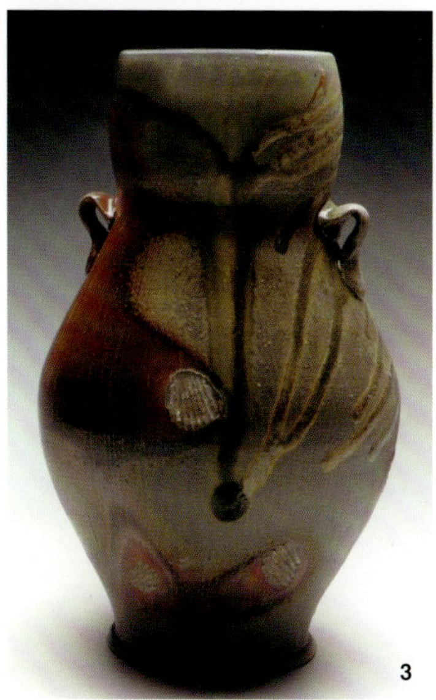

1 Matt Schiemann's vase, wheel thrown and altered using his clay body, Glass to Flash Flashing Slip, Leach Temmoku, wood fired, 2013. **2** Matt Schiemann's flask, wheel thrown and altered using his clay body, Glass to Flash Flashing Slip, Leach Temmoku, wood fired, 2013. **3** Matt Schiemann's vase, wheel thrown and altered using his clay body, Leach Temmoku, wood fired, 2013.

Ash Glazes and Overglazes for Cone 10 Firing

by Robert Briscoe

Interested in how Robert Briscoe achieves the surfaces on his pots? Check out his tried-and-true studio recipes.

STONEWARE CLAY BODY RECIPE (1–4)
Cone 10 Oxidation or Reduction

Custer Feldspar	12 %
Hawthorne Missouri Fireclay (20-mesh screened)	26
Hawthorne Bond Fireclay (35 mesh)	13
Kentucky Stone Ball Clay	13
OM4 Ball Clay	26
Virginia Kyanite (100 mesh)	10
	100 %
Add: Firebrick Grog (48 mesh)	10 %

I sometimes add acetic acid to the water when mixing this clay body. I use about 1 cup to 1 gallon of water for an acidity of 5%.

SLIP FOR ALL OCCASIONS
Cone 9–10 Oxidation or Reduction

Nepheline Syenite	20 %
OM4 Ball Clay	40
EPK Kaolin	20
Silica	20
	100 %
White	
Add: Zircopax	6 %

This slip can be used at any point in the process: wet (very thick); leather hard (thick); greenware (melted ice cream); and bisque (cream).

WHITE ASH GLAZE (2, 4)
Cone 9–10 Reduction

Mixed Unwashed Hardwood Ash	31.6 %
Dolomite	26.3
Nepheline Syenite	10.5
OM4 Ball Clay	31.6
	100.0 %

Works best in reduction. Very nice when applied thin. When applied thick, goes green. The mottled texture is lost if the ash is washed. Caution: wear gloves when working with the ash can be caustic.

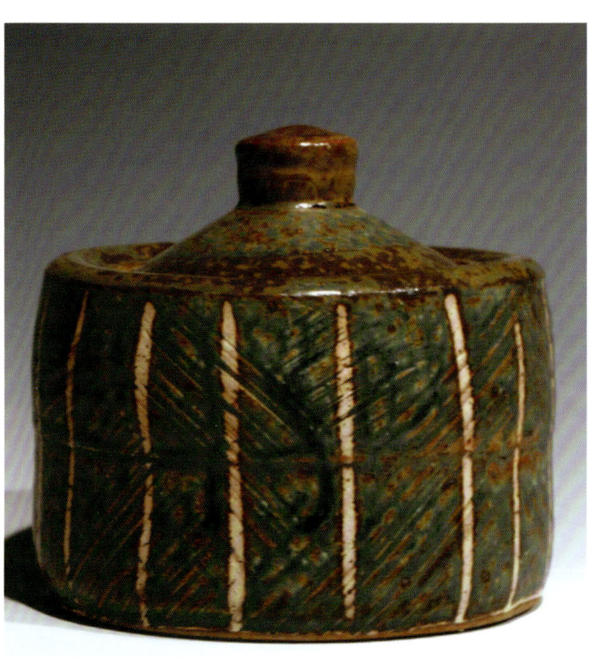

1

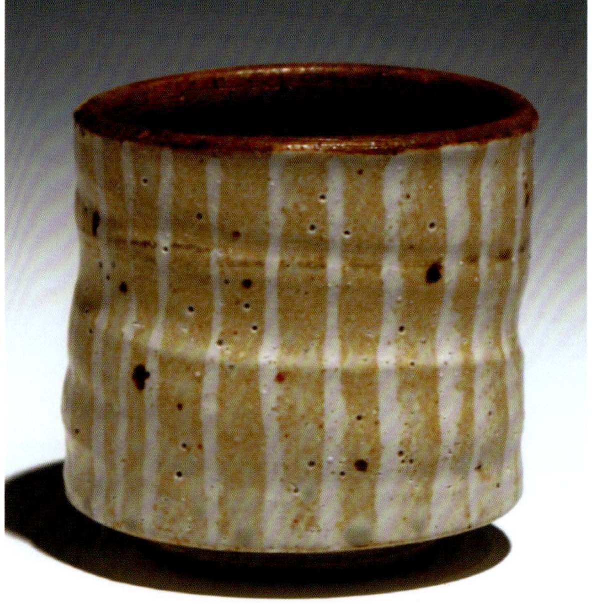

2

1 Sugar jar, gray-blue-green Base Ash Glaze, wax-resist brush marks over White Bisque Slip, overglaze stain. **2** Yunomi, White Ash Glaze wash, wax-resist brush marks over heavy White Bisque Slip, overglaze stains. **3** Noodle bowl, black Base Ash Glaze, wax-resist brush marks over heavy White Bisque Slip, overglaze stains. **4** Salad bowl, White Ash Glaze wash over heavy White Bisque Slip, overglaze stains. **1–4** Fired in reduction to cone 10.

BASE ASH GLAZE (1, 2)

Cone 9–10 Oxidation or Reduction

Mixed Unwashed Hardwood Ash	50 %
Cedar Heights RedArt	50
	100 %

Gray-Blue-Green

Add: Cobalt Carbonate	1 %

Mottled Yellow-Brown

Add: Nickel Oxide	3 %

Black to Greenish Black

Add: Chrome Oxide	1.0 %
Cobalt Carbonate	0.5 %

The color of the black/greenish black glaze depends on thickness. It is black when used thin and turns to a greenish-black with a thicker application.

ROBERT BRISCOE'S WHITE BISQUE SLIP (1–4)

Cone 9–10 Oxidation or Reduction

Borax	5 %
Minspar 200 Soda Feldspar	35
Georgia Kaolin	20
OM4 Ball Clay	20
Silica	20
	100 %

White

Add: Zircopax	5 %

Do not make substitutions for the Georgia Kaolin. Use in a half-and-half cream consistency applied in layers for a crackle surface. I use this slip to mask out iron in my stoneware and to change the glaze colors.

CELADON BASE (FROM JOHN GLICK)

Cone 9–10 Oxidation or Reduction

Bone Ash	4.5 %
Gerstley Borate	9.1
Whiting	4.5
Zinc Oxide (Calcined)	4.5
Minspar 200 Soda Feldspar	63.7
Silica	13.7
	100.0 %

Add: Vee Gum	0.5 %

Use as a clear glaze or as a stain flux for overglaze stains (see below). Add Vee Gum as a suspender.

OVERGLAZE STAINS (1–4)

Cone 9–10 Oxidation or Reduction

Yellow-brown

Add: Iron Oxide	2 parts
Rutile	1 parts
Celadon Base	6 parts

Aquamarine

Add: Copper Carbonate	10 parts
Cobalt Carbonate	1 part
Celadon Base	15 parts

Green

Add: Copper Carbonate	1 part
Celadon Base	15 parts

Black

Add: Mason Stain #6600	1 part
Celadon Base	2 parts

The amount of MS #6600 added depends on the density of the black desired.

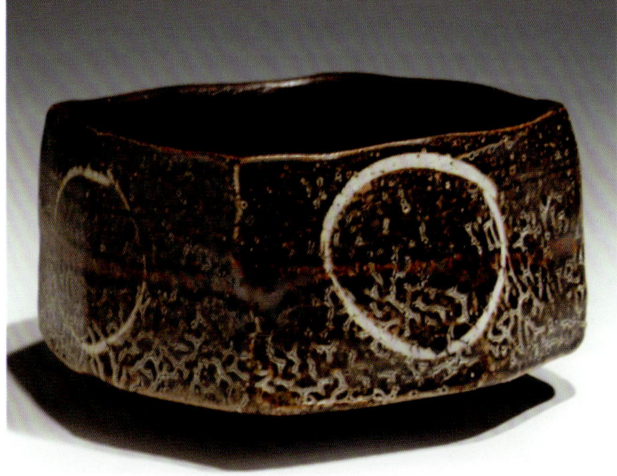

3

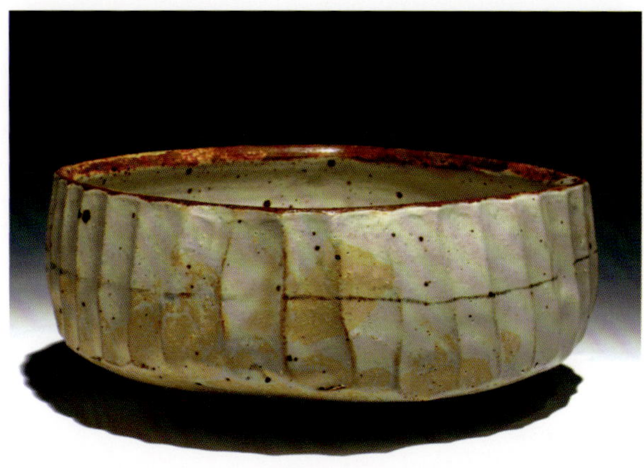

4

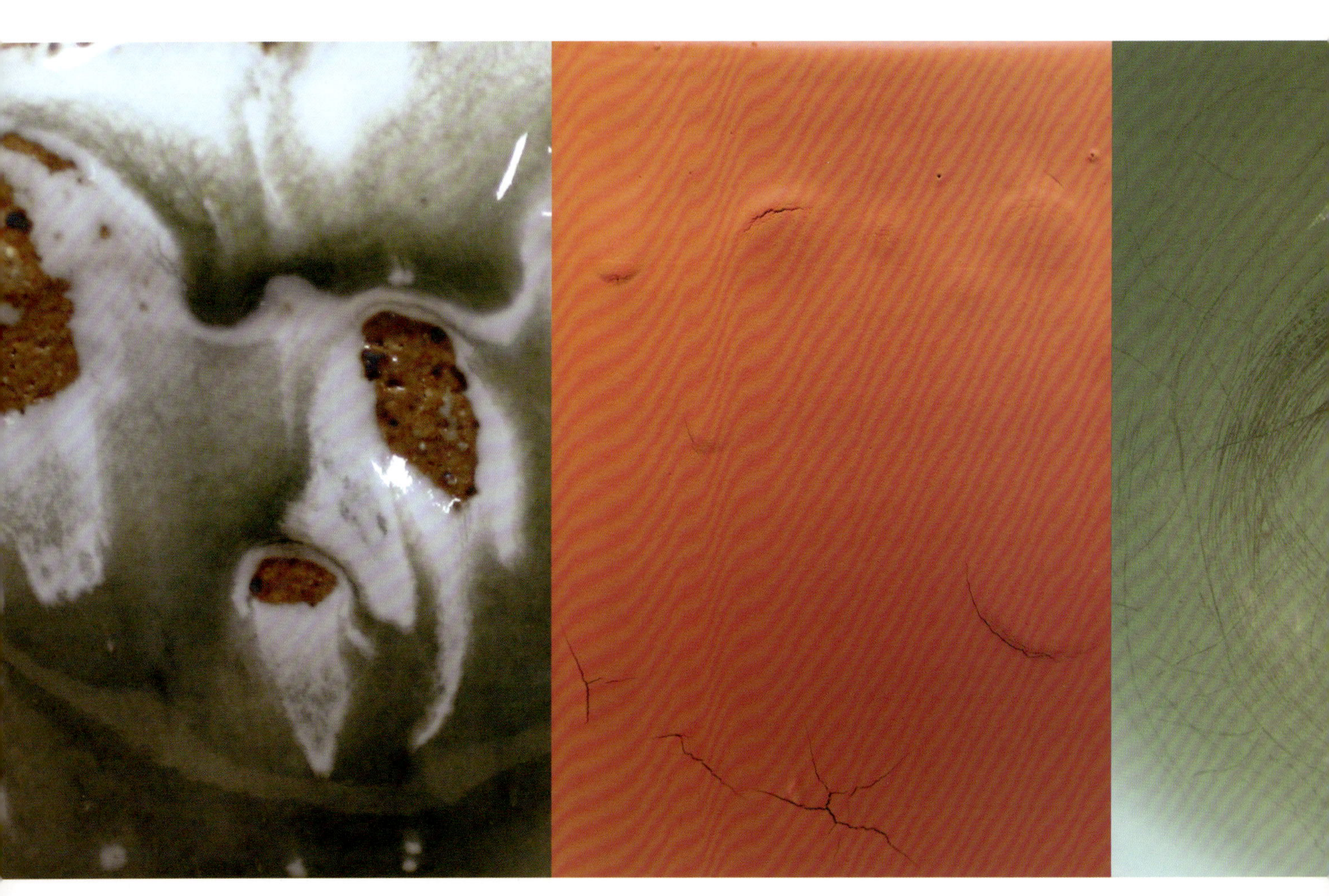

SECTION 4
Troubleshooting

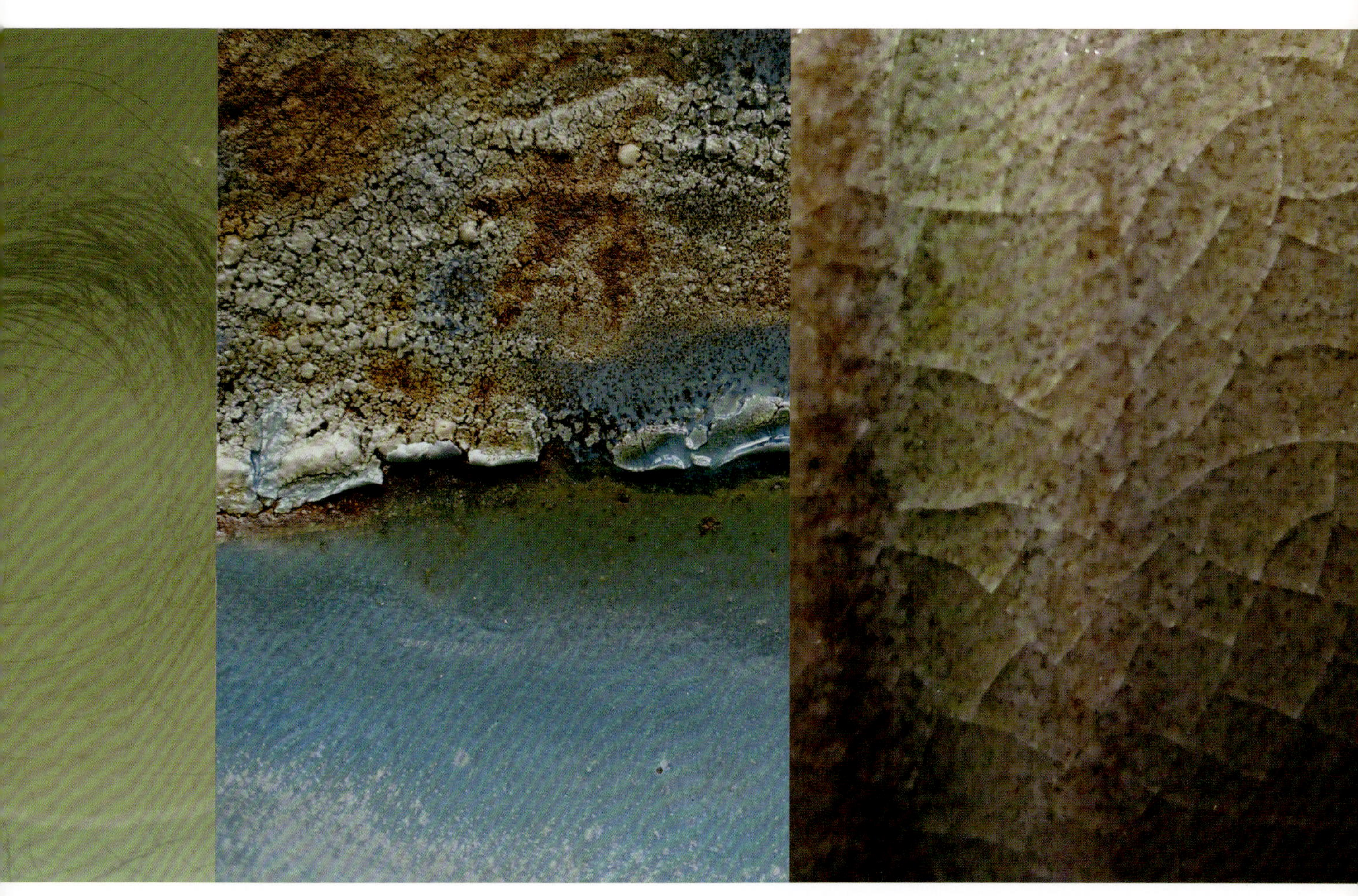

Blistering

by Johanna DeMaine

Defining the Terms

Glaze Blister: A bubble trapped within a glaze such that the glaze coating over the bubble is thin and fragile. The blister itself is unsightly. When it breaks during normal handling of the work the result is even less attractive!

LOI or Loss on Ignition: The amount of weight a material loses when it is fired. The loss is either free or chemically bound elements released as vapor by heating in the kiln or solids that react with oxygen in the kiln and burn away.

Surfactant: A chemical that reduces the surface tension of a liquid to which it is added. Also known as a wetting agent.

Viscous: Of a fluid, resistant to flow or deformation, even though liquid. A fluid which is thick, syrupy.

It's All About the Gas

Blistering is a glaze problem that occurs when a low-viscosity glaze traps a gas within it. Glaze blisters always have these two components. First, some sort of gas is trapped within the melted glaze. Second, the glaze is "thin," meaning it's been heated to the point that its consistency is watery rather than viscous.

Obviously a glass, which is a liquid, must first form. Then gases trapped within that glass expand due to the rising temperature in the kiln.

A very thick, viscous glaze may contain many bubbles of gas, but the viscosity of the glaze—its resistance to flow—will limit the expansion of the gas bubble. However, if the glaze is thin and watery, the bubble can expand greatly, in the process thinning the glass covering it.

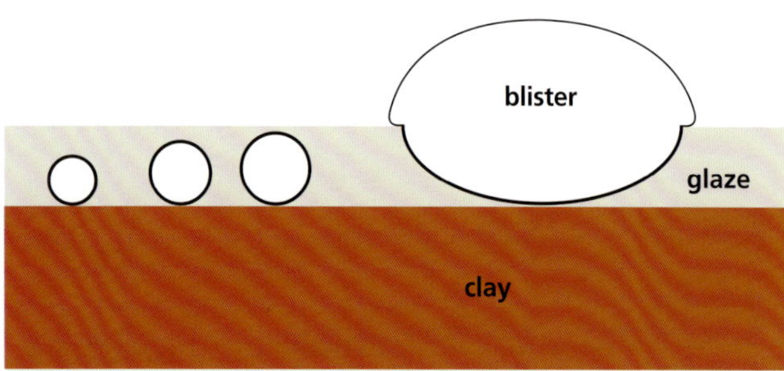

At the glaze-body interface, a bubble has formed and swollen well above the glaze surface. Note that the surface of the bubble is very thin and delicate. Within a glass (below the surface of the glaze), the bubble would be perfectly round, restrained by the glaze equally in all directions from the center of the bubble. However, in a blister the bubble is restrained by the glaze up to where the bubble swells above the glaze surface, but then the bubble tends to stretch and thin.

Glaze chemistry is a factor in blister formation because glaze chemistry controls glaze melting point as well as glaze viscosity. Obviously, the timing of melting matters. Low melting point glazes in mid- to high-fire applications are most likely to blister. That's because the later in the firing a glaze melts, the greater the odds are that problematic gases will have escaped being trapped in the glaze.

Before considering the glaze, it's critical to understand what is meant by gas. To begin with, the term gas is general rather than specific.

The gas trapped by a melting glaze may be any form of vapor:

- It can be air that was caught against the clay body as the glaze was applied over it.
- It can be oxygen given off by thermal decomposition of a glaze ingredient such as iron oxide.
- It can be a molecule of carbon dioxide given off, also by thermal decomposition, of a carbonate such as whiting.
- In the case of extremely low-melting-point glazes, it can even be water vapor given up by decomposition of clay body or glaze ingredients.

Short of firing in full vacuum with ingredients that do not off-gas upon heating, it is impossible to totally prevent gases from being trapped within a glaze. In that case, what's to be done? Ultimately, the answer is to change the glaze so it remains viscous enough that it does not blister, even though many gas bubbles may be trapped within it. Naturally it's also advisable to attempt to reduce the amount of gases trapped in the glaze.

The first step in modifying glaze viscosity usually involves the addition of kaolin or ball clay to the glaze recipe. Both are mainly kaolinite, a mineral made of equal parts of alumina and silica. Since most glaze recipes have between 3 to 15 or more times as much silica as alumina, adding clay quickly raises the proportion of alumina in the glaze.

This is important because alumina makes a glaze viscous. However, adding too much clay, (hence too much alumina), can produce a glaze that is refractory; in other words, one that will not melt. Reasonably viscous glossy glazes typically have between 5–15 times as many moles of silica as alumina.

An alternative is to reduce the quantity of glass formers and fluxes in a glaze recipe while leaving the alumina the same. Recall that boron is a glass former, as is silica, but boron melts at a lower temperature. If blistering is a glaze problem, boron should be used sparingly at higher glaze firing temperatures.

Choosing the Right Materials

It should go without saying that the traditional methods of minimizing bubble formation in glazes may help minimize glaze blisters. In particular, wetting the surface of work to be glazed prior to application of water-based glazes will help reduce air trapped between glaze and body. Likewise, use of a surfactant or wetting agent such as soap in the glaze slurry helps reduce air bubbles trapped under the applied glaze.

Use of frits as the source of glaze fluxes may help to prevent blistering of glazes that melt at low temperatures. This is because frits contain no carbonates that can decompose upon heating to release carbon dioxide gas. Obviously this gas can become trapped within a glaze if the melting temperature of the glaze is lower than the decomposition temperature of the carbonate present.

However, frits can still trap gases from other sources. Use of frits in a glaze recipe is no guarantee of blister-free firings. Testing is still necessary to determine whether frits reduce or eliminate glaze blisters from a given recipe.

Some argument is made that overfiring is the cause of blistering. Certainly, blisters would not appear if the ware had been fired to a peak temperature low enough that the glaze would have remained viscous. However, firing temperature alone is not the root cause of blistering. A high firing temperature simply reveals the glaze's susceptibility to this fault.

A truly overfired glaze, if from a well-formulated recipe, will flow uniformly—even flow off the pot—but without

LOI Isn't Important? Think Again!

The LOI (loss on ignition) of many common studio materials can affect your glazes, possibly even causing blisters. When choosing materials for your glazes, it's helpful to know when they are gassing and when they are melting in order to prevent or correct blistering. Note that some late gassers overlap early melters.

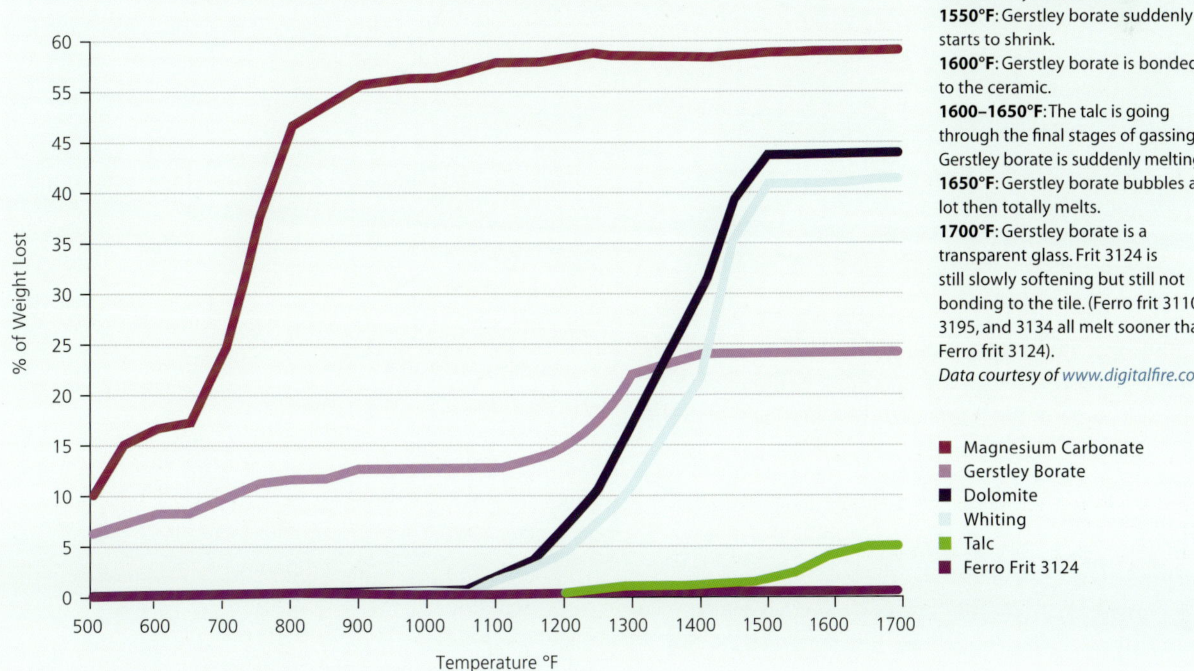

What's happening in the kiln:
1400°F: Frit begins melting. This happens well before calcium carbonate and dolomite finish gassing and before talc starts to gas. Gerstley borate stops gassing.
1500°F: The calcium carbonate and talc have stopped gassing before the Gerstley borate melts.
1550°F: Gerstley borate suddenly starts to shrink.
1600°F: Gerstley borate is bonded to the ceramic.
1600–1650°F: The talc is going through the final stages of gassing as Gerstley borate is suddenly melting.
1650°F: Gerstley borate bubbles a lot then totally melts.
1700°F: Gerstley borate is a transparent glass. Frit 3124 is still slowly softening but still not bonding to the tile. (Ferro frit 3110, 3195, and 3134 all melt sooner than Ferro frit 3124).
Data courtesy of www.digitalfire.com.

blistering. Blisters reveal a glaze that is not viscous enough at peak firing temperature.

Soaking the kiln at peak temperature for 15 minutes or more may reduce glaze blisters by providing time for the largest of them to burst and for glaze to subsequently flow into the crater left behind. Please do not ask how I know this is not a perfect cure for the problem.

If there is one piece of information that should be available with every glaze recipe, that would be the temperature at which the glaze melts. Draw trials—that, with care, can be safely removed from a fuel-fired kiln—will provide such information.

Draw trials, however, cannot be taken safely from electric kilns, so a small electric test kiln is the best alternative. Shutting the test kiln off at different temperatures to remove and examine glaze tiles will permit determining the melting temperature of a glaze.

Armed with that information, it is possible to consider which glaze ingredients may contribute to blister formation.

Bloating

by Dave Finkelnburg

Defining the Terms

Bloating: Formation, in a clay body during firing, of a gas bubble large enough to distort the surface shape of the fired ceramic. In severe cases the gas bubble will burst through to the surface of the fired work.

Oxidizing Atmosphere: An excess of oxygen from air in a kiln firing.

Reducing Atmosphere: A shortage of oxygen from air in a kiln firing.

Overfiring: Firing a ceramic body so hot that it begins to distort from melting.

There are three potential causes of bloating: over firing, "dirty" firing (reducing atmosphere in the early stages of firing), and poor clay mixing. Their cures are very different. Fortunately, they are easy to tell apart.

Fault: Over Firing

Overfiring is the easiest cause of bloating to recognize. Keep in mind that all ceramic bodies are intended to be formed at room temperature and then fired to durability while retaining that shape. However, if the firing is too hot, known as overfiring, the shape will be lost as the body just starts to melt.

Fault: Dirty Firing

Clays usually contain some organic materials which will burn in the presence of enough heat and oxygen. Some clays contain small to significant amounts of tiny crystals of pyrite, an iron sulfide. The sulfur in pyrite burns readily at moderate kiln temperatures and in a properly fired kiln has burned off by about 1300°F (700°C).

However, if the kiln is starved for air (unlikely in a well-vented electric kiln or a carefully tended fuel-fired kiln) the sulfur, as well as organic materials, can still be present. If oxygen gets into the kiln later in the firing, when the clay body is soft due to nearing its peak firing temperature, large volumes of gas will be generated by the combustion of the sulfur and organics and that will cause gas bloating in the ware.

Fault: Clay Mixing

When firing is clean and fully oxidizing until organics and sulfur are burned off, but bloating is observed, then the fault is not with the firing, but rather with inconsistencies in the clay body mixing. The fault is that flux in the clay body is concentrated in clusters, rather than being distributed uniformly throughout the body.

As any clay body approaches peak firing temperature, two features are always present in the work. There is a liquid glass phase formed from flux elements in the body melting the glass former present. There are also small bubbles of kiln gas left over as the body shrinks and becomes dense from the firing.

The glass phase, being a liquid, has almost no strength. At this point in the firing, the strength to keep the ceramic shape is supplied by the clay, quartz, and other more refractory materials in the body.

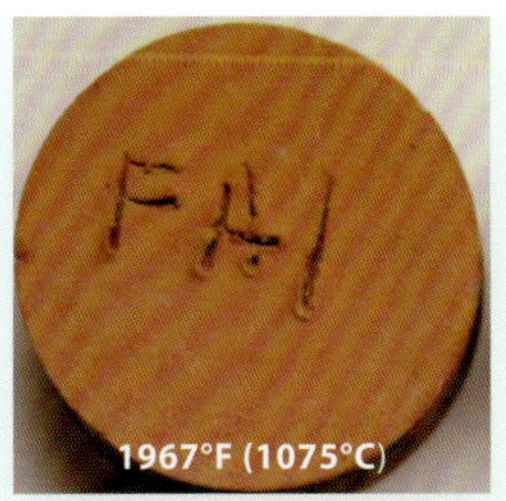

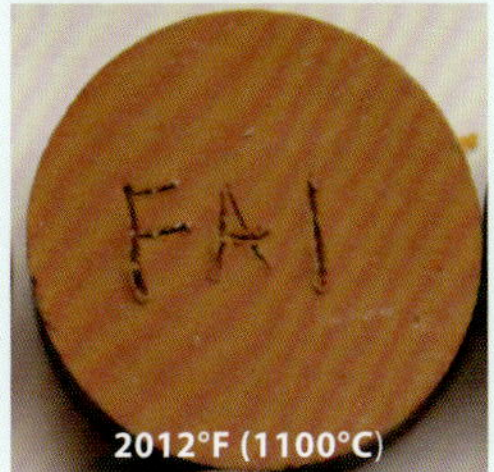

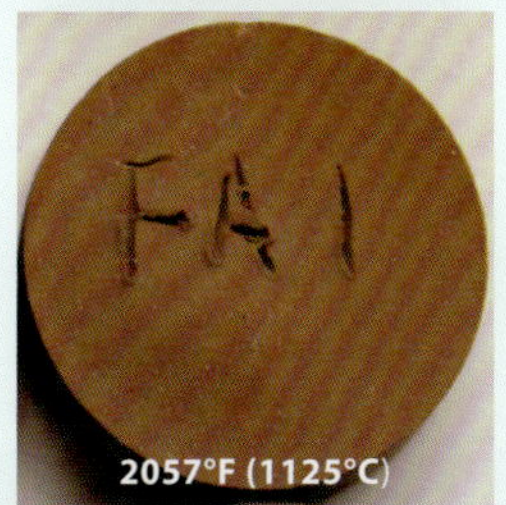

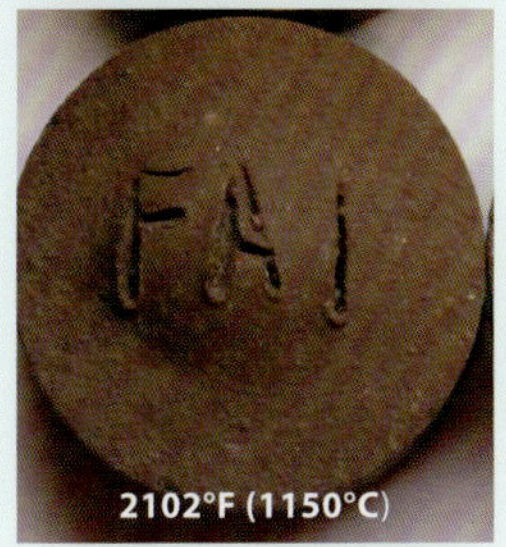

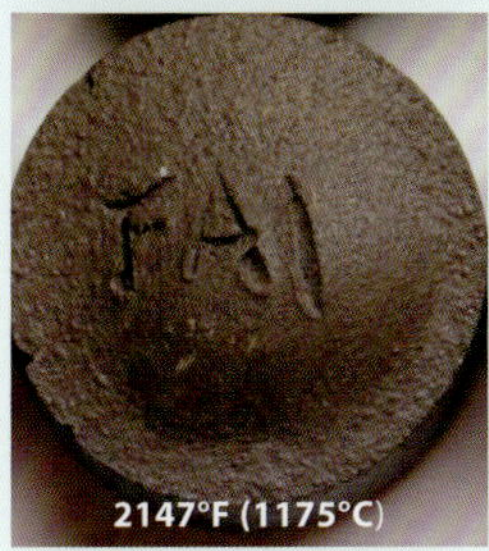

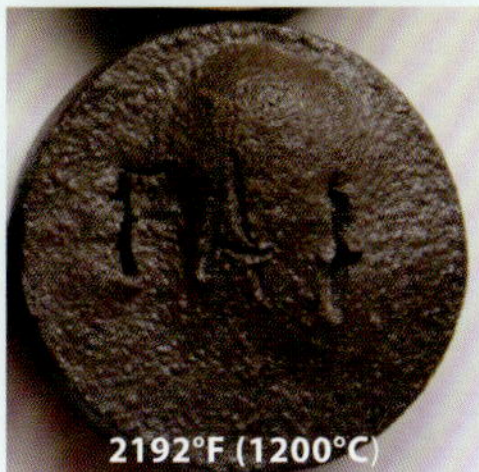

The gas bubbles naturally exert force to expand because the temperature everywhere in the kiln and ware is rising. The bubbles expand if they are not confined by the clay body.

In a well-mixed clay body, the liquid-glass phase is present in minute droplets too small to see with the naked eye. However, in the case of a poorly mixed body, or one contaminated with lumps of flux mineral, the glass phase forms pools just large enough that the clay-body structure is susceptible to being ruptured by expanding gas bubbles.

That's what happens when a clay body bloats due to poor mixing of its ingredients. An excessively large glass pool weakens the clay and expanding gas forms a bubble at the site.

Note that while the body is overfired locally, the body does not look overfired in general. Certainly, bloats would not appear if the ware had been fired to a lower peak temperature, but firing temperature alone is not the root cause of bloating. The firing simply reveals the poorly mixed body's susceptibility to this fault.

Troubleshooting the Basics

It is critical that the first firing of all ceramic work be done in a fully oxidizing atmosphere until all organics and sulfur compounds are burned off. This is especially critical with work that is to be fired to full density—functional work intended to be impervious to water or other liquids.

A good rule of thumb is, regardless of the heat source of the kiln, fire such work in a fully oxidizing atmosphere up to ~1500°F (~816°C). Organics and sulfur will have burned cleanly off by that point and will not cause problems later in the firing.

When bloating due to poor clay mixing occurs, the culprit is almost always feldspar in the clay body recipe. Feldspar, when handled dry, tends to form small clumps due to electrostatic attraction. Feldspar clumps, if blended into the body, cause bloats.

Such clumps can easily be prevented by simply mixing the water for the clay body recipe with 5 to 10% of the clay to be used, and then mixing the feldspar into that dilute clay slurry. This process, best done with a high-speed mixer, coats the feldspar particles with just enough clay to prevent feldspar clumping.

It is also possible for crystals of flux oxides to precipitate from clay slip found in recycled clay (crystals formed from soluble salts in studio water or dissolved from the body itself), and for those crystals to cause bloats. Where ware is formed from extensively recycled clay, but not from new clay of the same recipe, the safest remedy is to throw out the reclaim. Crystals can be removed by slurrying and screening, but the result will be a body of somewhat altered, and unknown, chemical composition. Clay is just not valuable enough to risk forming effort on a suspect body.

An example of a bloated cone 04 terra-cotta clay body. The body begins bloating by 2102°F (1150°C) and also becomes glassy and overfired at that temperature. *Photos: Matt Katz.*

Glaze Crawling

by Phil Berneburg

Defining the Terms

Absorption (absorb): The physical process whereby water penetrates into the porous clay underlying the glaze layer and is taken up and retained by the clay, and/or penetrates into a previously applied glaze layer.

Calcination: Heating a material to a specific temperature to drive off that part of the material which turns to a gas and is lost as a vapor at or below the calcining temperature.

Clay/Glaze Interface: The surface or boundary at which the clay and glaze layers meet or are in contact with each other.

Wetting: The establishment of intimate contact between a liquid and the surface of a solid such that the liquid can easily spread across the surface of the solid and penetrate the solid (if it is porous). In other words, the surface of the solid does not repel the liquid.

Of all the different types of possible glaze defects, the defect known as crawling probably has the greatest number of potential contributing causes. Why is that and what can you do to prevent it?

Cause and Effect

Crawling is characterized by the appearance after firing of generally irregularly-shaped bare or almost bare patches of the underlying clay body, surrounded by a somewhat thicker outline of the glaze (shown in the images below). While there are a lot of factors that can contribute to the occurrence of crawling, there is one predominant cause, a poor bond between the dried glaze layer and the clay beneath. If the adhesion is poor, when the ware is heated and the glaze melts, instead of adhering to the clay, the glaze tends to adhere to itself (because of the surface tension of

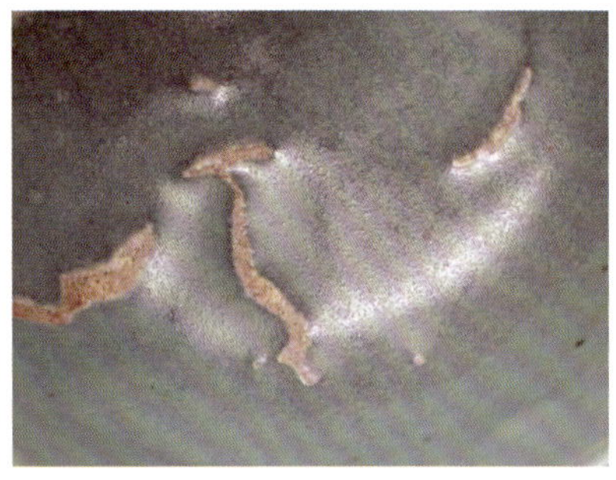

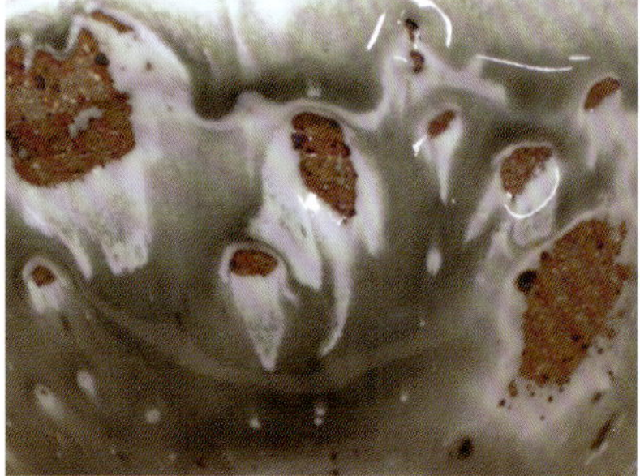

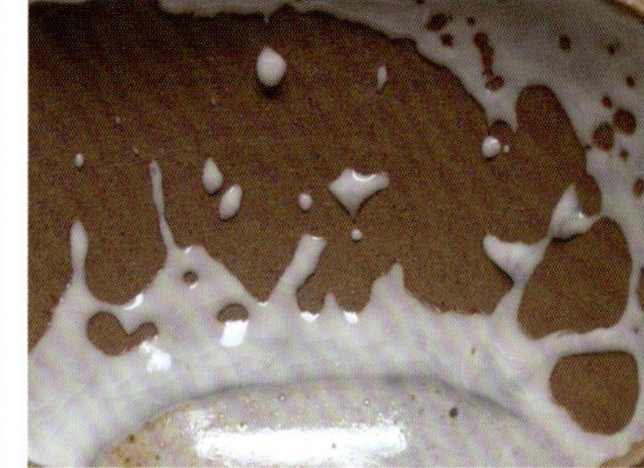

Glaze Application Tips

• Wipe a bisque-fired pot with a damp sponge just before glaze application. This removes any surface dust and assists in the liquid glaze wetting the surface of the pot, promoting good water absorption and adhesion of the glaze layer.

• If underglazes or stains are refractory (such as cobalt oxide or chromium oxide), their ability to repel glazes that are applied on top of them can sometimes be reduced by adding a flux to the stain or underglaze formula. In any case, such stains and underglazes should be applied only thick enough to yield the desired color; it is not necessary, and actually detrimental, to build up thick layers or surface coatings such as is commonly done with slips or engobes.

• Before glaze application, heat up pieces that have been severely over-fired in the bisque firing. This will help to evaporate some of the water in the glaze slurry and keep the glaze from running off of the pieces.

• The inherent stiffness (viscosity) of a glaze when it melts is due primarily to the chemical composition of the glaze, and thus cannot be changed without modifying the recipe. If a particular glaze is known to be stiff when it melts (i.e. shino glazes without soda ash), then the best approach for avoiding crawling is to try to minimize dusty or oily surfaces and avoid very thick applications of glaze, underglazes, and stains.

the glaze) and pulls away from the area of low adhesion with the clay.

Crawling is not caused by the firing, but only occurs during the firing as a result of pre-existing conditions. However, diagnosing the exact cause of crawling can be difficult because of the fact that anything in the processing of the ware before firing that results in a weakening of the bond, or a failure of a good bond to develop, can contribute to the occurrence of crawling. These factors can include composition of the glaze, application of the glaze, and drying and subsequent handling of the glaze. Furthermore, because the boundary between the dried glaze layer and the clay is hidden from view, the existence of a weakened bond is not visible early in the process.

If a glaze recipe contains too much clay or any other very fine or fluffy material that has the potential to absorb a lot of water, as the wet glaze dries, it can shrink sideways along the surface of the clay, as well as in thickness. This sideways shrinkage movement results in a weakening of the adhesion between the glaze layer and the clay. Alternatively, if a glaze recipe does not contain enough clay or other fine powders, but only relatively coarse or granular ingredients, there may not be enough fine material to create good contact and a good bond between the dried glaze and the clay.

If a glaze slurry is not well mixed and all the ingredients are not well suspended in the liquid before application of the glaze, the portion of the glaze that is used may contain mostly fine ingredients (that haven't settled out), resulting in greater than normal drying shrinkage and sideways movement.

Any loose debris or dust present on the surface of the clay before glaze application, as well as the presence of grease, oil, or any other water-repellent material, can reduce the bond. In order for a good bond to form, the water in the glaze has to wet the surface of the clay and be easily absorbed by the porous clay, pulling the solid ingredient particles into close contact with the clay surface. Wiping the bisqueware with a damp sponge just before glazing can eliminate dust and promote wetting.

If the surface of the clay has been smoothed by techniques such as burnishing or the application of fine-grained slips, the smooth surface can contribute to the failure of a good bond to form. This same principle is well known in the field of adhesives where it is frequently recommended that surfaces to be glued together be roughened slightly before joining (to increase the contact area and "interlocking" of the surfaces).

If a glaze is applied too thickly, or the porosity of the clay has been reduced by a higher-than-normal bisque firing, and the water cannot be absorbed rapidly by the clay,

The Three Stages of Glaze Crawling

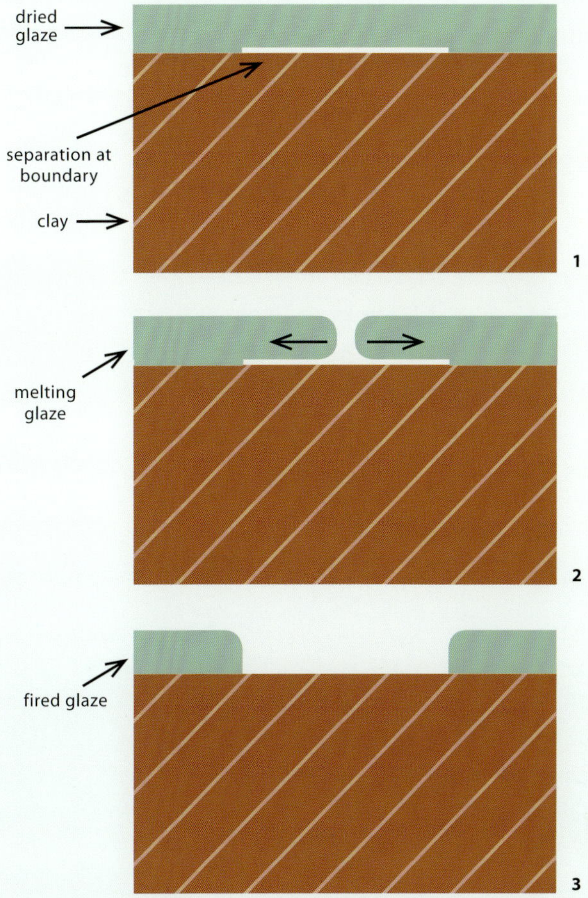

dried glaze
separation at boundary
clay
1
melting glaze
2
fired glaze
3

1 Dried glaze layer with the underlying area of separation/poor bonding to clay. **2** Early stage of melting of the glaze layer and the beginning of crawling over the area of poor bonding, due to surface tension of the liquid glaze (arrows indicate direction of glaze movement). **3** Final position of the glaze layer showing exposed clay surface.

the slower drying can lead to sideways shrinkage, loosening the original bond.

If the inside and outside surfaces of a pot are glazed separately, the water absorbed by the clay from the first application, which is still present in the clay, can prevent rapid absorption during the second application, resulting in a failure to form a strong bond. Alternatively, if the glaze from the first application has completely dried, the water that is absorbed by the clay during the second part of the application can soak through the wall and loosen the bond of the first layer, especially if the wall is thin. A similar situation can arise when glazes are layered. The water that is absorbed from the second application can soak through the underlying glaze layer and weaken the adhesion of the underlying layer, resulting in crawling of the bottom layer, carrying the upper layer along with it. Yet another related situation occurs when thin-walled ware is glazed by dipping. Water is absorbed from both sides of the wall and can very quickly saturate the wall, reducing further water absorption and preventing tight contact of any adsorbed glaze layer.

Base glazes that are naturally viscous (stiff) when melted, or the presence of excessive amounts of opacifiers or other additives that tend to increase the viscosity of the glaze, can result in poor wetting and adhesion of the melted glaze to the clay, and thus to crawling. Poor adhesion can also be caused by the presence of thick coatings of refractory (non-melting) underglazes and stains such as chromium oxide and cobalt oxide on the surface of the clay which prevent the melted glaze from sticking to the surface.

Conclusion

The important principle is that crawling is actually caused by conditions set up before, during, or right after glaze application. The solution is to examine the glazing process for any of the possible conditions described and make appropriate changes in the recipe or procedures.

As an example of a glaze recipe change, calcined kaolin can be substituted for part of the high kaolin content in a glaze recipe (86% as much calcined kaolin is needed to replace raw kaolin) in order to reduce drying shrinkage. When clay is calcined (heated to approximately bisque firing temperatures), bound water is driven off and the clay loses the ability to absorb large amounts of water and shows reduced drying shrinkage. Generally, only part (roughly 50%) of the raw clay is replaced, in order to retain the contribution of the fine, uncalcined clay to the formation of good adhesion, although this depends upon the actual amount of clay that is in the recipe. It is advisable to retain at least 10% of the total recipe as uncalcined clay.

Pinholing

by Dave Finkelnburg

Defining the Terms

Pinhole: A glaze flaw produced by a bubble bursting at the glaze surface, revealing the fired clay body beneath.

Viscosity: The ease or difficulty with which a glaze will flow when subjected to a given force.

Surface Tension: Internal cohesive force of a liquid that, as it increases, causes the liquid to resist wetting a surface of another material. A high surface tension glaze forms a bead on a clay body surface rather than spreading onto the body.

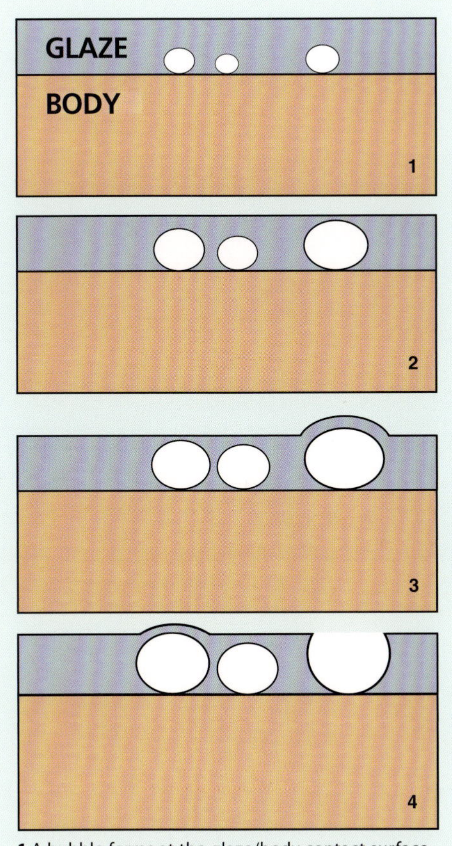

1 A bubble forms at the glaze/body contact surface. **2–3** The bubble grows, pushing through the melted glaze. **4** The bubble bursts, leaving a crater and exposing the clay body. Glaze surface tension and viscosity keep glaze from flowing into the void left by the bubble.

A pinhole marring a fired glaze is possibly the most troublesome of all glaze faults, disrupting an otherwise smooth surface. Slow firing at peak temperature helps heal pinholes, but preventing them in the first place is the holy grail of a smooth glaze.

The Root of the Problem

The root cause of any pinhole is a large glaze bubble. If no bubbles form in the glaze, no pinhole faults will blemish the glaze.

A pinhole starts as a bubble at the contact point between a glaze and the surface it's being fired on. During the firing, the bubble grows so large its diameter is greater than the thickness of the glaze and the bubble bursts at the surface of the glaze. At that point, either glaze flows into the crater left behind by the bursting bubble, or it doesn't. The latter case produces a pinhole.

The gases that form bubbles, leading to pinholes, have many potential sources. Decomposition of oxides in the body or glaze and gases trapped in pore spaces in both are obvious culprits. Because bubbles can come from many sources, most efforts to prevent pinholing focus on making glazes runny enough, and with low enough surface tension, so molten glaze fills the craters left by bursting glaze bubbles. To make runny, low-surface-tension glazes requires managing glaze composition.

Adjusting the proportion of clay in a glaze is the most common starting point. Alumina atoms raise glaze viscosity and thus also raise the surface tension. Adding clay, an alumina silicate mineral, will make a molten glaze "thicker," or more viscous. Reducing clay content thus makes the glaze runnier or less viscous.

An increase in the proportion of the flux element magnesium also raises glaze surface tension. In high quantities, magnesium makes a glaze with an excessively high surface tension (for example, crawl glazes). Flux, colorant, and glass-former atoms all influence glaze viscosity and surface tension to some degree. Given the virtually infinite number of possible combinations of these elements in a glaze, testing is necessary to balance glaze fluidity and surface tension for a given application.

In general, adding any flux element or colorant (with the exception of some commercial stains) will reduce glaze viscosity and surface tension. Since colorants are ordinarily used in small quantities, their effect is usually small. Cobalt may become an exception. When used to make an extremely dark blue, cobalt can make a glaze quite runny.

Increasing the proportion of fluxes in a glaze lowers its melting temperature. Adding the glass-former boron to a recipe, or substituting it for some of the silica in the glaze, has a similar effect. Both permit a glaze to remain molten longer during a firing, and that extra time can heal potential pinholes.

Healing Glazes

Adjusting a glaze formulation can help heal pinholes, but it's better to prevent them from forming in the first place.

Studio glazing is typically done with glazes applied to work that has been fired to a sturdy but still porous state. The porous ware absorbs water from the glaze, assuring that a glaze coating of adequate thickness adheres to the body.

The process of producing porous ware in the first firing makes later glaze application convenient, but also guarantees there will be air under the glaze in the pore spaces in the body. If the glaze melts before all air is driven out of the body by densification, the air coming from the body is trapped as bubbles in the glaze and can produce pinholes. To compound the problem, air can also be trapped between the applied glaze and the body.

Industry fights the first of these problems by firing hotter in the first firing, which is typically to full body density. However, the dense clay cannot absorb moisture so glazing is typically done by spray application onto heated ware. The heated ware dries the water from the glaze rapidly before the glaze has a chance to run off.

Industry also commonly uses some kind of surfactant or low-foaming soap as a wetting agent in the glaze mix. This helps the glaze wet the body and minimizes air trapping between the glaze and body.

In the glaze mixing studio one can also use a surfactant in the glaze mix. If twice-firing, wetting the surface of the ware before glazing can also be helpful. This will permit the glaze to more completely wet the surface of the ware. It is most convenient to do this while washing the ware to remove dust which may have accumulated during or after the first firing.

When using a fuel-heated kiln and firing to cone 10, firing in reduction up to peak temperature will reduce iron and prevent high-temperature off-gassing of oxygen from iron oxide. This is essentially preventing oil-spotting (created by thermal decomposition of iron oxide beginning around cone 8) by reducing the iron before the glaze melts in a thick, high-iron glaze. The oxygen given off creates craters that heal so the surface is relatively smooth but has a characteristic look.

In the final analysis, slowing the glaze firing near peak temperature to allow time for pinholes to heal over can be helpful. If the last 15 to 30 minutes of the peak cone bending occurs at a constant temperature and pinholing still occurs, then a less viscous glaze may be required.

Underfired Glazes

by Alisa Liskin Clausen

Defining the Terms

Glaze Slurry: The mix of glaze materials and water. Controlling slurry thickness is important to get a glaze to melt correctly.

Heat Work: The integrated effects of both temperature and time; heat saturation.

Specific Gravity (or Relative Density): The measure of how much more or less dense a specific liquid is than water.

Unity Molecular Formula: Also known as a Seger Formula. Glaze recipe format based on calculating the number of molecules of flux in a glaze to a total of 1.0 (which means they are in unity). The formula shows the ratio between fluxes, but perhaps more importantly, it shows the ratio of combined fluxes to the silica and alumina.

Viscosity: The resistance to flow; anti-flow. Low viscosity flows a lot. High viscosity flows only a little or not at all.

Detecting a Problem

Underfired glazes are usually matte and dry and can feel rough. Some gloss glazes seem like they were properly fired until you either look closely or use the object. For example, if you were to drink tea from a mug glazed with an underfired gloss, you might notice signs of crazing due to poor bonding, which become accentuated by the tea or coffee stains.

Glazes are complex and have many different melting points. The temperature at which a glaze melts and is considered mature depends on the balance of the three main glaze components in your glaze mixture. Silica forms glass. A flux makes otherwise very high-temperature melting silica (3110°F (1710°C)), melt at lower, more attainable temperatures such as 2232°F (1222°C) (cone 6). Alumina is added as a stabilizer to essentially keep the melted silica adhered to the ceramic surface. Making a glaze that's compatible with your clay and your firing temperature is all about balancing these materials.

If you open your kiln and your glaze looks underfired (for example, glossy glazes appear matte or the surface has an orange-peel texture), you have several factors to consider. To start troubleshooting, work from the easiest possible solution to the more complicated. This way you can systematically eliminate what caused the underfiring by starting with the simplest faults first, before speculating about more serious and time-consuming problems. After addressing the easy problems, if you determine that the glaze is the problem, you can alter the recipe.

Troubleshooting: Easy Fixes

If the underfired glaze is one you often use and it normally melts at your firing temperature, then you can look for these potential technical problems as possible causes for the under-matured glaze result.

Did the kiln reach the right temperature? When you open your kiln, and all of the glazes are underfired, then you can go ahead and check whether your kiln fired to temperature. The truest way to affirm how high your kiln fired is by placing cone packs in your kiln. Usually they are placed at different levels in the kiln, as temperatures can differ throughout a large and/or older electric kiln—typically, colder at the bottom and hotter at the top. Newer electric kilns are shamelessly even; so one cone pack on the middle kiln shelf can be sufficient. With a computer-controlled kiln, there will be a message on the digital display that the kiln fired as you programmed it. It will also give you a message if an error occurred during the firing. Hopefully, it will be clear to you what went wrong (maybe a power outage, or a circuit overload, etc.) and you can easily restart your kiln without a visit from an electrician.

Check your firing program: Did you set your kiln to fire to the right temperature? At this point in my career, I need reading glasses to ensure that I have keyed in the right temperatures, ramps, and holds. Glasses or not, small distractions can also lead to program errors. Check your program twice.

Troubleshooting: Intermediate Fixes

Placement in kiln: If you open your kiln and there are fired pieces with a good melt and others with the same glaze that are underfired, then we must look at where the underfired pieces are located in the kiln. This is an equipment-related issue again. Are they all near the same element or on the bottom of the kiln? If so, then I would suggest having a

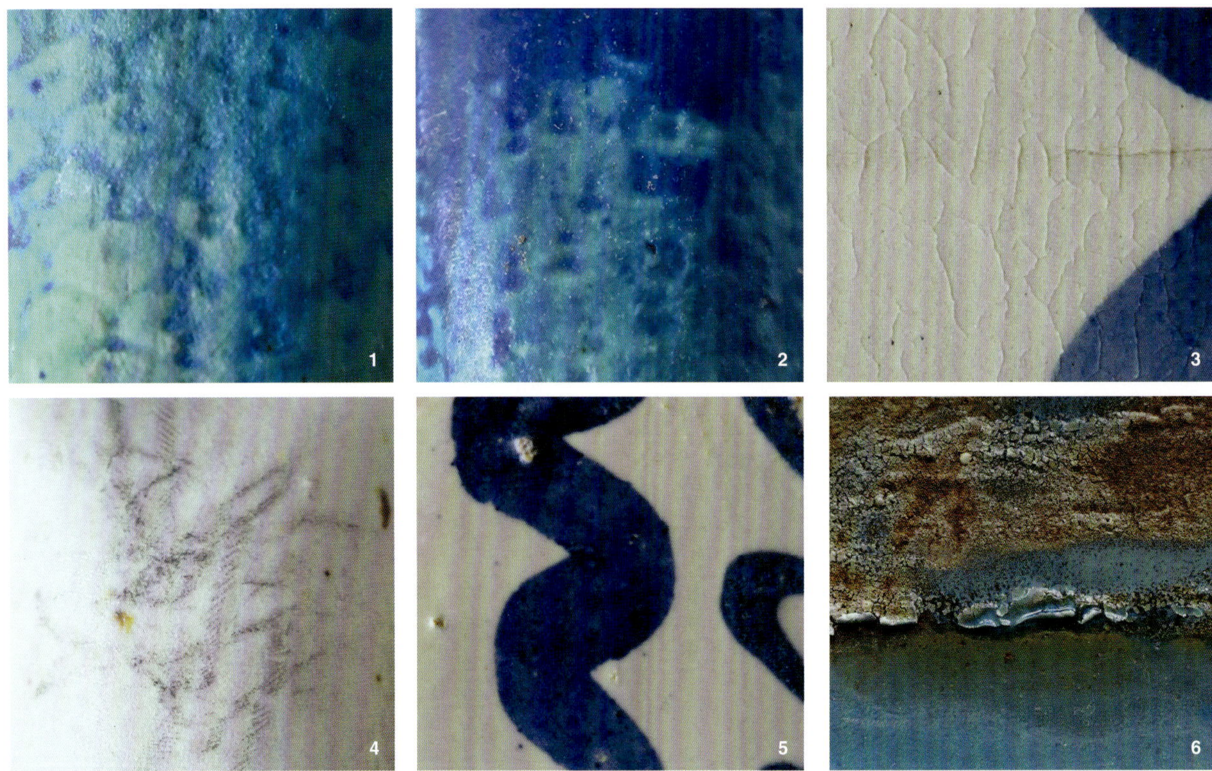

1 Fired glaze test with a thin glaze slurry where the glaze is underfired and matte. **2** Fired test showing a thicker glaze slurry, with a double dip of the glaze at the top showing a silky gloss. **3** Crazing may (or may not) be a caused by underfiring a gloss glaze. The glaze may be fired to the correct melting temperature, but crazed to due to low silica in the unity formula balance or because the bisque ware is too soft. **4** Cutlery marks on a matte white glaze. **5** An underfired transparent gloss glaze, which typically resulted in a milky surface, shows clumps of unmelted raw materials. **6** A mix of mattes with added Zircopax and borax are used to create texture and peeling. This would be an underfired and failed glaze if intended for dinnerware, but for my intentions on a non-food surface, it is a success.

kiln technician or electrician measure the heating elements. Maybe you just need new elements or, because the kiln is big and old, you need to increase your top temperature or increase your holding time at your normal top temperature to get more heat over time, so that the glazes have time to melt and smooth out. If the placement of the pieces seem to be irrelevant, for example if you have well-fired and underfired pieces on the same shelf, then we increase the difficulty of isolating the problem from looking at equipment to your bisque firing and glazing procedures.

Bisque firing too low: Underfired glazes can be a result of bisque ware that is underfired. That would mean that the bisqued surface is too porous and when you apply the glaze, the surface absorbs too much of it. The result could be underfired glaze, because there is too much glaze on the pot.[1]

Try increasing the top temperature of your bisque firing, making your bisque ware less porous. This may be enough to help the otherwise good balance of materials in your glaze melt as desired.

Troubleshooting: Viscosity and Density

How is your glaze slurry? Do you routinely mix it and/or sieve it every time you glaze or do you leave it in a bucket for long intervals and mix it up just enough to get it fluid and suspended enough to dip or pour it onto your piece? If so, the materials may not be evenly dispersed throughout the slurry.

Is the glaze in the bucket too thick or too thin? Either of these can result in underfired glazes. Glaze slurry that is too thick can cause underfiring because there is simply too much glaze on the surface, and glaze that is too thin can cause the same problem, simply because there is not enough glaze to melt smoothly (1). Be consistent. Each time you use a glaze, mix it well, making sure that any materials that have settled are mixed up into the slurry. If you do not mix the whole bucket, you will likely get a glaze that is unbalanced because key ingredients—or valuable amounts of them—are still sitting at the bottom of the glaze bucket. I like to sieve my glazes if I have not used them for a while (more than a month).

Measure the specific gravity using a hydrometer if desired. Otherwise do an educated dip test (for glazes you know well). Dip a test tile or your dry finger in the slurry and bend your finger. You can determine how thick or thin it is by how much or little it coats your knuckle. Each time you dip or pour your applied glaze, give it a stir first.

Remember the thickness of your glaze layer can also depend on the porosity of your bisque ware. Having these two variables in sync can eliminate an underfired glaze (2).[2]

If it is a new glaze that is underfired, make tests using a thin slurry, an average one, and a thicker one. Measure the specific gravity of these tests using a hydrometer and keep a record of the test tiles, so you understand what you are looking at after they are fired. Then you will be able to duplicate the specific gravity of the slurry that gave you the best melt.

Troubleshooting: Complex Solutions

If none of the above troubleshooting solves your underfired glaze problem, then look at the glaze formula for a possible solution.

Glazes are complicated: Underfired gloss glazes often show crazing because they have not bonded with the clay (3). They are sitting on the surface of the clay and are shrinking more than the clay. If this is the case, then you need to explore both your glaze and your clay body to find the right fit. Silica is essential in making a glaze, as it is the glass former. Look at your silica levels. If your glaze is crazed, too little silica may be the cause.

How you approach adjusting your glaze depends on you. Calculating the unity formula will allow you to add and decrease materials until you reach the right ratios between silica, flux, and alumina. Glaze calculation programs make it possible to do this easily, as you can add and adjust raw materials to make many different glazes and see and compare their analyses. Another approach would be to make lots of glaze tests. By testing glazes and actually seeing the results, you will learn quickly how materials react to each other in your glaze. You can use both methods: adjust your underfired glazes with glaze-calculation software, and test all the glazes you think will work or find interesting. You will have hands-on results and see the glazes that work.

Matte glazes are softer than gloss glazes and can appear underfired. Matte glazes look the way they do because of the presence of crystals under their surfaces and also because of the balance of the first three important glaze materials; silica, flux, and alumina. In reality, many matte glazes are underfired. Underfired mattes are most likely low in silica (in relation to the other two materials.) One way to determine if the glaze is underfired is to run a knife across the surface. Underfired mattes can be easily scratched with cutlery (4).

What if your glaze does not melt at your target temperature? If all of the ideas above are eliminated as the cause for the underfired glaze, consider the following:

Is this recipe intended for the cone range you fire to? Do you want to use this particular glaze recipe so much that you will fire an entire kiln load higher than usual to get it to melt, or fire separately in a less than full kiln to get the results you want?

Because I think the ultimate way of learning glaze chemistry and thus achieving rewarding results from your kiln is to know your raw materials characteristics, I would attempt to adjust the recipe.

Getting an underfired glaze to melt at cone 6 oxidation, for example, usually involves adjusting the fluxes. By adjusting the fluxes, I mean you have to find out which flux to use through testing. Remember that you may need to adjust the silica as well once you get the right flux. Coloring oxides can enhance the melt as much as opacifiers can inhibit it. Finding the right balance will yield a gloss with a smooth surface.

Hands-on Learning

There is no slam-dunk method for making or adjusting glazes. The difference between labeling a result as an effect or a fault depends on what your intentions are for the glaze (5–6).

Making lots of interesting tests, keeping good records, and understanding your materials and how they behave in the glaze balance form the hands-on way to learn how to adjust and lower the firing temperature of your underfired glaze. By lowering the maturing temperature, you may also slightly or completely alter the look of the surface. You may totally nail it. If it is not the glaze you are looking for, it is not a loss. You are one test closer to understanding how your materials work together and are learning what to explore in your next set of tests to fix the underfired glaze.

1 Frank and Janet Hamer *The Potter's Dictionary of Materials and Techniques*, Underfired, pp. 347.

2 Frank and Janet Hamer, *The Potter's Dictionary of Materials and Techniques*, Slop, pp 316.